FOLLOW THE LEADER, LOSE THE REGION

FOLLOW THE LEADER, LOSE THE REGION

CHARTING A CANADIAN
STRATEGY FOR
THE ASIA-PACIFIC

Jeffrey Reeves

UBCPress · Vancouver · Toronto

© UBC Press 2023

All rights reserved. No part of this publication may be reproduced, stored in a retrieval system, or transmitted, in any form or by any means, without prior written permission of the publisher, or, in Canada, in the case of photocopying or other reprographic copying, a licence from Access Copyright, www.accesscopyright.ca.

32 31 30 29 28 27 26 25 24 23   5 4 3 2 1

Printed in Canada on FSC-certified ancient-forest-free paper (100% post-consumer recycled) that is processed chlorine- and acid-free.

Library and Archives Canada Cataloguing in Publication

Title: Follow the leader, lose the region : charting a Canadian strategy for the Asia-Pacific / Jeffrey Reeves.
Names: Reeves, Jeffrey (Writer on Asian security issues), author.
Description: Includes bibliographical references and index.
Identifiers: Canadiana (print) 20220488800 | Canadiana (ebook) 20220488819 | ISBN 9780774868594 (hardcover) | ISBN 9780774868624 (EPUB) | ISBN 9780774868617 (PDF)
Subjects: LCSH: Canada—Foreign relations—Pacific Area. | LCSH: Pacific Area—Foreign relations—Canada. | LCSH: Pacific Area—Politics and government.
Classification: LCC FC251.A7 R44 2023 | DDC 327.7105—dc23

UBC Press gratefully acknowledges the financial support for our publishing program of the Government of Canada and the British Columbia Arts Council.

This book has been published with the help of a grant from the Canadian Federation for the Humanities and Social Sciences, through the Awards to Scholarly Publications Program, using funds provided by the Social Sciences and Humanities Research Council of Canada.

Printed and bound in Canada by Friesens
Set in Segoe and Charis by Artegraphica Design Co.
Cover designer: Will Brown
Copy editor: Frank Chow
Indexer: Noeline Bridge

UBC Press
The University of British Columbia
2029 West Mall
Vancouver, BC V6T 1Z2
www.ubcpress.ca

*To Oyun, Patrick, Julia, and Mochi.
Thank you for your love and support.*

Contents

Acknowledgments / ix

Introduction: Framing a Canadian Strategy in the Asia-Pacific / 3

1 The Basics: A Critical Examination of Western Narratives on Asia / 19

2 Asian Counter-Narratives: Indo-Pacific, Rules-Based Order, and Freedom and Openness / 40

3 Asian Counter-Narratives: Western State Identity in the Asia-Pacific / 54

4 Asian Narratives on Asia's Security Order: Western Hegemony as a Source of Instability / 76

5 Chinese Counter-Narratives: The Chinese Communist Party, Hong Kong, Xinjiang, and Foreign Affairs / 99

6 Mapping a Canadian Policy Approach to Asia: National Interests, Asian Narratives, and Network Analysis / 120

Conclusion: Toward Omnidirectional Diplomacy and
Strategic Integration / 144

Notes / 158

Selected Bibliography / 238

Index / 244

Acknowledgments

I would like to thank Stewart Beck, Marie-Lucie Morin, and Pierre Pettigrew of the Asia Pacific Foundation of Canada (APFC) for the time and space I needed to write this volume. I would also like to thank Jeff Nankivell, CEO and president of the APFC, for his support throughout the publishing process, as well as the APFC board of directors and staff. Thanks also to Professor Paul Evans for encouraging me throughout the writing process.

FOLLOW THE LEADER, LOSE THE REGION

Introduction

Framing a Canadian Strategy in the Asia-Pacific

In 2019, Canadian prime minister Justin Trudeau stood beside Japanese prime minister Shinzo Abe in Ottawa and called for greater Canadian-Japanese cooperation in the "Indo-Pacific." Hailed in the Canadian media at the time as a sign of Canadian middle-power diplomacy, Trudeau's comments left many in government and academic circles scratching their heads. Had Canada adopted an Indo-Pacific strategy toward Asia? Was the prime minister speaking off the cuff – perhaps inadvertently using Japan's preferred nomenclature around the Asian region's strategic environment – or was he purposefully and tactically aligning Canada's strategic posture in Asia with the Abe government's Free and Open Indo-Pacific (FOIP) vision? Did he understand that in adopting an Indo-Pacific framework for Canada's foreign policy approach to Asia he was positioning his country to be a part of a controversial US-led strategy that many Asian states viewed as anti-Chinese in spirit and practice?[1]

For some, such considerations were inconsequential. Canada should of course align its Asia-directed foreign and security policies with the United States and Japan – indeed, with any Western nation that shares Canada's values with respect to the international rule of law and a liberal "rules-based order."[2] At the time of Trudeau's comments, Canada was, after all, in the midst of a confrontation with the People's Republic of China (PRC) over Canada's decision to detain Meng Wanzhou, chief financial officer of the Chinese firm Huawei and a Chinese corporate celebrity, and China's reciprocal arrest of two Canadian citizens working in China, Michael Kovrig and Michael Spavor. In the face of increased Chinese pressure and growing uncertainty in Asia, surely Canada would want to work with the United States and other Western nations to secure its interests in the region?

For others, however, the prospect of Canadian alignment along an Indo-Pacific ideal was less than appealing. Far from being a workable vision of a future Asian order, some analysts argued, the Indo-Pacific ideal was instead a US-led, Defense Department–driven attempt to preserve American predominance over Asia's institutions.[3] The Trump administration, in particular, articulated its Indo-Pacific vision in largely antagonistic, militaristic terms, with Secretary of Defense Mark Esper pledging in a 2020 speech in Hawaii that the United States would "not cede an inch" of Asia to any other state.[4] Whatever Canada might gain from an Indo-Pacific alignment, these analysts warned, it equally stood to lose if it aligned itself with a consortium of states committed to self-preservation over regional stability.

For Canada, then, there seemed to be no clear answer in 2019 – or in 2020, 2021, or 2022 – as to the country's most effective approach to the Asia-Pacific, a region that Canadian policy-makers and businesspeople alike understood as full of opportunity but also as inherently difficult to navigate. Adding to this uncertainty was a hardening schism within the Canadian policy community over the approach Ottawa should take toward China, fostered in large part by commentary in the *Globe and Mail* that sought to frame those advocating Canada-China engagement as "naïve" or "soft on China" and those calling for Canada to adopt a harder line toward Beijing as "realists."[5] Mirroring the groupthink in the United States over China's role in Asia and adopting the US-based narrative that Asia's liberal order was under threat, Canada's policy writers entered a period of analytical malaise at exactly the time when Ottawa most needed strategic creativity.

The Heart of the Matter

Part of Canada's challenge in shaping a domestic approach to the Asia-Pacific is the lack of sophisticated domestic debate around the region's developing dynamics, the primary result of Canadian policy analysts' continued reliance on Western narratives and paradigms when conceptualizing the Asian region.[6] Rather than engaging in critical analysis of

Asia's security, governance, or economic trends – up to and including critique of Western assumptions toward the region – Canadian analysts instead almost uniformly frame their regional analysis within prescribed Western world views, many of which are either inherently biased or outright incorrect.[7] The shared belief among Canadian scholars on Asia that the country's membership in the G7 gives it a middle-power advantage in the region, for instance, is based on the mistaken belief that Asian states continue to look to Western economies as the standard-bearers for international governance norms. Similarly, the nearly universal belief among Canadian policy writers that the Communist Party of China (CPC) is illiberal, unstable, and repressive undermines the basis for a more robust – indeed, informed – Canadian policy toward China.[8]

Not only does this parochial world view set a false starting point for Canadian policy development, but it also contributes to an ossification of dialogue in Canada around Asia's primary strategic dynamics. Canadian advocacy for alignment with the US-led Indo-Pacific strategy is a case in point, as those pushing for it do so with little, if any, reference to the strategy's broader strategic context. In debating whether or not Canada should align with the United States, or Japan, or indeed any Western democratic state around an Asia-Pacific strategy, for instance, Canadian analysts make broad, often incorrect, assumptions about the nature of contemporary Asian order, including the region's existing and emerging institutions, its great power dynamics, its values and norms, and, most consequentially, Canada's place within the region.[9] More fundamentally, while an informed Canadian approach to Asia must necessarily address sensitive topics such as which states get to decide what constitutes Asian order, whether and to what degree China has a legitimate right to influence its own geographic region, and whether non-democratic states have the same legitimacy with respect to the international system, international institutions, and international mores, few Canadian policy analysts ever reference these issues in their writing.

From a policy development perspective, the lack of critical analysis in Canadian policy writing on the Asia-Pacific is problematic as there are a number of fundamental paradigms that Canadian policy-makers must address before developing an informed, national-level strategy toward the region. First, and arguably most consequentially, is whether the United States was, is, and will be Canada's best strategic partner for a bilateral approach to the Asia-Pacific region. For too many Canadian analysts, the answer to this question is an uncritical "yes," despite what many of these individuals identified as the Trump administration's shortcomings and the continued uncertainty about the Biden administration's approach to the Asia-Pacific.[10]

Canada and the United States share an ideational and civilizational identity, the argument goes, and therefore share the same national security goals in the Asian-Pacific region as a matter of course.[11] Further, only Washington has the capacity to shape Asian order with respect to institutions, international law, and great power relations, making it the most direct means for Canada to advance its own national interests within the region.[12] Moreover, Washington is the "indispensable nation" in Asia and has inarguably played a moderating role in the postwar era, structuring the region's security environment through its alliance system and providing security as a regional public good through its forward military presence.[13] For a state like Canada that lacks the agency to effect regional change on its own, partnership with the United States offers the clearest and arguably most natural path forward.[14] Failure to realize this value proposition in Canada-US relations is, according to some, a failure to understand the nature of international relations, particularly in a region where power is the ultimate arbitrator.

Closer analysis of the US role in Asia, however, suggests that such unmitigated optimism is unwarranted. Rather than providing a net strategic benefit, the Canada-US relationship can be a burden for Ottawa, particularly when Canada seeks to demonstrate autonomy in the region.[15] Further, far from offering a strategic way forward for Canada, the United States under the Obama and Trump administrations has become largely defence-dependent in both its strategic thinking and operational engagement and outreach, a policy approach the Biden administration is set to continue through its participation in newly minted, Western-led institutions like the AUKUS trilateral and the Quadrilateral Security Dialogue (the Quad).[16] No longer the regional hegemon, the United States is rather Asia's predominant security actor, running much of its diplomacy and engagement through the Department of Defense, not the Department of State.[17] As such, American policy-makers view Asia through a security lens, particularly with respect to China's activities in the region.[18] Washington's reliance on this framework for planning and operations neither offers Canada a model for engagement nor provides it with a non-securitized role for collaboration.

Second, and closely related, is the nature of Canada's relations with Western states and actors in Asia more broadly. Australia, the European Union, France, Germany, Japan,[19] the United Kingdom, and the United States have all articulated strategic approaches to the Indo-Pacific region predicated on Western state alignment and security cooperation through institutions such as AUKUS and the Quad.[20] These Western states have rationalized their strategic approaches to Asia as necessary to ensure a regional rules-based order, ostensibly one dependent on Western leadership, security cooperation, and regional intervention.[21]

Canadian policy writers almost uniformly assume that the country would benefit from closer cooperation and coordination with Western states in Asia, since Canada intrinsically shares these states' values (more on this below) and interests.[22] Western states, the reasoning goes, are better stewards of regional institutions such as human rights regimes, international rule of law, maritime security, and Asia's political economy than non-Western, illiberal states. For Canada, Western state alignment in the Indo-Pacific is therefore a clear "win" with respect to the country's regional positioning and its values-based foreign policy.[23]

As with Canada's relations with the United States, however, critical analysis of Asian narratives on Western state involvement in Asia suggests that the reality on the ground is more complicated. Within Asian discourse, for instance, one finds almost no demand signals for Western state involvement and/or leadership in or over the region's order. Neither does one find much reference in regional leadership statements, academic writing, media, or public polling that suggests Asian states and peoples share Western critiques of the region's order. Rather, one finds a well-developed body of literature among Asian commentators from Northeast and Southeast Asia identifying Western state (particularly US) involvement in Asia as a source of instability and ongoing conflict.[24] Even within Japanese and South Korean polling and writing, one finds deep skepticism over Western states' engagement in Asia and over Western concepts including the "Indo-Pacific" and "rules-based order." There is simply no regional evidence that Asian states are clamouring for Western leadership, or that they view Western states' relatively recent interest in Asia's order as a net-positive development for the region. The presumption that Canada would benefit from alignment with Western states in Asia is simply incorrect and easily dispelled through a critical analysis of Asian narratives.

Rather than prioritize Western state alignment, therefore, Canada should prioritize engagement with all Asian states that are interested in working toward a stable, inclusive, and cooperative Asian region. Rather than submit each bilateral relationship, each international institution, and each engagement to a "like-minded state" litmus test, Canadian policy-makers should pursue a policy of *omnidirectional diplomacy* and *strategic integration,* or the purposeful engagement with a myriad of Western and Asian states to ensure Canadian strategic, operational, and tactical cooperation throughout the region. Deep integration in multiple regional institutions, not ideological alignment with its Western partners, better serves Canada's national interests in Asia.

For many Canadian readers, the idea of a value-free foreign policy is anathema to how they view Canada's position in Asia and within the broader global community. The idea that the "world needs more Canada" has become central to how Canadians think about their country in general and their political and cultural values in particular.[25] Indeed, many Canadians are prepared are forgo deeper ties with states like China on the grounds that its government rejects Western concepts of human rights and governance. This leads to the third point of contention simmering within the larger debate over Canada's approach to Asia: the role of values in state relations.

For many Canadian policy-makers, there is a clear desire to align the country's foreign policy – or aspects of its policy – with other Western states, those that ostensibly share its values with respect to individual rights, state/society relations, and international law. There is a strong pull, then, from states like Australia and Japan that have integrated the idea of the like-minded state in their foreign and strategic policies so as to appeal, on a normative basis, to other Western democracies, like Canada, for cooperation and coordination.[26]

Inherently, this appeal to shared values offers a clear contrast with states like China that have different value systems – or lack values, as many Western analysts wrongly suggest – and are therefore deemed outsiders (at best) or disrupters (more commonly) to Asia's regional order. This appeal to common values, to like-mindedness, also provides Canada an opportunity to develop closer ties with Western states and institutions (as outlined above) and a clear rationale for selling its foreign policy approach to a increasingly skeptical Canadian public.[27]

Notably, the appeal for ideological alignment with like-minded states, particularly the United States, is especially pervasive in the Canadian policy and academic communities with respect to the country's China policy. One sees this most clearly in media opinion pieces on Canada-China relations, particularly in the *Globe and Mail*, Canada's most prestigious national media publication. Since early 2019, in particular, the *Globe* has published almost daily op-eds from Canada's most reliably anti-China commentators, contributing, at least in part, to a national conversation on China heavily biased against engagement.[28] The corollary to this position is the need for greater alignment with the United States, which, at least from the perspective of some of the paper's contributing authors, shares Canada's commitment to liberal norms.

It is not certain, however, that Canadian normative alignment with like-minded states is necessarily desirable, or even, ironically, ethical. Indeed, the idea of a coalition of liberal states – whether formal or informal – as a counterbalance to Asia's changing order is inherently chauvinistic, both with respect to the diversity of ideals and inclusivity of nation-states. At a time when democracy in Asia is in decline and when democratic states around the world have come under scrutiny for their widespread failures to arrest the spread of COVID-19 within their respective societies, the idea that Canada would predicate its approach to Asia on shared ideological alignment is both normatively arrogant and strategically inept.[29]

Neither is it certain that states such as India, Japan, and/or the United States do, in fact, share Canadian values, particularly with respect to state/society relations, democratic elections and accountability, economic governance, or "inclusivity toward immigrants and non-ethnic–majority citizens.[30] The United States under the Trump administration, in particular, demonstrated a very illiberal approach to foreign policy – supported by nearly half of Americans – that Ottawa would be foolish to support and should be loath to emulate.

Neither is it true that Asian states operate without foreign policy values, or that their different systems make them any less committed to Asia's regional institutions or stability.[31] China's foreign policy behaviour is directly correlated with the priorities it sets around domestic political stability, state/society relations, and national sovereignty for instance.[32] On the whole, therefore, Beijing prioritizes stability in its state relations in Asia, a prioritization that Asian states (as well as

Canadians) well understand and largely appreciate. Indeed, while Asian states clearly remain wary of China's influence, the old trope that these same states fear China and seek partnership with the United States to balance China is less true now than before.[33] States such as Indonesia, Malaysia, Thailand, and Vietnam, for example, have all demonstrated a keen ability to negotiate with China in ways that advance their own national interests and their national understanding of Asia's strategic environment, even on sensitive matters such as maritime disputes, while states such as Cambodia, Laos, and Myanmar have deepened their economic and political relations with China willingly, not as a result of coercion.[34]

Should Canada ultimately decide to align with its "like-minded partners," it will find itself squarely in the club of former colonial powers that are rejecting endogenous change in Asia and states that see China's "rise" (another unhelpful, outdated trope) as a security challenge rather than an opportunity for greater Asian integration and state-level cooperation.[35] Already an "outside" actor in Asia, Canada could find its opportunities for engagement further limited if regional actors see it – rightly or wrongly – as part of a Western coalition of states intent on arresting regional development for the sake of its continued predominance.

Omnidirectional Diplomacy and Strategic Integration
For Canada, conceptualizing and operationalizing a successful strategy toward Asia means navigating these competing narratives and dynamics to the extent that it can maximize its national interests in the region. As argued throughout this book, Canada cannot achieve this outcome through uncritical alignment with its traditional Western partners, as Western narratives toward Asia are largely biased and at times chauvinistic. Views from Brussels, Canberra, London, Paris, and Washington, far from representing regional dynamics and respecting regional developments, are too often grounded in Western-centric, neocolonial visions of global order and Western leadership and cannot offer Canada a sustainable, inclusive framework on which to build its own national strategy toward Asia. Rather, Ottawa must critically evaluate regional narratives on Asian order to find the correct path for Canada to follow. Through this approach, Canada can effect a strategic policy of omnidirectional diplomacy, avoiding ideological alignment for the sake of informed, non-ideologically based engagement.

Concurrently, Canada must seek concrete opportunities to work with regional actors and within regional networks to establish tangible relations with Asian states and actors and to advance its national interests and values through dialogue and cooperation. Central to this proposition is the need to understand more fully Asia's institutional architecture, primarily those ASEAN (Association of Southeast Asian Nations) and non-ASEAN institutions that enable Canada to work on issues of national priority. Through this policy of strategic integration, Canada can best position itself for non-ideological engagement, thereby raising its influence throughout the Asia-Pacific on issues of ideological importance to the Canadian people, such as human rights, climate change, and gender equality.

On Omnidirectional Diplomacy
There are many reasons why Canada would align its policy with that of Western states in Asia. In addition to Canada's having shared values with states like Australia and France, as well as shared interests with the European Union and the United States, these Western actors have all articulated a strategic approach to Asia, or the Indo-Pacific, based on these values and interests that Ottawa could adopt and implement with little effort. For Canadian policy-makers and strategic analysts, the common appeal from Western states to support the "rules-based order" is attractive as it reinforces their perception of Canada as a liberal state committed to international rule and international order and provides them with a means to amplify Canada's agency and voice on international issues. Further, the appeal among Canadian policy-makers in particular for conceptual and operational alignment toward Asia will grow as more and more Western states coordinate their activities through Western-oriented institutions such as the G7, NATO, AUKUS, and the Quad, and Western narratives toward Asia increasingly cast the region's order as being under threat from authoritarianism.

The pressure for Western alignment will increase even more as the Canadian public's views on the region harden, particularly with respect to Canada-China relations. Recent polls from the Asia Pacific Foundation of Canada suggest, for instance, that the Canadian public holds Beijing with as little regard as they do North Korea, and that they prefer that their government representatives deprioritize China's interests and reprioritize Canada's values when approaching Asia.[36]

Within Canada, there is a further predilection for cooperation with like-minded states, or Western state actors.

While the Trump administration's "America First" policy had the effect in Canada of raising questions among government officials and scholars over whether Canada and the United States are indeed like-minded with respect to their national and foreign policy values, the necessity for Canadian policy analysts to question Canada's relations with its most important Western partner quickly dissipated under the Biden administration. Indeed, calls within Canada for alignment with the Biden administration toward China have actually arisen as President Biden has used international forums to frame China as the West's predominant, if not existential, challenge and to call for Western states to align against Beijing around their shared values and US leadership.

Suffice it to say that Canada's natural inclination will continue to be alignment with Western states in its approach to Asia, particularly with the United States on matters related to governance, security, and human rights. As this book will demonstrate, however, wholesale Canadian alignment with the United States, or with any coalition of Western states, will come with significant costs as Western narratives and strategic assumptions toward Asia are not representative of regional views, and any state that fails to take regional perspectives into consideration will inevitably find regional states and institutions less interested in engagement.

To avoid a scenario where Canada's national interests are harmed through overreliance on Western states' approaches to Asia, Ottawa must critically examine its assumptions toward the region with the intent of decoding regional signals on issues of strategic importance. The critical evaluation of Western narratives on Asia is the necessary starting point, as many of the assumptions informing Western views of Asia do not stand up to scrutiny when held against regional dialogue, perceptions, or values. Concurrently, Canadian policy-makers and analysts must spend the time and effort to understand regional narratives regarding Asia's strategic environment. Doing so will enable Ottawa to approach the region from an analytical and conceptual position of strength, not from one based on chauvinistic, antiquated views of Western hegemony and Asian state subordination.

The end state of this approach is not complete strategic decoupling from Western states, particularly the United States. Canada's strategic interests are too intertwined with those of the United States for us to realistically expect it to ignore Washington's policy dialogues and processes for the sake of an entirely autonomous approach to Asia. Ottawa will always need to take US perspectives into account in its own policy deliberations, if for no reason other than the United States' geographic proximity and its direct impact on Canadian national interests through its proximity and power. Canada will also always find partnership in Western institutions such as the G7 and NATO to be force multipliers enabling it to exercise global agency disproportionate to its actual material and ideological strengths. Further, Canada is a quintessential Western state in its identity, governance, and values and will always seek to lead in these areas where it can – and rightfully so.

Canada should, rather, seek to establish equidistance between its natural Western orientation and the realities within the Asian region, particularly when such equidistance provides it greater opportunities to engage on issues such as human rights, gender equality, and climate change that are so central to it own priorities. Canada need not compromise its own values to do so. Indeed, in approaching the region through a position of humility and compromise, Canada can demonstrate to Asian states – including China – that it is committed to inclusivity and consultation.

What does a policy of omnidirectional diplomacy look like in practice? First, it requires a basis of strategic non-alignment, particularly around Western concepts such as the Indo-Pacific, which have become increasingly aligned with Western hegemonic ideals such as order preservation, Western leadership, and Western-directed security partnerships. Regional states are rightfully wary of these concepts, seeing the Indo-Pacific concept in largely confrontational, anti-Chinese terms. Canada should avoid aligning its foreign and security policies toward Asia with these Indo-Pacific strategies, particularly as they remain controversial throughout the region.

Second, Canada must work to understand and internalize regional perceptions of Asia's strategic environment, especially when these perceptions challenge Canada's assumptions toward the region. This book will identify many such instances and can therefore serve as a starting point for critical analysis of Canada's foreign policy approach to Asia. It alone cannot, however, serve as a strategic master plan toward the region. Rather, Canadian policy-makers must allocate resources to understand and respond better to Asia's changing environment and remain adaptive to shifts in regional perspectives and priorities, realizing all the while that regional dynamics shift as states' interests evolve.

Third, Canada must use this knowledge of regional dynamics to formulate tactical and operational relations in Asia that best enable it to advance its national interests in the region. This process is best understood as strategic integration, and it is to this point that we now turn.

On Strategic Integration

Within Asian narratives on regional state engagement and economic development, one of the most frequently recurring themes is "interconnectivity." Whether one examines China's Belt and Road Initiative (BRI), South Korea's New Southern Policy, or ASEAN's Economic Community, one sees repeated reference to interconnectivity as the primary means to strength ties between Asian actors and to establish further a community of Asian nations. Materially, Asian states and state actors establish interconnectivity through transnational infrastructure projects, cross-border special economic zones, and regionally based supply chains. Ideationally, these same states facilitate interconnectivity through free trade agreements, regionally agreed-upon standards and regulations, regional dialogue mechanisms, and sociocultural exchange. Whereas Western narratives on Asia are predicated on the idea the region's order is under strain from illiberal (read Chinese) sources, Asian narratives on Asian order instead describe a growing web of state and substate relations that constitute a regional ecosystem of networks and relations.

Interconnectivity, in this sense, is both a means to achieve Asian state cooperation and a strategic end state in that it provides a mechanism for the movement of Asian people, goods, and ideas. Across the region, Asian states are establishing new institutions designed to hasten this integration. These institutions are not, as Western narratives suggest, a source of regional instability. They are, rather, mechanisms designed by Asian actors to represent Asian interests within the Asian region.

For Canada, these institutions offer the most direct means of tactical and operational engagement in Asia. At the strategic level, they provide Canadian policy-makers and analysts with a venue for engagement and dialogue on issues of regional importance. At the working group level, they provide with Canada access to outcome-driven engagement on issues ranging from human rights to governance, from sustainable development to nuclear non-proliferation. More than any other means, these institutions provide Canada with a map of regional networks and ties through which it can work to engage.

Canadian policy-makers' priorities toward these networks should be non-ideological, non-restrictive engagement, or what this book calls "strategic integration." Whether with respect to the ASEAN+ mechanisms or the Conference on Interaction and Confidence Building Measures in Asia (CICA), the Canadian government should actively seek strategic-level representation in Asia's predominant institutions and tactical-level cooperation in the institutions' working and expert groups. As Asia's new institutions are increasingly one-stop shops for dialogue and work covering politics, economics, security, environment, and social engagement, Canada should be non-discerning with regard to an institution's ideological orientation, its membership, or its leadership, but should rather seek to engage with each institution on the conceptual grounds that Canada's interests in Asia are best served through dialogue and representation.

Equally, Canadian policy-makers should approach institutional engagement in Asia with the understanding that Canada's ability to influence regional discourse on issues the Canadian public prioritizes in its foreign relations, such as human rights and climate change, is dramatically expanded through non-paternalistic engagement. Rather than work with like-minded states to arrest Asia's institutional development, Canada can work with regional states, actors, and institutions to raise its values at the dialogue and working levels.

In addition to greater influence, a strategic integration approach to Asia's institutions and networks provides Canada with greater strategic flexibility in the region. Integration is not a dogmatic strategic ideal – unlike the Western "free" and "open" Indo-Pacific strategies – but rather one that prioritizes strategic engagement for tactical-level outcomes. Whereas Ottawa would necessarily lose the ability to engage with Asian states and Asian actors through alignment with the United States, for instance, a strategic integration approach would enable Canada to prioritize issue areas, relations, and networks depending on its national interests and its resources. If Canada decides human rights is its most important priority in Asia, for instance, it can work within Asian institutions and networks that address the issue, simultaneously learning from and influencing Asian discourse. Similarly, if Canada wants greater input on issues around a code of conduct for the South

China Sea, it can work with regional states to raise its concerns and viewpoints.

Importantly, strategic integration directly supports (and is dependent on) omnidirectional diplomacy. Canada is already integrated in Western-oriented institutions that are active, or are trying to become active, in the Asia-Pacific including the G7, the Five Eyes intelligence alliance, and NATO. Canadian policy-makers are further considering Canadian involvement in new Western-centric institutions such as AUKUS and the Quad. Canadian involvement in Asia's regional institutions, particularly ASEAN's working groups and non-ASEAN institutions such as the Lancang-Mekong Cooperation (LMC) forum and the Bay of Bengal Initiative for Multi-Sectoral Technical and Economic Cooperation (BIMSTEC), would provide counterbalance to its membership in Western institutions and increase its legitimacy as an independent strategic actor in the region. Far from diluting its existing relations with Western states and institutions, strategic integration in Asia would likely increase Canada's influence as it would enable Ottawa to "translate" Asian narratives for its Western partners.

Toward a More Informed Canadian Foreign Policy Approach to Asia

This book employs critical theory to examine and to critique the predominant Western narratives on Asia with the intent of informing a Canadian policy of omnidirectional diplomacy and strategic integration toward the region. Methodologically, the book examines scholarship, leadership statements, polling, and media from Northeast Asia (Japan, South Korea), Southeast Asia (Indonesia, Malaysia, Thailand, and Vietnam), and China to challenge Western narratives' predominant themes and assumptions and to provide alternative regional views. On issues ranging from the Indo-Pacific construct to Asia's "rules-based order," it undertakes textual analysis in Japanese, Korea, Indonesian, Malay, Thai, and Vietnamese to demonstrate Western discourses' misunderstanding of regional developments and to outline alternative, regionally based views of Asia's contemporary dynamics. It further details Mandarin-language scholarship, media, leadership statements, and polling to offer a counter-narrative to Western narratives on China's identity, its intentions, its institutions, and its state/society relations.[37] To ensure as accurate an account of Asia's counter-narrative as possible, it identifies scholarship and writing as part of each country's

Introduction

collective "mainstream" media even when such narratives constitute outsider perspectives vis-à-vis more dominant narrative strands. Identifying Japanese literature critical of the US-Japan security alliance, for instance, I took pains to review work from reputable publications and established, non-fringe authors.

Chapter 1 lays out the book's central argument, which is the idea that Western narratives on Asia are more representative of Western self-perceptions, Western beliefs, and Western-shared ideals than they are of regional realities. The chapter introduces concepts drawn from critical theory, critical security studies, and post-colonial literature, such as cultural hegemony and hegemonic socialization, to argue that Western narratives on Asia are a product of US hegemony, up to and including ideas around the region's international relations, Asia's rules-based order, the like-minded state trope, and the "free" and "open" concepts.

To elaborate this point further, Chapter 2 outlines narratives from Japan, South Korea, Indonesia, Malaysia, Thailand, and Vietnam on the Indo-Pacific as a geographic area and its conceptual foundations. Through close textual analysis, it demonstrates how Western assumptions around the Indo-Pacific are largely discordant with Asian thinking on the topic, including in Western-aligned states such as Japan.

Chapter 3 also employs non-English–language textual analysis to consider regional narratives on Western state involvement in Asia. Specifically, it examines how regional states view the United States, Europe and European states, Australia, Japan, and India as regional actors. It demonstrates that Asian narratives on US leadership and Western state involvement in Asia differ from Western discourse, which sees Western state leadership and involvement in Asia as a net positive for the region's stability. Chapter 3 also shows how the views of regional states toward Australia, Japan, and India diverge from the Western assumption that the three states are representative Asian actors and/or Western like-minded states.

Chapter 4 also explores regional narratives on three of Asia's predominant security issues: maritime security in the South China Sea, nuclear security on the Korean peninsula, and China-Taiwan security relations. It challenges Western assumptions about Asia's security regimes and the stabilizing effect Western states have on the region's security order. It demonstrates, for example, that the United States' predilection for Western security cooperation through institutions such as AUKUS are problematic as they totally ignore regional discourse that treats Western intervention in Asia as a source of *instability* rather than stability.

Moving from Asian narratives, Chapter 5 examines Mandarin-language writing and polling on China's predominant domestic and foreign issues, including Chinese domestic support for the Chinese Communist Party and the country's foreign policy motivations. It also outlines Chinese perspectives on issues central to Canada-China relations, such as the situation in the Xinjiang Uyghur Autonomous Region (XUAR), China-Taiwan relations, and governance in Hong Kong.

Chapter 6 builds on the previous chapters' analysis to undertake a brief network analysis of Canada's involvement in the Asia-Pacific's primary endogenous institutions and to identify further opportunities for Canadian engagement in the region's institutional networks. It outlines a networked approach for deeper Canadian engagement in the Asia-Pacific, setting the conceptual ground for the concluding chapter, which articulates a Canadian strategic approach to the region predicated on omnidirectional diplomacy and strategic integration.

1

The Basics

A Critical Examination of Western Narratives on Asia

Narratives are a foundational component of international relations, although scholars spend a surprisingly small amount of time considering their influence over global and regional systems and affairs. In addition to providing ideational frameworks for debate, narratives inform such intangibles as a state's identity, its national interests, its relations with its own society, and its ties with the rest of the world.[1] Narratives determine the language policy-makers and scholars use to articulate their state's priorities and values, thereby influencing the policies and analysis that result. They are the most basic component of how states view the world, determining, in the process, the nature of the international system.[2]

Narratives have the reiterative quality of both responding to and informing how states and state actors view their place in international society.[3] Canadian policy-makers, for instance, operate reactively to reinforce positive international narratives about Canada's national identity and proactively to advance Canada's narrative of its own foreign policy priorities and values. While having the positive effect of enabling states to engage, narratives can have the negative effect of reducing a state's perceived options regarding a specific issue area, within a specific institution, and toward a specific state. Narratives can also have the reductive quality of limiting a state's ability to maneuver in a dynamic environment, as they tend to evolve slowly and over time rather than in response to dramatic shifts in state relations and power dynamics.

Importantly, narratives are not neutral, as most of those who operate within their confines presume, but are the product of power dynamics.[4] Just as history is written by the victors, so dominant powers have a disproportionate influence over the formation and propagation of narratives. This effect is particularly pronounced when the dominant state operates not only through bilateral relations but also through multilateral institutions where appeals to common ideology, interests, and values are integral to an institution's structure and governance systems.[5] Antonio Gramsci described this process in his writing on cultural hegemony. G. John Ikenberry and Charles A. Kupchan expanded the concept to international relations in their writing on hegemonic socialization. Both of these concepts are addressed in more detail below.

Narratives are inherently value-laden, both responding to and reinforcing specific ideologies.[6] During the Cold War, for instance, concepts including historical materialism informed communist narratives on economics, politics, and security.[7] In contemporary Asia, the Democratic People's Republic of Korea (DPRK) relies on values around national struggle and self-reliance (*juche*) to inform narratives of legitimacy around North Korea's power structure.[8] Similarly, values of "freedom" and "independence" are central to US narratives around American exceptionalism.[9] These are, of course, only three well-known examples of the interplay between narratives and values that can be observed in national discourses throughout recorded history.[10]

Narratives are also fundamentally a collection of assumptions, not facts.[11] In this respect, they are closer to dogmas than to academic disciplines.[12] Quite often, narratives depend on their adherents' unquestioning loyalty for their survival, and wither under critical scrutiny. To prevent such scrutiny, narratives tend to include well-developed defence mechanisms. Those brave (or foolish) enough to question a narrative's validity, for example, often find themselves excommunicated, branded as traitors to the cause.

For Canada, the need to understand the role of narratives in Asian affairs is practical, not academic. As outlined in this book's introduction, policy-makers are disadvantaged by overreliance on Western narratives in formulating Canada's national approach to Asia, as Western narratives are largely based on assumptions around regional dynamics that do not correspond with reality. Whether having to do with concepts such as international law, the rules-based order, or the like-minded state, much of the Western narrative around Asia, as demonstrated throughout this book, is a function of Western self-referential identity, not regional perceptions.

US narratives, in particular, have become predominant to the extent that they now shape how other Western nations conceptualize the Asian region, primarily by setting narrative signs and signals through discourse on the region's dynamics. Canadian policy analysts too often accept these narrative indicators as a fixed sign of Asia's actual strategic realities, not, as they actually are, as reflections of US priorities and interests in the region.

Much of this book is dedicated to examining the assumptions within Western meta-narratives on Asia, specifically the contentions within Western discourse regarding the "Indo-Pacific," Western leadership, regional security, and China. Notably, to undertake an analytical exercise of this scope, it is sometimes necessary to employ simple analytical models in lieu of innately complicated constructs. Throughout this book, therefore, I will repeatedly reference Western, Canadian, and Asian narratives to describe discourses and perspectives across diverse peoples, states, and regions. In so doing, I knowingly reduce what are at times complicated narrative tributaries into common narrative streams.

Importantly, the use of these generic categories to inform my analytical approach is not meant to deny the richness of their component parts. There are, of course, divergent viewpoints and values across the Western world, within the Asian region, and across Canada. That said, it is this book's central premise that narratives are defining features of the international system that facilitate processes such as foreign and defence policy and inform regimes such as alliance relations and security communities. From this perspective, it is both necessary and appropriate to employ generalized classification systems to describe narrative alignment within and between states, particularly with respect to shared narratives that seek to define the nature of international order and to determine the legitimacy or illegitimacy of international actors.

Toward this end, we turn now to an outline of the conceptual approach employed in this book, addressing Western assumptions about Asia's international relations, Asia's "rules-based order," Asian institutions, international law, and like-minded states in the process.

Critical Theory as a Conceptual Framework
To build a "theory of the case" for how Canadian foreign policy toward Asia is hamstrung by policy-makers' overreliance on Western narratives, this book draws heavily from a body of literature known as critical theory. A relatively overlooked and often esoteric subfield within international relations theory, critical theory is primarily concerned with power dynamics between oppressors and the oppressed. For critical theory pioneers such as Antonio Gramsci, the world is divided between hegemonic powers and those states subordinate to the hegemonic system.[13] One can best understand all state relations, and international systems, therefore, as a function of inequality and exploitation.

Critical theorists draw heavily from Marxist and post-colonial writing to identify and explain how hegemonic actors use narratives, or social tools such as institutions, to shape the systems they control in order to ensure an unfair playing field, one in which they are better able to secure their predominance and propagate their interests.[14] For critical theorists, international society is fundamentally a rigged system designed to give states and state actors the perception that they have agency while systematically limiting their ability to take real independent action.[15]

These dynamics have necessarily produced winners and losers and, more importantly, promote the winners' interests through the propagation of their values and ideals. From a critical theorist's perspective, international institutions are tools of oppression as much as they are a component of global governance.[16] Similarly, universal values are a hegemonic means of social and cultural subjugation, not, as the system's dominant powers would have all states believe, an appeal to a common humanity.

Within the critical theorist's world view, narratives play a central role in propagating hegemonic control over subordinate states. Narratives enable dominant states to selectively build a normative rationale for their behaviour and an ideational framework for critique of other states.[17] Through narrative formation and control, hegemonic powers can determine, for instance, which states are "insiders" and which are "outsiders." In more extreme cases, hegemonic powers use narratives to justify interventions, conflicts, and war.[18] The American Cold War–era "domino theory" is an excellent example of a hegemonic narrative used to justify US military intervention in the Korean

Peninsula and Indochina, among other contingencies, all under the logic of containment.[19]

Critical theorists also argue that hegemonic powers use narratives to effect control over their partner states, primarily through a process Gramsci called "cultural hegemony," Ikenberry and Kupchan termed "hegemonic socialization," and Michel Foucault labelled "discursive power."[20] Through their dominance of international society's primary mechanisms (institutions, dialogues, regimes), hegemonic states advance their narratives and compel secondary states to adopt them. Secondary states either voluntarily or reluctantly internalize the hegemon's narratives as doing so increases their prestige and influence within the hegemonic system.[21] Once established, the hegemonic narrative "ecosystem" has a self-perpetuating quality. States with shared narratives validate one another and strengthen their narrative alignment accordingly.[22]

Narrative alignment, in turn, becomes an ideological litmus test for the hegemon's partners, or what analysts now refer to as "like-minded states." Those that share the hegemonic state's values and beliefs have access to its resources, networks, and support. Those that do not run the risk of becoming a target for hegemon-led collective action, with their beliefs, systems, relations, and ties cast as inherently "illegitimate" or, with respect to the Asia-Pacific, "illiberal."

From this book's perspective, critical theory provides an important conceptual means to evaluate contemporary Western narratives on Asia. Viewing them through the lens of hegemony, power dynamics, and cultural hegemony, one can see how Western narratives around the Indo-Pacific, for instance, are less about advancing Asian states' interests and/or perspectives than they are about ensuring Western (primarily American) hegemony and military predominance over the Asian region. Western narratives on China and Asian security, further, are more concerned with justifying Western predominance in Asia than they are with accurately reflecting regional realities, representing regional perspectives, or ensuring regional stability.

Similarly, Western narratives on Western leadership almost entirely discount Asian states' agency and mispresent the structure of Asian order to legitimize Western intervention in the region. Each of these areas is addressed in detail in subsequent chapters.

Critical theory's understanding of cultural hegemony, hegemonic socialization, and discursive power is also fundamental to this book's argument that the overdependence of Canadian policy-makers and analysts on Western narratives for their Asian policy development is a source of strategic vulnerability. Specifically, critical theory suggests that Ottawa's propensity to approach Asia through a Western analytical lens is not the result of thoughtful analysis over the best way to achieve Canada's national interests, but rather a function of US hegemony and Canada's place within the existing hegemonic system. Canadian policy-makers and policy analysts who uncritically employ terms like "Indo-Pacific," "rules-based order," or "like-minded states" to describe Canada's approach to Asia are propagating an externally constructed set of assumptions, not articulating a well-crafted national strategy for Canadian regional engagement. That these assumptions do not represent Asian narratives and priorities is particularly problematic for Canada as its policy-makers risk leaving the country isolated in the region if they uncritically internalize the assumptions as their own.

Finally, critical theory provides a starting point for the construction of an alternative narrative on Asia, one structured around regional discourse, perceptions, and priorities rather than Western assumptions. Critical theory's core tenet that hegemonic narratives are power constructs, not accurate descriptions of regional power dynamics, naturally lends itself to closer consideration of regional conditions and dialogues. In rejecting Western claims that Asia is moving toward an Indo-Pacific geographic construct, for instance, a critical theory approach necessarily identifies trends that support an alternative viewpoint – in this case, that the Asian region is becoming more inwardly focused through physical and ideational interconnectivity. The development of a counter-narrative is critical for Canadian policy-makers as it provides the basis for omnidirectional diplomacy and a strategic integration approach to Asia, one based on inclusive engagement, not ideological alignment.

The rest of this chapter employs critical theory to critique dominant Western meta-narratives around Asia's international relations, the rules-based order in Asia, international institutions, internal law, and the like-minded–state trope. The aim is to elaborate further on critical theory's core tenets while demonstrating its value as an analytical framework. To provide the most comprehensive critique possible of Western narratives on Asia, we go back to the very beginning – Western writing on Asia's international relations.

Critical Theory and Asia's International Relations

Within critical theory there are two main critiques of Western narratives on Asia's international relations. The first focuses on the tendency of Western scholars to employ Western standards to evaluate Asia's regional dynamics and experiences, and to assume that Western models of international relations are universal in their applicability to Asia.[23] Critiquing international relations (IR) theory in general, critical theorists argue that realism, liberalism, and constructivism are too Western-centric in their theorizing and biased in their analysis – a process that results in consistent misreading of regional affairs and under-theorization of regional international relations.[24] Western analysis on Asia often relies on Western historical experiences as conceptual baselines and analytical starting points, meaning that much of Asia's experience is treated as an adjunct to Western imperialism and colonialism, not as a unique set of relations and institutions that merit their own field of inquiry.[25]

Conceptually, Western-centric approaches to Asia's international relations too often result in a view of the region as institutionally underdeveloped and politically immature, two viewpoints that informed colonial-era rationales for Western intervention and involvement in the region.[26] By applying Western concepts such as sovereignty to Asia's political regimes, for example, Western scholars have argued that the concept of statehood was underdeveloped in Asia, thereby suggesting the region lagged behind Europe, in particular, in terms of its political sophistication.[27] Central to this perspective is the belief among past scholars, in particular, that the West had a responsibility to "educate" Asia's political elites on modernity, a belief that informed racist ideals, including the "white man's burden" in Asia.[28] In its most virulent form, Western actors employed these narratives to justify "nation building" in Asia or to countenance Western intervention in Asian states' political affairs, a process most recently observed in Afghanistan.

Western-centric IR theories also employ Western paradigms to critique Asia's political regimes, economic institutions, and state/society relations, measuring their "legitimacy" against Western liberalism.[29] Western IR scholars' critiques of the Chinese Communist Party, for instance, tend to focus not on its effectiveness at governing but rather on its lack of political transparency, representation, or accountability – all Western standards for good government.[30] Western critiques of the

Association of Southeast Asian Nations (ASEAN) also tend to use Western models, particularly the European Union, as global standards against which they judge ASEAN's "effectiveness" and/or "success." Western narratives further suggest that economic liberalism and democracy remain the standards against which Asian states' "openness" and "freedom" must be measured.[31] In each instance, the presumption of Western institutions as the global standard dismisses Asia's regional experiences, histories, and innovations.[32]

As demonstrated throughout this book, these ideational Western assumptions regarding Asia's institutions have real-world strategic outcomes for the region, and indeed for Canada's foreign policy toward Asia. The view that Asia is a dependent region within the broader Western-dominated global system, one that requires Western leadership, informs Western strategies on the Indo-Pacific, for instance, in ways that will almost certainly lead to future instability (more on this later). Similarly, the Western proclivity to judge Asia's internal institutions against Western standards creates a paradigm across the Western world that non-democratic states are somehow simply out of equilibrium rather than operating in line with their own internal political traditions.[33] Western ideas around economic "openness" and political "freedom" similarly inform a sense of hubris across Western states leading to the view that an Asian region moving away from these values is one in need of Western leadership and guidance.

Critical theory's second critique of Western IR scholarship on Asia is its lack of inclusivity, equality, and representation from Asian scholars and scholars from the Global South.[34] First, critical theorists argue that Western scholars largely discount Asian viewpoints on Asia's international relations, seeing them as somehow irrelevant to the larger field of international relations, which is primarily theorized around Western experiences.[35] Rather, Western scholars largely ignore regional debates on Asia's past and present experiences, seeing these as little more than outliers to the more established Western system of international relations.[36]

One sees this most clearly with respect to China, where Western scholars overlook the country's rich, unbroken discourse on state/society relations, governance, and international relations only to critique the country in line with Western standards, such as representative democracy. Similarly, Western scholars' near-universal rejection of regional voices on Asia's predominant security regimes – whether the South China Sea, North Korea, or Taiwan – results in a similar biased view of the region's strategic environment. As Western states are more and more willing to tie their own legitimacy in Asia to their support for outcomes that fit their world view of Asia's order, not the ideas regarding order one finds in regional discussions, the dependence on Western narratives once again raises the prospect of regional instability.

Second, critical theorists argue that non-Western voices are structurally underrepresented in IR scholarship as the ability to write and to publish effectively in English has become a structural prerequisite for engagement.[37] The field's most prominent journals and university presses publish almost exclusively in English, all but ensuring that scholars from North America and Europe dominate IR-related discourse. Western scholars then cite these English articles, books, and journals almost exclusively, leading to an echo chamber of analytical debate that is functionally exclusive. Further, Western editors are largely dismissive of those untrained in Western methodologies regarding international relations, an editorial development that has moved IR scholarship markedly toward a US system that privileges quantitative over qualitative analysis. For those more interested in approaching international relations through a humanities lens, particularly those unable to publish in English, there is less and less opportunity for publication. Emanuel Adler and Steven Bernstein label this process "epistemic colonialism."[38]

Again, there are real-world consequences to these outcomes. Western scholars, particularly non-area specialists, who rely on English-language literature to frame their understanding of Asia are necessarily engaging with only a fraction of available scholarship – *a fraction that is exclusively informed by Western narratives and assumptions*. This suggests that even the most conscientious scholars working exclusively in English will find their understanding of alternative viewpoints artificially limited. For policy analysts, the implications are even greater. Rather than presenting a balanced, informed account of ideas, dialogues, and debates to a policy community charged with shaping the state's regional approaches, those working only in English and with English-speaking counterparts will instead present a skewed perspective as a matter of course.

Critical Theory and the "Rules-Based Order"
Within the broader Western narrative on Asia's international relations, the concept of the rules-based order (RBO) in Asia has emerged as a predominant theme. Across Western academic and policy writing, the concept now appears with such frequency that Western analysts uncritically assume its form and function and reference it in their writing as if it were a fixed, observable, and uncontroversial constant within the international system.[39] More specifically, and relevant to discussions of Canada's foreign policy approach toward Asia, the Biden administration now references RBO "preservation" as a key driver behind its Indo-Pacific strategy and its approach to China.[40] Indeed, RBO "protection" is now central to Western states' strategic narratives around and policies toward the Asian region, as outlined below. While the next chapter examines Asian perceptions of the rules-based order in detail, this chapter is concerned with a critical analysis of the rules-based order as a Western meta-narrative.

The rules-based order is a nebulous concept, as exemplified in one well-known Western scholar's observation that defining it is like "wrestling fog."[41] Conceptually, one can trace its genesis to George Kennan's early writing on containment, according to Anne-Marie Slaughter, one of the concept's principal architects.[42] G. John Ikenberry initially used the term with reference to liberal democratic alignment, Western defence of the "liberal international order," and Western military preponderance, all with the expressed intent of preventing great power conflict with autocratic states.[43] Other scholars have used the term interchangeably with concepts that include US hegemony, US unipolarity, and US global leadership, both positively and negatively.[44] Still others have defined the rules-based order as a US-provided "public good," conveniently ignoring the number of times the United States has violated the rules-based order when it has suited its national purpose.[45]

More relevant to this book, Western scholarship on Asia now routinely employs the term "rules-based order" in opposition to China's "revisionism," implying that it is under attack while failing to define its exact parameters.[46] For Western policy analysts, in particular, rules-based order in Asia is as much a rallying cry for Western engagement in Asia as it is a tangible, observable entity.[47] Indeed, more and more Western scholarship treats the rules-based order as a strategic end state in Asia rather than a functioning regime, one that requires concerted Western partnership to secure.[48]

Operationally, one can trace the rules-based order's first regular appearance in the American political and strategic lexicon to 2003, when US policy-makers and policy analysts used the term to justify the United States' unilateral decision to invade Iraq, despite opposition from the United Nations.[49] Within Asia, both the Trump and Biden administrations have invoked the rules-based order to legitimize US military operations and partnerships and to rally Western state cooperation in the Indo-Pacific.[50] President Biden, in particular, has used it to call for Western political and military coordination in Asia and vis-à-vis China with the G7, the European Union, NATO, and the Quad, and with Australia and the United Kingdom through the AUKUS framework in 2021.[51] Within US narratives on Asia, references to the rules-based order are particularly pronounced with respect to US-China competition and the need for the United States to maintain military predominance to defend the rules-based order in Asia against Chinese "revisionism."[52] The US Department of Defense, for example, identified China's challenge to the Indo-Pacific rules-based order and the need for US-led RBO preservation in Asia as the key strategic objective informing its 2021 Pacific Deterrence Initiative, for which it requested US$5 billion.[53]

Outside the United States, one finds repeated reference to RBO preservation as a strategic end state and as an "international public good" in Japan's Free and Open Indo-Pacific concept.[54] The Abe/Suga/Kishida governments, in particular, referenced RBO preservation to justify closer alliance with the United States on regional security matters, up to and including Japan's support for "peace and stability" in the Taiwan Strait.[55] The European Union's Indo-Pacific strategy similarly identifies the rules-based order in Asia to countenance a more robust European (and European naval) presence in Asia, all for the sake of regional "stability."[56] France's Indo-Pacific strategy includes repeated reference to rules-based multilateralism and the rules-based order, as do the Indo-Pacific concepts of the Netherlands and Germany.[57] Somewhat perversely, both London and Berlin have identified the need for RBO preservation in the Indo-Pacific as justification for their respective naval deployments to Asia, including to highly sensitive areas such as the South China Sea and Taiwan Strait.[58]

Support for the rules-based order in Asia is now arguably Australia's predominant strategic objective in the Asia-Pacific.[59] Across its Foreign Policy White Papers and throughout Australian academic writing on the region, one finds repeated mention of Australia's need to work with regional democracies to defend the Indo-Pacific rules-based order.[60] Notably, Australian policy writers and strategists tend to identify the rules-based order's importance in line with Australia's national interests and democratic values, not with respect to Asia's overall stability and security.[61]

Far from a stabilizing regime, critical theorists see the rules-based order as a hegemonic system of oppression designed by predominant powers to ensure their interests vis-à-vis the developing world.[62] Their cynicism comes, in large part, from the fact that Western states established the rules-based order from a position of power and privilege, not through a process of collaboration and consultation.[63] For critical theorists, it is an inherently exclusionary construct, despite Western scholars' claims that states such as China have benefited from the stability it provides. More specifically, critical theorists argue that the rules-based order is a great power means of ensuring an operational space for advancing Western states' economic, diplomatic, and security interests – a space these same states purposefully designed and effectively control.[64]

For critical theorists, the concept of the rules-based order as a fixed entity, particularly when its principal architects use its preservation as a rationale for aggression within the international system, is especially problematic. The United States, in particular, has used perceived threats to the rules-based order as a justification for military action on multiple occasions, the most glaring instance being Iraq, as noted above.[65] Indeed, the United States has similarly referenced its need to protect the rules-based order with respect to its Iran and North Korea policies, up to and including the threat of military force against both states.[66] Most relevant for the sake of this book are US references to the rules-based order in Asia being under "attack" from China.[67]

More specifically, critical theory suggests that the rules-based order is a problematic concept on three salient grounds. First, in order to have legitimacy, the rules-based order cannot be a fixed constant, but must have the ability to adapt to the system it supposedly represents in line with natural systemic changes. This would include the ability to adapt to shifts in relative balances of power between states, to divergences between state types, and to changes in states' values, norms, and principles.[68] Second, critical theorists would reject the premise that the rules-based order can come under attack from any state or coalition of states, as its only "vulnerability" comes from antiquated, unresponsive mechanisms for change. There is no single, fixed rules-based order, so it is more accurate to view its evolution as a contest of ideas or state influence, both of which require ideational buy-in for legitimation.[69] Finally, critical theorists reject the idea that any single state, or consortium of states, has the right to "protect" the rules-based order, particularly if the only "threat" to the system comes from alternative institutions, values, and norms.[70] The rules-based order cannot belong to any single state, short of coercive hegemony, and therefore has value only in its ability to represent all states. US claims that it is protecting the rules-based order through military action, therefore, are not the actions of a benevolent state, but rather a clear example of hegemonic aggression and of the hegemon's willingness to use force to ensure its predominance within the international system.[71]

Other strands of critical theory relevant to analysis of Western narratives on Asia include those concerned with institutions and international law, both of which are central to Western discourse on the rules-based order and Western leadership in Asia. On institutions, for example, critical theorists reject the Western claim that existing global institutions are inclusive and impartial, arguing instead that these institutions are largely skewed in favour of the Western states that established them and consequently resistant to reform.[72] Rather than evolving in line with Asia's development and/or demographic trends, these institutions are instead a primary means through which powerful, wealthy states maintain power, often at the expense of weak, developing states.

Closely related to critical theory's critiques of international institutions are its critiques of international law. As with institutions, critical theory scholars argue that international law is not the result of state consensus, but rather an institution the world's predominant powers established in line with their own understandings of jurisprudence and their own geopolitical and geo-economic interests.[73] International law, in this sense, is not the sacrosanct institution Western analysts often identify as key to a rules based order, but is rather a tool for oppression that the system's established powers use to ensure their privileged positions within the international community and to prevent rival states from upsetting the international status quo.[74] From this perspective, international law, rather than being an impartial tool to effect transnational justice, is a hegemonic instrument designed to ensure the established powers' continued systems-level predominance.[75]

From this perspective, Canadian policy-makers should be wary of the rules-based order as a narrative foundation on which to build a foreign policy approach toward Asia. In addition to its vagueness, the concept remains uniformly Western-centric and does not accurately represent regional trends around order formation, state relations, and strategic priorities. As with the rules-based order, a clearer understanding of the controversies attached to international institutions and law can help inform a more balanced Canadian approach to Asia, particularly as one finds clear skepticism around both concepts within Asian narratives.

Critical Theory and the "Like-Minded State"
Another problematic meta-narrative within Western discourse on Asia is the idea of the like-minded state. Under the Trump administration, the concept emerged as a rallying cry for Western democracies to work together to protect the rules-based order in the Asia-Pacific. Encoded in the United States' 2017 National Security Strategy, the like-minded state concept built on the Obama administration's more measured used of the term to call for a US-led coalition of states, organized primarily to push back against Chinese and Russian revisionism.[76] Conceptually, the Departments of State and Defense furthered the idea of like-minded state cooperation in their respective Indo-Pacific strategies since neither document referenced in the note has the title *Free and Open Indo-Pacific Strategy*?[77] Operationally, President Trump's National Security Council identified like-minded coalition building as key to its plan to maintain US pre-eminence in the Indo-Pacific theatre.[78]

In keeping with Trump-era usage, the Biden administration has embraced the like-minded state paradigm; indeed, it has expanded its usage to describe the return of US leadership on issues as diverse as humanitarianism, climate change, alliance relations, and security cooperation in the Asia-Pacific.[79] As with the Trump administration, the Biden team has similarly identified US like-minded partnership as a cornerstone of its policy to "manage" China.[80]

With such a purposely vague concept, there is no formal constitution of like-minded states in Asia. Indeed, both the Trump and Biden teams have used the concept to call for closer US cooperation with ASEAN member states, many of which neither share US values nor interests toward the region.[81] Part of the US like-minded state paradigm is therefore aimed at fostering an inclusive community of states to advance US interests in the region.

The larger part of the like-minded state model is, however, closely aligned with a US-centric alliance of Western democracies, all of which share the United States' priorities around preserving the rules-based order in Asia and managing China's regional rise. This reading of the like-minded state construct becomes clear in US statements on AUKUS, the Quad, US Indo-Pacific strategies, US commentary on its alliance relations, and US leadership statements on democratic coalitions.[82] Functionally, this grouping of like-minded states includes Australia, France, Germany, Japan, the Netherlands, and the United Kingdom, all of which have embraced the like-minded state approach as a means to further their own national interests in the Asia-Pacific.

For Australia, for instance, like-minded state cooperation is central to the Morrison government's approach to preserving the "durable strategic balance" in the Indo-Pacific.[83] Australian policy-makers and politicians also use the like-minded state model to justify the country's "forever partnership" with the United States and the United Kingdom in the Indo-Pacific through AUKUS.[84] Similarly, the Abe/Suga/Kishida governments in Japan incorporated the idea of like-minded state cooperation in the country's Free and Open Indo-Pacific vision, and reiterated the importance of like-minded state cooperation as a cornerstone of Japanese security engagement in the Indo-Pacific and with the Quad.[85]

Likewise, the United States' predominant European partner states have adopted the like-minded state paradigm to describe their intentions, approaches, and priorities vis-à-vis the Indo-Pacific theatre. Indeed, whether it be France, Germany, or the Netherlands, all the European states with committed Indo-Pacific strategies have referenced like-minded state cooperation as a critical component.[86] The United Kingdom, too, has identified its strategic role in the Indo-Pacific as a "convener of likeminded states."[87] Indeed, whether in Canberra or London, policy-makers now reference a conceptual cohort of like-minded states as critical to their achieving all their strategic ends in Asia, whether defined in terms of preventing climate change or preserving the region's rules-based order.

Critical theory would suggest that there are clear historical overtones to the like-minded state construct in Asia that make it particularly problematic. Whether with respect to colonialism, imperialism, or anti-communism, one finds extensive reference to like-minded state consortiums in Cold War–era accounts of Western state alignment.[88] Washington, in particular, used "like-mindedness" as a justification for supporting European colonial efforts in Asia, to justify military intervention in Indochina, and to countenance regime change in states such as Indonesia. While Western state cooperation under the like-minded state mantra in Asia today has not yet reached the Cold War–era fever pitch, critical theorists note all current like-minded states are former colonial powers in Asia, at least one of which maintains colonial-era territories (New Caledonia) in the region even today.

In Canada, a growing chorus of policy analysts are calling for conceptual alignment with the United States and other like-minded Western states in Asia.[89] Central to their logic is the belief that as a Western middle power, Canada can, and should, advanced its national interests through close coordination with Western democracies. In working with like-minded states, the argument goes, Canada can best support the rules-based order in Asia, push back against Chinese aggression throughout the region, and ensure the preservation and/or promotion of democracy within certain Indo-Pacific states.[90] Further, in working with like-minded states, Canada can best leverage its status as a G7 country in Asia and best position itself to be an active member of any emerging democratic coalition of states.[91]

Yet a full embrace of the like-minded state paradigm would be a strategic mistake for Canada, much as it might ultimately prove to be for its most vocal proponents. Far from enabling Canada to work more effectively in the region, prioritizing like-minded state relations over a more diversified strategy based on national security interests will place Canada firmly inside a Western-aligned camp of states, many of which are declining, outside powers and all of which – as noted above – are former colonial states.[92]

Critical Theory and the "Free" and "Open" Concepts

While there are differences in their respective approaches, Western narratives on the Indo-Pacific have uniformly identified the maintenance of "freedom" and "openness" as a strategic end state within the region. France's Indo-Pacific strategy, for instance, identifies "free" movement and "free" trade as strategic priorities, while Germany's Indo-Pacific approach calls for "freedom of opinion and freedom of the press" and "freedom of religion and belief, religious tolerance and the responsibility of the religions for peace."[93] Japan defines the "free and open Indo-Pacific" as a regional public good, where states have freedom of movement and freedom of navigation and can engage in free trade.[94] Within Australia's various policy statements on the Indo-Pacific, one finds regular reference to "open markets facilitat[ing] flows of goods, services, capital and ideas" as a strategic priority, as well as "the right of individuals to practice their religion free from government interference."[95]

The United States, under both the Trump and Biden administrations, has been more explicit in its articulation of a free and open Indo-Pacific. For instance, the State Department's 2019 document *A Free and Open Indo-Pacific: Advancing a Shared Vision* defines the United States' strategic end state in the Indo-Pacific as the "preservation of the free and open regional order," an order based on "freedom and openness rather than coercion and corruption."[96] Former Secretary of Defense Mark Esper was even more specific in a 2020 speech at the Asia-Pacific Center for Security Studies (APCSS) in Honolulu, stating that the United States' Indo-Pacific strategy was designed to ensure that China does not undermine the region's "free" and "open" regional order through its coercive activities.[97]

While anodyne at first glance, Western narratives on freedom and openness in the Indo-Pacific amount to a shared normative framework for state relations rooted in Western concepts of democracy and economic liberalism.[98] With respect to democratic freedom in the Indo-Pacific, Western states are advocating for democratic systems of government, individual human rights, and political liberalism while pointedly critiquing autocratic states in the region such as China.[99] With respect to economic freedom, the Western states advocate for the free movement of people or goods, free markets, and free trade.[100]

With respect to an "open" Indo-Pacific, Western states are committed to maritime openness, the openness of societies, and openness to Western activities and influence. Similarly, Western policy-makers use the word "open" with respect to markets, trade, and investment, all in contrast to the "closed" modes of protectionism, state-directed investment controls, and import substitutions.[101]

Freedom and openness, in this regard, are concepts distinctly aligned with Western values around liberal economics and democracy as well as the Western states' self-perceived right to "fly, sail, and operate" anywhere within the Asian region permissible under international law.

Far from being universal in their application, they represent a Western hegemonic view of Asia's international relations and regional order that does not take the region's endogenous economic and governance systems and values into any account.[102]

Viewed from this perspective, there are inherent contradictions in the "free" and "open" normative framework that informs Western and Western-aligned policy making toward the Indo-Pacific. Regarding the idea of freedom within the Asian region, Western concepts assume that Asian states and societies somehow lack freedom or that their understanding of freedom is somehow underdeveloped and in need of Western guidance and support. One need only view the Washington-based Freedom House's 2020 freedom index to see, for instance, how Asia is almost entirely composed of states lacking "freedom," defined in terms of democracy, civil liberties, and political rights.[103]

Yet Western assumptions about Asian states' freedom deficits do not reflect Asian perceptions of freedom so much as they demonstrate Western paternalism.[104] Western scholarship tends to assume that lack of institutionalized freedom – such as constitutionally guaranteed freedoms of the press, of expression, or of religion – necessarily means that Asian societies lack freedom in practice.[105] While formalized political freedom in some Asian states is indeed limited, it is equally true that Asian societies are generally content with their political systems, often seeing Western-style democracy and freedom as little more than an excuse for ineffective governance (more on this topic in the next chapter).[106] Neither is it certain that Asian societies across the region see democratically defined freedom as the most effective means of ensuring their individual or collective rights.[107] The 2020 global pandemic, in particular, has greatly undermined the appeal of democracy and freedom in Asia, particularly in states like Indonesia where citizens express a willingness to trade nominal ideas of freedom for effective government.[108]

Neither does the concept of openness as used in Western narratives about the Indo-Pacific accurately reflect the economic or security priorities of Asian states. On economic openness, for instance, many Asian nations (including, ironically, Japan) have relied, or are relying, on protectionism as a primary means of ensuring stable and continued economic growth.[109] For Asian states from Vietnam to Indonesia, from Malaysia to Thailand, industrial policies designed to provide state subsidies to specific companies and to limit foreign investment and competition in industries deemed strategically significant are a feature of their economic systems, not a bug.[110] The idea that Asian economies would somehow become more competitive through deregulation, or through more openness to foreign capital, is particularly out of step with Southeast Asian nations still scarred from the 1997 Asian Financial Crisis and the 2008 Global Financial Crisis, both of which clearly demonstrated the risk of too much "openness."[111]

On security openness, Western states are primarily concerned with maintaining their ability to operate without restriction within the Asian region, whether in the South China Sea or off China's coastal waters, in line with their own interpretations of international law. For the United States in particular, strategic openness is closely related to its ability to intervene effectively in regional contingencies, most notably with respect to Taiwan and North Korea.[112] Similarly, Australia and Japan have equated Indo-Pacific openness with their ability to operate across with region with minimal restriction, and have identified Indo-Pacific security institutions such as the Quad and AUKUS as means of ensuring their operational openness.[113] Western narratives on security openness in the Indo-Pacific are thus more about maintaining US-led military predominance in Asia than they are about responding to any particular threat.[114]

The belief that the United States and its allies need to preserve this level of security openness is based, however, on the strategic assumption the US-led alliance system is the most legitimate regional security institution and that any decrease in the system's influence, power, or ability to direct regional security outcomes is unacceptable. Corollary to this is the idea that no other regional actor should have the means to resist US-led security pressure or to shape Asia's security order in ways inimical to Western states' strategic interests.[115] Western narratives on the Indo-Pacific's openness are less about ensuring inclusivity within Asia's strategic environment than they are about preventing the regional development of a near-peer power, specifically China, that could potentially limit Western hegemony.[116]

There is, arguably, some regional demand for US-led military cooperation in Asia to counterbalance China's growing influence. Scholarship on international security in Asia, for instance, has identified strategic balancing as an important component of Southeast Asian states' foreign and security policies, in particular.[117] Where Western narratives on Indo-Pacific openness exceed this regional demand is in their unwillingness to account for change at the regional level that excludes Western state predominance. For instance, no Western narrative on Asia's security has identified support for China's ongoing negotiations with ASEAN over a code of conduct in the South China Sea as a potential instrument for achieving regional stability. Rather, the United States and its partners have summarily rejected the idea of a regional accord on maritime disputes as counter to international law and as a covert means for China to expand control over Southeast Asia.[118] To suggest alignment between regional support for continued US and Western state engagement and regional support for openness in the Indo-Pacific is therefore to offer a false equivalence. Whereas Asian states welcome the former for its contribution to regional stability, they view the latter as a mechanism for continued US-led Western hegemony.[119] Chapter 2, on Asian perspectives of Asian security regimes, addresses this divergence in greater detail.

To Construct a Strategy, Deconstruct the Region

For Canada as well as for other democratic middle powers, challenging the American hegemon's predominant narrative is inherently problematic as it is, in many ways, intrinsically tied to the country's own identity as a liberal power. For instance, when the Trump administration first outlined its "free" and "open" Indo-Pacific strategy, most Canadian scholars rushed to endorse the idea, as freedom and openness are Canadian values as much as they are American values. Similarly, when Canadian media portrayed China's foreign policy as inherently anti-democratic or as a threat to the rules-based order in Asia, few Canadian academics or policy-makers publicly disagreed. As Gramsci noted in his writing on historical materialism, there is little to no room for a dissenting voice within hegemonic discourse, as such discourse appeals to the very values that distinguish insiders from outsiders.[120]

Such uniformity of thought is, however, antithetical to effective strategic development. Indeed, there is a broad body of literature ranging from business studies to corporate governance to military science that identifies diversity of thought as a critical input into any successful outcome, whether in product development or the drafting of a theatre campaign plan. States that adhere unquestioningly to the hegemon's viewpoints are therefore disadvantaged with respect to developing a national strategic approach that accurately reflects the operational environment as it relates to the state's national security, economic, and political interests, or, collectively, national interests.

There is a clear responsibility, therefore, for those who study Asia's security environment to examine, to outline, and to present alternative scenarios that can contribute to greater situational awareness that Canadian policy-makers can, in turn, use to inform their policy processes and deliberations. In line with Kenneth Booth's admonition that the scholar's first role is that of advocate, scholarship, in its most fundamental form, should concern itself with critical examination of predominant systems to ensure that these systems are just and are not, conversely, tools for oppression.[121] Indeed, it is the scholar's duty to challenge prevailing narratives through informed analysis, thereby ensuring greater diversity of thought and inclusivity of non-dominant yet equally valuable viewpoints.

This chapter has employed critical theory as an analytical framework for examining some of the primary meta-narratives in Western discourse on Asia. Its purpose has been to problematize the key concepts that inform Western strategy toward the region and to suggest that more critical analysis of Asia's primary institutions is needed, particularly analysis that includes reference to Asian narratives, viewpoints, and priorities. Too much of Western policy analysis and scholarship is built around narrative assumptions that are exclusionary, that are inherently biased in their formulation, and that prioritize Western state interests over regional stability. For Canadian policy-makers in particular, understanding the deficiencies in Western narratives on Asia is critical to successful strategy building in the region.

The remaining chapters build on this chapter's use of critical theory to demonstrate further areas where Western narratives fail to accurately represent Asia's emerging dynamics and state relations. Parallel to this, regional narratives on Asian developments at the strategic, operational, and tactical level are identified and described, including Asian perceptions on Western states' activities and identities in the region. Through this process, an alternative narrative is established that Canadian policy-makers can use to formulate a more holistic approach to Asia, one built on the core principles of omnidirectional diplomacy and strategic integration.

2

Asian Counter-Narratives

Indo-Pacific, Rules-Based Order, and Freedom and Openness

The "Indo-Pacific" concept sits at the heart of contemporary Western narratives on Asia. First used to advocate for greater interconnectivity between Africa, the Middle East, and Asia, the concept has evolved to become an organizing mechanism for Western state engagement in Asia. Japan and the United States, for instance, use the term "Indo-Pacific" as a catch-all strategic ideal to add value to their alliance relations, to justify their joint military operations in the Asian theatre, and to coordinate their foreign and security policies, among other aspects of their bilateral relations.[1] The European Union and member states such as France, Germany, and the Netherlands have similarly articulated Indo-Pacific visions and strategies to justify an increase in European military activity in Asia, French security support for its overseas Asian territories, and German force projection in areas including the South China Sea.[2] Australia, more than any other state, has integrated the Indo-Pacific concept into its foreign and defence white papers to raise its international profile in institutions such as AUKUS, the G7, the Five Eyes intelligence alliance, and the Quad.[3]

While the term "Indo-Pacific" fundamentally references a supraregional geographic area, Western states now also use the concept to articulate a shared, Western-centric vision of Asia's "rules-based order" (RBO).[4] As outlined in Chapter 1, the Indo-Pacific's rules-based order has emerged as a Western strategic end state in Asia, one based on

Western economic, political, and security predominance and dependent on the region's remaining "free" and "open" to Western activities, values, and interests. Indeed, more and more, Western narratives on the Indo-Pacific are less concerned about its precise geographic demarcations, on which there are disagreements, and more concerned with its ideational and institutional architecture, on which there is general accord. For all its Western proponent states, the Indo-Pacific's real value is in its expressed economic and political liberalism and its Western-dominated structure.[5] More precisely, Western narratives on the Indo-Pacific highlight its importance in balancing "illiberal," "revisionist" China, although few Western policy-makers outside the former Trump administration are brazen enough to openly admit it.[6]

The problem with the Indo-Pacific concept is not in its conceptual construction per se. Where it falls short is its failure to account for critical voices from the Asian region, particularly from states like Japan and South Korea, where one finds well-developed counter-narratives on their relations with the West, and Indonesia, Malaysia, Thailand, and Vietnam, all of which sit at the geographic, conceptual, and strategic heart of the Indo-Pacific. The tendency of Western narratives to ignore Asian voices on the region's geography and order and to assume Asian actors' acceptance of and agreement with paradigms of Western origin such as "freedom" and "openness" means that much of the Western narrative takes place in effectively an echo chamber, where all opposition to the concept goes unheard. This proclivity leads to dissonance between Western and Asian narratives that have real-world consequences, up to and including their contribution to regional conflict and/or war.[7]

This chapter continues the previous chapter's use of critical theory to challenge the Western Indo-Pacific narrative as a hegemony ideal, one that ignores regional narratives in its assumptions. It accomplishes this by examining local-language sources from Japan, South Korea, Indonesia, Malaysia, Thailand, and Vietnam to provide a counter-narrative to Western narratives on the Indo-Pacific, rules-based order, and freedom and openness.

Asian Narratives and the Indo-Pacific as a Geographic Construct
Examining discourse on the Indo-Pacific from Asian states, one sees significant divergence between regional and Western narratives. Whereas Western policy-makers and academics use the term "Indo-Pacific" to

describe Asia's geographic and conceptual parameters, many Asian scholars and analysts, conversely, reject the term as a misrepresentation of Asia's scope and as a discursive turn of phrase that marginalizes Asian states within their own region.

Some Japanese scholars, for instance, remain resistant to the Indo-Pacific as a strategic ideal, even as Tokyo has unambiguously structured its foreign policy around the concept.[8] Such resistance comes from concern that Japan's relations with Asia-Pacific states could suffer if Tokyo aligns too closely with US strategy and expands the country's foreign policy scope into the Indian Ocean area.[9] More specifically, Japanese scholars worry that the country will dilute its influence in Asia and create unnecessary tensions with China, one of Asia's most important actors, if Tokyo continues to pursue an Indo-Pacific strategy.[10] The counterpoint to the Indo-Pacific concept is the belief that Japan should develop its own Asia-Pacific strategy, one that involves cooperation with China and other Asian states to strengthen the region's endogenous institutions, such as the Comprehensive and Progressive Agreement for Trans-Pacific Partnership (CPTPP) and Regional Comprehensive Economic Partnership (RCEP), even in the absence of the United States.[11] Only through this more inclusive, Asia-Pacific–focused approach is it possible to ensure Japan's national security interests in Asia.[12]

In South Korea, similarly, both policy-makers and academics have been hesitant to adopt the Indo-Pacific nomenclature, despite the Moon Jae-in administration's 2021 usage of the term in a joint statement with President Biden.[13] In outlining its New Southern Policy, for instance, Korean policy-makers assiduously avoid propagating the Indo-Pacific narrative, for both geographic and strategic reasons. Geographically, Seoul's strategic focus is entirely Asia-Pacific in orientation, particularly with respect to Southeast Asia, which South Korean strategists have identified as Asia's geographic, economic, and political centre of gravity.[14] Strategically, South Korean policy-makers avoid the Indo-Pacific ideal to ensure a more inclusive, equidistant approach to great power relations in Asia, an approach based on balanced engagement with ASEAN, China, Japan, India, the United States, and Russia in the Asia-Pacific.[15] Among Asia's endogenous institutions, South Korea has identified the CPTPP and the RCEP agreements – both inherently Asia-Pacific institutions – as its primary means of achieving economic diversification and integration in Asia.[16]

One sees similar hesitancy around the Indo-Pacific concept among scholars and policy-makers in Southeast Asia. Indonesian scholars, for instance, are cynical about the Indo-Pacific as an externally costructed, hegemonically imposed geographic area that undermines the country's centrality in the Asia-Pacific.[17] Although Indonesia is naturally positioned to benefit from an Indo-Pacific geography, and its strategic analysts see value in the country's development of a "two-oceans" approach to its foreign policy, the analysts are equally unified in their belief that the US-led, Western Indo-Pacific concept is overly militaristic and overtly antagonistic toward China.[18] Rather, Indonesian policy writers prioritize the country's engagement with institutions such as the Indian Ocean Rim Association (IORA) that are more inclusive of regional voices and representative of regional interests.[19]

Malaysian scholars take an even more critical view of the Indo-Pacific concept, seeing it as a US hegemonic construct designed to advance American interests in Asia to the detriment of regional actors.[20] Rather than seek alignment within an Indo-Pacific vision, Malaysia's Prime Minister Muhyiddin Yassin has outlined a foreign policy approach for his country based on closer ties with the Islamic world, China, and ASEAN.[21] As with South Korea, the Malaysian government also purposely avoids referencing the Indo-Pacific in its foreign policy white papers, preferring instead to use the term "Asia-Pacific" to describe the country's operational environment.[22]

Even in Thailand, a formal US ally in Asia, one finds hesitancy regarding the Indo-Pacific concept. Thai scholars question the Indo-Pacific's relevance as a geographic construct, arguing instead that the concept is a strategically driven redefinition of the Asia-Pacific to facilitate cooperation between Australia, Japan, and the United States in response to China's Belt and Road Initiative (BRI).[23] Rather than seeking stability in Asia through its Indo-Pacific redesign, Thai scholars argue, the United States uses the concept to advance an "America First" approach to Asia that ignores the interests of Asian states, including those of key US allies such as Japan.[24] Vietnamese scholars, similarly, are resistant to the Indo-Pacific concept, which they believe fails to take the perceptions and interests of Asian and African states into account and is overly antagonistic toward China, thereby making it unpalatable for Asian states that do not want poor relations with Beijing.[25]

Vietnamese writers have also contextualized ASEAN's "Outlook on the Indo-Pacific" as *defensive* in nature, not the result of ASEAN alignment with the Western states' Indo-Pacific concept.[26] According to this perspective, ASEAN articulated such an outlook out of strategic necessity to reject the concept's most anti-China principles, to call for Southeast Asian centrality, and to insist that the Indo-Pacific region remain inclusive rather than exclusive. Indonesian scholarship, in particular, supports the position that ASEAN's Indo-Pacific Outlook is not an affirmation of the Western Indo-Pacific geographic ideal but rather a strategic rebuttal of the US-led "free and open Indo-Pacific," which is more about the United States creating "living space" (*lebensraum*) in Asia and is therefore an intrinsically destabilizing concept.[27] Further, one also finds deep ambiguity toward the Indo-Pacific concept in regional polling on Southeast Asian elite perspectives, with over 60 percent of respondents arguing that the Western concept of the Indo-Pacific is a geopolitical construct and that ASEAN member states need to articulate an ASEAN view of the Indo-Pacific to stay relevant.[28]

Asian Narratives on the Rules-Based Order

As outlined in Chapter 1, the rules-based order is central to Western narratives about Asia, particularly with respect to Western views that Asia's rules-based order is under strain and in need of Western support. While one does find reference to the rules-based order in Asian leadership statements, particularly those advocating moderation in US and Western engagement in Asia to avoid regional conflict with China, one also finds critiques of the concept across Asian scholarship, particularly with respect to US hegemony and a free and open Indo-Pacific.

Japanese scholars, for instance, question the stability of the rules-based order, arguing that the US propensity to use force or the threat of force to advance its strategic interests in Asia has the self-defeating quality of undermining Washington's claims that it supports a rules-based order in the region.[29] Japanese academics have further questioned the rules-based order's overall sustainability, particularly with respect to its democratic ideals and within East Asia, where order evolves more quickly than at the global level.[30] To position Japan most effectively to engage in Asia's emerging order, Japanese scholars argue, its leadership should work toward a consensus-based order in Asia, not toward a Western-aligned rules-based order. Japan should also prepare for a

Sinocentric Asian order and be ready to rethink its strategic alignment in response, much as it did in the Meiji Restoration era.[31]

In South Korean scholarship, there is broad agreement that the liberal rules-based order is a US-constructed hegemonic system through which Washington exercises power in the Asia-Pacific.[32] Korean scholars have likened it to a US Cold War–era containment strategy, one designed to arrest China's rise in the region through the US's Indo-Pacific strategy.[33] Rather than align with the US hegemonic rules-based order, Korean scholars have argued, Seoul should undertake an active middle-power diplomacy approach toward Asia and act as a "civilized regional leader" in the Asia-Pacific.[34]

Indonesian writers are also largely cynical about the US rules-based order, arguing that its institutions, such as the World Trade Organization (WTO), the Organisation for Economic Co-operation and Development (OECD), and the dollar-dominated financial system, propagate US interests, relations, and power rather than represent Asian interests.[35] The rules-based order is especially rigged to advance US and Western values around democracy promotion, even to the detriment of Asian, non-democratic states.[36] Some Indonesian scholars are particularly critical of the rules-based order's rejection of Islamic values and its promotion of modernity and secularism over religion.[37]

One finds similar critique of the rules-based order in Malaysia, particularly around its appeal to "universal values."[38] Indeed, Malaysian scholars are largely critical of the rules-based order as a tool of Western colonialization, arguing that the United States, in particular, has used it to undermine national identity politics and counter post-colonial nationalism.[39] Far from bringing stability to the developing world, in particular, US hegemonic discourse around the rules-based order has led to a growing anti-hegemonic movement against the United States, particularly involving Islamic states.[40]

In Thailand, scholars argue that the rules-based order does not reflect Thai politics or society, that its application to Thailand delegitimizes the country's historical and contemporary experiences, and that it advances Western over Asian interests.[41] Thai critical theorists have further identified it as a corrosive force in the country's intellectual tradition and economic development path, particularly as it presents liberalism as a universal value for all states in the international system.[42]

One finds similar critiques in Vietnamese narratives on the rules-based order, particularly with respect to its capitalist roots, anti-socialist rhetoric, and role in advancing liberal globalization.[43] In particular, Vietnamese scholarship is deeply cynical about its financial institutions, its reliance on economic liberalism, and its Western-centricity as having contributed to the 1997 Asian Financial Crisis and the 2008 Global Financial Crisis.[44] Far from bringing stability to Asia, the rules-based order has disadvantaged development states such as Vietnam, which lack the domestic institutions necessary to mitigate its associated risk.[45]

As with Asian narratives on the Indo-Pacific concept, one finds far greater cynicism in regional discourse around the rules-based order. Whereas Western narratives focus on its ability to bring stability to Asia, Asian scholars and policy writers view it as a Western-constructed and Western-dominated regime that is unrepresentative of Asian states' interests, histories, or cultures. Asian narratives largely reject the idea that the rules-based order is inclusive, and question the extent to which its liberal institutions allow for the participation and representation of non-democratic states. Indeed, one finds more and more reference in regional writing to the important role played by Asia's regional institutions – such as the CPTPP, the RCEP, the BRI, and ASEAN's communities – in regional governance, state relations, and people-to-people exchanges.

Japanese policy analysts, for instance, have identified Asia's emerging institutions as the future building blocks of a regional order, one more representative of Asian relations and Asian states' interests, where Japan can implement a foreign policy predicated on "comprehensive and multilayered engagement."[46] South Korean writing on Asia's institutions also highlights their importance in Seoul's approach to regional affairs.[47] Rather than seeking alignment with the Western rules-based order, Korean scholars identify the need to link the country's New Southern Policy with regional and Asian states' domestic economic development institutions.[48] One sees similar narratives on the importance of Asia's endogenous order in Indonesia and Malaysia, where scholars identify state engagement with regional institutions and people-to-people engagement through ASEAN as the foundations for the future stability of Asia's order.[49] Thai and Vietnamese writing also regularly call for closer intra-regional and "cultural" engagement to strengthen Asia's regional order, and more direct state engagement to expand Asia's order.[50]

Asian Narratives on the "Free" and "Open" Concepts

One also finds a far different regional narrative with respect to what Western narratives term "free" and "open" systems in Asia than that found in Western discourse on the subject. Rather than enthusiasm for free markets, freedom of expression, and freedom of the high seas, for example, Asian narratives instead raise concern over how "freedom" contributes to instability at the domestic and regional levels. Rather than unfettered support for regional "openness," open societies, and open economic systems, one finds a more nuanced discussion of regionalism and state/society relations than in Western narratives. Across the region, therefore, one finds little endogenous support for the Western concepts of freedom and openness as articulated in line with the Indo-Pacific concept. Indeed, arguably, Asian narratives suggest that the region is perhaps one global area where both concepts face a skeptical public.

While it is beyond this book's scope to examine the expansive literature in Asia around economics, governance, and state/society relations, some contextualization of regional discourse is necessary for more targeted analysis of contemporary narratives around the Indo-Pacific freedom and openness concepts. On economics, for instance, one finds far greater support within Asian scholarship for state intervention and state-directed development than in Western writing on the region's political economics. Asian scholars and analysts, for example, routinely identify industrial policy, protectionism, state subsidies, and export incentives as key components of the region's development success, rightly arguing that states such as China, Japan, Malaysia, Singapore, South Korea, and Vietnam have used such measures to achieve unprecedentedly high levels of development and economic growth.[51] Similarly, regional polling suggests that Asian societies support government management of their respective economies and, indeed, see effective state intervention in economic development as a key indicator of a state's performance and legitimacy.[52] Far from a desire for greater economic freedom and/or openness, regional narratives suggest that Asian states and societies are more supportive of mixed-model economic systems where central authorities have a clear role in managing economic development to benefit society over capital.

In addition to regional support for mixed-model systems, one sees extensive criticism of capitalism in Asian narratives on political economics. Rather than viewing capitalism as a net-positive system leading to high levels of sustainable growth, discourse in Asian tends to view market fundamentalism as a source of instability, vulnerability, and inequality.[53] Regional commentary on the 1997 Asian Financial Crisis and the 2008 Global Financial Crisis, in particular, tends to identify "crony capitalism," free markets, and deregulation as systemic risks, and argues the need for regional institutions such as the Chiang Mai Initiative Multilateralization (CMIM) and the ASEAN+3 Macroeconomic Research Office (AMRO) to mitigate global capitalism's risks.[54] One sees a similar critique of capitalism in regional polling on social sentiments. Indeed, social antipathy toward capitalism in arguably more acute in Asia than in any other region, with opposition to free markets the highest in India and Thailand.[55]

Neither is support for state activism and opposition to open markets limited to theoretical debate in Asia. Across the region, for example, states such as China, Japan, South Korea, Singapore, Malaysia, Thailand, and Vietnam have also published national development plans that prioritize state-led investment in and support of domestic industries, including technology, education, and manufacturing. While China's "Made in China 2025" is the most well-known and criticized example of a state-led industrial plan, one finds a similar approach to state-directed development in Japan's 2020 "Strategy for Semiconductors and the Digital Industry," South Korea's "New Deal," and Indonesia's "National Long-Term Development Plan" among other national policies in the region.[56]

One finds similar critiques with respect to the ideas of freedom and openness in Asian narratives on the region's politics. Within Asian scholarship on governance, for instance, one finds a clear preference for accountability, effectiveness, and responsiveness over personal freedom or political openness.[57] Indeed, regional polling suggests a decided move away from democratic liberalism in Asia toward mixed-model and authoritarian governments, due largely to perceptions among Asian individuals – including those in the region's most established democracies – that values such as freedom and openness lead to ineffective governance, not greater rights and/or actual freedom. Rather than seeking to emulate these Western political values, Asian states and societies increasingly look to regional states like China and Singapore as governance models.[58]

Indeed, rather than treating freedom and openness as necessary conditions for democracy or good governance, Asian scholars and individuals increasingly see these as excuses that Western states and policy-makers use to rationalize poor policies, poor performance, and systemic corruption.[59] The miserable performance of Western states during the COVID-19 pandemic are a case in point. Rather than address the pandemic directly, Western states, particularly the United Kingdom and the United States, employed half measures to ensure their societies' freedom and openness. The result of such value-driven policy, from an Asian perspective, was not government efficiency but rather systemic breakdown, with Western states experiencing the world's highest morbidity and mortality rates, with more than 1 million deaths in the United States alone.[60] Asian narratives suggest that Asian actors are unwilling to pay such a high price for freedom, and indeed see the West's messianic obsession with liberal democratic values as little more than dereliction of duty by the Western political class.[61]

Within this broader context, one finds a more detailed Asian narrative around the Western free and open Indo-Pacific construct. In Japan, for instance, policy-makers and scholars raise concerns that Japanese alignment with the Western free and open ideals will isolate the country in Asia and unnecessarily antagonize China.[62] Rather than seek ideational alignment with respect to liberal democracy, these scholars argue, Japan's interests are better served through issue-specific alignment and coordination, including with China on issues such as pandemic response and recovery and climate change.[63] Neither can Japan rely on free markets alone to achieve its economic security; Tokyo must maintain a "defensive" policy of state intervention and activism to ensure the country's long-term prosperity.[64]

South Korean scholarship on the free and open aspects of the Indo-Pacific is even less supportive of normative alignment with respect to economic and governance policies. South Korean scholars argue, for instance, that it is in Seoul's best interest to maintain a foreign policy based on strategic neutrality, not ideational alignment.[65] In particular, Seoul should studiously avoid "values diplomacy" – or diplomacy designed to advance liberal values – as it has the potential to foment nationalism and contribute to regional tensions between Western states, China, and Russia.[66] As Seoul's primary foreign policy aims in Asia are stable, inclusive relations with all states, Korean scholars argue that its interests are better served through advancement of neutral ideals such as peace and coexistence.[67]

In Southeast Asia, one finds similar hesitancy toward normative alignment with the free and open concepts in leadership statements, policy documents, and scholarship. At the subregional level, for instance, ASEAN member states multilaterally adopted language around "inclusivity," "non-alignment," "equality," "mutual respect," and "non-intervention" to frame their collective Outlook on the Indo-Pacific statement.[68] According to regional analysts, ASEAN member states deliberately eschewed reference to "free" and "open" in their Outlook to avoid polemics that would anger China and Russia and to focus on pragmatic engagement.[69]

At the national level, one also sees a clear ideational and semantic movement away a free and open Indo-Pacific and toward one predicated on "inclusivity," even among states like Indonesia that are active in the Indian Ocean region. The Indonesian leadership, for instance, routinely uses terms like "stable," "prosperous," "inclusive," "transparent," and "peaceful" to describe the country's approach to the Indo-Pacific, which is predicated on state cooperation, not confrontation.[70] Indonesian scholarship suggests that such language is purposeful as alignment with a US-led free and open Indo-Pacific model would result in conceptual "bandwagoning" and undermine the country's preference for strategic equidistance.[71] Malaysian scholars similarly warn against normative alignment with Western liberal values, arguing that such alignment with any single state or coalition of states would undermine the country's ability to hedge its relations.[72]

Thai scholarship on the Indo-Pacific is also skeptical of Western usage of "free" and "open" to describe the region's normative regimes. Thai (and Malaysian) scholars argue that Western ideas of freedom and openness are less about a fair, stable system than about the desire of Western states to project force and exert influence throughout the region at will, even at the cost of ASEAN centrality.[73] Thai commentators also express concern that Western free and open Indo-Pacific strategies are threatening ASEAN neutrality and leading toward greater intra-regional instability and conflict, an outcome made more likely as Western opposition to China's BRI grows and Western institutions such as the Quad become more active in Southeast Asian security matters.[74] Vietnamese scholars, while more supportive of Vietnam's cooperation with the United States on national security issues, express similar concerns that Western free and open Indo-Pacific strategies may have a destabilizing effect on the region's security and on ASEAN unity.[75] Vietnamese commentators are particularly wary of Western attempts to impose liberal economic and governance models on Asian states as a means to expand Western influence throughout the region.[76]

Where one does see some alignment between Western ideals of freedom and openness and Southeast Asian narratives is on maritime security in the South China Sea. Uniformly, ASEAN and ASEAN members states are committed to freedom of navigation, freedom of access, and openness of Asia's maritime commons. One finds repeated reference to maritime freedom throughout regional discourse, often in line with Western concepts of freedom and openness and Indo-Pacific maritime security.

Where such concepts differ between Western and Asian narratives, however, is in their overall understanding of Asia's maritime domain and its strategic parts. Whereas Western accounts of freedom of navigation focus exclusively on China's maritime activities in the Indian Ocean and the South China Sea, Southeast Asian narratives instead highlight the importance of collaboration, consultation, and conflict prevention as informing Asian maritime freedom. Indonesian writing on maritime security in Asia, for instance, regularly identifies China as a net-positive actor in Asia, arguing that cooperation between Jakarta and Beijing is a critical source of regional *stability*, not instability.[77] Malaysia scholarship similarly identifies cooperation between Asian states, including China, as the key to ensuring freedom in the South China Sea, and treats Western involvement in the region as a source of instability.[78] Thai analysis of freedom of navigation in the South China Sea also identifies a negotiated code of conduct between ASEAN and China as the most effective means of ensuring maritime stability.[79] Even Vietnamese analysts rarely identify Western state involvement as a necessary condition of regional maritime freedom, but rather treat the US military presence in Asia as an important balancing tool against Chinese claims to maritime territories Hanoi sees as its own. In Vietnamese narratives, the US military presence does not directly result in regional maritime freedom or openness but rather ensures that Vietnam's interests are secured against China.[80] These differences in regional perceptions of the South China Sea dispute are addressed in more detail in subsequent chapters.

Asian States' Adoption of an Indo-Pacific Framework

Considering the foregoing Asian narratives on the Western Indo-Pacific concept, it becomes necessary to question why some Asian states have in fact incorporated aspects of the concept into their strategic policies and outlooks. In 2019, for instance, ASEAN member states issued their Outlook on the Indo-Pacific, which many Western analysts argued constituted strategic alignment with Western states with respect to an Indo-Pacific ideal.[81] Prime Minister Narendra Modi similarly adopted an Indo-Pacific framework for India's foreign policy during a 2018 speech at the Shangri-La Dialogue in Singapore.[82] Both Singaporean prime minister Lee Hsien Loong and Indonesian president Joko Widodo have also referenced the Indo-Pacific with respect to their strategic engagement in Asia.

These states and actors' adoption of the Indo-Pacific as a strategic framework for engagement is indeed notable, although not for the reasons most Western analysts would suggest. While ASEAN, New Delhi, Singapore, and Jakarta have all accepted the Indo-Pacific as a contemporary strategic reality, they have equally rejected its strategic and normative assumptions in multiple official statements.

ASEAN's Outlook on the Indo-Pacific, for instance, is more a summary refutation of Western assumptions about Asia than a confirmation of regional alignment with Western Indo-Pacific ideals. The Outlook's "Background and Rational," "Objectives," and "Principles" all reiterate the importance of ASEAN centrality, of regional dialogue and engagement, of inclusivity, of non-alignment, of non-interference, and of non-intervention in state affairs in Asia, while tacitly rejecting the more divisive, polemical, and paternalistic aspects of Western Indo-Pacific narratives.[83]

Similarly, India's official statements on the Indo-Pacific repeatedly reject Western alignment in favour of a balanced approach to US and China relations, identify the importance of ASEAN as Asia's economic and political core, and call for inclusivity within Asia's order formulation to account for regional developments.[84] Singapore, in particular, has publicly refuted the idea of Western-led containment of China in the Indo-Pacific and has argued for regional engagement predicated on inclusivity, ASEAN centrality, great power restraint, and middle-power neutrality.[85] Even more pointedly, Indonesia's Joko Widodo has largely stopped referencing the Indo-Pacific in his speeches on the country's foreign policy, out of concern that it might indicate Indonesian acceptance of US strategic aims in Asia.[86]

What these Asian states' adoption of aspects of the Indo-Pacific framework shows, then, is not strategic alignment with Western Indo-Pacific ideals but the extent to which Western hegemonic discourse necessitates a strategic response from Asia's regional states. Far from reflecting the states' own strategic priorities or representing their regional strategic views, their adoption of the Western-propagated Indo-Pacific ideals is more accurately seen as a secondary state strategy of hedging.[87] Indeed, one need only review statements from the leaders of these states to see such hedging in action, as regional leaders are often more careful to identify what the Indo-Pacific *is not* than they are to outline their own Indo-Pacific visions. For Asian states, therefore, the Indo-Pacific is a negative concept – one that requires subtle refutation through engagement – rather than a positive one outlining their strategic priorities in the region.[88]

Implications for Canada

This chapter provides a standing point for a more informed Canadian policy toward Asia – a policy formulated to address regional narratives and views covering issues such as Asia's geographic scope, its rules-based order, and its economic, governance, and security trends. By examining non-English–language, regional policy statements, scholarship, and media, it provides a baseline for Canadian policy analysts to use in considering regional discourse as a counter to dominant Western narratives. As Canada must ultimately execute its policy within Asia, clearer understanding of regional views on regional developments should be a prerequisite for policy formulation.

Indeed, if Canada is to effect an approach to Asia predicated on omnidirectional diplomacy and strategic integration, as this book suggests, it is essential that Global Affairs Canada provide its Asia-based diplomats a framework for sustainable engagement based on regional realities, not Western assumptions. Any policy that fails to consider the regional narratives outlined above is more likely than not to fail, particularly as regional actors become more inwardly focused and Asian regionalism becomes more advanced.

3

Asian Counter-Narratives

Western State Identity in the Asia-Pacific

Inherent in Western narratives on the Indo-Pacific is the assumption of Western state benevolence, an assumption predicated on the belief that Asia needs Western leadership and Western state/coalition intervention to ensure its stability and "rules-based order." So ingrained is the idea of Western benevolence within such narratives that one sees it uncritically employed in Western leadership statements, policy writing, scholarship, commentary, and media as an immutable fact.[1] All the Western states' Indo-Pacific concepts, for instance, are premised on the understanding that Western institutions such as AUKUS, NATO, the Quad, the G7, the Five Eyes, and Western military alliances are essential to ensure Asia's strategic equilibrium and human security.[2] Operationally, perceptions of Western benevolence have led Berlin, London, and Paris to unilaterally dispatch frigates and aircraft carriers to Asia to ensure its security (despite regional opposition), and Australia, the United Kingdom, and the United States to establish AUKUS, an extra-regional military alliance expressly designed to counter China's rise in Asia.[3]

Closely related to this idea of Western benevolence is the newly resurrected Cold War–era concept of the "like-minded state." Western policy-makers and scholars now use this concept to countenance Asian-based military alliances between Australia, European states, Japan, the

United Kingdom, and the United States and to justify Western institution building in Asia, including the Quad, the Summit of Democracies, and AUKUS.[4] Central to the like-minded state model is a shared national commitment to a "free" and "open" Indo-Pacific and the belief that Western democracies can, and must, work together to ensure an Asian rules-based order.[5]

More specifically, Western narratives employ the like-minded state concept as a litmus test to determine "insider" and "outsider" states, or those states that constitute the Western coterie versus those that contribute to regional "instability."[6] Western narratives also use the like-minded state paradigm to determine which states have strategic value within the Indo-Pacific and to understand how that value plays out within the region.[7] Western narratives on Australia, for instance, routinely identify it as a model Asian democracy and a net contributor to Indo-Pacific stability.[8] Similarly, they identify Japan as a Western-aligned state, one that shares Western values, views, and strategic interests in Asia, including such constants as opposition to China, a commitment to liberalism, and a determination to partner with Western states.[9] Western narratives on India are equally sanguine, seeing New Delhi as innately a part of the Western system of like-minded states.[10]

Conversely, Western narratives identify China as Asia's predominant source of instability, one that uses coercion, "debt trap diplomacy," and gray zone tactics to reshape the region through "revisionism" and to advance its influence and control over regional developments, states, and institutions.[11] The need to counter Chinese "revisionism" and "aggression" sits at the heart of Western narratives on Asia.

As with other aspects of such narratives, however, one finds alternative views in Asian discourse, particularly around the ideas of Western benevolence and the like-minded state. In particular, Asian narratives diverge significantly from the assumption of Western narratives with respect to the identities, roles, and effects in Asia of Australia, Europe, European states, India, Japan, the United Kingdom, and the United States. Neither does one find widespread agreement among Asian narratives that China is a revisionist or aggressive actor. While all Asian states share some degree of concern over China's disruptive potential, they also view China as a largely rational and responsible actor and see it as a source of regional stability, prosperity, and leadership rather than as the unhinged, aggressive state found in Western narratives.

To demonstrate these narrative tendencies in Asia, this chapter identifies and outlines regional writing on the identities, actions, and motivations of Western states within Asia. Through close textual reading of policy writing, scholarship, and media from Japan, South Korea, Indonesia, Malaysia, Thailand, and Vietnam, it identifies a regionally based counter-narrative to the predominant Western view that informs much of the domestic debate in Canada.

The United States as a Benevolent Leader in Asia
There is arguably no more central assumption within the Western narrative on Asia than that the United States is a benevolent actor and that its leadership is critical to the region's stability.[12] US government publications, for instance, are uniformly premised on the belief the United States is an unselfish provider of public goods in Asia and that regional states benefit from its leadership in the region.[13] Western academic, media, and policy writing similarly proceeds with the assumption that US foreign policy is fundamentally selfless and its intentions, if sometimes misguided, are essentially noble.[14] In Asia, however, regional perceptions of the US role are decidedly mixed. While one does see in the regional literature repeated references to the importance of the United States as a security provider, one also sees deep cynicism and concern over US intentions, behaviours, and policies toward the region, particularly with respect to China, even among its closest Asian allies.

In Japanese writing, for instance, one finds a body of scholarship questioning whether Tokyo's reliance on Washington as a security partner ultimately disadvantages its long-term national security prospects.[15] Japanese scholars regularly question whether the country's overreliance on the United States has created a dynamic where Japan's strategic options are limited, particularly with respect to China, and whether Japan could be "trapped" in the event of a US-China conflict.[16] Japanese policy-makers raise similar concern over the Abe/Suga/Kishida government's strategic alignment with the United States on issues such as Taiwan, China, and the Indo-Pacific, arguing that Japanese security dependence on the United States undermines the country's ability to act autonomously in Asia and to seek proactive engagement with Beijing.[17] Similarly, Japanese diplomats criticize US efforts to isolate China and to pressure Japan to limit its engagement with Beijing, arguing that such measures raise the potential for regional instability.[18]

South Korean scholarship similarly identifies the US drive for regional hegemony as deleterious to Asia's stability, particularly with respect to US security policy toward China and its tendency to involve other states, such as South Korea, in its drive to contain China.[19] South Korean analysts identify the United States' willingness to wage "war" against Chinese companies such as Huawei as evidence that the Trump and Biden administrations are using coercion to protect US economic and strategic primacy in Asia at the potential cost of Asian states' economic development and opportunities.[20] Korean scholarship is particularly focused on the United States' Indo-Pacific strategy as a source of instability on the Korean Peninsula, in Northeast Asia, and in the South China Sea, as Korean analysts largely see the strategy in antagonistic terms.[21]

Neither is Japanese and South Korea concern over the US role in Asia limited to policy and academic debates, as one sees a clear decline in public approval of the United States in local-language polling. A 2020 Government of Japan Cabinet Office poll, for instance, found that only 24 percent of Japanese respondents thought Japan-US relations were "good."[22] Even more pointedly, a 2020 NHK poll showed that 92 percent of Japanese respondents thought Japan-US relations were inherently unequal, 46 percent that the United States was an untrustworthy partner, 81 percent that Japan should not do more to contribute to Japan-US security relations, and 24 percent that the two states' bilateral relations would decline, while 52 percent do not support the Abe/Suga government's foreign policy, which is predicated on alignment with the United States in the Indo-Pacific.[23] Further, 80 percent of respondents identified US foreign policy toward Asia as inherently "bad," while over 40 percent cast Japan-US relations in negative terms. Most tellingly, when asked to identify characteristics that describe American society, most Japanese respondents chose negative terms such as "racist," "unequal," "drugs," and "guns."[24]

US approval ratings in South Korea have similarly dropped from a high of 84 percent in 2014 to a new low of 59 percent in 2019, while only 17 percent of respondents expressed confidence in US leadership, according to a 2020 Pew poll.[25] Similarly, in a 2020 poll by the Korea Institute for National Unification, 38 percent claimed South Korea–US relations had deteriorated, while 50 percent of those respondents blamed the United States for the deterioration.[26] Further, 56 percent of Korean respondents to a 2020 Gallup poll suggested that US foreign policy toward Asia made the region less stable.[27] While support for the alliance with the United States remains strong in South Korea, over 47 percent of respondents claimed that the alliance would be unnecessary if (and when) North and South Korea established peace.[28] This suggests that South Korean support for the alliance relationship is limited to contingencies on the Korean Peninsula and does not extend to broader security interests. Indeed, South Korean support for the security alignment with the United States falls precipitously on matters such as China, with over 40 percent of South Koreans supporting a policy of "strategic ambiguity" over US alignment toward Beijing, according to a 2020 Dong-A Ilbo poll.[29]

Disillusionment with the United States as a responsible, stabilizing actor in Asia is even more prevalent in Southeast Asian literature. Indonesian scholarship is replete, for instance, with writing on US hegemony in Asia and Washington's willingness to use unilateral, bilateral, and multilateral means to ensure its ongoing regional primacy vis-à-vis China, even at the cost of regional stability.[30] Indonesian academics regularly criticize Washington for acting as Asia's self-appointed security leader and for opposing regional developments that challenge its authority as its right and, indeed, duty.[31] Since the Trump administration, in particular, Indonesian analysts have argued that US chauvinism has destabilized Asia and that China, not America, is now the region's most responsible and influential actor.[32] Malaysian scholarship, similarly, identifies the United States' military "pivot" to Southeast Asia, its control over international institutions such as the United Nations, International Monetary Fund, and World Trade Organization, the global primacy of the US dollar, and Washington's willingness to use all these resources to contain China in Asia as a recipe for regional conflict that will ultimately involve all Asian nations.[33] Malaysian analysts also express concern about the US effect on ASEAN unity and centrality, particularly as the Trump and Biden administrations have increased pressure on regional states to align with the country's strategic posture against China.[34]

Thai discourse on the United States in Asia also tends toward cynicism, with Thai scholars arguing that US elites routinely conflate the idea of US leadership in Asia with US hegemony.[35] Thai analysts also argue that US-led initiatives such as the Quad are inherently destabilizing and that Washington treats Southeast Asian states as tools in its

China containment strategy, believing it can compel them to participate in anti-China activities by tying Western provision of the COVID-19 vaccine, among other issues, to their support.[36] Thai commentators are particularly worried that the United States seems intent on pulling their country and ASEAN into a "Cold War 2.0," despite the clear desire of Southeast Asian states to remain neutral in any great power conflict between the United States and China.[37]

Vietnamese scholars express concerns over US pressure on Vietnam to side with it in its efforts to contain China through military means, and over Washington's willingness to turn Asia into a "hegemonic battleground" to further its national interests.[38] Vietnamese strategists also warn of the US effect on their country's strategic autonomy, even as they remain largely supportive of US security relations as a strategic buffer against Chinese activities and claims in the South China Sea.[39] As in other ASEAN member states, Vietnamese academics are also vocal in their concern over US tendency to treat ASEAN as a strategic lever in its ongoing conflict with China, particularly as Washington weakens ASEAN in the process.[40]

In addition to these Southeast Asian narratives, one finds in regional polls growing cynicism toward US leadership, US institutions, and US trustworthiness. In 2020, for instance, 47 percent of Southeast Asians surveyed in a poll conducted by the Institute for Southeast Asian Studies (ISEAS) in Singapore expressed little or no confidence in Washington as a strategic partner. A further 56 percent characterized the US-led Indo-Pacific strategy in largely negative terms, classifying it as a China containment strategy and as a threat to ASEAN unity.[41] At the same time, over 76 percent of respondents claimed that US engagement in Asia had either "substantially declined" or "declined," with 40 percent suggesting that US decline was irreversible.[42] Most consequential for this chapter's purposes, seven out of ten Southeast Asian states – including Brunei, Cambodia, Indonesia, Laos, Malaysia, Myanmar, and Thailand – chose China, often by a significant margin, when asked whether they would prefer alignment with Washington or Beijing.[43]

Many of these same states have lost faith in the US governance model, with regional polling suggesting a growing preference within Southeast Asia for autocratic and/or mixed-model over democratic governance systems. According to Asian Barometer Survey results published in 2020, more and more regional states look to Singapore, China, and Japan as models of good governance, or increasingly prefer their own national models to that of the United States.[44] A long-term trend with respect to Asia's marked move away from democratic systems of governance is the growing disillusionment in Southeast Asia with US governance, with polling suggesting that 86 percent of respondents believe the US response to the COVID-19 pandemic – the greatest socio-economic challenge any Asian state has faced in decades – was the world's worst.[45]

The European Union and European States: Regional Actors and Honest Brokers

Prior to 2018, regional discourse on the involvement of Europe and European states in Asia was predominantly focused on matters related to colonialism and trade. Despite widespread interest in European languages, history, and culture throughout Asian capitals, regional narratives tended to either ignore France, the Netherlands, the United Kingdom, and Germany or treat them as historically significant but contemporarily irrelevant strategic actors. This is not to suggest that Asian scholars were uninterested in European affairs, but rather that European actors lacked sufficient agency within Asia to affect the region's broader geopolitical environment.

After 2018, however, one finds a decided uptick in regional writing on Europe and European states, particularly with respect to their adoption of and involvement in the Indo-Pacific ideational concept and geographic area. In 2018, for instance, France announced its Indo-Pacific strategy, which was predicated on Paris's self-identification as a "Pacific power."[46] In 2020, both the Netherlands and Germany similarly published Indo-Pacific visions, followed in 2021 by the European Union and by the United Kingdom's "tilt" to the Indo-Pacific, as outlined in its Global Britain strategy.[47]

At the institutional and state levels, one finds broad support for European engagement in Asia, particularly with respect to the economic components of European Indo-Pacific strategies. In 2021, for instance, ASEAN agreed to make the United Kingdom its eleventh full dialogue partner, despite its ongoing moratorium on new members, and enhanced its relations with the European Union to a strategic partnership.[48] Australia and Japan also expressed enthusiastic support for European involvement in the Indo-Pacific, support Western analysts referenced as evidence of widespread enthusiasm in Asia.[49] Proponents of European engagement in Asia point to such outcomes as evidence that Europe and European states are now serious actors in the Asian geopolitical arena.

Within regional discourse, however, one sees a decidedly less enthusiastic view of Europe's security and political involvement in Asia. While overall regional discourse on Europe is more sanguine than writing on the United States, one sees an equal amount of skepticism over European intentions in the region, particularly with respect to regional security, Western hegemony, and China's regional influence. Indeed, aside from Asian commentators' broad support have for Europe's role as a trade partner, there is decidedly little support among regional scholars and analysts for a more developed European presence in the region's security or political sectors.

Japanese scholars argue, for instance, that the European Union's engagement in Asia contributes to a disequilibrium between Asian states, making regional conflict more likely. This is not because European involvement is particularly deleterious, but rather because outside powers such as France, Germany, the Netherlands, and the United Kingdom create artificial divisions between states like Japan, South Korea, and China.[50] In dispatching military assets to Asia, in particular, European states are contributing to a Chinese siege mentality and potentially undermining regional public support for their engagement.[51] Neither are Japanese analysts convinced that European states have the capacity to operate in the Indo-Pacific, despite their self-identification as Pacific powers.[52] Japanese writers express widespread skepticism, for instance, that France can achieve its strategic goals in the region, particularly as its colonial territories, such as New Caledonia, question their relations with Paris.[53]

South Korean discourse also questions the intentions, motives, and capabilities of European states in engaging in the Indo-Pacific, particularly France, which has prioritized security engagement over economic integration in the region.[54] South Korean analysts also argue that European states' military activities in Asia are part of a US-led China "containment" strategy and could lead to a new Cold War in Asia between Western states and China.[55] Notably, South Korean commentators also express concern that EU involvement in Asia could isolate Seoul on issues such as North Korea and China, as the strategic alignment of

France, the Netherlands, Germany, and the United Kingdom with a US-led, values-based approach to regional security issues could challenge South Korea's preference for pragmatism.[56]

In Southeast Asia, one also finds concern over European intentions in Asia, particularly with respect to China. Indonesian media, for instance, has questioned European states' purposes in deploying naval vessels to Asia, arguing that such measures will likely contribute to rising tensions and regional perceptions that the Western world has aligned to contain China.[57] Malaysian commentators have cited French and British naval activities in the South China Sea as evidence that both powers are intent on using Asia to advance their global reputations and to challenge China in order to demonstrate their strategic resolve.[58] Thai writers have argued that US-EU security relations are entirely anti-Chinese in nature, warning that the West's military collaboration in Asia will increase tensions in the region to no apparent end.[59] Vietnamese writers – largely more supportive of the efforts of European states to challenge China in the South China Sea – have nevertheless argued that such European activity in Asia is largely reminiscent of the Eight-Nation Alliance of European powers that invaded China in the early 1900s – a historical parallel, they warn, that Beijing will interpret as a threat to its sovereignty.[60]

In addition to regional scholarship, one also finds lukewarm sentiments toward Europe and European states in regional polling. In the 2020 ISEAS poll, for instance, only 0.6 percent of Southeast Asian respondents saw the EU as an important economic actor in Asia, and only 1.1 percent saw it as an important strategic actor in the region.[61] While showing clear support for an ASEAN-EU free trade agreement, 44 percent of the same respondents rejected EU involvement in the Regional Comprehensive Economic Partnership (RCEP), stating that the agreement should be open to Asian states only.[62] When asked whether they trusted the EU, those who expressed distrust argued that the EU and its member states lacked the capacity to act on the global stage (34 percent), that they lacked knowledge of local cultures or political systems (17 percent), and that the EU was too divided internally to maintain a long-term strategic presence in the Asian region (35 percent).[63]

Neither did the Boris Johnson government's attempt to advance a Global Britain strategy born fruit in Asia, with most Asian states expressing little interest in closer engagement with the United Kingdom.

In a 2021 poll on Southeast Asian perceptions, for instance, only 3.7 percent of respondents identified it as a desirable strategic partner, and only 2 percent expressed confidence in its ability to provide leadership on international issues.[64] Further, while London has made "deep engagement" in Asia a pillar of its post-Brexit foreign policy strategy, few in Asia see potential engagement in positive terms or, indeed, as strategically significant.[65] Rather, there is a clear sense in Asia that the United Kingdom's ambitions in the region – up to and including its participation in AUKUS – are based on an outdated sense of regional power dynamics, an inflated sense of Britain's regional influence, and postcolonial nostalgia.[66]

Australia, Japan, and India

Australia, Japan, and India are all central actors in the Western narrative on the Indo-Pacific. Actively, the three states self-identify as Indo-Pacific states and predicate their regional strategies on Western-state alignment and cooperation, to varying degrees. Indeed, Australia and Japan, in particular, have been instrumental in the development and propagation of the Indo-Pacific ideal, using their dual roles as "Western" and "Asian" states to reshape the Asia-Pacific's geopolitical boundaries and to drive cooperation with other Indo-Pacific like-minded states, including India. Passively, the three states serve as legitimating sources within non-regional Western state discourse on the Indo-Pacific, the liberal rules-based order, freedom and openness, and like-minded state cooperation. For Washington and Brussels, for instance, the engagement of Canberra, New Delhi, and Tokyo around the Indo-Pacific ideal is evidence that "Asia" is accepting of Western values, intentions, and viewpoints.

Within Asian narratives, however, one sees different views of the three states that challenge Western assumptions, particularly when viewed in parallel to their roles as Indo-Pacific actors. On Australia, for instance, one finds a high degree of cynicism in Northeast and Southeast Asian discourse with respect to its status as an Asian actor, its autonomy from the United States, its relations with China, and its understanding of Asia's regional security environment. On Japan, regional discourse, including within the country itself, questions Japan's status as a Western-aligned state, its dependence on US strategic support, and the staying power of its current anti-Chinese foreign policy in the post-Abe/Suga era. On India, regional discourse questions the country's status as a Western like-minded state, as a "balancer" to China's regional influence, and as a Western state strategic partner. Each of these narrative strands is outlined in greater detail below.

Japanese narratives on Australia do not identify it as an Asian state but instead treat it as an outsider Western nation with deep cultural and political ties with the United States and Europe and an interest in expanding its influence within Asia through bilateral and multilateral engagement.[67] Japanese scholars argue, for instance, that Australia's foreign policy in Asia reflects Western values and norms, not Asian ideals, and that Canberra is often challenged to engage in Asia on Asian terms.[68] While Japanese commentary on Australia is largely positive, a body of contemporary writing also focuses on Australia's "racist" policy history toward Asian states, peoples, and diasporas in Australia, and identifies areas where the country's past foreign policy has prioritized "whiteness" over inclusivity.[69]

Critical narratives of Australia in South Korea also focus on its role as a Western state operating in Asia, particularly with respect to its near-total alignment with the United States and its anti-China policy in the Indo-Pacific.[70] Korean scholarship treats Australia, along with New Zealand, as an outsider power in Asia, one intent on achieving its economic aims in the region through strategic engagement.[71] This is not a criticism per se of Australia's foreign policy (South Korean writing on Australia is also relatively positive); nevertheless, Korean analysts do see Canberra's strategic interests in Asia as deriving from its status as a Western state, particularly with respect to its alliance with the United States.[72]

Southeast Asian scholarship also treats Australia as an outsider Western power intent on using its alliance with the United States and its involvement in Western institutions such as AUKUS and the Quad to increase its influence in the Indo-Pacific region, a region that reflects Australian national priorities, not Asian realities. Indonesia scholarship, for instance, points to Australia's "assertive" foreign and security policy toward Asia as a potentially destabilizing factor in Southeast Asian and Indonesian affairs, and warns Jakarta to take measures to ensure the country's stability in the face of future Australian aggression.[73] Indonesian analysts also suggest that ASEAN-Australian relations, while beneficial, are vulnerable to shifts in the region's geopolitics and thus inherently unstable and unpredictable.[74] Australia's predilection to view regional events such as the South China Sea territorial disputes as related to its national interests, Indonesian commentators argue, leads it to securitize the region in ways that create tensions, particularly with China.[75] Malaysian scholars question Australia's self-appointed role as a security provider in Southeast Asia, particularly Canberra's decision to align with the United States through the AUKUS mechanism, which Malaysian analysts fear will lead to an arms race and instability in the Asia-Pacific.[76] Indeed, Malaysian commentators argue that Australian participation in AUKUS is evidence that the Australian government maintains a colonial, chauvinistic view of Asia predicated on the belief Asian states require Western leadership – a "white man's burden" view of Asia.[77]

Thai scholars also argue that Australia's propagation of the Indo-Pacific concept is more about the country's national interests and its desire to demonstrate value as a US ally and as a Western state than it is about advancing a sustainable theory of state relations and strategic trends in Asia.[78] Further, Australia's decision to align unambiguously with the United States against China contributes to new Cold War dynamics that have short- to long-term negative implications for the region's peace and stability.[79] Thai commentators specifically point to Australia's active participation in Western-led military operations in Asia as evidence that Canberra sees engagement with Western state coalitions in the region as its principal foreign policy tool.[80]

Critical Vietnamese narratives on Australia also identify the country as part of a US-led anti-China coalition in Asia, one designed to perpetuate US and Western state hegemony even at the potential cost of instigating a new regional Cold War.[81] While Vietnamese commentators express largely positive views with respect to Vietnam-Australia bilateral relations, they also register concern that Canberra's approach to China and its reliance on Western security partnerships to advance its interests in Asia, in particular, contribute to greater regional tensions between Beijing and Western states.[82]

Aside from the above narratives, one does not find much preoccupation in Asian discourse over Australia's influence as a regional actor, despite Western assumptions that Canberra is a representative Asian actor. Regional polling suggests, for instance, that hardly any Asian respondent sees Australia as a notable economic, strategic, or military force in the region. Just 0.3 percent of ASEAN respondents to the 2020 ISEAS poll identified Australia as a leading economic power in Asia, while just 0.4 percent identified Canberra as a significant strategic regional power.[83] Further, only 2.3 percent respondents identified Australia as having a capacity to preserve Asia's regional order, and only 7.5 percent identified it as a desirable third-party state for cooperation.[84] There is therefore a significant gap in Western perceptions of Australia as an impactful Asian power and the realities around regional views of Australian identity and influence.

Japan, on the other hand, is an influential regional actor that enjoys a high degree of strategic trust throughout Southeast Asia, in particular. The same polls that highlight Australia's status weakness in Asia, for instance, routinely identify Japan as one of the region's most important economic and strategic actors, albeit a distant fourth behind China, the United States, and ASEAN. Western state narratives that identify Japan as an important regional actor are correct in this respect.

Where Western narratives fall short, however, is in their assumption Asian state support for Japan is predicated on its identity as a Western-aligned state and as a free and open Indo-Pacific proponent. Rather, Asian narratives around Japan's value as a regional actor focus on its role as an economic rather than a security provider, and on its contributions to regional development, not its coordination with Western state coalitions in Asia. Indeed, Asian narratives, including Japanese narratives, become markedly less supportive when addressing Tokyo's cooperation with Washington, its participation in the Quad, and its approach to China. Asian perceptions of Japan as a state actor drop sharply when viewed in parallel to Western state intervention in the region.

Within Japan scholarship, for instance, there is a clear and developed counter-narrative to the more predominant writing on the country's free and open Indo-Pacific foreign policy.[85] Central to this counter-narrative is the belief that Japanese overreliance on the United States as a security provider has undermined the country's ability to act independently and created unnecessary friction between Tokyo and Beijing.[86] More specifically, Japanese policy-makers and analysts argue that Japan's current prioritization of strategic alignment with the United States and engagement in Western institutions in Asia undermines its relations with other Asian states.[87] These Japanese analysts call for a more independent Japanese foreign policy, one that works through regional institutions such as the Comprehensive and Progressive Agreement for Trans-Pacific Partnership (CPTPP) and the RCEP, not the Quad, and includes a clear prioritization to work with China to become more integrated in regional institutions.[88]

Korean scholarship argues that Japan's Indo-Pacific strategy is a function of its desire to expand its relations with Western states, including Australia, Europe, the United Kingdom, and the United States, and to use such ties to counter China's rise in Asia, not the direct result of its national security interests.[89] Japan's policy, in this respect, is inherently exclusionary and carries strategic echoes of Imperial Japan's Imperial Defense Policy, which sought to emulate Western state development to strengthen its position in Asia.[90] The result, Korean analysts argue, is a deterioration in the region's overall security environment, particularly with respect to China and North Korea, and a regional arms race.[91]

One finds a somewhat more measured but similar critique of Japanese foreign and security policy in Southeast Asian discourse. In Indonesia, for instance, scholars argue that Japan's Indo-Pacific concept is a means for Tokyo to develop markets overseas, particularly in developing economies, making it little different from China's Belt and Road Initiative (BRI).[92] Indeed, Indonesian writers argue that Japan and China are engaged in a zero-sum competition for economic dominance of the Indo-Pacific region, most especially within Southeast Asia.[93] Tokyo's attempt to use the Indo-Pacific to advance its economic interests in Southeast Asia, in particular, brings it into direct competition with Indonesia and other developing Asian economies.[94]

Thai writing similarly identifies Japan's engagement in Southeast Asia as an extension of its competitive policy toward China, an approach that the Abe/Suga government crafted in line with US policy toward China.[95] In this view, Japan's foreign policy motivation in Asia is as much about arresting China's regional influence as it is about providing support for states like Vietnam and Indonesia.[96] Further, Japan's motivations for working with Australia and India through the Quad, Thai analyst argue, is a reflection of the country's strategic dependency on the United States.[97]

Conversely, Vietnamese scholarship argues that Tokyo is not as aligned with the United States on security issues in the Asia-Pacific as it first appears. Rather, Japan has its own foreign policy goals that often conflict with those of Western states, such as maintaining good relations with Russia, and that it will moderate its foreign engagement in Asia as its interests evolve, not in alignment with the United States.[98]

While Japan is clearly aligned with the Western-led Indo-Pacific strategy in Asia, it is far from certain whether it will maintain such alignment in the long term or whether it will pivot to a more regionally focused, inclusive policy predicated on maritime security and closer alignment with China, among other regional states.[99] Such discourse specifically prioritizes Japan's role as an Asian state over its identity as a Western-aligned actor and argues that Tokyo's longer-term interests are regional stability and growth, not Western predominance and American hegemony.

On India, Asian narratives diverge from Western views in their treatment of New Delhi as a non-aligned, subregional power with little ability to influence developments in the Asia-Pacific, much less the ability to balance against China in the Indian and Pacific Ocean regions. Japanese scholarship, for instance, argues that India remains firmly committed to its foreign policy legacy of non-alignment and that Western commentators mistake the pragmatism in its foreign policy approach for de facto alignment.[100] Even if India were more decidedly pro-Western, Japanese analysts argue, it lacks the ability to effect real change outside of South Asia, and indeed struggles even within that subregion to establish meaningful influence.[101] India's withdrawal from the RCEP free trade agreement, in particular, undermined its effectiveness as an actor in Asia.[102] Neither should Japan assume that India will remain a stable bilateral partner, as its domestic politics veer toward authoritarianism and "Hindu-nationalism" pervades its social institutions.[103]

In South Korea, one finds a decidedly mixed view of India's role in Asia. Korean analysts argue, for instance, that the Modi government's foreign policy in Asia is the direct result of the country's internal politics, particularly the Bharatiya Janata Party's (BJP) Hindutva agenda, and that its partnership with Western nations is little more than BJP posturing.[104] Korean scholars reject the idea that India has become a de facto pro-Western state, and argue the Modi government's approach to foreign affairs is more similar to the Chinese than to the American approach.[105] Korean commentators do, however, argue for closer Korean-Indian ties as an effective means for Seoul to diversify its relations, seeing India's primary value as a non-aligned state.[106]

In Southeast Asia's predominantly Muslim states, scholars express deep concern over the BJP's Hindutva policies. Indonesian scholarship, for instance, is replete with writing on the Modi government's policy approach to Kashmir, with academics sharply criticizing the BJP's use of Hindu nationalism to define a Indian national identity that marginalizes the country's Muslim communities and contributes to sectarian violence.[107] Malaysian commentary on India similarly criticizes the Modi government for its "weaponization" of Hindu identity against India's Muslims, and suggests that the country's domestic politics are undermining its influence in Southeast Asia, within ASEAN, and across the Muslim world.[108]

Above and beyond these critiques, Southeast Asian narratives largely focus on the gap between New Delhi's stated policy of "Acting East" and the country's actual influence in Southeast Asia. Indonesian narratives suggest that India is preoccupied with foreign and security policy issues in South Asia, such as its relations with Pakistan, China, and Afghanistan, and is therefore unable to operationalize its engagement with Southeast Asia to any meaningful degree.[109] New Delhi's failure to negotiate entry into the RCEP is a case in point of its inability to integrate more effectively with Asian states.[110] Malaysian scholars similarly argue that the Modi government's Acting East policy has yet to differ significantly from its predecessor's "Look East" policies in form and function.[111] This gap between Indian rhetoric and action will likely grow in the short to medium term due to the Modi government's mishandling of India's COVID-19 pandemic response and the country's developmental setback and reputational cost.[112]

Thai scholars argue that the Modi government has found it difficult to extend India's geographic and foreign policy scope beyond South Asia, with the exception of getting Myanmar and Thailand to join the Bay of Bengal Initiative for Multi-Sectoral Technical and Economic Cooperation (BIMSTEC).[113] While India is an influential cultural and political partner for Southeast Asian states, Thai scholars argue, its diplomatic and economic influence in the region remains limited, particularly as New Delhi opted out of the RCEP and the BJP failed badly in its response to India's COVID-19 crisis.[114]

Vietnamese scholars argue that India is an underperforming Asia-Pacific actor that has not realized its potential to emerge as a regional great power.[115] While the Modi government is more ambitious than the previous Indian administrations with respect to the country's foreign relations, New Delhi's diplomatic efforts remain primarily focused on South Asia, where it seeks to improve relations with neighbouring states, manage its border disputes with China, and pursue greater subregional economic integration.[116] Outside of South Asia, Vietnamese policy analysts argue, India continues to pursue and prioritize a policy of non-alignment and multipolarity that includes relations with states such as Russia and Iran, albeit to limited effect.[117]

China as a "Revisionist" and "Coercive" Power
Whereas Western narratives on Asia tend to overestimate the identities, reputations, alliances, and influences of United States, Europe, Australia, Japan, and India in the Asia-Pacific, they underestimate regional sentiments toward China, particularly the degree to which Asian states see China as a desirable, responsible, and stabilizing actor. In contrast to Western assumptions about China as a revisionist state, for instance, Asian narratives tend to identify it as an irreplaceable actor within the region and a critical partner for Asian states on sustainable economic development, infrastructure investment, climate change, and pandemic response, recovery, and preparation. While Asian discourse on China includes the perceived need to work with Beijing to address areas where its foreign engagement leads to regional tensions, it also sees China as part of any long-term solution, not as the sole source of the problem.

On China's place in Asia, for instance, Asian states differ markedly from Western assumptions about China's "rise" and its putative potential to destabilize the Asian region. At least part of this disagreement comes from the Asian perspective that China is already Asia's predominant economic, political, and security actor – that it has in fact already risen. Regional polling from 2019 to 2021 shows, for instance, that around 75 percent of Southeast Asians already see China as the region's most influential economic actor, and around 50 percent see China as the region's most important strategic and political actor (polling puts the United States at just 7 percent and 30 percent, respectively).[118] Similarly, Asian Barometer polling from 2017 shows that the vast majority of Northeast Asian actors, including South Korea, Japan, and Taiwan, believe that China is Asia's predominant power, both with respect to its "hard" power (military capacity) and "soft" power (cultural appeal).[119]

Polling also shows that most Asia-Pacific respondents (57 percent) view Chinese influence in largely positive terms.[120] Indeed, under the Trump administration, in particular, Asian states largely viewed China as a *more stable, more responsible power* than the United States. On free trade (a key component of the Western free and open Indo-Pacific concept), Asian respondents in 2020 identified China as more committed to the ideal than the United States.[121] When asked in 2020 whether they would align with China or the United States if forced to choose, seven out of ten Southeast Asian respondents chose China.[122]

While these numbers declined somewhat for China in 2021 following the Biden administration's conceptual commitment to re-engage with Asia, polls still showed a high degree of approval (44 percent) for China's regional leadership during the COVID-19 pandemic, compared with relative disapproval for Japan (18 percent), Europe (10 percent), and the United States (9 percent).[123] More importantly, over 40 percent of respondents predicted that their countries' relations with China would improve in the immediate future. More than any other poll, arguably, this registered sense of optimism toward China's future influence represents a stark break with Western narratives on the danger that China's rise poses to regional stability.

Even with respect to ongoing territorial disputes in the South China Sea, the majority of respondents (74 percent) identified China as part of the solution to regional tensions in 2021, arguing that a negotiated code of conduct between ASEAN member states and China was the best path forward to achieve regional stability.[124] Similarly, 66 percent of respondents called for coordination between China and ASEAN member states through subregional institutions to address security and environmental issues around the Mekong region, a main area of tension between Asian states.[125] These findings also differ markedly from Western views of China as a regional disrupter, and suggest a clear regional prioritization of dialogue to address instability in the South China Sea over the Western preference for shows of force.

It is beyond the scope of this book to map comprehensively regional discourse on China. There is simply too much written in Asia on China's domestic and foreign affairs to articulate any but the most truncated of accounts. Nevertheless, within the broad body of such literature, one does find well-articulated narratives that are worth highlighting to demonstrate the differences between regional views and the assumptions that have informed Western narratives' treatment of China. In Japan, for instance, scholars argue that China's foreign policy is not inherently antagonistic or exploitative as Western scholarship suggests, but rather an outcome of China's historical approach to foreign policy, which prioritizes domestic and foreign stability, interconnectivity, multilateralism, and the development of an Asian "community."[126] Further, Japanese academics argue, China is a necessary actor in Asia and a key contributor to regional order, despite Western states' maneuvering to position the Indo-Pacific concept in opposition to China's Belt and Road Initiative.[127] Chinese foreign policy and foreign engagement is driving economic modernization in developing Asia with respect to telecommunications, digital trade, and public health, and its foreign policy norms have evolved to include issues related to environmental sustainability and social development.[128] While Japanese commentators certainly see China as a regional competitor of Japan, they also see the two states' competition as non-zero-sum and argue that China and Japan can work together where possible.[129]

Korean scholarship is also more positive with respect to China's contributions to regional development and security, and more critical of Western narratives that suggest Beijing is somehow more aggressive and/or assertive than other states.[130] Rather than treat the Belt and Road Initiative as a source of instability, for instance, Korean scholars suggest instead that Western securitization of Chinese foreign policy and Western policies predicated on containment of China are contributing to Asia's instability.[131] Korean analysts note further that no Asian state is interested in alignment with the United States or a Western coalition of states against China, but rather all seek to engage with Beijing on issues ranging from military joint training to shared maritime awareness.[132] Far from being a disruptive power, Korean writers argue, China is a regional core state that contributes in a major way to Asia's overall economic development and order.[133]

Indonesian discourse on China is also largely positive, particularly with respect to China's influence on the country's economic growth, stability, and security.[134] Indonesian commentators see China as an irreplaceable source of investment in Indonesia's domestic economy, for instance, and advocate for closer trade, finance, and investment ties.[135] Even on matters of conflict between the two states, such as overlapping maritime claims in the South China Sea, Indonesian security analysts argue against alignment with the United States and for dialogue and partnership with China on the grounds that the United States, not China, is an untrustworthy partner.[136] On pandemic cooperation, in particular, Indonesian discourse on China points to its role as a provider of regional public goods, such as vaccines and personal protective equipment.[137]

One finds similar discursive trends in Malaysian scholarship on China, albeit with a greater focus on socio-cultural relations between the two states.[138] More than in other Southeast Asian states, for instance, Malaysian media regularly highlight the country's cultural "closeness" with Beijing as a source of strength in their bilateral relations.[139] Malaysian scholars identify China's opposition to Western colonialism, its relations with the Global South, and its support for the Palestinians as drivers behind closer Malaysian-Chinese relations.[140] Indeed, while Malaysia has traditionally adopted a balanced approach to US-China competition in Southeast Asia, a sizable number of Malaysian policy-makers and commentators advocate for more direct alignment with China on economic, political, and security matters in Asia.[141]

Thai narratives on China are also uniformly supportive of closer bilateral ties, even those that raise concerns about China's influence in the country and in Asia.[142] Generally, Thai scholars see China as a responsible regional actor and reject Western assumptions about its "disruptive" foreign policy.[143] Thai media, in particular, regularly identify China as a positive source of regional development, of stability operations (such as peacekeeping), and of public health, particularly with respect to China's support for Thailand over the course of the COVID-19 pandemic.[144] Vietnamese scholars see China's overall regional role in positive terms, with the notable exception of its maritime claims around the South China Sea.[145] Even on these security issues, however, Vietnamese policy-makers and commentators advocate for *closer*, not lesser, ties with Beijing, seeing dialogue with China as the most promising avenue for crisis management and avoidance.[146]

What these narratives demonstrate is that among Asian states there is a decidedly more complex and complementary view of China's behaviours, activities, and influence in the region than one sees in Western narratives. Rather than seeing China as a destabilizer, Asian nations view it as an integral political, strategic actor with an outsized ability to shape the region. Where Asian states do see China as a challenge, such as in the South China Sea or in the Mekong, they also see it as part of the solution, prioritizing dialogue over confrontation. Whereas the Western narrative of China securitizes nearly every aspect of China's foreign and security policies, Asian states, conversely, seek greater interconnectivity for the sake of their own economic opportunity and regional stability.

Implications for Canada

Canadian policy discourse shares many of the same chauvinistic assumptions that constitute Western narratives on Asia. The idea that Western like-minded states occupy a privileged position in Asia's security and governance architecture, for instance, is ubiquitous throughout Canadian policy writing. The belief that Western states are best positioned to ensure Asia's rules-based order is ubiquitous throughout Canadian leadership statements and media. And the certitude that Canada's best partners in Asia are Australia, Europe, Japan, and the United States (only one of which is an Asian state) influences Canadian scholars' view of the country's need to adopt an Indo-Pacific approach to Asia, an approach informed by the supposed superiority of Western leadership in the region.

As this chapter demonstrates, however, this view is fundamentally flawed. Asian states do not share Western assumptions about the importance of Western state leadership in the region, nor do they share Western states' self-perceptions concerning their regional roles and identities. Rather, Asian narratives on the roles and involvement of Western states in Asia are far more critical, up to an including discourse that identifies Western states, particularly the United States, as the greatest contributor to regional instability.

Neither do Asian states agree with Western assumptions about the roles of Australia, Japan, and India in Asia, instead differing significantly in how they view the three states as regional actors. Whereas Canada, for instance, routinely identifies Australia as a model Asian state toward which it should strive, Asian states do not even recognize it as Asian. Whereas Western narratives identify Japan and India as Western-aligned actors, Asian states see the two as intrinsically bound to their own immediate strategic environments and likely to adapt their foreign and security policies within Asia accordingly.

Neither do Asian states share Western views about China as a "revisionist" state. Rather, Japan, South Korea, Indonesia, Malaysia, Thailand, and Vietnam all see Beijing as a regional actor with huge potential to contribute to regional stability, economic growth, and interconnectivity. While these same actors remain concerned over China's deleterious effects on stability in the region, they also see China as a critical part of any solution to any regional problem.

Any Canadian strategy toward Asia that fails to privilege these regional narratives over the assumptions that inform Western states'

Indo-Pacific strategies will fail. While Western states possess huge material capacity to interfere in Asia's regional dynamics, history is not on their side. Asian states and societies, rather, have developed their own narrative lenses to understand the region's developments, and these run counter to Western views and assumptions. For Canada to establish a lasting presence in Asia not predicated on Western military predominance, listening to these regional voices is a prerequisite.

4

Asian Narratives on Asia's Security Order

Western Hegemony as a Source of Instability

In *The Hell of Good Intentions,* Harvard University professor Stephen Walt demonstrates how policy-makers in the United States have used exaggerated threat narratives to justify the country's overseas operations as a matter of policy up to the present day. Walt notes how US policy elites have constructed these narratives to rationalize American involvement in assassinations, interventions, regime change, and war when their real purpose was not national defence but the propagation of American hegemony through the expansion of democracy, liberal values, and open markets. Walt further argues that US narratives of global insecurity have, ironically, led to a breakdown in the very liberal order that policy-makers sought to promote, and has all but ensured an end to US global hegemony. A consummate realist, Walt concludes that in oversecuritizing its foreign affairs, the United States has contributed to global insecurity, undermined its international reputation, and hastened its decline.[1]

This is very much the case of US security involvement in Asia, which is full of historical examples where existential threat rhetoric has been used to justify American involvement in some of the region's poorest, most underdeveloped states. In 1898, for instance, President Theodore Roosevelt invoked Alfred Mahan's naval theories as justification for the Philippine-American War, arguing that the United States needed overseas colonies to defend American interests abroad.[2] In this brutal war, more than 250,000 Filipinos had been killed by 1902.[3] President Harry Truman also framed US involvement in the 1950 Korean War in existential terms, arguing that US intervention was needed to check the spread of global communism.[4] While an enduring narrative of US involvement, modern-day historians now largely reject this interpretation of the Korean War's origins, instead focusing on the war as a continuation of Japanese occupation and intra-Korean tensions between those who had resisted and those who had supported Japanese colonialization.[5]

US strategists similarly referenced the "domino theory" to justify the American war in Indochina, arguing to the American people, among others, that all Southeast Asia could turn communist if the North Vietnamese were allowed to consolidate power.[6] As with the Korean War, historians now view the Vietnam War as a by-product of decolonialization and US intervention as an effort to preserve aspects of Asia's imperial order.[7] Washington similarly used fear of an unsubstantiated communist takeover in Indonesia to effect regime change in the 1960s, from the nationalist, anti-colonial Sukarno to the despotic, dictatorial, yet pro-Western Suharto. As many as a million Indonesians died in the anti-communist purge that followed.[8]

Importantly, US threat exaggeration and US security narratives have not just provided Washington with a domestic rationale for its overseas operations but, as argued throughout this book, have facilitated a hegemonic socialization process that, in turn, has shaped the broader Western narrative around Asia's security environment, particularly among US allies and partners. Georgetown University professor Victor Cha outlines this process in *Powerplay: The Origins of the American Alliance System in Asia,* noting that the United States built and maintained is alliance system in Asia by propagating its threat perception and seeking conceptual alignment with states like Japan, South Korea, Australia, and New Zealand.[9] Amitav Acharya argues that the United States used the Southeast Asia Treaty Organization (SEATO) to inculcate its strategic narratives in regional and extra-regional Western states and US allies, including Australia, France, New Zealand, Pakistan, the Philippines, Thailand, and the United Kingdom, to the point that the institution became a mechanism for US hegemonic control in Asia.[10]

One sees similar behaviour in contemporary US narratives about Asia, particularly in Washington's propagation of its Indo-Pacific strategic vision and its predilection for vilifying the People's Republic of

China (PRC). As in the past, there is also clear evidence that Western states and Western-aligned states have uncritically accepted the US hegemonic narrative as their own. As noted in earlier chapters, Australia, the European Union, France, Germany, Japan, the Netherlands, and the United Kingdom have all identified the need to "manage" China as a primary security challenge in the Asian region. Further, these states have all internalized the Indo-Pacific and its component parts in their own strategic thinking, almost entirely in line with US strategic views on the region.

Above and beyond the Indo-Pacific construct, one also finds universal agreement among Western states on what issues constitute Asia's primary security areas, how to conceptualize these issues in line with Asia's strategic environment, and, indeed, how to respond to these security challenges. Among Western narratives on Asia's security, for instance, one finds broad consensus that North Korea's nuclear program, Taiwan's national security, the militarization of the South China Sea, and territorial disputes in the East China Sea over the Diaoyu/Senkaku Islands[11] are Asia's primary security issues, and that each requires continued Western oversight and involvement – to varying degrees – to prevent further escalation. Further, Western states view their involvement in these security areas in entirely positive terms, seeing it as an essential part of any potential solution. Indeed, one finds nearly no scholarship in the Western world considering whether Western state involvement in Asia contributes to *insecurity* rather than security, or whether Western disentanglement from the region's primary security areas may, in fact, have a stabilizing effect.

This chapter demonstrates that regional narratives differ markedly from Western discourse with respect to the three main security issues outlined above and Western involvement in Asia as it relates to stability. The chapter outlines thinking from China, South Korea, and Japan on the North Korea (Democratic People's Republic of Korea, or DPRK) and the East China Sea, scholarship from Southeast Asia on the South China Sea, and regional commentary on Taiwan that presents a dramatically different narrative from that dominant in Western policy statements, media, and academic and other scholarship. It further identifies a strand of strategic thought across Asian states that securitizes Western – especially American – involvement in Asia as a source of insecurity and instability.

North Korea

North Korea occupies a privileged position in Western narratives on Asian security. It is the quintessential rogue nation, impervious to Western sanctions and pressure. Isolated within Northeast Asia while surrounded by some of the world's most advanced economies, it is the "Hermit Kingdom," resistant to modernization and closed to foreign influence. Routinely the subject of Western satire, it is the "inscrutable" country ruled by a dynasty with a flare for theatrics and odd-sounding rhetoric. Alone among America's adversaries, it is simultaneously a weak state and an existential threat. It is part of the "axis of evil," a nuclear power just crazy enough to use it nukes.

For decades, Western scholars have treated North Korea as the boogeyman of Asia, presenting its leadership, military, and society as innately alien and, consequently, as incapable of constituting a modern nation. Pointing to its use of terrorist tactics and militarized violence, Western strategists have routinely branded the North Korean state as a "criminal" regime, thereby delegitimizing its sovereign rights and national security interests.[12] Indeed, among Western analysts, there is a tendency to portray the North Korean regime as more akin to a mafia than a legitimate government, particularly as it relies on activities such as currency counterfeiting, weapons proliferation, and cybercrime to generate funding.[13]

Starting with the Six-Party Talks (6PT) in 2003, Western analysts have also pointed to North Korea's nuclear program as evidence of its belligerence and its threat to international security. Following the country's successful 2016 test of a hydrogen bomb and intercontinental ballistic missile, US policy-makers have further identified North Korea as a threat to US domestic security, a move that countenances increased and indeterminant American economic and military pressure and unrelenting North Korean isolation.[14] While denying that North Korea is a nuclear state, Western policy-makers now call for North Korean nuclear disarmament as a precondition of sanctions relief.[15] At the same time US presidents have threatened the country with "total destruction" and "fire and fury" on behalf of America's allies.[16]

Western policy-makers have long used the North Korean "threat" as a justification for the continued deployment of Western "sending state" troops from Australia, Belgium, Canada, France, Luxembourg, New Zealand, South Africa, the United States, and the United Kingdom to

South Korea under the United Nations Command (UNC) and to Japan under the UNC (Rear).[17] US government and military leaders now identify the ongoing "crisis" on the Korean Peninsula as the primary rationale for US troop and materiel deployment to South Korea and Japan.[18] Since the end of the Cold War, in particular, US policy-makers have used instability on the Korean Peninsula to justify the United States' ongoing alliance relations in Northeast Asia, having relied on the threat of communism to legitimize the US security presence in the region for much of the twentieth century.[19] From its annual multilateral Rim "of the Pacific Exercise (RIMPAC) to the US–South Korea Foal Eagle Exercise, the United States also routinely points to its need to deter North Korea as justification for its numerous, Asia-Pacific–based military engagements.[20]

Following the breakdown in the Six-Party Talks, Western strategists have argued for a policy approach to North Korea predicated on deterrence, "strategic patience," and sanctions, with the ostensible hope that the North Korean regime would collapse under the weight of Western pressure. Under the Trump administration, US policy toward North Korea veered toward one of "maximum pressure," up to the point of US threats of war and North Korean threats of nuclear retaliation.[21] While the Biden administration has yet to adopt a distinctive approach to North Korea, it continues to rely almost exclusively on sanctions regimes toward Pyongyang as a matter of policy, threatening secondary sanctions to any country or company that fails to follow these sanctions.

While this view of North Korea is unarguably the dominant narrative in Western strategic writing – to the point that one has a hard time finding any alternative account of North Korean security dynamics in English – it is, in fact, just one perspective on Korean Peninsula affairs, one that is entirely Western-centric, intrinsically biased, and chauvinistically self-serving. Within South Korean scholarship, policy commentary, and security writing on the DPRK, for instance, one finds a dramatically different perspective of North Korea as a security actor with respect to its history, its motivations, and its activities, as well as divergent opinions about what policy Seoul and the international community should take toward Pyongyang, what strategic ends are desirable with respect to the country, and what role the United States plays in Northeast Asia's security architecture.

Among Korean historians, for instance, there is a growing view that the situation in North Korea is rooted in America's postwar "colonialism" of South Korea, its involvement in the Korean civil war, its Cold War isolation of North Korea, and its use of sanctions against North Korea, not in some inherent deficiency among North Korean leaders and society as the Western narrative suggests.[22] From this perspective, North Korea is the victim of American and Western state aggression, and its behaviour is that of a weak state seeking survival in a system over which it has no control.[23] One can best understand North Korea's foreign and security policy, these analysts argue, as desperate attempts to stave off collapse in the face of direct pressure from the world's most powerful nation and its regional allies, not as the behaviours of an irrational state.[24]

Korean analysts also see US-led sanctions regimes as a direct cause of North Korean "provocation." Cut off from legitimate means of economic growth, such as trade, foreign direct investment, or overseas remittances, Pyongyang is left with no choice but to engage in criminal behaviour such as drug trafficking, currency counterfeiting, and cyberattacks.[25] In what amounts to a perverse cycle, the United States then identifies North Korea's mafia-type behaviour as justification for further sanctions.[26]

There is a South Korean narrative that also identifies American aggression, not North Korean belligerence, as the source of North Korea's nuclear weapons program.[27] According to this narrative, having endured American attacks, threats, and punitive action and having had to exist with US nuclear weapons, missile defence, and 28,500 troops on its borders since its founding, North Korea was forced to develop a nuclear deterrent capability as a matter of existential survival.[28] Far from a demonstration of state aggression, North Korea's nuclear program is entirely defensive in nature and, considering rhetoric from past US administrations threatening it with "total destruction," understandable in practice.

Within Japanese counter-narratives on North Korea, one finds many similar viewpoints. For instance, on the US decision to divide Korea after the Second World War and to engage in war to ensure that the Koreans remained divided during the Cold War, Japanese scholars have argued that the United States has prioritized its own global strategy over peace and security on the Korean Peninsula, and that it has taken advantage of its protectorate over South Korea (and, indeed, Japan) to cement American predominance in Northeast Asia through the deployment of US troops and military assets to the region.[29] On sanctions, Japanese analysts have raised similar concerns as their Korean counterparts as to their overall effectiveness as well as their stated purpose, which is to disrupt North Korea's nuclear program and to effect regime change. Far from improving the security dynamics in the Korean Peninsula, these analysts argue, Western sanctions actually worsen its strategic environment, both by making North Korea more desperate and by creating distrust between North Korean and Western state leadership.[30]

Japanese scholars also question the underlying assumption in Western scholarship that North Korea's leadership is inherently irrational and that the country is a rogue nuclear power. They argue instead that all North Korean behaviour is both rational and understandable when viewed as a deterrent to Western aggression or as a response to Western threats.[31] On the US reliance on military diplomacy to engage with North Korea, Japanese academics argue that Washington's approach puts South Korea and Japan at risk, even as the US mainland sits largely outside the range of most of North Korea's ballistic missile capabilities. Indeed, Washington's lack of coordination with Seoul and Tokyo means both states are vulnerable to American whims and North Korean responses, even to the point of being overly vulnerable to nuclear, chemical, or biological attack.[32]

Critique of Western involvement in Korean security matters is even more pronounced in Chinese narratives, particularly with respect to US provocations, troop and weapons deployments, and unilateralism toward North Korea. Chinese scholars argue, for instance, that the United States has used Western involvement in the Korean Peninsula to prolong the Korean conflict in ways that suit American strategic interests in Northeast Asia. Rather than seek a negotiated solution, they assert, the United States is incentivized to maintain the perception of a North Korean threat to justify its troops presence not only in South Korea but also in Japan.[33]

Chinese scholars also argue that the United States uses the North Korean "threat" to justify deployment of controversial military technologies such as the Terminal High Altitude Area Defense (THAAD) system to South Korea – systems that have a dual-use purpose of providing the US military with signals intelligence (SIGINT) and missile defence capabilities directed toward China and Russia and that therefore increase security tensions in Northeast Asia.[34] Similarly, US military commanders use North Korea as a pretext to maintain forces in Japan, with the real intent of using these forces to defend Taiwan and to counter mainland China.[35]

Chinese narratives also accuse Western states of engaging in unnecessary provocation of North Korea, up to and including the implied use of nuclear force against the country, and of acting unilaterally, or without reference to other regional powers such as China and Russia that have a direct interest in North Korean outcomes.[36] Chinese scholars also criticize Western state charges that Beijing is North Korea's patron and that it could influence Pyongyang. They argue that it is instead the United States' responsibility to solve the North Korean "problem," which it can do through direct policy actions such as sanctions relief and diplomatic normalization.[37]

South China Sea and East China Sea
Just as Western narratives use the North Korean threat to justify Western and US troop deployments in the Korean Peninsula and Japan, so they use China's presence and activities in the South and East China Seas to rationalize US alliance relations, to countenance Western naval deployments throughout the Asian region, to legitimize US-led freedom of navigation operations (FONOPs) in the South China Sea, and to advocate for Western-oriented security institutions such as AUKUS and the Quad. Chinese activity in the South China Sea has become the rallying mark for Western states' conceptual and operational alignment around assumptions such as Chinese "coercion," "revisionism," "aggression," and "unilateralism."[38] These assumptions, in turn, inform Western Indo-Pacific strategies and validate individual state action, such as the British deployment of an aircraft carrier and Australia's decision to dispatch nuclear submarines to the South China Sea.[39]

On the South China Sea, Western narratives identify China's island reclamation, its claims over maritime features, it base development, and its use of its coast guard, navy, and "maritime militia" to enforce its claims as evidence that China is intent on replacing the United States as the region's predominant naval presence to control the region's sea lines of communication (SLOCs) and to deny access to Western navies and international shipping in the event of conflict.[40] Western analysts point to China's "hardening" of island and land features in the

South China Sea as evidence that it is militarizing the region, and to its rejection of an international tribunal's findings that some of its activities and claims in the region are illegal according to the United Nations Convention on the Law of the Sea (UNCLOS) as confirmation of Chinese "revisionism" and "rejection" of international law.[41]

For the United States in particular, China's activities in the South China Sea have become a rallying point for increased military spending in the Asia-Pacific, for further US naval deployment throughout the region, and for US military engagement with and support for other South China Sea claimant states, including Vietnam.[42] The need to deter Chinese activities in the South China Sea is at the centre of the AUKUS trilateral, Washington's Indo-Pacific strategy, and its outreach to other like-minded states to manage China's rise.[43] Indeed, the topic has given rise to a cottage industry within US think tanks, defence contractors, and war colleges, where individuals and institutions have developed entire careers and initiatives around monitoring Chinese activity in the region through satellite imagery and textual analysis.[44]

Western policy-makers now frame their engagement with Southeast Asian states and with the Association of Southeast Asian Nations (ASEAN) as Western "support" for Asia's liberal order, arguing that China's activities in the South China Sea are undermining this order.[45] From Berlin to Canberra, from Paris to Washington, Western politicians routinely identify Chinese "aggression" in the South China Sea as confirmation that Western involvement in Asia is critical and, indeed, a function of Western benevolence and leadership.[46]

On the East China Sea, the Western narrative focuses on alleged Chinese aggression and territorial violations with respect to the Chinese-claimed and Japanese-administered Diaoyu/Senkaku Islands, which Japan nationalized in 2012.[47] Led by Tokyo and Washington, this narrative frames Chinese naval and air force activities in the region as provocative and as violations of Japanese sovereign maritime and air space.[48] Western analysts have further pointed to China's 2013 establishment of an air defence identification zone (ADIZ) in the East China Sea as evidence of Chinese revisionism and coercion and China's destabilizing effect on regional stability.[49]

Importantly, Western narratives routinely classify Chinese activity in the South and East China Seas – including its use of fishing vessels to disrupt US and Japanese naval and coast guard activities and its reclamation and development of maritime features in the South China

Sea – as "gray zone" activities, or "operations short of war."[50] Through this rhetorical tactic, Western analysts now identify almost any Chinese activity within Asia's maritime domain as a precursor to armed conflict, thereby justifying Western security operations against China as defensive in nature.[51]

One finds far more diversity of opinion within Southeast Asia narratives on the involvement of the United States and other Western states in the South China Sea, particularly in local-language scholarship. In Indonesia, for example, writing on maritime security in the South China Sea largely ignores the excessive territorial claim narrative that informs Western strategic writing to focus on American hegemony and greater power competition between the United States and China as the source of regional instability.[52] Indonesia's leadership, including senior military leaders such as the secretary general of the National Defense Council Rear Admiral Harjo Susmoro, have further identified "hegemonic conflict" in the South China Sea – not Chinese "aggression" – as the defining feature for their country's strategic environment.[53] Indonesian media coverage of US activity in the South China Sea, including the US Navy's use of freedom of navigation operations, suggests that the United States is operating in the region primarily to ensure continued US naval control in Asia by denying China space to develop.[54] Indonesian analysts, in this respect, see Beijing and Washington as equal contributors to instability in the South China Sea (and, indeed, the East China Sea, on which more is found below).[55]

In Malaysia, one finds a similar narrative about Western states' involvement in the South China Sea, albeit one generally more sympathetic to China's position and more critical of American intentions. While Malay-language media identifies great power competition in Southeast Asia as the primary driver behind tensions in the South China Sea, Malaysian analysts largely blame the United States and its Western allies – including Australia and Japan – for destabilizing the region through their provocative naval operations.[56] Central to this contention is the belief that China and ASEAN have managed, and can manage, tensions in the South China Sea through negotiation, especially on a code of conduct, and that Western involvement undermines regional efforts at conflict mitigation.[57]

While more sympathetic to the United States than Malaysians, Thai analysts also argue that Western operations in the South China Sea, including FONOPs, are less about ensuring Asia's order or protecting international law than they are about ensuring Western and American predominance and prestige in Asia, which is threatened by China's rise.[58] Thai strategic writers argue that Western states' credibility and reputation as regional actors are now tied to their ability to deter China's activities in the South China Sea, which suggests that US/Western operations in the region are more about prestige preservation and reputation management than strategic necessity.[59]

Even Vietnamese writers routinely and openly question the United States' stated intentions in the South China Sea, arguing that US operations are more about ensuring American security interests than supporting regional order or regional states' conflicting claims with China.[60] Indeed, Vietnamese support for US operations (which Western analysts routinely invoke in justifying a Western presence in the region) does not come from the belief that the United States is in the region to secure order, maintain neutrality, or support international law, but rather from the hope that it will act against China so Vietnam can advance its own maritime claims in the South China Sea – many of which are just as "illegal" as Chinese claims under UNCLOS.[61] Rather than viewing Vietnam-US relations as an indication of regional support for US operations in the South China Sea, therefore, it is more accurate to view the two states' bilateral relations as a function of a Vietnamese security policy rooted in the logic of "the enemy of my enemy is my friend."

On Western involvement in the East China Sea, Chinese-language literature provides the fullest counterpoint to the Western narrative, a counterpoint that rests on the belief that Japan – not China – caused the current crisis by nationalizing the Diaoyu/Senkaku Islands in September 2012.[62] Chinese scholars argue, in particular, that Tokyo's decision to claim sovereignty over the islands forced Beijing to react, whereas China had been content to avoid conflict through a status quo predicated on strategic ambiguity before Japan's nationalization.[63] Chinese analysts also argue that US support for Japan's claim of sovereignty over the islands is antagonistic and destabilizing, noting (correctly) that the Obama administration warned Japan against taking such a step – seeing the move as unnecessarily provocative – only to later confirm that US support for Japan extended to its defence of the islands.[64]

Commentators from Taiwan similarly identify Japan's nationalization of the Diaoyu Islands (which Taiwan claims) as a provocation contributing to instability in the East China Sea.[65] Indeed, Taiwan's ruling

Democratic Progressive Party (DPP) resolutely claims Taiwanese sovereignty over the islands, rejects any historical or contemporary Japanese rationale regarding their ownership, and calls for US neutrality on the islands' sovereign status.[66] Taiwanese scholars have further accused Tokyo of acting with a colonial logic toward the Diaoyu Islands, claiming that its actions amount to bullying and calling for international arbitration to challenge its "occupation."[67]

South Korean discourse on East China Sea security issues contains similar critiques of Japan's territorial claim and administrative control over the Diaoyu/Senkaku Islands, albeit mostly in reference to Japan's similar claim over the Dokdo/Takeshima Islands, which Seoul controls, and in the context of South Korea–Japan foreign relations.[68] Korean commentators, for instance, have argued that Japan's nationalization of the Diaoyu/Senkaku Islands is a feature of is expansionist archipelago policy, by which it seeks to gain control over islands in the East China Sea that were never historically Japanese.[69] Korean analysts have further argued that Japan's approach to both the Diaoyu/Senkaku and Dokdo/Takeshima Islands is evidence of Japanese "diplomatic incompetence" and of Tokyo's lack of interest in maintaining good relations with China and South Korea in Northeast Asia.[70]

Taiwan
The Western narrative on Taiwan is divided into two parts: one focused on cross-strait relations, Taiwanese democracy and sovereignty, and Chinese coercion; the other focused on Taiwan as a Western security partner, as an "unsinkable aircraft carrier" in Asia, and as a bulwark against Chinese naval expansion beyond its "first island chain." In the Trump and Biden administrations, US narratives on Taiwan have grown to include diplomatic normalization, or the US intent to "lift self-imposed restrictions" on bilateral relations, in what amounts to a unilateral attempt to alter the conceptual status quo governing relations between mainland China and Taiwan. Unifying all these different narratives on Taiwan are Western deliberations on war with China, whether with respect to China's military modernization, US operational contingencies for the Taiwan Strait, or US allies' roles in the event of US-China conflict.

On cross-strait relations, Western narratives concerning Taiwan start with the understanding that relations between mainland China and Taiwan exist under a "one-China policy." This policy, rooted in Washington's

1979 decision to switch diplomatic recognition from the Republic of China (Taiwan) to the People's Republic of China, holds that there is only one China, controlled by the PRC, and that the United States (and other Western states) acknowledge that the PRC sees Taiwan as part of China. Western policy-makers do not *accept* that Taiwan is part of China – as Beijing's "one-China principle" states – but only *acknowledge* that Beijing believes it is.[71] While a seemingly modest conceptual difference, Western narratives have latched on to the variation in practice to challenge Beijing's claims to sovereignty over Taiwan.

Western scholars have pointed to Taiwan's democratic institutions and the Taiwanese people's increasing identification as "Taiwanese" rather than "Chinese" to challenge China's sovereign claim and to argue that Taiwan is an independent entity, if not an outright "state."[72] Western analysts consider Beijing's use of economic linkages and incentives to enhance ties between the mainland and Taiwan as coercion, and argue that its refusal to renounce the use of force to prevent Taiwan from declaring independence constitutes bullying.[73] They regularly point to Taiwan's democracy as evidence that Beijing's autocratic system of government is illegitimate, and that democracy and Chinese culture are compatible.[74]

The Western narrative on Taiwan's security focuses on the need for its defence, on the strategic value it provides as a bulwark to China's naval expansion into the Pacific Ocean, and on its role in Chinese military modernization and strategic planning. Referencing the 1979 Taiwan Relations Act, for instance, US policy-makers and strategic analysts argue that the United States has a legal and moral obligation to defend Taiwan while remaining "strategically ambivalent" about how, when, and where it will provide such defence.[75] Australian defence officials have indicated their country's willingness to use force to defend Taiwan against mainland China, particularly as part of a US-led coalition.[76] France and the United Kingdom have also dispatched naval warships to the Taiwan Strait to demonstrate their military support for Taiwan.[77] Even the European Union has committed itself to Taiwan's defence, albeit focusing on dialogue and crisis management mechanisms rather than military options.[78]

Part of these Western actors' justifications for defending Taiwan is the need for democratic alignment against Beijing's regional influence and the desire to preserve Taiwan's democratic institutions.[79] Another part, however, is Taiwan's geographic proximity to mainland China and its importance as an "unsinkable aircraft carrier" from which Western states – primarily the United States – can act against China in the event of conflict or war.[80] Western strategic writing has long identified Taiwan as both a potential base of operations for Western forays into mainland China and as an immovable obstacle to Chinese naval deployment into the Western Pacific, or beyond what Western strategists refer to as the first island chain.[81] Indeed, the concern that Beijing could use Taiwan as its own base to deploy its naval assets into the Pacific has preoccupied Western strategists much longer than concerns about Taiwan's democratic institutions, and continues to be the predominant reason in Western strategic writing for countering Beijing's efforts to "reincorporate" Taiwan.

Closely related to Taiwan's strategic significance is the Western discourse on mainland China's coastal defence, or its anti-access/area-denial (A2AD) capabilities. Western defence analysts routinely identify Beijing's development of asymmetric defence, including its "carrier killer" ballistic missiles, as a function of its intention to use force against Taiwan, or to deny Western intervention in a potential China-Taiwan contingency.[82] In presenting Beijing's military development and deployment as part of a plan to intimidate Taiwan, Western analysts identify its domestic defence systems in entirely offensive terms, meaning that Western strategies to counter China's A2AD capability become defensive in nature.[83]

In addition to these long-standing Western narratives, policy-makers and analysts under the Trump and Biden administrations have adopted a new strand of discourse toward Taiwan predicated on "normalization" of relations, "strategic clarity," and a rejection of "self-imposed restraints" in dealing with Taipei.[84] Most fully articulated by former secretary of state Mike Pompeo, this US narrative holds that Taiwan is a like-minded actor that deserves unrestricted support from the United States and other Western states.[85] While a seemingly minor policy adjustment to the uninitiated, the Trump/Biden discourse with respect to Taiwan represents a fundamental departure from the United States' decades-long one-China policy and, arguably, a conceptual realignment of cross-strait relations.[86] Predictably, Australia, France, the United Kingdom, and the European Union have all announced similar policies in what amounts to a break in long-standing Western discourse on Taiwan.[87]

On the other hand, regional discourse on Taiwan differs from predominant Western narratives that assume instability in cross-strait relations, China's predilection for coercion, Taiwan's desire for independence, and the desirability of Western state engagement with Taiwan. In Southeast Asia, for instance, writing on cross-strait relations largely eschews the Western perspective that Taiwan is under threat from China. Rather, Southeast Asian security writing on Taiwan and cross-strait affairs tends to focus on the need for dialogue and crisis management between Beijing and Taipei, not on the need for military multilateralism to "manage" the threat from Beijing. Where Southeast Asian writers do venture into security analysis of the Taiwan Strait, they tend to take a critical perspective toward the United States, not China.

Malaysian analysts, for instance, are highly critical of American military activity in the Taiwan Strait, seeing it as unnecessarily provocative.[88] In Indonesia, writing on Taiwan tends to focus on US hegemony and US containment of China as the underlying cause of cross-strait tensions, not on Beijing's policies or Taiwan's democratization.[89] Somewhat more measured, Thai analysis identifies the underlying security dynamics as great power competition, albeit with an understanding that US military activity is the primary provocation within these dynamics.[90] Vietnamese media identifies Western states – including France, the Netherlands, and the United Kingdom – as acting in ways that lead to greater instability in the Taiwan Strait, seemingly without close coordination with Taipei.[91] While there is significant variation in these states' precise narratives concerning cross-strait affairs, one can identify the common themes of greater respect for Beijing's position and interests with respect to Taiwan, greater cynicism regarding the intentions and activities of Western states, particularly the United States, concerning Taiwan, and greater concern that Western/US provocation could lead to a worsening security environment across the region.

One finds more divergent views on Taiwan in writing across Northeast Asia, including well-developed discourses that align with Western narratives. There are, however, significant oppositional voices in South Korea and Japan over Western/US policy toward Taiwan that are entirely ignored in Western analysis of cross-strait relations as they largely undermine Western assumptions. In South Korea, for instance, analysts identify US policy toward Taiwan as a primary cause of ongoing cross-strait tensions. Whereas the United States is ostensibly opposed to Taiwan's formal independence, it provides Taipei with the military means to defend itself and the diplomatic top-cover for it to rebuff negotiated settlements with Beijing. Rather than seeking a solution to cross-strait tensions, US policy is fundamentally designed to perpetuate the problem.[92] While the Trump and Biden administrations have moved the United States' historical approach to Taiwan away from a policy of status quo maintenance, they have done so in an entirely antagonistic and escalatory fashion that challenges mainland China's sovereign claims and thereby raises the potential for cross-strait conflict.[93] Indeed, US policy toward Taiwan is less about supporting the Taiwanese people – who stand to lose the most from conflict – than it is about US competition with Beijing and Washington's desire to use Taiwan as leverage.[94]

In Japan, critical narratives on Taiwan focus on the Abe/Suga government's approach to cross-strait relations, contemporary Japan-US cooperation on Taiwan, and Western/US cross-strait foreign policy approaches. Japanese analysts argue, for instance, that the cross-strait policy of the government of former prime minister Shinzo Abe was rooted in the "Kishi diplomacy" advanced by Nobusuke Kishi, Abe's maternal grandfather and Japanese prime minister from 1957 to 1960, which sees support for Taiwan primarily as a tool to pressure China. Kishi policy toward Taiwan (which the government of Prime Minister Yoshihide Suga has continued) does not consider what is best for cross-strait relations, but rather seeks to "play the Taiwan card" to undermine the Chinese Communist Party. It is consequently predicated on confrontation and therefore more likely to undermine regional stability.[95]

Relatedly, Japanese politicians warn against US and Japanese misreading of Chinese intent, particularly with respect to the People's Liberation Army (PLA) and tendencies in Washington to view PLA military development in offensive terms. China is developing the PLA as a modern military force and tasking it with national defence. Using Chinese military modernization as a justification for an aggressive Taiwan policy raises the potential for strategic misunderstanding and resulting conflict between Beijing, Tokyo, and Washington.[96] Former Japanese cabinet officials, academics, and researchers have also warned against Japanese security alignment with the Biden administration on Taiwan, arguing that the Suga government should resist pressure to align with US policy discourse and activity, and should even, where appropriate, criticize US actions against China as "excessive" in nature.[97] Others warn of the damage to Japan-China relations if Tokyo aligns with the US on Taiwan, arguing that doing so would amount to Japanese involvement in China's internal affairs and would go against China's "core interests."[98] Rather, Japan should develop its own approach to Taiwan that respects the one-China principle and advances Japan-Taiwan relations in ways that are mutually beneficial to both actors.[99]

Even within Taiwan, one finds a far different narrative on cross-strait relations than within Western discourse. Taiwanese policymakers and academics, for instance, routinely identify dialogue with Beijing as a critical factor in cross-strait relations, and many Taiwanese analysts raise concern over whether the United States considers Taiwan's national interests when formulating its own Taiwan policy.[100] On the United States' contemporary policy toward cross-strait relations, in particular, Taiwanese academics have been more critical than Western academics of US intentions toward Taiwan, and wary of Washington's strategic use of Taiwan to undermine Beijing's regional security.[101] As with scholarship from South Korea and Japan, Taiwanese scholars are especially concerned that Western support for the island could have the adverse effect of undermining Asia's security.[102]

In mainland Chinese scholarship on Taiwan, one finds a robust narrative concerning Taiwan's historical ties to the mainland, cross-strait relations and Chinese sovereignty, Taiwan as a core issue in Chinese national security, and PRC plans for peaceful reunification, among other issues. Central to this narrative is a critique of the US approach to cross-strait relations, which Chinese authors uniformly see as ill informed, chauvinistic, aggressive, ahistoric, and strategically designed to ensure ongoing conflict between Beijing and Taipei, to the advantage of the United States.[103]

Chinese analysts, in particular, identify US support for Taiwan as part of Washington's broader strategic policy to contain China through encirclement and to foil China's rise by forcing Beijing to use force to prevent Taipei from declaring formal independence.[104] Chinese scholars argue the US strategic commitment to Taiwan is less about protection of democracy than about pressuring China, pointing, correctly, to US support for Taiwan's past authoritarian governments.

On the Trump/Biden approach to Taiwan, in particular, the Chinese narrative is deeply cynical about US intentions, seeing Washington's move toward more direct support for Taipei as designed to challenge the CPC's legitimacy, even at the potential cost of war between mainland China, Taiwan, and the United States.[105] Chinese analysts warn against a move toward "strategic clarity," which would see the United States declare its willingness to use force to "protect" Taiwan's independence from mainland China, arguing that a policy shift of this type would compel the latter to use force and undermine Asia's regional stability.[106]

Western Leadership

Another pervasive theme in the Western narrative on Asian security is the importance of Western leadership and Western involvement as stabilizing factors in the region.[107] Closely related to discourse on Asia's "rules-based order," these narratives suggest that the region's stability is inherently fragile and Western involvement in and leadership over key institutions is necessary to ensure that Asia remains "free" and "open" to outside powers.[108] A long-standing theme traceable back to the postwar years of the 1950s, particularly in rhetoric around the need for Western intervention in the Korean War, the idea that Asia's stability necessitates Western intervention has grown in recent years in parallel to China's regional integration and the Indo-Pacific's conceptual development.[109]

Indeed, a predominant feature of the contemporary Western narrative on Asia is an assumption that Western states – led by the United States – have an entirely positive role to play in Asia through the provision of security guarantees, through the establishment of like-minded state partnerships and institutions, and through their support for Asian democracy.[110] Whether through their respective Indo-Pacific strategies, their G7 engagement, their NATO alignment, or their cooperation through the Quad, Western nations now routinely identify a responsibility to maintain Asian order as a defining characteristic of Western global leadership, with states like Australia, France, Germany, Japan, the United States, and the United Kingdom acting as global stewards of the region's order.[111]

In the Western narrative, the preservation of order involves Western state engagement in Asia's predominant security areas, as outlined above.[112] Western narratives now routinely identify Taiwan's defence, Asian maritime security, or North Korea's nuclear program as factors compelling their proactive military involvement in the region, whether through unilateral or multilateral means.[113] Western policy-makers increasingly justify their Asian regional security cooperation and co-ordination in terms of stability maintenance, arguing that Western alliance systems remain a critical feature of Asia's security environment from which all Asian states benefit. More and more, Western states are coming to define their common commitment to democracy as a further justification for their intervention in Asia's security order, with the underlying assumption being that Western democracies have greater legitimacy in global governance than non-democratic states.[114]

Beyond their involvement in Asia's outstanding security areas, Western states now collectively identify management of Chinese "assertion" as a factor driving their common approach to the region's order preservation. This view is arguably nowhere more clearly stated than in the 2021 NATO communiqué, which singled out China's growing influence, its assertiveness, its stated ambitions, its nuclear arsenal, and its asymmetric capabilities as "systemic challenges" to the Asia-Pacific's order necessitating a Western response.[115] One sees similar commitment to collective security against China in Western narratives on the Indo-Pacific region, both in national strategic documents, such as the United States' Indo-Pacific strategy, and in joint Western statements, such as the 2021 G7 communiqué.[116] Indeed, as highlighted throughout this book, the perception that Western states share a responsibility to ensure the stability of Asia's order by countering China's illiberalism has become a dominant feature of Western narratives on Western involvement in the region's security order.

One gets a picture of Asian narratives concerning Western leadership in the above discourse on Western – primarily US – involvement in the South China Sea, the East China Sea, North Korea, and Taiwan. Whereas Western narratives portray states such as Australia, France, Germany, the Netherlands, Japan, the United Kingdom, and the United States as security providers and stabilizing actors, regional narratives on Western "leadership" are far less sanguine, particularly on matters related to Asian state relations, security dynamics, and great power competition (outlined in greater detail in the previous chapter). In Southeast Asian narratives, one finds little demand for greater involvement of Western states, outside the narrow, state-specific examples related to Vietnam and the South China Sea, for instance. Even on these issues, support for Western involvement is limited to national interests, and does not include a desire for greater Western support of Asia's order. Indeed, in Southeast Asian narratives, one is more likely to see concern over the intentions and activities of Western states, and their potential to destabilize the region through uncoordinated policy, than one is to see support for Western involvement in Asia.

In Indonesia, for instance, one sees deep cynicism over the idea of Western leadership in Asia, particularly Western states' attempt to reclassify the Asia-Pacific region as the Indo-Pacific region, a reclassification that plays to Western states' strengths but marginalizes Southeast Asian actors.[117] Western state "leadership," particularly US leadership, is a misnomer, as its strategic end state is hegemonic consolidation for the sake of competition with China.[118] Malaysian scholars similarly question Western state and US leadership in Asia, arguing that their primary goals are not strengthening Asia's security order but shaping the perceptions and narratives of ASEAN and ASEAN member states so as to control their behaviour.[119] These analysts argue that the Biden administration would not employ anti-Islamic rhetoric and impose economic sanctions against Muslim states, such as Malaysia, Iran, Turkey, and Indonesia, if indeed it were a real leader in Asia.[120]

In Thai analysis, one also sees criticism of Western states' preoccupation with China and the US pursuit of hegemony under the guise of regional leadership, both facets of Western foreign policy that Thai scholars worry could lead to a Cold War 2.0 in Asia.[121] Thai analysts also largely reject Western concepts of the Indo-Pacific, seeing the construct as predicated on American predominance and American determination to challenge China in Asia.[122] Vietnamese analysts reject Western claims of benevolent leadership, seeing European and US activity in Asia in largely, if not entirely, self-serving terms, particularly with respect to countering China's influence to preserve Western pre-eminence.[123] While generally more accepting of a US military presence in Asia in light of its conflicts with China, Vietnamese defence analysts have also suggested the need to develop countermeasures to the Western/US Indo-Pacific strategy to ensure that Vietnamese interests are not undermined by its implementation.[124]

Neither is there consensus in Northeast Asia on Western state leadership in Asia, particularly with respect to the United States' role as the self-appointed regional hegemon. In Japan, for instance, a minority narrative among policy-makers, strategists, and academics argues that Japanese reliance on US leadership undermines Japan's relations with China and increases Japan's strategic risk of entrapment and/or abandonment.[125] To offset this vulnerability, Japanese policy-makers have called for greater security collaboration between Japan and other Asian states, including China and Russia, through the establishment of an "Asian NATO."[126] Japanese analysts have also advocated for closer Japan-China ties on matters of security, economic development, and governance within Asia to balance against the United States' increasingly unpredictable behaviour, including bilateral Japanese-Chinese engagement in countries such as Bangladesh, Cambodia, and the Maldives.[127]

South Korean scholars also express concern over Western state leadership in Asia, and argue the need for more inclusive state representation, including from China and Russia, on matters of regional importance, such as North Korean security.[128] Korean analysts further question the United States' actual resolve to lead in Asia, noting a perennial gap between its rhetoric and its actions in Asia and its ongoing strategic preoccupation in the Middle East.[129] As with other Asian states, Korean narratives raise concerns over Western antagonism toward China, arguing that efforts to contain China could lead to conflict in the near to medium terms.[130]

Predictably, the Chinese narrative on Western/US leadership in Asia is extensive, sophisticated, and critical. On US leadership, for instance, Chinese scholars argue that Washington's preoccupation with unipolarity undermines regional security systems by preventing an evolution of power dynamics, where China, in particular, can develop capabilities, relations, and strategies in proportion to its material means.[131] While US hegemony might have been a feature of the post–Cold War 1990s, the idea that one state, or even a coalition of Western states, can set global rules and then use threats to enforce the rules is at best archaic and at worst openly hostile to other states.

Chinese writers also argue that in their attempt to lead in Asia, Western states and the United States are, in fact, engaged in revisionism, the very thing they accuse China of undertaking through its foreign policy engagement throughout the region.[132] Chinese scholars point to the establishment of Western institutions such as AUKUS and the Quad, the expansion of Western coalitions such as NATO, the intensification of Western multilateral military training and operations, the formulation of Western alternatives to China's Belt and Road Initiative, and the deployment of Western military assets to Asia as clear evidence that Western states are more interested in *shaping* than in *preserving* Asian order, in ways that ensure Western pre-eminence vis-à-vis China.[133]

Finally, Chinese analysts reject the preconception that Western states are leading international efforts to preserve a rules-based order that is ostensibly under strain from China's activity. They question the precise nature of the rules-based order, suggesting that Western states, particularly the United States, have routinely violated international law when it suits them and engage in extrajudicial policies like sanctions when and where doing so suits their purposes. Western leadership, in this respect, is not about strengthening international institutions but rather about maintaining Western systemic hegemony, even at the cost of conflict with China.[134]

Implications for Canada

Successful strategic development depends in large part on a comprehensive understanding of one's operational environment. For Canadian policy-makers attempting to formulate a national approach toward Asia, a fuller account of regional narratives on key security issues is critical. Yet all too often, Canadian analysts and commentators forgo any attempt to understand Asian view concerning the region's security environment, relying instead on dominant narratives from the United States and Europe in the belief that these Western-centric viewpoints are universal and unassailable. Consequently, Canadian policy-makers are far more likely to employ biased, incomplete views of Asia in their security policy planning processes, believing, incorrectly, that they are drafting such policy in line with regional demand signals. The end result is an unbalanced security strategy that fails to advance Ottawa's national interests, that demonstrates ignorance of regional states, and that amplifies the sense that Canada is an outside power in the Asian region.

Conversely, Canada can better position itself within the region as an unbiased, informed actor by taking the time and effort to listen to Asian voices on Asian security issues. On the South and East China Seas, for instance, Ottawa can better understand how regional actors might interpret its cooperation with the United States and other Western actors in largely negative, provocative terms, and can subsequently plan strategic engagement with regional actors to offset these perceptions. On North Korea, Canada can similarly design a strategic approach that engages multiple actors and stakeholders in a way that demonstrates a sophisticated understanding of regional affairs, a sensitivity to regional concerns, and independence of action from Western and US policies. Canada can also develop a multi-actor, multi-pronged approach to Taiwan that addresses Taipei's interests, assuages Beijing's concerns, and incorporates regional priorities with respect to stability and interconnectivity.

Through a more developed account of regional state perceptions and narratives around Western leadership, Canada can also develop a sense of humility that will, ironically, increase its ability to advance its national interests in Asia and make it a more knowledgeable and sympathetic actor in the region. Such knowledge is the starting point to a more informed Canadian strategic approach to Asia, one that requires understanding of regional networks, relations, and ties for operationalization.

5

Chinese Counter-Narratives

The Chinese Communist Party, Hong Kong, Xinjiang, and Foreign Affairs

In January 2021, just days after angry protesters descended upon the US Capitol Building, Chinese president Xi Jinping delivered a speech at the World Economic Forum's Davos Agenda that, for a brief moment, upset the predominant Western narrative about China's place in the world. Drawing exclusively from Western discourse around a liberal rules-based order, Xi called on the global community to work together to combat climate change, strengthen multilateralism, preserve globalization and open markets, and ensure that global economic growth was balanced, inclusive, sustainable, and equitable.[1] Further, he called on states to eschew ideological alignment and to pursue a "path of peaceful co-existence," one more accepting of countries' diverse cultural and historical backgrounds.[2] Most importantly, Xi called for a common commitment from states to adhere to international law, to avoid "selective multilateralism," to reject "Cold War thinking," and to pursue consultation and communication as the primary means for crisis avoidance and management. Following four years of the Trump administration's "America First" policy, Xi's articulation of China's world view struck many Asian analysts as measured, reassuring, and responsible.[3]

Western commentators were, however, uniformly critical of Xi's speech, arguing, fundamentally, that China remained an "illiberal" actor despite its leadership's attempt to co-opt Western language around multilateralism and the rules-based order.[4] Western authors and policy-makers instead pointed to the "illegitimacy" of the Communist Party of China (CPC), China's treatment of its Uyghur population, its ongoing conflict with Taiwan, its undermining of Hong Kong's democracy, and its foreign policy behaviour as evidence that Xi's comments were cynical and disingenuous.[5] Predictably, Western policy analysts also attacked those with dissenting views of the predominant Western narrative on Xi's speech and China's behaviours as "self-serving lackeys" and "useful idiots," thereby narrowing Western discourse on China to include only views critical of Beijing.[6]

When the episode involving Xi's Davos speech and the Western response is seen in its entirety, two important lessons can be drawn that have significant implications for this book's core argument. First, nowhere is Western cultural hegemony clearer than in Western narratives about China, which almost exclusively employ US-origin threat narratives to describe the country's behaviour.[7] Indeed, whether with respect to Chinese foreign policy, military development, technological innovation, corporate policy, state governance, national security, social affairs, investment and trade, or indeed any other China-related issue, the contemporary tendency among Western policy writers is to securitize China as a "threat" and as an "'illiberal" power.[8] Notably, this Western narrative both contributes to and is influenced by Western policy-making toward China, all but ensuring that Western states' relations with China will remain contentious, if not conflictual, in both tone and practice for the foreseeable future.[9]

Second, Chinese narratives about the country's domestic and foreign affairs differ from predominant Western views to the extent that they are often polar opposites. Where Western narratives on the CPC focus on its "illegitimacy," for instance, Chinese narratives focus on its effectiveness, its inclusivity, its "democracy," and its support from the Chinese people. Where Western narratives accuse the CPC of genocide in the Xinjiang Uyghur Autonomous Region (XUAR), Chinese narratives insist that the party acting to prevent social instability, political violence, and terrorism within the country. Similarly, Chinese narratives on the South China Sea point to US-led freedom of navigation operations (FONOPs) as the primary source of maritime instability and characterize Chinese activity as entirely defensive in nature.

Importantly, Chinese narratives are not, as Western commentators suggest, cynical. Rather, they reflect Chinese scholarship, political commentary, values, and public opinion on foreign and domestic affairs, as outlined below. As such, the tendency of Western policy-makers and scholars to summarily dismiss them carries significant risks, the most immediate of which is armed conflict resulting from misunderstanding and miscommunication.

Nobel Prize–winning economist Thomas Schelling wrote extensively about how miscommunication between states raises the potential for unintended consequences such as war, and how clear communication and a concerted effort by both sides to understand their mutual perspectives are preconditions of crisis management.[10] As Western narratives around China routinely securitize all aspects of Chinese foreign policy to the point of treating China as an existential threat – all the while refusing to engage in critical examination of China's own narratives – conflict stemming from miscommunication is not only possible but likely.

A less immediate, but no less real, threat for Canada is that its policy-makers will employ biased logic in formulating the country's strategic approach to China, thereby preventing it from achieving its maximal national interests with China or, in a worst-case scenario, raising the likelihood of miscommunication and conflict with China.[11] Canadian policy analysts' calls for regime change are a good example of how a Western-dependent mindset toward China could undermine the states' bilateral relations and strengthen Beijing's perception that Canadian policy-makers seek to destabilize it.[12] To balance against such self-defeating demagoguery, critical analysis that provides insight into China's perceptions is needed.

This chapter provides a much-needed starting point for a more informed understanding of China's intentions, perspectives, and behaviours in Asia in order to contribute to Canada's domestic policy dialogue. It starts with the assumption, outlined above, that much debate in Canada is based on Western narratives concerning China's behaviour, underdeveloped analysis of China's domestic policy priorities and intentions, and biased accounts of China's state/society relations. To remedy these deficiencies, this chapter outlines Chinese narratives on a number of issues relevant to Canadians' views of China and Canadian-Chinese relations, starting with Chinese narratives around the CPC.

Notably, it is not the intention here to whitewash areas where China's leaders have fallen short of their self-assigned roles as the country's political and moral standard-bearers, of which there are many – as there are with all states. Rather, this chapter's intention is to establish the basis among readers for cognitive empathy toward China for entirely selfish, if not nationalistic, reasons. As former FBI chief negotiator Chris Voss notes in his classic book *Never Split the Difference*, empathy with one's "opponent" is the necessary starting point for getting what one wants in a negotiation.[13] As bilateral relations between states are fundamentally negotiations, where both sides work to advance their own interests to maximum effect, failure to approach China with cognitive empathy is a failure to take all necessary means to achieve one's strategic end state.

Domestic Support for the Chinese Communist Party
During the Trump administration, senior US officials, including Vice President Mike Pence, Secretary of State Mike Pompeo, and Deputy National Security Advisor Matthew Pottinger, reverted to Cold War–era rhetoric to characterize the Chinese Communist Party, presenting it as the modern-day "evil empire" and urging the Chinese people to "change" their leadership.[14] Taking their cues from Washington, US-based analysts upped their criticism of the CPC, arguing that it was illegitimate, repressive, and corrupt.[15] To demonstrate the "universality" of Western values and to avoid well-justified criticism of xenophobia and racism, US policy-makers and analysts stressed that their criticism of China was limited to its political system and was a function of their support for the Chinese people, for whom they appointed themselves unofficial spokespersons.[16] Challenged with polling that showed widespread support among Chinese for the CPC, these same US-based commentators dismissed the findings as propaganda and as evidence of widespread repression.[17]

The Biden administration continued to demonize the CPC from the very beginning of its tenure, with Secretary of State Antony Blinken arguing during his January 2021 Senate confirmation hearing that the party's primary foreign policy goal was to speed US decline and to establish an alternative world order.[18] Indeed, under President Joe Biden, official criticism of the CPC became a decidedly bipartisan phenomenon in the United States, with House Speaker Nancy Pelosi calling for a 2022 Olympic boycott over the CPC's human rights abuses and the Congressional-Executive Commission on China charging the CPC with acts of "genocide," on which more is written below.[19]

Over the same period, anti-CPC rhetoric flourished across the Western world, with policy-makers and analysts from Australia, Canada, the United Kingdom, and European Union member states trying to outdo each other in criticizing the CPC and calling for regime change.[20] In one particularly jarring instance of Western chauvinism, Canadian scholar Charles Burton claimed that the CPC "is ultimately not really Chinese" and insisted that China's Confucian heritage was more in line with liberal democracy – a breathtakingly patronizing claim that discounts the CPC's origins and the Chinese people's agency, overstates Western influence on China's domestic experience, and ignores more than 3,000 years of Chinese political history.[21] Whether attacking the CPC on functional or cultural grounds, these Western critiques share common thematic undercurrents: that the party is autocratic and therefore illegitimate; that Chinese support for the party is irrelevant as the party suppresses the people; and that it is the West's moral responsibility to oppose the CPC so as to bring freedom and democracy to the Chinese people.

While Western audiences tend to be sympathetic to critiques of the CPC, these same critiques ring hollow within China, where the CPC enjoys widespread, multi-generational support.[22] Neither is Chinese public support for the CPC the result of societal repression, as the Western narrative would suggest, but rather the result of the Chinese people's shared belief that the CPC has been a largely effective – if not infallible – governing body that has raised Chinese living standards, led China's economic modernization and growth, and ensured China's foreign and domestic stability in the face of internal and external pressures.[23] Far from seeing the CPC as a problem in line with Western narratives on Chinese leadership, the Chinese people, rather, see the CPC as a highly valuable solution to the country's challenges, broadly defined.[24]

On quality-of-life and economic development issues, for instance, one finds broad public agreement across Chinese social media, Chinese print media, and Chinese scholarship that CPC leadership has contributed to the unprecedented rise in living standards and economic growth across the country since the founding of the People's Republic of China.[25] Although such achievements would clearly be impossible without the Chinese people's ingenuity, resilience, and perseverance, the Chinese people equally credit the CPC's leadership for the country's development since 1949, which has been consistent and comprehensive.[26] While some Western scholars have suggested that China, more specifically the Chinese people, could have accomplished even more under a democratic government that was more committed to liberal economic principles, such counterfactual exercises are entirely irrelevant. The fact remains that modern-day China's economic development, its burgeoning role as an international superpower, and the Chinese people's growing sense of nationalism, in both its benign and virulent forms, is the result of the CPC's leadership, not in spite of it.[27]

While almost certainly a point of controversy for Western readers, the CPC's central role in providing China with growth and development opportunities, as well as security and international prestige, is widely understood in China.[28] Since 2008, in particular, Chinese scholars have routinely identified the CPC's leadership as a critical component in the maintenance of the country's internal stability – especially as Western states (particularly the United States) have struggled with their own forms of democracy in the face of the Global Financial Crisis – and in the provision of fundamental public goods such as domestic stability and security.[29] Chinese academics, in particular, have offered the CPC as a conceptual counterpoint to what many view as Western states' failures of governance, up to and including their inability to provide equal access to development and education opportunities, and their unwillingness to address their own internal domestic issues around race relations and to avoid plunging their states and militaries into long-term, costly wars.[30] For many Chinese writers, the CPC's focus on internal metrics such as employment opportunities for recent college graduates, on national poverty reduction, on internal stability and anti-terrorism (on which more is written below), and on health and sanitation rather than on global predominance or the ability to project power on the global stage is evidence not only of the CPC's policy pragmatism but also of its function as a true representative body for the Chinese people, one more focused on delivering tactical results than engaging in ideological infighting.[31]

Indeed, it is the CPC's pragmatism, its commitment to use whatever means necessary to achieve it policy goals, that most Chinese identify with the party, not its Marxist-Leninist ideological roots, which so many Western observers insist on referencing when writing about (or criticizing) the party.[32] The CPC's pragmatism, in turn, allows it to be extremely flexible in its policy prescriptions, changing course where needed.[33] The CPC is, in this respect, naturally attuned to China's domestic needs and uniquely suited to developing non-ideological responses to address the country's challenges.[34] Chinese writers tend to view this governance trait and characteristic as desirable not only from a domestic standpoint but also in contrast to other modes of governance, which approach policy-making not with the intent to solve the problem but with a set of prescribed ideological viewpoints.[35]

Similarly, while there is certainly agreement among Chinese scholars and academics, and even the Chinese media, that the CPC can and should do more to address issues such as endemic corruption, environmental problems, and poverty, among other pressing domestic concerns, there remains a sense among the Chinese populace that the CPC is part of the solution, not part of the problem.[36] One can see this Chinese perception of the CPC in protest language and action, both of which routinely appeal to the CPC to address social issues at the local level.[37] Indeed, central to most social protests in China is an appeal to higher-level CPC authorities to become more involved, to intervene, so as to address directly the source of unrest, even if that source includes local-level government or military officials.[38] Chinese social views of the CPC, in this respect, are of an institution that has the Chinese people's best interests at heart, but that, as with all things human, is only as good as the people that constitute it.[39]

Neither is support for and approval of the CPC limited to Chinese academics and analysts or the Chinese media. According to a 2021 poll from the Edelman international public relations firm and Tsinghua University, for instance, 82 percent of Chinese respondents expressed "trust" in the CPC, the highest level of government trust recorded among respondents from twenty-four Asian states.[40] Asked to define government trust, Chinese respondents identified the CPC as "ethical" and "able." Similarly, a 2020 Chinese Academy of Social Sciences (CASS) poll showed that 80 percent of Chinese respondents believed the CPC had the ability to solve the country's most pressing problems, including the COVID-19 pandemic.[41] Further, a 2020 poll from the Harvard Kennedy School's Ash Center for Democratic Governance and Innovation found that over 95 percent of Chinese respondents were satisfied with the CPC as a ruling party.[42] The poll, conducted over the course of fifteen years and covering Chinese public opinion at multiple jurisdictional levels, also noted that public support for the CPC had actually *increased* across nearly all issue areas, including its management of economics, environmental issues, and domestic security. Similarly, a 2020 survey by the Chinese Global Times Public Opinion Survey Center showed that Chinese support for Western models of government had dramatically *decreased* over the past fifteen years, particularly among China's youth. Asked whether they admired Western states' models of governance, for instance, only 8.1 percent of respondents between fifteen and thirty-five years old expressed support, while 48.3 percent expressed distaste.[43]

Hong Kong as a Chinese City

Within the Western narrative on China, Hong Kong has emerged as a particularly potent symbol of Western "freedom" and "democracy" versus Chinese "repression" and "authoritarianism." Western reporting on the months-long 2019–20 protests, for example, invariably framed the instability in the Hong Kong Special Administrative Region (HKSAR) as a clash between political types, with pro-democracy activists standing against pro-Beijing autocrats.[44] Western scholarship at the time treated the protests as evidence of China's political ineptitude, pointing to the Hong Kong authorities' proposed extradition law as an unnecessary provocation, and as indicative of an emerging pro-democracy movement in the HKSAR.[45] Even as the protests continued and became unrulier, Western media portrayed events on the ground as pro-democracy civil disobedience and as a harbinger of generational change in Hong Kong, change resulting from widespread dissatisfaction with the CPC in Hong Kong.[46] As the demonstrations progressed, some Western observers warned of the potential of a violent response from Beijing, citing the Tiananmen Square incident in 1989 as a precedent.

Following the protests, the Western narrative on Hong Kong became even more negative, particularly once Beijing implemented a national security law (NSL) for the HKSAR on July 1, 2020. Even before the full text of the NSL became available, Western scholars decried Beijing's legislation as an abrogation of the 1984 Sino-British Joint Declaration and the "one country, two systems" formulation that governed Beijing–Hong Kong relations after the 1997 handover of Hong Kong from the United Kingdom to China.[47] Western media wrote of Beijing's "betrayal" of the Hong Kong people, and Western scholars warned that Hong Kong's democratic foundations and civil liberties were at risk.[48] Australia, Canada, the United Kingdom, and the United States enacted legislation offering Hong Kong citizens residency, citizenship, or refugee status, primarily in response to Western concerns that Beijing would use the NSL to target Hong Kong dissidents.[49]

For Western observers, these concerns were validated in January 2021, when more than 1,000 Hong Kong police undertook a city-wide campaign to detain fifty-three individuals – many of them former pro-democracy lawmakers and activists – on charges of subversion.[50] Western scholars were quick in their near-universal condemnation of the mass arrest, arguing that the move undermined Hong Kong's autonomy and that Beijing's actions violated its international obligations under the Sino-British Joint Declaration.[51] Western leaders, including then Canadian foreign affairs minister François-Philippe Champagne, called for greater coordination between democratic states to put pressure on China, while others, including Canada's shadow foreign minister, Michael Chong, called for Western states to implement Magnitsky sanctions against Hong Kong officials in response.[52]

While Western policy-makers and academics often frame their commentary on Hong Kong as acts of justice, or as support for justice or for Hong Kong's democratic institutions. Chinese observers almost uniformly view the Western narrative as a cynical attempt by outside powers to interfere in China's domestic affairs, much as they did in the past, particularly when Chinese leadership and society were divided and weak.[53] Indeed, much of the Chinese narrative on Hong Kong is rooted in a post-colonial understanding of the HKSAR as a product of Western imperialism, where Western concerns over Hong Kong are more about maintaining a regional balance of power in Western states' favour than about achieving justice for the Hong Kong people.[54] The British, after all, had more than 150 years to establish democracy in Hong Kong but chose instead to administer it as a colonial outpost, limiting the Hong Kong people's freedoms as a result.[55] For many Chinese, the fact that the United Kingdom advocated for democracy in Hong Kong only in the final years before its return to China in 1997 is more than enough reason to reject any Western concern over Hong Kong's future as political posturing.[56]

Related to this point is the belief in China that Hong Kong is a Chinese city and that any attempt by outside Western powers to influence its internal development is illegitimate. The claims of Western states that China is betraying the provisions of the Sino-British Joint Declaration, for instance, garner little support in China as Beijing fundamentally rejects the idea that outside powers can limit its sovereignty, particularly now that China has developed into a wealthy and powerful nation.[57] Further, China's leadership and people are unwilling to abide by agreements Beijing negotiated while in a relatively weak position. In this respect, the need to rectify Hong Kong's historical and political division from China provides a compelling reason to hasten reunification, one far more important to Chinese territorial and political integrity than Western claims to Hong Kong as a kind of international protectorate.[58]

Neither, importantly, does China see its involvement in Hong Kong as a violation of its "one country, two systems" formulation with respect to the HKSAR, as the two-systems formulation was never about democratic autonomy but rather about ensuring political stability in Hong Kong for the sake of economic opportunity.[59] Western assumptions that "two systems" meant democracy for Hong Kong and autocracy for China are thus fundamentally mistaken. Rather, "two systems" implies market liberalization and rule of law in Hong Kong and a controlled and planned economic system in in the rest of China.[60] From Beijing's point of view, nothing it has done in Hong Kong has changed this fundamental balance.[61]

Viewed from this perspective, Beijing understood the 2019–20 protests in Hong Kong primarily as a socio-economic issue resulting from overdependence on market fundamentals, where young Hongkongers felt left behind as the gap between the city's wealthy and its average citizens grew. As with capitalism around the world, Beijing saw a system in Hong Kong that had benefited the few at the cost of the many, and understood that it needed to take a more direct role in Hong Kong's management to address the issues exacerbated by laissez-faire capitalism.[62] Where the protests veered toward pro-democracy or, in extreme instances, pro-independence advocacy, China identified a small group of Western-backed agitators and claimed that their activities were unrepresentative of Hong Kong's majority, which prioritized stability and economic equality over democracy.[63]

Quite rightfully, China rejected Western charges of suppression and violence, arguing that it showed great restraint in its use of force by allowing the Hong Kong Police Force to manage the protests, which it did with marked professionalism. To highlight the hypocrisy surrounding Western charges of coercion, Beijing contrasted policing in the United States in 2020 and police use of violence in American cities such as Portland, Oregon, with the Hong Kong Police's restraint.

On the national security law, Chinese narratives reject Western criticisms that it limits individual Hongkongers' rights, and argue that the law aims exclusively to deal with individuals and movements in the HKSAR that seek to undermine stability and challenge China's sovereignty.[64] The Chinese leadership has argued that the months-long protests in Hong Kong and the HKSAR government's failure to pass a comprehensive national security law (as it was required to do under Hong Kong Basic Law Article 23) necessitated Beijing's direct involvement.[65] Chinese lawmakers argue that, far from a threat to Hong Kong's domestic governance institutions and its rule of law, the NSL is directly aligned with the HKSAR's Basic Law, or its "mini-constitution."[66] The NSL's purpose, therefore, is not to undermine Hongkongers' rights but rather, in keeping with China's policy priorities toward the HKSAR since the 1997 handover, to facilitate Hong Kong's full political and economic integration with mainland China and its long-term political and economic viability.[67]

With respect to the 2021 arrest of the fifty-three pro-democracy lawmakers and activists, Chinese commentators fundamentally rejected Western narratives around political oppression and instead argued that Hong Kong officials had acted against organized (and Western-supported) state subversion.[68] Whereas Western media portrayed those arrested as democratic activists, Chinese leadership statements and media labelled them as strategic saboteurs intent on undermining the HKSAR's seventy-member Legislative Council through a plan they called the "35+." Spokespersons from both the Hong Kong Office for Safeguarding National Security and the Beijing-aligned Hong Kong Liaison Office identified what they called the group's "10-step mutual destruction plan," which called for legislative paralysis, mass public protests, and international sanctions to undermine Hong Kong's stability.[69] In Chinese and Hong Kong narratives, therefore, those arrested were seen as a clear and present danger to the city's governance institutions, its rule of law, and its social stability, not a group of well-intentioned, pro-democracy activists intent on challenging the NSL through civil disobedience.

Xinjiang

Few issues evoke as visceral a response in Western discourse as Xinjiang. Under the Trump administration, for example, Secretary of State

Pompeo accused the CPC of engaging in genocide in the region, a charge the Biden administration has repeated through its own State Department.[70] Across the Western world, leaders from Australia, Canada, and the United Kingdom have also used the "genocide" label, employing the term in its more expansive usage to criticize China's attempts to erase its Uyghur minority group's ethnic identity through forced re-education in "concentration camps" and through systemic demolition of Xinjiang's "old towns" and historical areas.[71]

Western media has also accused Chinese authorities of religious persecution in the XUAR.[72] Western activists have reported state-directed activities such as the destruction of mosques, the targeting of Islamic scholars, and the requirement that Uyghur students forgo fasting during Ramadan while at school. Chinese officials have reportedly banned religious symbolism such as the hijab and beards throughout the XUAR, and punished individuals who have failed to comply with the restrictions.[73]

Citing China's own internal statistics on childbirths in the XUAR, Western activists have also accused Beijing of forcing ethnic minority women to have abortions and undergo sterilization.[74] Western media has reported on rape in Uyghur women's centres, suggesting that the CPC may be using systematic rape as a tool of its ethnic policy.[75] From London to Ottawa to Washington, elected officials called for a political boycott of the 2022 Winter Olympics, labelling the event a "genocide Olympics."[76]

More recently, Western academics have accused Beijing of using forced labour in Xinjiang, particularly within the region's vast cotton and tomato industries.[77] This charge has led a number of Western activists to call for a boycott of Chinese apparel and agricultural products, and Western states, most notably the United States, to block imports of Chinese cotton and tomatoes. Politicians from the European Union, in particular, have suggested that China's actions in Xinjiang will prevent the bloc from signing a general agreement on investment with Beijing.[78]

Unsurprisingly, Chinese narratives on Xinjiang differ greatly from Western narratives. For Chinese academics and writers, for instance, government activity in the XUAR is a function of the CPC's minority policies, an outcome of its commitment to poverty reduction through remote area development, and a matter of national security, particularly with respect to the "three evils" of radicalism, separatism, and terrorism.

On China's minority policies, for instance, Chinese policy-makers and scholars take a paternalistic view of the CPC's responsibilities toward Xinjiang's ethnic minorities, a view predicated on party responsibility to ensure a "people-centred" approach to ethnic and cultural preservation that prioritizes individual civil, economic, and human rights over ethnic and cultural "purity."[79] More specifically, while Chinese policy-makers acknowledge the importance of ethnic and cultural diversity in the XUAR, they also insist that cultural determination cannot stand in the way of economic and social "modernization."[80] One can trace this understanding of state/ethnic community relations back to Mao Zedong, who put a particular stress on the need for party intervention in the affairs of ethnic minorities to ensure intergenerational economic and social development, and who saw such development as critical to China's national stability.[81]

In this respect, Chinese narratives on the XUAR tend to focus on the region's ethnic and cultural "backwardness" and the party's responsibility to raise the Uyghurs' living standards through education, training, and indoctrination.[82] Party/state activities in Xinjiang, therefore, are not about cultural erasure or forced assimilation. They are, rather, about nation building and providing support for those the CPC believes need it most, even if there are short- to medium-term costs to providing such support.[83] Indeed, Chinese scholars regularly identify opposition to the CPC's development and education programs in Xinjiang as evidence that they are desperately needed.[84]

Closely related to the country's minority policies is the issue of Xinjiang's overall development. The XUAR has been, and continues to be, one of China's poorest regions, primarily as a result of its remoteness and isolation. For the CPC, XUAR development is a national priority, both with respect to its people's living standards and to its role in China's domestic economy. Under the economic policy of "dual circulation," for instance, the CPC sees the need to develop its internal markets and the need to increase the Chinese people's consumption as national development imperatives, which means the party cannot afford to leave any part of China underdeveloped. This is particularly the case with the XUAR, as its proximity to Central Asia and its role as a Chinese "gateway" to Europe's markets make it a valuable entrepôt for overland Chinese trade.[85]

At the more micro level, the CPC has also committed itself to the ambitious goal of eradicating poverty nationwide by 2021, which, of course, includes within the XUAR.[86] To accomplish this objective, the CPC has pushed for economic modernization and intra-national connectivity between provinces and autonomous regions, and has prioritized education and training programs for the country's minority groups, which tend to lag behind the majority population with respect to human development indexes such as education and gender equality.[87] Whereas Western narratives classify China's education and training centres in Xinjiang as "concentration camps," Chinese commentators see them as a means to bring economic, educational, and training opportunities to one of the country's most marginalized populations, a minority group with lower human development indexes with respect to issues such as literacy and gender equality than the rest of the Chinese population.[88]

Overlying the CPC's development priorities in the XUAR are ongoing concerns among Chinese policy-makers and scholars that the region is home to domestic terrorist organizations.[89] At least one of these groups, the East Turkistan Islamic Movement (ETIM), was on the US terrorist list from 2002 until 2020, when the Trump administration declassified it as a terrorist group for political purposes.[90] Chinese scholars believe that ETIM terrorists have deep training and operational ties to the ungoverned spaces in Afghanistan and Pakistan, and that they have been involved in acts of terrorism in China, including the 2009 Urumqi riots, which left nearly 200 civilians dead; the 2013 Tiananmen Square suicide bombing, which killed 5 civilians; and the 2014 Kunming rail station attack, where knife-wielding terrorists killed 31 people, among other instances of localized violence across China.

Within Chinese discourse, therefore, one finds broad-based support for Chinese security operations in the XUAR, particularly with respect to aspects of radicalism, separatism, or terrorism or with regard to political Islam.[91] While there is a clear differentiation within Chinese literature between the Uyghur population and the ETIM, there is also a developed understanding that the XUAR's distinct socio-economic and ethno-cultural conditions make radicalization more likely among the minority populations.[92] The XUAR's relative underdevelopment, its proximity to countries and areas with active terrorist education and training camps, and outsider attempts to radicalize its Islamic minority all feature prominently in Chinese literature on the region's particular vulnerabilities.[93]

Chinese narratives on Xinjiang, therefore, include assumptions that the region is impoverished, that poverty leads to radicalization, that radicalization leads to terrorism, and that the Uyghurs' Islamic faith makes them particularly vulnerable to political Islam imported from Pakistan and Afghanistan.[94] Within this narrative, it is the CPC's responsibility to provide education, training, and work opportunities for the Uyghur population, regardless of any localized opposition these policies might face. From this perspective, Chinese scholars see Western charges of genocide as not only a hegemonic tool to undermine China's international legitimacy but also a cynical means to destabilize China by pressuring it to alter its development and security approach to the XUAR.[95]

Chinese Foreign Policy

As noted throughout this book, the assumption that China is a coercive and revisionist actor in Asia is an important discursive theme in Western narratives on the region. Conceptually, the belief that China is an aggressive state informs every Western Indo-Pacific concept, every account of Asia's rules-based order, and every formulation of the Western like-minded state paradigm. Operationally, Western assumptions regarding Chinese aggression provide a common enemy for Australia, the United Kingdom, and the United States to justify Anglo-American military cooperation through AUKUS, and for Australian, Indian, Japanese, and American coordination through the Quad. While critiques of Chinese foreign policy behaviour vary between states, one can divide the broader "China threat" thesis into two main themes.

First, Western narratives argue that China is a coercive actor, particularly with respect to economic statecraft. Western analysts point to China's use of "illegal" trade restrictions to punish states with which it has ongoing diplomatic or security disputes as evidence that China employs coercive diplomacy, up to and including state-directed boycotts and informal sanctions. Western narratives claim, for instance, that China imposed a comprehensive embargo against Australia for questioning its human rights record and for calling for international investigations into the origins of COVID-19.[96] China's similar use of economic statecraft against Canada, the Philippines, South Korea, and Sweden, Western analysts argue, shows that Beijing sees informal sanctions and trade restrictions as legitimate reactive tools for state coercion.[97]

Western narratives also suggest that China proactively uses "debt-trap diplomacy" to coerce developing states, in particular, to concede strategic national assets to Chinese control. According to Western analysts, China uses predatory lending to seize control of infrastructure such as Sri Lanka's Hambantota International Port, and to gain access to natural resources, as in the case of Zambia.[98] Closely related to the debt-trap diplomacy critique is the Western narrative surrounding China's Belt and Road Initiative (BRI), which Western policy-makers and analysts routinely argue is Beijing's long-term, deliberate grand strategy to displace the United States as the predominant global power.[99] Criticism of the BRI comes from the Western belief, in particular, that China is using the strategy to build influence and to gain political control in areas like Africa, Latin America, and Southeast Asia and across the Global South.[100]

Second, Western narratives argue that China is a revisionist actor determined to undermine the international liberal rules-based order and to replace the United States as the predominant global power. Central to this assumption is the belief that China seeks to disrupt, dismantle, and replace predominant Western-centric institutions with less liberal institutions that propagate its values, priorities, and leadership.[101] These institutions include formal organizations, such as the United Nations; normative institutions, such as the rule of law; and conceptual institutions, such as the global security order, which depends in particular on US hegemony.[102] As outlined in earlier chapters, the need to secure the liberal rules-based order lies at the heart of Western strategy toward China, particularly those intent on preserving "freedom" and "openness" and Western dominance in the Indo-Pacific region.[103]

Predictably, Chinese narratives on Chinese foreign policy are very different from their Western counterparts. Chinese analysts fundamentally reject the idea that China is a coercive actor, and instead argue that China's foreign policy behaviour prioritizes stability, "win-win" relations, non-interference, and common development, among other issues.[104] Pointing to the tendency among Western powers (especially the United States) to use military force and/or broad sanctions regimes to achieve their diplomatic ends, Chinese analysts even question the fundamental logic of what in the Western narrative constitutes coercion, particularly as China has no record of using force abroad in the modern era.[105]

Where China has restricted trade, Chinese commentators argue that it has done so for defensive reasons, not as punitive action. On economic measures taken by China after South Korea's deployment of the Terminal High Altitude Area Defense (THAAD) system, for instance,

Chinese analysts note that system enabled the United States to spy on China, a situation, these analysts argue, that necessitated a Chinese response.[106] On import restrictions placed by Beijing on Australian goods, Chinese narratives similarly identify Australian "provocations" as the source of conflict, noting that China suspended economic dialogue and exchange with Australia *in response* to the Morrison government's "antagonism."[107] Indeed, much of the Chinese narrative on the country's foreign policy is defensive in nature, arguing that China has little choice but to engage in reciprocal actions when Western states work against its international interests, either directly (as when Japan nationalized the Diaoyu/Senkaku Islands) or indirectly (as when the Norwegian Nobel Committee awarded Liu Xiaobo, a prominent, Chinese, pro-democracy dissident, the Nobel Peace Prize).[108] From China's perspective, such actions are not single-issue but rather part of a broader US-led attempt by Western states to delegitimize it as an international actor.[109] China sees its responses as not only justified but moderate in comparison with the United States, which regularly uses dollar "weaponization" to punish states, institutions, and individuals at will.[110]

Chinese analysts also reject charges of dept-trap diplomacy, arguing that China's lending – whether through the Silk Road Fund or the China Development Bank – relies on commercial logic and adheres to international standards with respect to repayment.[111] Chinese policy analysts refute the Western assumption that Beijing uses predatory lending to secure access to assets, noting, in particular, that Chinese firms prefer debt collateral in the form of bank accounts with minimum balance requirements, meaning that they want repayment guaranteed in *cash*, not *assets*.[112] Chinese commentators also point to Beijing's willingness to defer debt service payments, particularly during the COVID-19 pandemic, as evidence that China is a responsible lender, even compared with Western states and financial institutions.[113] As for charges of foreign policy coercion, Chinese commentators see Western claims of debt-trap diplomacy as nothing more than a smear campaign to undermine China's foreign relations with the Global South, in particular.[114]

Chinese analysts also reject Western criticism of the Belt and Road Initiative, arguing that the initiative, far from being a grand strategy for world dominance, is a strategic means to address China's domestic economic challenges through win-win foreign and economic relations.[115] The BRI provides a blueprint for how China can expand its overseas export markets, thereby enabling it to deal with issues of excess internal capacity, and identify opportunities for Chinese investment in regional infrastructure that can lead to common development in Asia. First and foremost, the BRI is a strategic means of integrating China's peripheral states in Northeast, Southeast, South, and Central Asia into the Chinese market, creating growth opportunities for both China's landlocked provinces and some of Asia's poorest developing states.[116] Again, Chinese scholars argue that investment through the BRI finances projects within Asia, in particular, that Western states and institutions would not touch, and that the BRI's investment vehicles, such as the Silk Road Fund, operate with market principles, not strategic aims.

In this respect, the BRI differs little from South Korea's New Southern Policy, Taiwan's New Southbound Policy, and Japan's Free and Open Indo-Pacific vision – all of which are industrial policies that use state-directed investment to promote regional interconnectivity and integration to further national trade.[117] That Western states criticize China while supporting the other states is further evidence of a Western double standard toward China and Chinese foreign relations.

The Chinese narrative on China and the rules-based order is also dramatically different from the Western narrative. Whereas Western scholars argue that China is undermining the rules-based order, Chinese scholars argue that China supports international order but rejects Western hegemony.[118] The difference between "order" and "hegemony," these scholars argue, is that while order is an inclusive, responsive, and equitable system for organizing and managing state relations, hegemony is a system of great-power–dominated institutions designed to perpetuate the dominant state's power and prevent rival powers from gaining influence.[119] China is a "responsible stakeholder" in propagating inclusive and equitable order, but rejects the idea that order is a fixed constant that cannot adapt to changes in the global balance of power without faltering.

To be clear, China does advance a new order in Asia, albeit one that includes institutions from both the existing and emerging orders.[120] Beijing believes this reconstituted order is necessary as Asia has fundamentally changed since the end of the Cold War and the existing, Western-led order no longer represents regional dynamics and/or trends.[121] There is a compelling logic, therefore, to a new regional order in which China has a predominant role due to its size, influence, and historical relations with other Asian states. This is not to say that China seeks domination within Asia, as Western scholars often suggest, but rather that China supports an endogenous order that reflects the regional balance of power while also respecting state sovereignty.[122]

Implications for Canada

There is arguably no greater gap in perceptions concerning Asia's strategic environment than that between China and the Western world. Indeed, as demonstrated above, the views expressed by Beijing, on the one hand, and by Washington, Canberra, or Ottawa, on the other, are often polar opposites, with the Western world ascribing to China a particular set of motivations and behaviours that China fundamentally rejects. While some Western policy-makers have attempted to account for such divergence in viewpoints by invoking a "clash of civilizations," or by pointing to it as an outcome of Western universalism versus Chinese repression, such logic is not only chauvinistic but flawed. One does not have to rely on cultural determinism to account for the Chinese narrative with respect to the country's domestic institutions and foreign policy, for instance. Rather, as demonstrated above, Chinese views of issues, including the country's governance, its role in Hong Kong, its approach to Xinjiang, and its foreign policy, are rooted in endogenous understanding of Chinese national interests, particularly with respect to the country's stability, security, and prestige.

The tendency within Western scholarship and among Western policy-makers to summarily dismiss China's perspectives in their own strategic calculation, therefore, inevitably leads to a lopsided strategic narrative built on righteous indignation rather than sound strategic calculation. Failure to admit any Chinese perspective into one's strategic calculation allows for the development of neither strategic empathy nor an informed understanding of China's motivations, behaviours, or actions. Ultimately, the result is a poorly conceptualized approach to China that fails in any strategic purpose other than the propagation of animosity between states.

From this perspective, it is critical that Canadian policy-makers consider Chinese perspectives when developing the country's strategic approach to China and, indeed, to the Asia-Pacific. On the CPC, for instance, Canadian politicians and diplomats must understand Chinese narratives around the party's centrality, its popularity, its legitimacy, and its effectiveness in order to ensure a productive working relationship between Ottawa and Beijing. The contention in Western discourse that one can work with the Chinese people while marginalizing the

CPC, for instance, has no basis in Chinese social narratives and will almost certainly lead to state-level tensions, such as those between Australia and China. If Canadian policy-makers prioritize stability within Canada-China relations, as it is in Canada's interests that they should, an understanding of Chinese narratives on the CPC is a prerequisite.

Canadian politicians and policy analysts would benefit from a clearer view of Chinese narratives on Hong Kong, particularly those that prioritize the HKSAR's stability, prosperity, and security. Instead of adopting the predominant Western narrative that China is undermining Hong Kong's democracy, for instance, Canadian policy-makers should take seriously Chinese concerns over sovereignty, political legitimacy, and Western interference in Hong Kong, as these core concerns inform Beijing's approach to the region. While they may not agree with Chinese narratives, respect for and understanding of these narratives will secure Canadian commercial, diplomatic, and consular interests in Hong Kong and enable Ottawa to engage more effectively with local and central government officials on issues like human rights, free speech, and freedom of assembly.

Similarly, Ottawa needs to maintain clear and stable lines of communication with Beijing on Xinjiang if it wants the ability to influence the CPC's approach to human rights in the region. While the CPC will pursue whatever policy toward the XUAR supports its domestic economic, social, and security agendas, Canada will be able to raise its voice on issues such as forced labour and detainment if Beijing sees it as an honest broker, not simply a Western agent intent on challenging China's rise. This simple truth exposes a stark irony in Western approaches to Xinjiang, namely, that the more Western states criticize China or charge it with genocide, the less ability they have to convince China to modify its behaviour. Canadian understanding of and respect for Chinese narratives in Xinjiang are the necessary starting point if Ottawa is to have even a limited ability to affect developments there.

On cross-strait relations, it is also in Canada's national interests to understand and to address Chinese views and concerns regarding Taiwan, if for no other reason than to preserve Taiwan's autonomy and to avoid conflict in the Taiwan Strait. Indeed, Canadian strategic empathy toward China's perspectives on Taiwan have never been more critical as Australia, France, Germany, Japan, the United Kingdom, and the United States have all increased support for Taiwan in ways that are leading to greater tension between Beijing and Taipei. As a result, Canada's most effective strategic role vis-à-vis Taiwan is to act as a neutral broker, one that works with mainland China, Taiwan, and Western states to avoid conflict. For Ottawa to fill this role, Canadian policy-makers must understand and take Chinese concerns regarding cross-strait relations seriously.

Finally, Canada must consider China's perspectives on the Asian rules-based order, its BRI engagement, and its foreign policy behavior. Rather than assume that China is a revisionist power or that it engages in predatory economic activity, Canadian strategic analysts must instead examine Chinese narratives to understand Beijing's foreign policy intentions, behaviours, and actions more fully. Taking China's viewpoints into consideration, Ottawa can then develop a more informed approach to the region that maintains its ability to work with China when, where, and how it chooses.

Conversely, there are clear costs to ignoring Chinese narratives on issues such as the CPC's legitimacy, its approach to Hong Kong, Taiwan, and Xinjiang, and its foreign policy motivations, actions, and relations. One can see this most clearly with respect to Australia-China relations. When the Morrison government employed a biased Western viewpoint to critique China's foreign and domestic politics in 2020, Beijing responded by essentially severing relations with Canberra. To offset this loss of bilateral ties, and to address the strategic instability that accompanied it, Canberra deepened its defence relations with Washington, functionally choosing to side with the United States against China in Asia. Far from bringing greater stability, prosperity, and security to the Australian people, the Morrison government has instead limited Australia's strategic room for maneuver, increased the country's dependency on the United States, and ensured that Australia-China relations will remain conflictual for the foreseeable future.

6

Mapping a Canadian Policy Approach to Asia

National Interests, Asian Narratives, and Network Analysis

For Canadian policy-makers, Western narratives on Asia have clear appeal. Normatively, they identify Canada as a like-minded state, a part of the international elite responsible for the defence of international liberalism and the propagation of progressive values. They frame Canada as a global leader on issues that matter deeply to the Canadian public, such as the protection and propagation of democracy, international law, and human rights. They create space for Canadian foreign policy within Western-dominated forums such as the G7 and NATO, acting as force multipliers that enable Ottawa to "punch above its weight" on global governance and security issues. They reinforce Canadian world views on democracy versus authoritarianism and on the importance of freedom and openness, and they align with the Canadian sentiment that the country can and should act as a force for good within the international system.

Western narratives further play to the Canadian ego, particularly the idea that Canada can intervene at the highest levels of global society to influence security, economic, and governance outcomes through fiat and partnership. Western narratives inflate Canada's identity as a critical "middle" power and increase it policy-makers' sense that Ottawa can tip the balance of global power through its alignment and support. However, they also feed a sense of Western chauvinism in Canada around its role as a global "saviour" that has achieved domestic enlightenment and is therefore responsible for bringing such enlightenment to other, less enlightened states, particularly those non-democratic developing economies in Asia.

Operationally, Western narratives also provide Ottawa with a set of prescribed policies that its leadership can use to formulate national strategy toward Asia, assuming that Canadian policy-makers and academics uncritically accept Western narratives around Asia's strategic environment, state identities, and regional dynamics. The Western states' Indo-Pacific strategies, for instance, outline plans for cooperation on security and defence, democratic global governance, "high-quality" economic investment, and countering China – among other policy approaches – that provide Canada with a clear Asia policy framework should its leaders choose to align its interests with those of other Western states. That these states have already identified a role for Canada within their narratives and strategies – whether as an "alliance partner," "middle power," "developed democracy," or "like-minded state" – increases the likelihood that Canadian policy-makers will ultimately opt for alignment.

Such conceptual and operational alignment is obviously attractive. Canada is, after all, a democracy and has long-term strategic interests in remaining an active participant in transatlantic affairs and Anglo-Saxon affairs. For instance, Canada is not interested in breaking with the G7 over a common Western approach to Asia, as the institution provides Ottawa with a powerful network of states and a critical forum for values-based discourse. Canadian policy-makers and politicians also see irreplaceable value in working with NATO on Asia-Pacific issues as NATO provides it with a security community of democratic states and a means to project influence disproportionate to its national material strength.

Yet, as this book has demonstrated, the massive discrepancy between Western and Asian narratives on Asian dynamics means that Canadian policy-makers cannot expect to approach the region through a Western analytical lens and operational framework and still achieve their national strategic end states, whether defined in political, economic, or security terms. While alignment with Western states can help Canada achieve certain strategic ends, such as increasing its international influence and global prestige, the same alignment can disadvantage Canada in Asia to the point that it risks its ability to operate effectively within the region at all. It is simply not enough for Canada to approach Asia as a subregion of a Western-dominated global system. The region has moved too far away from this subordinate role, and has far too much momentum for us to expect anything but further consolidation.

It is this very consolidation of state ties that provides Canada with the clearest blueprint for developing a strategic approach to Asia, one based on regional dynamics, relationships, linkages, values, and priorities. While a potential obstacle for Western-aligned engagement, this same regional network can facilitate Canadian tactical, operational, and strategic integration in Asia in ways that will subsequently lead to greater Canadian understanding of Asia and to improved regional perceptions of Ottawa's strategic intentions in the region.

Through this approach, one based on "strategic integration," Canadian policy-makers can better position the country to contribute to Asia's strategic stability and to influence the evolution of Asia's regional order, up to and including issue areas of importance for the Canadian public, such as democracy, human rights, and international law. Canada's ability to realize its national interests in Asia, therefore, comes not from its participation in a Western-led coalition of states working within a Western-devised strategy for Asia's "preservation" but rather from its willingness to engage with regional actors and networks on their own terms.

These dynamics compel a strategic rethinking of Canada's approach to Asia, one predicated on the country's national interests, not on its ideational alignment with Western narratives and Western approaches. To facilitate this process, an analytical "blank slate" is critical – one that considers Canada's national interests, internalizes Asian narratives, and identifies specific institutions and actors for engagement. Nothing in this approach requires wholesale rejection of Western strategic thought toward the region, but it does necessitate critical examination of many assumptions in Canadian strategic writing on Asia, particularly with respect to the region's primary dynamics.

Canada's National Interests in Asia

The essential starting point for developing a Canadian approach to Asia is consideration of the country's national interests in the region. Although this is a basic enough principle, there is unfortunately a dearth of scholarship on this topic, despite Canadian strategic analysts' regular invocation of interests to justify Western state alignment in the

Indo-Pacific. Where one does see reference to Canadian national interests is largely with reference to its support for the regional "rules-based order," a reference that avoids the tricky task of either defining specific national interests or the precise nature of the rules-based order, which, as addressed in preceding chapters, remains an ill-defined and controversial concept, particularly in Asia.

If not with respect to the rules-based order, how does one define Canada's national interests? International relations theory provides a starting point, with the general consensus being that all nations share the common interests of maximizing their power, ensuring their security, and enabling their economic growth.[1] These fundamental interests have both singular and iterative qualities. With respect to power, for instance, states seek to develop material and influential means to effect regional change and to ensure room for maneuver within their bilateral and multilateral relations. Power is also a function of security, and states seek the ability to counter threats, deter aggression, and engage in successful military operations where necessary. Power and security also enable state-oriented commercial activity, whether state- or private sector–directed, which in turn enables the generation of more power.

Within this national interest triad, one can further develop an understanding of states' interests resulting from less tangible aspects, such as national identity and national values. More specifically, one can see variations in states' national interests around the nature of power, the understanding of security, and the utilization of economic power and statecraft, among others.[2] Western states, for instance, have prioritized the propagation of liberal democracy in their national interests, believing (often falsely) that democratic governments are more accountable, responsive, and representative and that democratic systems moderate state behaviour. China, conversely, has deprioritized ideological alignment and prioritized "win-win" relations with states, seeing its expanded influence as more important than the propagation of its governance and economic systems. European Union and ASEAN member states have also prioritized supranational governance in their national interests, albeit to different degrees. While one can attribute these variations in national interests to the core tenets of power, security, and economy, they vary by wide enough margins to suggest that states often prioritize one national interest over others, and that national-level analysis is still necessary to determine an individual state's foreign policy priorities.

Canada clearly has national interests that span the conceptual gamut from power to security to economic growth. With respect to power, Canada seeks to play a role in regional governance around issue areas including international law and economic systems, and to contribute to the development of regional standards around emerging issue areas such as climate change and digital trade. Canada also wants to increase its representation and influence within regional forums on strategic issues, such as the ASEAN Regional Forum (ARF), and within dialogue mechanisms such as Council for Security Cooperation in the Asia Pacific (CSCAP). Through these efforts, Canada works to increase its influence both within multilateral institutions and across its bilateral relations, and prioritizes deepening its relations with emerging markets in Southeast Asia such as Malaysia and Indonesia. Canada also desires to advance issues such as gender equality, human rights, and inclusive, sustainable economic growth throughout the region, particularly in Asia's developing economies. Most importantly, Canada prioritizes stability in the region and aims to leverage its position as a trusted regional actor to contribute to such stability.[3]

On security, Canada's national interests also focus on stability, albeit through the lens of military power rather than governance and international law.[4] Canada seeks to play a stabilizing role in the Korean Peninsula, around the Taiwan Strait, and within the South China Sea with respect to maritime security, for instance. Canada engages with regional states on humanitarian and disaster relief and provides troops for peacekeeping activities in North Korea, for demining in the Solomon Islands, and for enforcing fishing regulations in the Pacific.[5] On great power competition in Asia – the predominant strategic security theme in the region – Canada's national interests rest on equidistance between China and the United States, not alignment with one side over the other. Canada seeks to engage more in middle-power groupings in Asia and has prioritized greater strategic integration with ASEAN in its approach. Canada does not maintain a significant military presence in Asia, although it does deploy naval vessels to the region several times a year.[6] During these deployments, Canada prioritizes relationship building and maritime law. Canada also engages in military dialogue and joint-training activities in Asia.

On economics, Canada approaches Asia with an intent to diversify its trade and investment away from North America, where it is overly dependent on the US market, and to provide micro, small, and medium-sized Canadian enterprises with growth opportunity in the region.[7] With bidirectional investment flows still relatively underdeveloped, for instance, Canada wants to increase inbound Asian investment to Canada and outbound Canadian investment to Asia.[8] On trade, Canada also sees Asia as a potential market for expansion and has entered into a bilateral free trade agreement (FTA) with South Korea and a multilateral FTA with Australia, Brunei, Chile, Japan, Malaysia, Mexico, New Zealand, Peru, Singapore, and Vietnam through the Comprehensive and Progressive Agreement for Trans-Pacific Partnership (CPTPP).[9] Notably, China remains Canada's second-largest trade partner, despite the downturn in relations between the two states since 2019, and Canada-China economic relations continue to expand.[10] Canada has also prioritized deeper economic integration with ASEAN member states and India as part of its diversification push toward the region, and is currently negotiating FTAs with both, albeit with limited success. Canadian universities, similarly, have become financially dependent on students from Asia (particularly China, India, and the Philippines) and on investments from Asian states for research and development, among other activities.[11]

Notably, all Canada's national interests in Asia, as defined above, share two common determinants. First, they depend in large part on regional stability from the bottom up, meaning stability resulting from Asian state integration, communication, and collaboration, not a Western-imposed rules-based order designed to arrest Asian's regional development to ensure Western predominance. Second, they require Canadian bilateral and multilateral involvement and integration with Asian states, including China, on Asian, not Western, terms. In both instances, Canada would be disadvantaged by alignment with any Western-origin Indo-Pacific ideal, particularly one predicated on Western military involvement and Western support for a regional order that neither includes the region's predominant economic and political actor (China) nor takes regional perspectives, perceptions, and priorities into consideration. To ensure that its strategic approach toward Asia appropriately advances its national interests, Canadian strategists must consider how these very interests align with Asian narratives, starting with the issue areas critical to regional stability and Asian state relations.

Normative Realignment

As demonstrated throughout this book, there are significant differences between the way Western and Western-aligned actors view Asia's strategic environment and the way Asian actors view the region's dynamics, up to and including the desirability of Western state involvement and leadership. Canadian analysts and academics almost universally employ Western narratives to articulate Canada's interests in Asia and to advocate for Canadian alignment with Western-formulated strategies, such as the Indo-Pacific concept. Canadian policy-makers must reject this heuristic in favour of one that is more rooted in regional narratives, particularly those that problematize Western state involvement, if they are to develop a policy that facilitates omnidirectional diplomacy and strategic integration and maximizes Canadian's strategic options. In particular, Canadian policy-makers must consider six points.

(1) Western Views of Governance, Economics, and Security Are Not Universal

While one sees clear support for responsive and effective governance across Asia, there is within the region clear and growing skepticism of Western democracy with respect to its stability, its responsiveness, and its flexibility. Asian societies are no less interested in good governance or personal freedom than their Western counterparts, but are less convinced that democratic governments are capable of providing these public goods to their people. Neither are Asian states and societies broadly supportive of economic liberalism, having seen first-hand how open markets lead to vulnerabilities and how managed economies can contribute to domestic development. There is, rather, more acceptance in Asia for mixed models of economic governance and development. Further, the Western narrative around a "free" and "open" Indo-Pacific is more a product of Western state priorities and identities than a response to Asian demand signals. Indeed, one finds little support in Asia for greater openness to Western involvement unless on distinctly Asian terms, such as through regional trade agreements (CPTPP, Regional Comprehensive Economic Partnership [RCEP], Asia-Pacific Economic Cooperation [APEC]) or through bilateral free trade agreements.

Canadian policy-makers must take these perspectives into consideration when pursuing aspects of the country's national priorities that touch on governance, economic priorities, and security relations. The predilection of Asian states for *flexibility* in governance and economic systems necessitates a similarly adaptive approach by Ottawa, one that forgoes ideological rigidity in favour of process-based outcomes. Through non-deterministic engagement, Canada will find far more opportunities for meaningful exchange, including on issues such as gender equality, human rights, and sustainable development, than if it adopts a Western approach that seeks, above all, to preserve a rules-based order in Asia based on Western, not Asian, priorities.

(2) Regionally, China Enjoys Greater Support and Suffers Less Criticism than in Western Discourse on Chinese Domestic and Foreign Affairs

While Chinese "revisionism" is at the heart of Western discourse on Asian order and stability, regional states are far more interested in engaging with China than critiquing its foreign and domestic policies. In regional polling, scholarship, and policy statements, one finds greater support for China's activities in Asia and sympathy toward its domestic approach to issues such as Xinjiang and Hong Kong. Even Asian states that are wary of China's growing influence are not interested in sidelining it from regional developments or alienating it from regional institutions. Indeed, Asian states largely prioritize integration with China, seeing more ties with Beijing as economically desirable and strategically stabilizing.

Ottawa must approach the region with the understanding that Asian states see China's activities in Asia in largely positive terms and that any attempt by Canada or a Western coalition of states to vilify China will likely find little regional support. Rather, Asian states are interested in finding positive ways to engage with China that adjust for China's growing economic and political centrality and preclude regional instability. As China is central to Asia's regional order, maintaining a positive relationship with China will be critical to deeper Canadian integration in the region.

(3) Within China, One Finds Broad Support for the Chinese Communist Party (CPC) and Well-Developed Counter-Narratives Concerning its Foreign and Domestic Policies

In striking contrast to Western narratives on China, Chinese scholarship, media, and polling show that the Chinese people support the CPC, seeing it as legitimate, responsive, trustworthy, and accountable. Further, Chinese narratives suggest that the Chinese people view the CPC as integral to China's domestic stability and to China's growing international prestige.

Chinese narratives on Hong Kong, cross-strait relations, Xinjiang, and foreign policy frame Chinese policy priorities in terms of national security, sovereignty, poverty reduction, and minority development. Chinese critiques of Western discourse on these issues draw heavily on anti-colonial and anti-imperialist logic to argue that Western states' narratives are formulated to undermine China's domestic stability, to tarnish its international reputation, and to perpetuate Western hegemony.

For Canadian policy-makers, it is critical to incorporate Chinese perspectives into the country's approach to China, even if only to reject such views through policy deliberation. Rather than dismiss Chinese narratives out of hand as propaganda or as coerced, Canadian policy analysts must instead understand that Chinese views come from a domestic sense of Chinese interests and China's identity. By taking the time and energy to understand China's viewpoints, Canadian policy-makers can develop cognitive empathy, which will increase their ability to engage with China on positive terms and as an honest broker.

(4) Asian States Are Wary of Western Involvement in the Region and Are Opposed to Any Western Strategy Predicated on Competition with China

There is little to no demand in Asia for greater Western state involvement, except in the case of narrow national self-interests, such as Vietnam's desire for US partnership in order to advance its maritime claims against China. In this respect, the ASEAN Outlook on the Indo-Pacific is correctly seen as a response to Western hegemonic discourse and as a rejection of Western assumptions about the Indo-Pacific's strategic underpinnings. All Asian states express concern over the Western proclivity to treat China as a regional threat, and over any Western strategy to contain China's activities, influence, or relationships. Across Asian narratives of the West, one finds repeated concern over Western state intentions, behaviours, and activities, and a deep cynicism over Western intentions to "lead" in Asia, particularly on issues related to Asian "order."

Canadian policy-makers must understand that adoption of an Indo-Pacific strategy toward Asia will place it firmly in a Western-aligned camp of outsider powers (on which more is written below). An Indo-Pacific conceptual alignment will also burden Canada with strategic baggage with respect to issues ranging from Chinese containment to Western state paternalism. Far from benefiting from such an alignment, Canada will find its room for strategic maneuver curtailed, and will ultimately find it more difficult to achieve substate integration and cooperation within the Asian region.

(5) Western Narratives on Australia, Japan, and India Are Ill-Informed and Self-Serving

While Western states routinely identify Australia as an "Asian" actor, for instance, Asian narratives on Australia focus primarily on its status as a Western power in Oceania, particularly one with deep historical and cultural ties to the West. Far from representing Asian interests in its foreign and security policies, Australia is seen by Asian states as a regional agent of the Western world, one clearly ingrained in Western institutions and openly committed to preserving Western aspects of regional (and global) order. Western assumptions that Australian support is synonymous with Asian support are therefore largely misleading.

Western claims that alignment with Japan indicates widespread regional acceptance of an Indo-Pacific paradigm also fail to take Japan's unique regional identity into account. Within Asia, for instance, Japan has the status of a Western-aligned and Western-influenced state, particularly with respect to its strategic dependence on the United States. This status complicates its relations with other Asian states, a paradigm that Japanese policy-makers, academics, and analysts clearly understand. In Japan, for instance, one finds well-developed narratives that call for the country to reject its status as a Western partner and to integrate itself more into Asia, particularly toward China. Thus, Western narratives on Japan fail on two important accounts: first, their assumption that Japan is a representational Asian state, and second, their assumption that Japan is firmly in the Western camp.

Western narratives on India are arguably even more convoluted and self-serving, particularly those that identify India as a like-minded state. Under the Modi government, India has moved in a decidedly illiberal direction both with respect to its domestic political system and in its treatment of its minority Muslim population. Further, Western assumptions that India can "balance" China in Asia ignore India's political and social instability, laid particularly bare before and during India's COVID-19 outbreak, and its problematic relations with other South Asian states. Western views of India as a Western-aligned actor also ignore the country's long history of multidirectional relations, including with Western opponents such as Iran and Russia.

Canadian policy-makers must be discerning and critical in reading regional signals around these states' identities. They must also realize that Australia, Japan, and India are not representative of Asian regional discourse, and work to understand different narratives in Asia around non-Western-centric security issues. While Canada must continue to work with Canberra, Tokyo, and New Delhi, it should do so with a clear understanding that each state has a unique viewpoint on Asia's dynamics, with a clear bias stemming from its own domestic and foreign policy priorities. Canada should also question Western assumptions concerning Japan's and India's Western alignment, and presume that both Tokyo and New Delhi will act first and foremost according to their national interests and their evolving relations with China.

(6) Asian States Differ Significantly from Western States in How They View Asia's Regional Security Order

Regional narratives on Asia's predominant security challenges includes critique of Western states' involvement in and of US "leadership" across the region. In Northeast and Southeast Asia, for instance, one finds scholarship and policy writing identifying the United States, in particular, as a source of regional instability and arguing that Western state engagement in Asia has prevented conflict resolution. Asian narratives further question Western states' foreign policy motivations, particularly with respect to Western intentions to preserve Asia's order. Asian scholars argue instead that Western actors seek preservation of their hegemony in Asia, even at the cost of the region's overall stability. From this perspective, Western states, not China, are the greatest threat to Asia's stability, especially as they engage in revisionist activities such as institution building (AUKUS and the Quad, for instance) and work collectively to contain China, despite regional opposition to such containment.

Canada must realize that Asian states are no longer interested in playing subordinate roles within their own region, and are no longer willing to accept Western leadership at the cost of their agency. Rather than seeking condominium with Western states intent on preserving Western hegemony in Asia, Canada would better serve its national interests through engagement with Asian states on equal grounds, up to and including on issues that challenge Canadian preconceptions and values. While, as noted above, Canadian policy-makers will almost certainly be tempted to use the country's place in Western institutions like the G7 and NATO as force multipliers, they must consider the potential cost to Canada's reputation and identity that such alignment will inflict.

Networks, Linkages, Nodes, and Relations

If Canadian policy-makers consider Canada's national interests in tandem with the above views on Asia's predominant geostrategic dynamics, they will almost certainly find it necessary to develop an alternative regional approach to the US-led, Western state–aligned Indo-Pacific concept. Indeed, with the gaps between Asian perceptions and the Indo-Pacific's core assumptions as significant as they are, uncritical adoption of the concept by Canadian officials would be tantamount to a strategic dereliction of duty. Canada cannot realize its national interests in Asia through a strategy based on exclusion, particularly one that discounts Asian states' agency and prioritizes Western state hegemony. Rather, Canada's national interests are best served if it works in Asia on Asian states' terms and within their network relations.

To facilitate a reconceptualization of Canada's approach to Asia – one that takes all the above considerations into account in its formulation – greater clarity is needed with respect to Asia's institutional architecture and ecosystems. Arguably the most direct way to achieve this operational clarity is through network analysis. Through network analysis, one can start to identify areas where Asian states and state actors engage and to consider the nature of their engagement. The process of network mapping can provide a tactical and operational blueprint for Canadian integration that takes actors, interests, values, and issues into direct consideration. Further, in determining which networks are the most developed, or the "thickest," Canadian policy-makers can identify regional "nodes," or dense areas of Asian state/actor activity, and prioritize them in Canada's foreign policy according to its own national interests and plans.

A network analysis approach of this type is predicated on the following logic. First, network analysis provides a direct methodology for gathering empirical data on state engagement at the substate level. As state relations are a function of interaction, identification and examination of networks also provide the most measurable means of determining the nature of state relations. Networked states have linkages, for instance, that facilitate the movement of goods, people, and ideas. The more linkages states share, the stronger their base relations, in both ideational and material terms. Linkages can exist between states (bilateral linkages) or between multiple states (state systems), and can extend across political, economic, and social sectors.

States, actors, or individuals with extensive bilateral or multilateral linkages can, in turn, become nodes. These nodes can serve as regional "influencers" and "facilitators" around specific issue areas and are critical components of state systems. Identification and examination of key nodes provides critical information about networks' constituent actors, component parts, and values, among other useful information. Nodes also provide important insight into the nature of state relations and into the evolution of regional ecosystems and regional order.

Operationally, analysts can undertake network analysis in Asia by identifying regional networks, determining the thickness or thinness of network linkages, and isolating key regional nodes. Subsequently, they can critically assess whether these networks, linkages, and nodes represent activities, behaviours, and values that match their own national interests and consider whether engagement within the networks is possible and/or desirable. Once analysts have a clear picture of the networks' constituent actors and density, policy-makers (or other actors) can approach these networks through the predominant nodes to pursue engagement. Through this approach, Canada can undertake tactical-level engagement on specific issue areas to support the broader goal of omnidirectional diplomacy and strategic integration, working from the bottom up to inform a regionally determined, non-biased approach to relationship building.

Network Analysis and the Making of a Canadian Strategy toward Asia

Asia, or the Asia-Pacific, is deeply integrated across institutional lines, many of which facilitate dialogue and cooperation between regional states on transnational political, economic, social, environmental, and security issues. Indeed, Asia has an entire ecosystem of institutions that ties its regional states together in dense networks that, in turn, constitute a bottom-up Asian order. Together, these institutions act as regional arteries for the movement of ideas, people, and goods that contribute to a regional body politic, one that gains strength with each passing year of increased Asian integration.

Canada has already taken some limited steps toward regional network integration through its participation in some of Asia's more prominent institutions. Canada is a founding member of the APEC mechanism, for instance, and engages with the twenty-one APEC member states on trade promotion, economic reform, and economic integration.[12] It is also a member of the CPTPP multilateral free trade agreement, through which it has worked to set region-specific trade and tariff standards in Asia and Latin America.[13] Canada also has limited engagement with ASEAN (on which more is written below), particularly around economic issues. Lastly, Canada is also a member of the Asian Development Bank (ADB) and the Asian Infrastructure Investment Bank (AIIB), although some Canadian policy-makers have advocated disengagement with the latter to demonstrate resolve against Chinese "aggression."[14]

While a start, Canadian network integration in Asia is far from sufficient. Canadian institutional involvement in Asia remains almost exclusively limited to economic issues and largely geared toward institutions with more international scope and Western state involvement. Indeed, with the notable and limited exception of ASEAN, Canadian representation is almost completely lacking in Asia's endogenous institutions, particularly those with non-economic focuses.

To address this deficit, greater understanding of Asia's institutional ecosystem is needed, as well as an understanding of its constituent networks. The rest of this chapter identifies the region's most influential institutions, examines Canada's current engagement (if any) with each, and offers recommendations for Canadian institutional and network engagement going forward. As ASEAN and its subsidiary dialogues and working groups dominate Asia-Pacific institutionalism to a significant extent, the first part of the network analysis focuses exclusively on ASEAN and its ecosystem. The second part examines Asia's non-ASEAN institutions with an eye toward potential Canadian involvement.

ASEAN

If Asia's institutionalism is a body politic, as described above, ASEAN serves as its beating heart. Organizationally, ASEAN draws Southeast Asian states together into a supranational set of institutional arrangements through which they seek consensus on issues ranging from the transnational movements of people to climate change to nuclear proliferation. Through its ASEAN+ mechanisms, ASEAN brings China, Japan, and South Korea (ASEAN+3) together in Asia's only region-wide institution. The ASEAN+6 dialogue expands the institution's geographic reach even further, to include Australia, India, and New Zealand. ASEAN also facilitates the East Asia Summit (EAS), which includes all ASEAN+6 members and the United States and Russia; the ASEAN Defence Ministers' Meeting-Plus (ADMM+), which includes these same states; and the ASEAN Regional Forum, which includes all the EAS states plus Europe, Canada, Bangladesh, the Democratic People's Republic of Korea, Mongolia, Pakistan, Sri Lanka, East Timor, and Papua New Guinea. All these high-level dialogues focus on strategic issues, making them key intra- and extra-regional dialogues.

In addition to these high-level dialogue groups, there are literally dozens of subordinate ASEAN dialogue mechanisms organized under the broader thematic areas of political, economic, socio-cultural, and community and corporate affairs.[15] Far less known than ASEAN's marquee dialogue series, these institutions are essentially ASEAN's working groups and represent the most tangible areas where ASEAN member states and their dialogue partners focus on and achieve tangible, tactical-level outcomes that lead to state and substate ties.

For Canada to take full advantage of ASEAN as a regional institution for strategic integration, it must develop a two-level approach. At the strategic level, Canada must establish deeper relations with the ASEAN Secretariat, ideally in the form of its inclusion in one of ASEAN's "plus" mechanisms. Only through this degree of integration can Canada effect the sort of operational and tactical-level engagement it needs to integrate itself in ASEAN's institutional process. The inclusion of Australia and New Zealand in the ASEAN+6 mechanism (through their East Asia Summit status) could provide a framework for Canada's eventual inclusion, particularly if Ottawa is able to demonstrate an appropriate strategic commitment to ASEAN engagement beyond the efforts it has made to date. One potential starting point for Canadian "plus" status could be the ongoing discussions between Canada and ASEAN over a free trade agreement. Negotiation topics should include the expansion of a Canada-ASEAN comprehensive and strategic partnership and Canadian inclusions in the EAS.

Seen from this perspective, Canada's strategic-level engagement with ASEAN to date is disappointing. Canada-ASEAN relations are primarily limited to Canadian involvement in the ASEAN Regional Forum and the Canada-ASEAN Post Ministerial Conference Plus One (PMC+1) mechanism, neither of which provides Canada with access to ASEAN's broader institutional framework.[16] While Canada has used these ties to establish a permanent ASEAN ambassador in Jakarta and to engage in confidence-building measures with ASEAN aimed at transnational crime, terrorism, and peacekeeping, it has not been able to translate these ties into more substantial participation, such as involvement in the ADMM+'s Expert Working Group (EWG). Notably, Canada's failure to leverage its existing ties with ASEAN for more formal engagement is due partly to Chinese opposition to its inclusion, particularly in the ADMM+ EWG.[17] Such exclusion should serve as a wake-up call for Canadian policy-makers who argue that Canada can undertake a strategy toward Asia while maintaining contentious relations with China.

If Canada can achieve deeper strategic integration with ASEAN, it will find multiple opportunities to engage with ASEAN member states on issues ranging from climate change to economic affairs to sociocultural engagement, which will having long-lasting effects on setting regional governance standards going forward. On climate change, for instance, Canada could replicate Chinese, Japanese, and Australian efforts to work with the ASEAN Ministerial Meetings on the Environment (AMME), the meetings of ASEAN Senior Officials on Environment (ASOEN), and the ASEAN Working Group on Climate Change (AWGCC) under the ASEAN Socio-Cultural Community (ASCC) pillar.[18] While largely limited to ASEAN member states, these groups also engage with ASEAN+ members on parallel efforts, such as the China-ASEAN Clean Coal Conversion Technology Exchange and Promotion, the ASEAN-Australia Smart Cities initiative, the ASEAN-Japan Energy Efficiency Partnership (AJEEP), and the ASEAN-Korea Network on Climate Change Adaptation in Aquaculture.[19]

On economic issues, where Canada is already the most active, Ottawa could leverage a strategic partnership with ASEAN to operationalize its ongoing dialogue efforts with the ASEAN Economic Ministers Meeting (AEMM) and the ASEAN Senior Economic Officials Meeting (SEOM), which, to date, have resulting in little more than joint statements about shared interests and values.[20] Japan, for instance, has used its ASEAN+3 status to establish an ASEAN-Japan Economic Resilience Action Plan and a Dialogue for Innovative and Sustainable Growth (DISG), all with the intention of coordinating ASEAN-Japan economic cooperation in the Asia-Pacific in the post-pandemic era.[21] South Korea, similarly, has built on its strategic relationship with ASEAN to establish a South Korea-ASEAN free trade agreement and to integrate its New Southern Policy into the ASEAN Economic Community.[22] Australia and New Zealand have used their status as ASEAN+6 states to establish the ASEAN-Australia-New Zealand Free Trade Area (AANZFTA).

China has also used its strategic relationship with ASEAN to good economic effect, aligning its Belt and Road Initiative (BRI) engagement in Southeast Asia with the ASEAN Economic Community to the extent that the two are now formally linked through the China-ASEAN Connectivity Cooperation Committee.[23] China has also established a China-ASEAN Investment Cooperation Fund, a China-ASEAN Maritime Cooperation Fund, an ASEAN-China Transport Ministers Meeting, an ASEAN-China Customs Directors General Consultation Meeting, and a Special Fund for Asian Regional Cooperation.[24] As a result, China-ASEAN economic relations are driving Asian economic integration in large part, reinforced by the ASEAN-driven Regional Comprehensive Economic Partnership.[25] This suggests that, as with its engagement with the ADMM+ EWG, Canada will ultimately require Beijing's support for deeper economic cooperation with ASEAN, even if it can develop a Canada-ASEAN strategic partnership or settle on a Canada-ASEAN free trade agreement.

Canada would also benefit from a strategic partnership with ASEAN to establish political and security linkages with ASEAN member states, which, at the time of writing, it largely lacks. As noted above, Canada is a member of neither the EAS nor the ADMM+, and is integrated only into the ASEAN Political-Security Community through its participation in the ASEAN Senior Officials Meeting on Transnational Crime (SOMTC).[26] Australia, on the other hand, has used its strategic ties to ASEAN to establish the ASEAN-Australia Special Summit, the ASEAN Post Ministerial Conference with Australia (PMC+1), the ASEAN-Australia Forum, and the ASEAN-Australia Joint Cooperation Committee (JCC) Meeting. Japan, similarly, has established an ASEAN-Japan Defence Ministers' Informal Meeting and a Japan-ASEAN Dialogue on Defence Cooperation in dealing with non-traditional security threats.[27] South Korea's political and security involvement with ASEAN includes the ASEAN–Republic of Korea Summit, ministerial meetings, and the ASEAN–Republic of Korea Dialogue and Senior Officials Meetings.[28] Through these mechanisms, the three states work directly with ASEAN member states and China on security issue areas such as maritime security, human rights, cybersecurity, humanitarian and disaster relief, governance, non-traditional security, transnational terrorism, and demining.

China, more than any other actor, has integrated itself into the ASEAN Political-Security Community through ASEAN+1 dialogues on a code of conduct for the South China Sea, maritime emergencies, transnational crime, non-traditional security, nuclear proliferation, human rights, anti-corruption, defence cooperation, and illicit drug trafficking.[29] Beijing is active across all of ASEAN's political and security dialogues – EAS, ARF, ADMM+ – and deeply integrated in working groups that facilitate tactical engagement and substate security cooperation such as the ASEAN and China Cooperative Operations in Response to Dangerous Drugs (ACCORD).

On socio-cultural engagement, Canada would also benefit from deeper strategic integration in ASEAN as its efforts to date are extremely limited. Whereas Japan has agreements with ASEAN covering health (including pandemic), environment, sports, science and technology, youth, and intellectual exchange, as well as cultural cooperation and disaster management, Canada's engagement is limited to a scholarship program that provides 125 students from Southeast Asia the opportunity to study in Canada.[30] For perspective, Australia has provided 1,715 scholarships for Southeast Asian students through its ASEAN Australia Awards–Endeavour Scholarship and Fellowships, and has announced plans to expand this number through a new Australia for ASEAN Scholarships and the New Colombo Plan Scholarship Program.[31] South Korea, similarly, has expanded its socio-cultural ties with ASEAN through the ROK-ASEAN Consultative Group in the Employment and Labour Sector under the ASEAN Socio-Cultural Community.[32] At the time of writing, Canada has no equivalent programming.

China, predictably, has done the most to establish socio-cultural ties with Southeast Asian states through ASEAN's mechanisms, establishing the China-ASEAN Expo; China-ASEAN Education Cooperation Week; ASEAN-China Science, Technology and Innovation Cooperation; ASEAN-China Health Ministers Meeting; ASEAN-China Senior Officials' Meeting on Health Development; ASEAN-China Young Leaders

Scholarship Program; and Special Fund for Asian Regional Cooperation.[33] China has also implemented an ASEAN-China Work Plan on Cooperation in Culture and Arts and a China-ASEAN Cultural Forum, and has drafted a Joint Statement on Strengthening Media Exchanges and Cooperation between ASEAN and China.[34]

For ASEAN's strategic partners, primarily those part of the ASEAN+ mechanisms, there are therefore clear opportunities for engagement above and beyond participation in ASEAN's primary institutions, such as the EAS, ARF, and ADMM+. Australia, China, India, Japan, New Zealand, and South Korea have all leveraged their strategic engagement with ASEAN to facilitate operational and tactical-level participation on issues ranging from human rights to labour to gender equality, all in line with Asian priorities and values. For each state, the end result is greater network integration the Asia-Pacific on issues directly related to their national interests.

This pattern of engagement provides Canada with a clear model for achieving deeper participation in Asia's pre-eminent multilateral institutions. Rather than prioritizing a Canada-ASEAN free trade agreement, for instance, Ottawa would do better to negotiate a broader Canada-ASEAN strategic partnership, particularly one that leads to Canadian ASEAN+ status and enables Canada to expand its network engagement within Southeast Asia beyond its traditional economic relations. Canada would subsequently increase its access to ASEAN's operational and tactical-level institutions, which are often more focused on specific issues and outcomes than the EAS or ARF, and which Canada can determine based on its national interests. Through this access, Canadian participation in Asia's predominant institutional network system would deepen and Canada's ability to contribute to discussions on regional approaches to human rights, non-traditional security, and humanitarian issues would increase. Rather than effecting change through a top-down, Western-led strategy predicated on order preservation, Canada would instead be involved in bottom-up order formation.

The challenge, of course, lies in demonstrating Canada's added value to ASEAN, particularly to the degree that Canadian involvement in an ASEAN+ mechanism adds to its functionality at the regional level. In establishing Canada as an ASEAN dialogue partner, Ottawa has taken the first necessary step forward. Canadian involvement with ASEAN at present is not enough, however, to convince ASEAN member states that the institution would be stronger for greater Canadian participation. Ottawa must invest more time and resources in its ASEAN relations, particularly around non-economic issues, to demonstrate its strategic resolve and its long-term commitment to ASEAN's centrality and functionality.

Canada-China relations will also remain a stumbling block for Canadian involvement in ASEAN, as outlined above. Beijing's support will be critical for Canadian participation in ASEAN+ mechanisms, but at present it is not forthcoming. As noted above, regional perspectives on China are more accommodating than Western views. Canadian policy-makers must revisit the prevailing assumption in Ottawa that Canada can have a balanced approach to Asia without stable, amicable relations with China.

Non-ASEAN Asian Institutionalism

While deeper integration with ASEAN will be challenging for Canada, it is also the most direct (and arguably the easiest) means for Canada to develop network ties in Asia. ASEAN is the region's predominant institution, and with four distinct communities addressing economic, political and security, socio-cultural, and corporate issues, it provides an easily navigable blueprint for substate, micro-level engagement. ASEAN is also largely open to cooperation with extra-regional powers, including the United States and Europe, on issues relevant to its mandate, which provides Canada an opportunity to advance its relations with the institution.

Outside of ASEAN, on the other hand, Asia's institutional ecosystem is more diverse, less inclusive, and more issue-specific. Asia's endogenous institutions, in particular, are largely uninterested in Western narratives on the region's dynamics, governance, and development economics, and see Asian control as a strategic end in and of itself. One finds no discussion of the importance of Western leadership in these institutions, nor a broad willingness to pursue Western institutional support. Rather, many Asian institutions are predicated on a sense of regional political and economic autarky, or the pursuit of "Asian solutions to Asian problems."[35] One can attribute the preference for regionalism over internationalism to the fact many of Asia's predominant institutions have their roots in the region's anti-colonial era and are inherently "anti-Western" in form and function.

Canada will be challenged to establish cooperation with these institutions and within Asia's institutional networks, particularly if its policy-makers continue to approach the region through Western paradigms and with Western assumptions. Indeed, as noted above, Canadian normative realignment away from Western narratives around Asian viewpoints is a prerequisite for deeper Canadian institutional involvement in the region, particularly on matters of deep regional importance such as security and economic development. While the learning curve for such engagement is undoubtedly steep, the return on investment is proportionately high.

Conceptually, one can divide Asia's institutional architecture into dialogue and working groups. Across these two institutional types, one can further divide Asia's institutions into those addressing security, economics, governance, socio-cultural issues, and the environment. Increasingly, however, the divide between institutional type and institutional scope is becoming less clear as the region's predominant institutions are becoming more multifunctional and multidirectional.

For instance, take the Lancang-Mekong Cooperation (LMC) forum, which started as a subregional security dialogue and expanded into one of continental Southeast Asia's most important multilateral institutions, complete with joint working groups. Established in 2016 with China, Cambodia, Laos, Myanmar, Thailand, and Vietnam as original members, the LMC has grown from being the only endogenous institution in Southeast Asia addressing water and river security to becoming the subregion's most representative and inclusive mechanism for discussing transnational matters, including agriculture, poverty reduction, cross-border economic cooperation, production capacity, and connectivity.[36] Founded on the principles of conflict prevention, dialogue, and non-interference in domestic affairs, the LMC is in many ways a prototypical Asian institution, as it prioritizes Asian narratives, priorities, and shared interests while eschewing outside interference.[37] Largely unknown outside Asia, the LMC has emerged as a regional counterpart to the United Nations–established Mekong River Commission (MRC), the Mekong-US Partnership, and the Mekong-Japan Cooperation, all of which include Western states while excluding China.[38]

The Bay of Bengal Initiative for Multi-Sectoral Technical and Economic Cooperation (BIMSTEC), which includes Myanmar, Thailand, Bangladesh, Bhutan, India, Nepal, and Sri Lanka, is another example of a regional institution that started with a focus on economic cooperation among geographically collocated states but expanded to address non-economic issues, including environment and disaster relief, transnational crime and terrorism, and public health.[39] In addition to its annual Heads of State and Ministers Summits, BIMSTEC also coordinates expert working groups and engages in multilateral research and development through its functional centres on energy, weather, and climate change.[40]

The Conference on Interaction and Confidence Building Measures in Asia (CICA) dialogue has also grown from a niche dialogue on Central Asian security to a prestigious multilateral organization with working groups on environmental, economic, political, social, and security issues.[41] Based on non-interference, consultation, and crisis management, CICA's remit has expanded to environmental, economic, social, and political issues.[42] CICA summits are now among the most prestigious in the world, where regional leaders like Xi Jinping introduce paradigm-shifting concepts such as the "New Asian Security Concept" and Eurasian heads of state from countries as diverse as Israel and Iran come together to discuss confidence building.[43] As with the LMC, membership is limited to Asian states and the institution is exclusively concerned with Asian affairs, albeit with a more Eurasian focus.[44]

The Belt and Road Forum for International Cooperation has also become an influential, regionally based, broadly inclusive mechanism for economic, political, and development cooperation in Asia and across the Global South.[45] Initially formed to advance a "new type of development" between China, Asia, and the developing world, it now addresses issues such as vaccine allotment, pandemic recovery and response, social resilience, and "green" development. Twenty-nine heads of state from across Asia and Eurasia attended the 2020 Forum, making it one of the Asia-Pacific's most inclusive mechanisms for dialogue and engagement.

Closely related is the Silk Road NGO Cooperation Network Forum, which in its inaugural phase already includes 170 civil society groups from twenty-two countries across Asia.[46] Focusing on sustainable development goals such as poverty alleviation, education, and medical care, the NGO Cooperation Network Forum facilitates substate cooperation between different development actors and strives to create a civil society "web" and a "people's network" across Asia and the Global

South.[47] Its focus on outcomes rather than dialogue also ensures its relevance as a regional network multiplier, particularly on issues related to livelihood projects.

In Northeast Asia, the Greater Tumen Initiative (GTI) has emerged as a regional mechanism for multilateral consultation between China, Mongolia, Russia, and South Korea. The institute has evolved from a cross-border economic development program to become a forum for dialogue and joint activity around the region's sustainable development and economic integration. With Japan and North Korea as observers, the GTI is arguably Northeast Asia's most inclusive institution and the most direct means of dialogue and cooperation among its states.[48] The GTI's value, in this respect, is not limited to its scope and resources but lies in its function as a regional network for the exchange of people and ideas.

In addition to these institutions, Asian states increasingly interact through annual dialogues such as the Boao Forum for Asia and the Beijing Xiangshan Forum on Asian economic and security interests, respectively. Often referred to as the "Asian Davos," the Boao Forum has become Asia's pre-eminent economic dialogue forum, with twenty-nine member states and a charter to advance Asia's economic integration and regionalization.[49] The Beijing Xiangshan Forum serves much the same purpose for regional dialogue on hard-security issues.[50] Both forums have become critical mechanisms for advancing Asian narratives on the region's economic and security dynamics and for establishing institutional linkages between Asian political, military, business, and academic leaders.

Canadian involvement in any or all of these institutions would provide its policy-makers and diplomats with greater access to regional networks and a greater understanding of Asian states' priorities and perspectives. With engagement, Canada's ability to influence regional development through dialogue and practice would increase, thereby providing Ottawa with greater ability to advance its values throughout the region on issues such as human rights, gender issues, and governance. Through network participation, Canada would also demonstrate its willingness to learn from regional experiences, its ability to act outside a Western-centric system of institutions and values, and its humility in engaging Asian actors though Asian institutions on Asian terms. All these benefits would increase Canada's ability to achieve its national interests in Asia, whether defined in economic, political, or security terms.

Engagement will not be easy, however, and will require a fundamental rethinking of how Canada approaches Asia. As argued above, it will require a cognitive shift in how Canada sees the region, and a subsequent re-evaluation of its regional partnerships. Engagement also requires the acceptance of regional realities with respect to Asia's institutions, the most important of which is China's central role in regional networks and its ability to act as a regional spoiler to outside powers with which it has poor relations. Should Canadian policy-makers approach their Asia policy with these considerations in mind, Canada can achieve omnidirectional diplomacy and strategic integration in the Asian region. It is to this concept that the final chapter is dedicated.

Conclusion

Toward Omnidirectional Diplomacy and Strategic Integration

In July 2021, President Joe Biden addressed the Asia-Pacific Economic Cooperation (APEC) Virtual Leaders' Retreat and outlined his vision of US leadership in the "free" and "open" Indo-Pacific. In addition to bringing a values-driven approach to foreign and security engagement, Biden argued, the United States would ensure that all states in the region abided by a "rules-based order."[1] Biden further elaborated on the US-led "Build Back Better World Partnership" – a Western-led alternative to China's Belt and Road Initiative (BRI) – and pledged to supply COVID-19 vaccines in a US-led bid to end the pandemic.[2]

Predictably, Chinese media pounced on Biden's comments to accuse the United States of ignoring regional realities, overestimating US influence and strength in the region, and politicizing APEC to divide the Asian region into spheres of influence.[3] Chinese scholars pointed to the United States' domestic political instability and its poor pandemic response to question its relevance as a regional leader, and argued that China, not the United States, had provided the Asian region with upward of 300 million doses of COVID-19 vaccine.

President Xi Jinping's own comments to APEC further underscored differences between US and Chinese visions of Asia's internal dynamics. Rather than focusing on regional tensions, Xi highlighted the importance of multilateralism, economic integration, continued economic development, and collaboration in science and technology between

Asian states. He pointed to the Belt and Road Initiative as a source of regional growth, and promised China's support to raise living standards throughout Asia, particularly among Asia's developing economies.[4]

Western media, also predictably, dismissed Xi's comments as propaganda and focused their analysis on China's ongoing campaign against the Uyghurs in Xinjiang and its repressive policies in Hong Kong. On the same day as Xi's speech, as if to emphasize these points, Western media also carried coverage of the Biden administration's warning to US companies operating in Hong Kong.[5]

While a single event, the 2021 APEC virtual summit provided a powerful hermeneutic for understanding how narratives affect the way states conceptualize Asia's strategic environment, how they define their national interests, and how they subsequently formulate their national strategies toward the region. The United States and its Western partners, including Australia, France, Germany, Japan, and the United Kingdom, see Asia as a region adrift from its traditional Western institutions and leadership, and have developed Indo-Pacific narratives to justify and formulate their respective policy responses. China and most Asian states, conversely, see the region as moving more toward its natural equilibrium, where Asian interests override Western intentions and Asian leadership is key to regional stability.

For Canada, conceptualizing and operationalizing a successful strategy toward Asia means navigating these competing narratives and dynamics in order to realize its national interests in the region. As argued throughout this book, Canada cannot achieve this outcome through uncritical alignment with its traditional Western partners, as Western narratives are largely biased and at times chauvinistic. Far from representing regional dynamics and respecting regional developments, views from Washington and Brussels are too often grounded in Western-centric, neocolonial visions of global order and Western leadership and cannot offer Canada a sustainable, inclusive framework on which to build its own national strategy toward Asia. Rather, Ottawa must critically evaluate regional narratives on Asian order to find the correct path for Canada. Through this approach, Canada can effect a strategic policy of omnidirectional diplomacy, or avoidance of ideological alignment for the sake of informed, non-ideologically based engagement.

Concurrently, Canada must seek concrete opportunities to work with regional actors and within regional networks to establish tangible relations with Asian states and actors and to advance its national interests and values through dialogue and cooperation. Central to this proposition is the need to understand more fully Asia's institutional architecture, primarily those ASEAN and non-ASEAN institutions that enable Canada to work on issues of national priority. Through this policy of strategic integration, Canada can best position itself for non-ideological engagement, thereby increasing its influence throughout Asia on issues of ideological importance to the Canadian people, such as human rights, climate change, and gender equality.

On Omnidirectional Diplomacy

Omnidirectional diplomacy, as the name suggests, rests on a policy of non-aligned, active engagement designed to ensure that a state maintains positive, non-ideological, and independent relations with as many states as possible to ensure maximum room for maneuver. A preferred strategy of small, middle, and developing powers, in particular, the concept prioritizes realism over ideology, flexibility over rigidity, and adaptability over intransigence.[6] In contemporary international relations, the approach is most prevalent among Asian states. Indeed, omnidirectional diplomacy draws much of its strategic logic from Asian foreign policy principles, including non-interference, non-alignment, mutual respect, mutual non-aggression, respect for sovereignty, and territorial integrity.[7]

By most accounts, Japan pioneered omnidirectional diplomacy with its 1977 Fukuda Doctrine (based on a speech by Prime Minister Takeo Fukuda) through which it sought to engage with as many states as possible to maximize its influence as a middle power and to lessen its dependence on the United States.[8] China has similarly used omnidirectional diplomacy since its "reform and opening" era to establish relations with international and regional institutions and to initiate ties with developing and developed states to ensure its domestic and international legal sovereignty.[9] North Korean leadership employed omnidirectional diplomacy in its bilateral and multilateral relations with China, the European Union, Japan, and the United States during the Six-Party Talks, and continues to use omnidirectionality to manage inter-Korean affairs.[10]

In Southeast Asia, Vietnam and Singapore employ omnidirectional diplomacy to maintain purposeful, pragmatic approaches to great power relations, regional institutionalism, and ASEAN, with the express purpose of ensuring freedom of movement within Asia's regional system.[11]

Thailand used omnidirectional diplomacy to significant effect throughout the Cold War to avoid colonialism, and continues to employ the approach to manage the effects of US-China competition on its strategic posture.[12] Indonesia, perhaps more than any other Southeast Asian state, has made omnidirectional diplomacy the foundation of its foreign and security policy approach to Asia, a policy that Jakarta calls "pragmatic equidistance" and that rests on non-alignment, multilateralism, and flexible diplomacy.[13]

For Canada, a strategic approach to Asia predicated on omnidirectional diplomacy carries distinct advantages. First, as noted above, Asian states are unequivocally comfortable with the approach's core tenets, specifically its assumptions with respect to non-alignment and pragmatic engagement. Canada will likely find broad regional support for its diverse engagement throughout Asia if it demonstrates strategic resolve and commitment to the region. Asian states, further, will not fault Canada for working with multiple institutions and partners, at least as long as Canada refrains from joining inherently antagonistic coalitions, such as AUKUS or the Quad, or aligning with Indo-Pacific strategies predicated on Western predominance and exclusivity.

Australia's contemporary strategic approach to Asia provides a cautionary tale. Under the Morrison government, Australia became increasingly isolated in the Asia-Pacific by advocating an Indo-Pacific ideal, by antagonizing China through chauvinistic diplomacy, and by deliberately aligning with the United States against China through AUKUS.[14] Whereas its strategic analysts see strength in the country's new resolve, opposition toward Australia's new "aggression" is growing across Asia, as is the regional view that Canberra has prioritized its role as an Anglo-Saxon state over Asian regional stability.[15] Any advantages Australia may have gained through its alignment with the United States against China it stands to lose through its rejection of regional norms and values concerning non-alignment and non-aggression. In the long term, it is highly likely that Australia will suffer from a reputational cost in Asia that will augment its identity as an outsider power and reduce its ability to act as an honest broker in the region. Canada should studiously avoid following Australia's example and instead focus on omnidirectional diplomacy in Asia.

Second, by taking an omnidirectional approach, Canada can leverage its status as a Western actor to add value to its engagements in Asia. Canada's ability to bring its relations with the G7, the United

Nations, and NATO to bear in Asia, for instance, raises its strategic value as an interlocutor between the West and the Asia-Pacific. Canada's strategic proximity to the United States, further, provides it with the ability to act as a strategic broker in Asia, an ability that is unique to Canada's national identity and rests on its ability to "translate" North American intentions to Asian actors. Canada's firm support for aspects of the international system, such as the rule of law, climate change mitigation, gender equality, and sustainable development, will also serve it well in Asia, as many Asian states remain firmly committed to and interested in these aspects of the international order.

As argued throughout this book, however, there is a fine line between proactive Canadian engagement in Asia and Western state alignment toward the region. To ensure its reception among Asian states as an honest broker or a strategic partner, Canada must internalize Asian narratives around the region's primary dynamics to avoid bias and chauvinism in its approach. This normative shift depends on the willingness of Canada's leaders to engage with uncomfortable regional narratives around Western leadership, the desirability of free and open systems, and the Western-determined rules-based order, as well as their readiness to develop strategic empathy toward China's viewpoints, even those with which they fundamentally disagree.

Third, in utilizing an omnidirectional diplomacy approach, Canada is best suited to navigate Asia's increasingly complex strategic environment. On China-US competition, for example, Canada's national interests are best served by a policy of non-alignment and equidistance, particularly as overreliance and/or dependence on either actor would necessarily limit Canada's ability to engage effectively within regional institutions and with regional states. Omnidirectional diplomacy also positions Canada best to work with ASEAN and ASEAN member states, all of which employ the approach in their own foreign and security policies to varying degrees. It will also increase Canada's prospects for engagement with non-ASEAN institutions such as the Conference on Interaction and Confidence Building Measures in Asia (CICA).

As with its engagement as a Western actor, Canada's ability to use omnidirectional diplomacy to manage Asia's strategic dynamics more effectively depends on the ability of its policy-makers to understand, respect, and internalize regional narratives on issues of regional importance. Correspondingly, Canada's ability to undertake such an omnidirectional approach will suffer if its leaders adopt an Indo-Pacific approach to the region, as most Canadian policy analysts currently advocate.

On Strategic Integration

Whereas a policy of omnidirectional diplomacy prioritizes a broad approach to foreign affairs predicated on a diversity of international partnerships, a strategic integration approach idealizes "deep" relations, or the development of multi-sector, multi-level, multi-issue relations with states and institutions. In international relations theory, for instance, one finds reference to strategic integration in works on alliance relations, strategic partnerships, and international organizations.[16] Among the concept's primary assumptions are that integration leads to more enduring partnerships, that it enables states to learn from one another, that it enables confidence building between actors, and that it provides a means for states to demonstrate strategic commitment.[17] Importantly, while states are the ultimate beneficiaries of a strategic integration approach, they are not the only actors involved. To realize the approach's full potential, engagement between non-state actors such as institutions and firms, and between social groups such as international students and diasporas, is essential. Nevertheless, states can and should take the lead role in facilitating strategic integration where possible.

Operationally, one sees examples of strategic integration in the European Union, where state and substate actors work purposefully to build on the EU's supranational structures to strength the idea of a European community, and across Asia.[18] The drive for strategic integration among the ASEAN member states and between these member states' institutions, societies, and economies, for instance, sits at the heart of the ASEAN Community Vision 2025 concept, the Master Plan on ASEAN Connectivity, and, of course, the Initiative for ASEAN Integration (IAI) Strategic Framework.[19] China's BRI, South Korea's New Southern Policy, Taiwan's New Southbound Policy, and, indeed, Japan's Free and Open Indo-Pacific (FOIP) vision all also identify strategic integration between states and substate institutions as strategic ends, ways, and means – in other words, they classify national and regional integration as a strategic method, tool, and goal in and of itself.[20]

Central to the regional drive for strategic integration is the assumption that integration develops and strengthens regional networks and provides additional avenues for state and substate exchange. China's leadership, for instance, has identified Asian integration as essential to regional stability, to the establishment of an Asian community, and to the achievement of regional prosperity, and has prioritized multi-sector, multi-level integration in the country's foreign and economic policies.[21] ASEAN states have similarly identified Asia-Pacific regional integration as the foundation of an ASEAN community, whether defined in terms of institutions, bilateral state relations, or people-to-people exchanges. Indeed, from Jakarta to Seoul to Singapore, one finds repeated references to integration as the key to Asian regionalism and to Asian regional order in leadership statements and strategic policy guidance.[22]

Although one can argue that Canada has a base within Asia on which it can build an omnidirectional diplomatic approach, one cannot say the same for a Canadian policy of strategic integration. Indeed, Canada's absence from in Asia-Pacific affairs is a common theme one encounters in the region – an absence that polling by the Asia Pacific Foundation of Canada captured clearly in its six-country survey of Asian perceptions toward Canada, where respondents identified "lack of knowledge" of Canada as a major obstacle to closer state, commercial, and people-to-people relations.[23] In a region where networks and relations facilitate inter-state engagement, Canada's diminutive status is a strategic liability, one that Ottawa must address if it truly seeks to advance the country's interests in Asia.

This books provides the fundamental components Canadian policy-makers can use to effect strategic integration in the Asia-Pacific region: a detailed account of Asian narratives, a brief network analysis of the region's primary institutions, and a framework for omnidirectional diplomacy. More specifically, for Canada to implement a strategic integration policy, Ottawa will need to consider regional viewpoints, identify regional institutions, and engage with as wide a variety of Asian actors as possible. Only by addressing each of these prerequisites in their policy formulation will Canadian policy-makers best secure the country's long-term strategic integration in the Asian region.

On Asian narratives, for instance, this book has argued at length the need for Canadian policy-makers to listen to and learn from regional voices on key strategic issues, not, as many Canadian policy analysts would urge, to uncritically adopt Western narratives on issues such as Asia's rules-based order, its freedom and openness, and Western leadership. Canadian policy-makers should studiously avoid alignment with

Western Indo-Pacific visions, in particular, as these visions depend on assumptions about Asia that privilege ongoing Western predominance over the region's long-term stability and development. While Canada may achieve short-term benefits from Indo-Pacific alignment in terms of Western state partnership, the medium- to long-term costs of such alignment will almost certainly erase those gains and diminish the country's regional stature.

Further, by internalizing Asian narratives in their planning processes, Canadian policy-makers can determine where and how to expend Canadian resources and efforts. They should understand Asian narratives concerning non-aggression and dialogue as evidence that Canadian involvement in Western military coalitions, such as AUKUS or the Quad, or in Western-aligned military activities, such as freedom of navigation operations, will result in regional opposition particularly if Canada chooses to engage in such activity without counterbalancing engagement, or omnidirectional diplomacy. Conversely, Canadian policy-makers should look to engage in the Asia-Pacific through dialogue and around conflict mitigation and resolution issues, such as with China and the ASEAN member states on a code of conduct for the South China Sea that reflects regional, not Western, concerns. Part and parcel to such efforts is the understanding that Canada makes reputational gains from its presence and participation in regional dialogues even when progress is halting and outcomes uncertain.

On Asian institutionalism, Canadian policy-makers must look beyond surface-level engagement with ASEAN to integrate more fully into its working groups and dialogues, particularly across its political, economic, socio-cultural, and corporate affairs communities. As noted in the previous chapter, Canada's ASEAN engagement remains largely underdeveloped, meaning that Ottawa has clear room for deeper integration within ASEAN and with its member states. One clear way to achieve such integration is to link Canadian involvement in an ASEAN+1 mechanism with any discussion of a Canada-ASEAN free trade agreement. Indeed, Canada should prioritize closer strategic integration over economic engagement with ASEAN, as the former will provide a more solid foundation for the latter in the long term.

Simultaneously, Ottawa must find ways to work with Asia's non-ASEAN institutions, particularly those like CICA, the GTI, and the LMC mechanism that are endogenous to the region and are becoming more influential, prestigious, and inclusive. As full participation is unlikely in the short term, Canada should seek observer status where and when possible. Alternatively, it can request dialogue partnership with each institution around specific issue areas with institutional relevance, such as confidence building and/or water security. Canada can increase these institutions' receptiveness to its overtures if it can demonstrate knowledge of regional narratives and neutrality in its strategic engagement. To demonstrate neutrality, Canada will need to pursue a strategy of omnidirectional diplomacy, particularly with respect to China, as outlined above.

On bilateral relations, Canada should pursue formal strategic partnerships with as many Asian states as possible, emphasizing political, social, and economic integration as its primary objectives. A relatively underutilized tool in Western state foreign policy engagement, strategic partnerships are an important means of establishing and deepening state-to-state, multi-sector relations in Asia.[24] China uses strategic partnerships, for instance, to establish bilateral ties short of formal alliances, and has created a network of strategic partner states in Asia through concerted effort.[25] India, Japan, South Korea, and the ASEAN member states similarly use strategic partnership agreements to establish state and substate mechanisms for closer integration across their respective political, economic, societal, and security sectors.[26] Relatedly, Canada should also expand the number of sister city and twinning agreements it has with Asian states and cities. As with strategic partnerships, Asian states use such agreements to facilitate trade, investment, and social exchange, and to increase substate integration, coordination, and communication.[27]

In addition to these state-led initiatives, Canada must create opportunities for its firms, non-governmental organizations, and people to integrate into the Asia-Pacific's existing networks and institutions. Canada can accomplish this most expeditiously by increasing its Asian-based diplomatic missions and trade commissioner services' resources and by posting individuals with requisite regional knowledge and language skills throughout the region. In the short term, Global Affairs Canada can work with Canada's Asian diaspora communities to recruit individuals with deep knowledge of and ties to the region, a recruitment strategy that could help achieve diversity and inclusivity in a foreign policy system that prioritizes French-language cultivation and preservation over critical-needs languages like Korean, Japanese, Mandarin, and Vietnamese. In the long term, the Canadian government must cultivate the Canadians' Asian "literacy" to ensure their ability to engage effectively with the region, on which more is written below.

Concurrently, Canadian diplomats should work directly with in-country, non-governmental institutions such as Canadian chambers of commerce, overseas diaspora groups, university alumni networks, and business leaders to create a networked community of Asian-based Canadians and Asians with ties to Canada. This community can advise Canadian public and private sector actors on opportunities and strategies for regional engagement, and facilitate Canadian integration in Asian institutions, mechanisms, and forums. To further support integration, the Canadian government could increase funding for Canadian firms' market entry in Asia through Export Development Canada (EDC), enabling them to compete with companies from Japan and Singapore, for instance, that receive substantial government support for market expansion in Asia.

Canadian policy-makers should also leverage existing efforts, such as the Asia Business Leaders Advisory Council (ABLAC) to listen to and learn from Asian business leaders' perspectives on regional opportunities and challenges for Canada.[28] To ensure that its strategic approach to Asia is diverse and inclusive, Ottawa should also fund more missions to Asia for underrepresented Canadian communities, such as First Nations groups, mirroring the efforts of the Asia Pacific Foundation of Canada with its Women-only Business Missions to Asia.[29] Finally, Canadian policy-makers should work with Canadian industry groups such as the Institute of Corporate Directors to raise awareness of the opportunities provided by free trade agreements like the Comprehensive and Progressive Agreement for Trans-Pacific Partnership (CPTPP) in the Asian region.

To strengthen Canadian social integration with Asia, the Canadian government should prioritize and fund educational exchange and Asian literacy programs at the primary, secondary, and tertiary levels. On educational exchange, the Canadian government should increase scholarship funding for exceptional Asian students from developing economies to study at Canadian universities, while also providing them with a clear path to permanent residence after graduation. Ottawa could also increase research grants for university scholars and centres with partnerships in Asia through the Natural Sciences and Engineering Research Council of Canada (NSERC) and the Social Sciences and Humanities Research Council (SSHRC), for example, to ensure Canadian universities' competitiveness and enhance their prestige in Asia. As a corollary, Canadian policy-makers should revisit the requirement of the 2021 New National Security Guidelines for Research Partnerships that universities and university researchers submit risk assessment forms to the Canadian intelligence community as a prerequisite for federal research partnership funding.[30] Securitization of Canada's research and development activities, particularly through processes that lack transparency and accountability, raises the potential for politicization of Canada's research partnerships. Canadian policy-makers should develop an alternative means of assessing Canadian research ties with Asian states, one that minimizes the intelligence community's oversight while ensuring that national security concerns are addressed in a transparent, equitable, and accountable manner.

On Asian literacy, the Canadian government should invest in Asian language programs at the primary and secondary levels to ensure that our next generation of businesspeople, diplomats, and scholars have the skills necessary to succeed in Asia. Ottawa can provide funding for provinces to develop language "feeder" schools, enabling secondary students to transfer directly to a university program to continue their Asian language and cultural studies. These programs should emphasize overseas experiences for students, and Canadian universities should develop ties with credible colleges throughout Asia to provide students the opportunity to live and study in the region.

While the above recommendations would provide Canada with the means to effect a policy of strategic integration in Asia, they are by no means an exhaustive list. Canadian policy-makers must constantly seek out areas where closer engagement between Canada and Asian states and institutions is possible, and cultivate them as a matter of national strategic priority. The more Canada can integrate throughout Asia at the state and substate levels, the better positioned it will be to achieve its strategic ends in the region.

Conclusion

Geographically and demographically, Canada is an Asia-Pacific state. Through British Columbia, for instance, Canada has a direct pathway to Asia's markets and direct linkages to Asian communities from China to India to Indonesia. Economically, Canada also has distinctive interests and advantages in the Asia-Pacific. There is huge demand in the region, for instance, for Canadian natural resources such as oil and gas, timber, rare earths, agri-food, and, indeed, fresh water. Canada's participation in the Comprehensive and Progressive Agreement for Trans-Pacific Partnership, a region-wide free trade agreement, gives its firms further access to regional markets, including Japan. As economic growth and regional integration continue throughout the Asia-Pacific, Canada's opportunities in the region will grow, provided its leaders understand and seize these opportunities through a concerted, informed foreign policy.

As of 2022, however, Canada lacked a strategic plan toward the Asia-Pacific designed to ensure its long-term national interests, as defined in previous chapters. Rather than focus on Canadian engagement in the Asia-Pacific, for instance, the Trudeau government has sought to develop Canadian leadership in Western-aligned institutions such as the G7 and NATO and in the United Nations Security Council.[31] Within the Canadian foreign policy community, in particular, the Asian region largely remains an afterthought, one primarily seen through the strategic prism of the country's relations with the United States and Western opposition to China, not with respect to Canadian-Asian relations.[32]

Indeed, where Canadian policy-makers and policy analysts do think about the Asia-Pacific, they share an almost universal tendency to frame Canada's national approach and national interests in line with Western narratives, and to argue for Canadian alignment with Western strategic assumptions and plans, primarily the Indo-Pacific paradigm. To parry criticism of Western-centrism in their analysis and policy design, Canadian "experts" on Asia routinely point to the adoption of the Indo-Pacific concept by Australia and Japan as evidence of regional acceptance, wrongly arguing Canberra and Tokyo represent regional sentiments and assumptions.

Rather than offering Canada a sustainable strategic path forward in the Asia-Pacific, these analysts' reliance on Western-centric thinking creates a strategic risk for the country. Nowhere is this clearer than in their widespread push for Canada to adopt an Indo-Pacific approach to the Asia-Pacific – a recommendation that runs counter to Canada's national interests, to Asia-Pacific dynamics, to regional sentiments and assumptions, and to global geopolitical trends and developments.[33] Far from enabling Canada to advance its interests in Asia, such an alliance would disadvantage it in the short, medium, and long terms by leaving it isolated, dependent, and vulnerable to countermeasures.

Canada's strategic interests in Asia would be better served, conversely, by deep, sustained engagement in the Asia-Pacific *in line with Asian narratives and sentiments.* Rather than aligning with outsider powers like Canberra, Brussels, and Washington to execute a strategy informed entirely by Western narratives and assumptions, Ottawa should turn to voices from states like China, Indonesia, Japan, Malaysia, South Korea, and Thailand to determine where, when, and how it can engage with Asia to best effect, both for its national interests and for regional stability. Canadian policy-makers should then internalize these regional narratives in their policy processes and prescriptions and map their engagement priorities accordingly.

The implementation of Canadian policies should be informed by omnidirectional diplomacy and strategic integration. As outlined above, such an approach would prioritize broad engagement and deep participation with Asian states and institutions, all designed to enmesh Canada in the region's existing networks, institutions, and relations. In the short term, Canada can advance its most vital national interests through diplomacy. In the long term, regional integration strengthens Canada's strategic position by providing it with diverse, substantial, and meaningful partnerships.

While the idea of listening to Asian narratives to frame one's Asian engagement is a seemingly modest one, critical theory suggests that its adoption will be problematic. Cultural hegemony and hegemonic socialization are theories built on the idea that those part of the hegemon's "inner circle" will internalize its ideas, beliefs, and values as their own, and that states will shape their polices and practices to accord with the hegemon's priorities. Over time, the hegemon's ideas become so predominant and entrenched that questioning them becomes an existential issue – a questioning of one's identity in relation to one's culture, society, and history. Michel Foucault labelled this process "discursive power," identified it as central to hegemonic systems, and argued that it was key to understanding hegemonic control.

In practical terms, these theories suggest that Canadian policy-makers and policy analysts will reject the proposition that their viewpoints are biased toward hegemonic narratives and that their policy recommendations are more reflective of the hegemonic state's strategic objectives than their own. They will likely claim instead a clear-eyed understanding of Canada's national interests and bristle at the idea that Canada's interests are best served through omnidirectional diplomacy,

Conclusion

in particular, seeing Canada's closeness to the United States and its status as a Western state as a strategic advantage. No one, after all, responds positively to the suggestion that their ideas are anything but their own, that they are anything but the outcome of clear, unbiased deliberation.

Such may indeed be the case. Perhaps Canada's interests are ultimately best served by wholesale alignment with a Western Indo-Pacific ideal. If so, however, it is incumbent on Canadian policy-makers and policy analysts to articulate why Canada gains more from aligning its interests in Asia with outsider Western powers than it does from cooperation with Asian states and institutions in line with their regional priorities and perspectives. They must then formulate a strategic approach to Asia that addresses the issues raised by this book, particularly the demonstrable fact that Asian states largely reject the fundamental assumptions of the Western Indo-Pacific world view. They must then communication their rationale, vision, and strategic plan to the Canadian public, a public whose interests in Asia depend on their leadership's crafting of a policy that maximizes their opportunities and minimizes their risk. The Canadian people deserve this much from their government and should see anything less as a dereliction of duty.

Notes

Introduction: Framing a Canadian Strategy in the Asia-Pacific

1 Uri Friedman, "America Is Alone in Its Cold War With China," *The Atlantic*, February 17, 2020, https://www.theatlantic.com/politics/archive/2020/02/us-china-allies-competition/606637/.
2 Jonathan Berkshire Miller and Thomas Wilkins, "The Role for Middle Powers in the Free and Open Indo-Pacific: Looking at Opportunities for Canada and Australia," *Japan Review* 3, 1 (Summer 2019): 1–11.
3 Jeffrey Reeves, "Canada and the Free and Open Indo-Pacific: A Strategic Assessment," *Asia Policy* 15, 4 (October 2020): 51–64.
4 "US 'Won't Cede an Inch' in Pacific, Esper Says in Swipe at China," *CNA*, August 27, 2020, https://www.channelnewsasia.com/news/world/united-states-mark-esper-china-indo-pacific-territory-influence-13058668.
5 Doug Saunders, "'Tough on China' Is a Winning Idea for Erin O'Toole – if He Can Decide What 'Tough' Means," *Globe and Mail*, September 18, 2020, https://www.theglobeandmail.com/opinion/article-tough-on-china-is-a-winning-idea-for-erin-otoole-if-he-can-decide/.
6 Lucas Donovan, "Situating Canada in the Free and Open Indo-Pacific: Lucas Donovan for Inside Policy," Macdonald-Laurier Institute, March 16, 2020, https://www.macdonaldlaurier.ca/situating-canada-free-open-indo-pacific-lucas-donovan-inside-policy/.
7 Preston Lim, "Now Is the Time for a Canadian Pivot to the Indo-Pacific: Preston Lim for Inside Policy," Macdonald-Laurier Institute, November 17, 2020, https://www.macdonaldlaurier.ca/now-is-the-time-for-a-canadian-pivot-to-the-indo-pacific-preston-lim-for-inside-policy/.

8 Charles Burton, "The Chinese Communist Party Is Not Really Very Chinese at All: Charles Burton in the Globe And Mail," Macdonald-Laurier Institute, July 6, 2020, https://www.macdonaldlaurier.ca/chinese-communist-party-not-really-chinese/.
9 Jonathan Berkshire Miller, "It's Time for Ottawa to Rethink How It Sees Asia," *Globe and Mail*, April 18, 2019, https://www.theglobeandmail.com/opinion/article-its-time-for-ottawa-to-rethink-how-it-sees-asia/.
10 Diane Francis, "In Picking Sides between China and the U.S., Canada's Choice Is Clear," *Financial Post*, January 16, 2020, https://financialpost.com/diane-francis/diane-francis-in-picking-sides-between-china-and-the-u-s-canadas-choice-is-clear.
11 Pierre Colautti and Jonathan Paquin, *Between Alignment and Distancing: The Strategic Dilemma of Washington's Allies in the Biden Era*, Policy Brief 8 (Network for Strategic Analysis, 2021), https://ras-nsa.ca/publication/between-alignment-and-distancing-the-strategic-dilemma-of-washingtons-allies-in-the-biden-era/.
12 Jeremy Paltiel, "Canada's Middle Power Ambivalence: The Palimpsest of US Power under the Chinese Shadow," in *America's Allies and the Decline of US Hegemony*, ed. Justin Massie and Jonathan Paquin (New York: Routledge, 2020), 126.
13 See, for instance, Brian Lee Crowley, *What's a Middle Power to Do? Protecting What Matters in a Dangerous World*, Commentary (Ottawa: Macdonald-Laurier Institute, 2014), 7, https://www.macdonaldlaurier.ca/files/pdf/MLICommentaryKorea11_14_3.pdf.
14 David Dewitt et al., "AWOL: Canada's Defence Policy and Presence in the Asia Pacific," *International Journal* 73, 1 (2018): 16, https://doi.org/10.1177/0020702018768474.
15 Reeves, "Canada and the Free and Open Indo-Pacific."
16 Lu Zhenhua, "Biden's 'Asia-Tsar' Likely to Continue Trump's China Policy, Experts Say," *Caixin Global*, January 17, 2021, https://www.caixinglobal.com/2021-01-17/bidens-asia-tsar-likely-to-continue-trumps-china-policy-experts-say-101651793.html.
17 Mira Rapp-Hooper, *Shields of the Republic: The Triumph and Peril of America's Alliances* (Cambridge, MA: Harvard University Press, 2020), 176.
18 See, for example, Lindsey W. Ford and James Goldgeier, "Retooling America's Alliances to Manage the China Challenge," Brookings Institution, January 25, 2021, https://www.brookings.edu/research/retooling-americas-alliances-to-manage-the-china-challenge/; US National Intelligence Council, *Global Trends 2040: A More Contested World* (Washington, DC: Government Printing Office, 2021), https://www.dni.gov/files/ODNI/documents/assessments/GlobalTrends_2040.pdf.
19 This book addresses Japan's national identity as a "Western" and "Asian" state in subsequent chapters. Broadly speaking, it argues that Japan is a "Western" state in its institutional, relationship, and strategic orientation and an "Asian"

state in all other practical terms. There is a robust body of literature to support the classification of Japan as a "Western" state, although I acknowledge the conceptual awkwardness of the classification. As such, I take great pains to outline Japan's unique role in Asia and its complex internal discourse around its national identity through close contextual reading of Japanese leadership statements, academic articles, and public opinion polls.

20 Edward Fishman and Siddharth Mohandas, "A Council of Democracies Can Save Multilateralism: Boris Johnson's 'D-10' Is the Club the World Desperately Needs," *Foreign Affairs,* August 3, 2020, https://www.foreignaffairs.com/articles/asia/2020-08-03/council-democracies-can-save-multilateralism; C. Raja Mohan, "A New Pivot to Asia," *Foreign Policy,* January 15, 2021, https://foreignpolicy.com/2021/01/15/biden-china-asia-allies-strategy-pivot/.

21 White House, "U.S.-EU Summit Statement," news release, June 15, 2021, https://www.whitehouse.gov/briefing-room/statements-releases/2021/06/15/u-s-eu-summit-statement/; White House, "Carbis Bay G7 Summit Communiqué," news release, June 13, 2021, https://www.whitehouse.gov/briefing-room/statements-releases/2021/06/13/carbis-bay-g7-summit-communique/.

22 John Ivison, "How Canada Can Resist China's Intimidation by Teaming up with Like-Minded Allies," *National Post,* June 1, 2020, https://nationalpost.com/opinion/john-ivison-how-canada-can-resist-chinas-intimidation-by-teaming-up-with-like-minded-allies.

23 "G7 Public Engagement Paper – Building a More Peaceful and Secure World," Government of Canada, January 8, 2019, https://www.international.gc.ca/world-monde/international_relations-relations_internationales/g7/documents/secure_world-monde_sur.aspx?lang=eng.

24 Michael D. Swaine, "The Deepening U.S.-China Crisis: Origins and Solutions," Carnegie Endowment for International Peace, February 21, 2019, https://carnegieendowment.org/2019/02/21/deepening-u.s.-china-crisis-origins-and-solutions-pub-78429.

25 David Webster, "UN Security Council: Actually, the World Doesn't Need More Canada," The Conversation, June 23, 2020, https://theconversation.com/un-security-council-actually-the-world-doesnt-need-more-canada-141092.

26 Jonathan Berkshire Miller and Stephen Nagy, "Post-Abe, Japan Matters Even More for Canada," *Japan Times,* September 24, 2020, https://www.japantimes.co.jp/opinion/2020/09/24/commentary/japan-commentary/post-abe-japan-matters-even-canada/.

27 Craig Singleton, "G7 Powers Must Confront the Chinese Threat Together," *National Post,* October 21, 2020, https://nationalpost.com/opinion/craig-singleton-g7-powers-must-confront-the-chinese-threat-together.

28 See, for example, Charles Burton, "America Shouldn't Go It Alone in Containing China," *Globe and Mail,* August 6, 2020, https://www.theglobeandmail.com/opinion/article-america-shouldnt-go-it-alone-in-containing-china/; Robert Fife and Steven Chase, "Trudeau Vows to Stand up to China's 'Coercive Diplomacy,'" *Globe and Mail,* October 13, 2020, https://www.theglobeandmail.com/politics/article-trudeau-vows-to-stand-up-to-chinas-coercive-diplomacy/; Charles Burton,

"In Canada, the Tide of Opinion Is Turning on China," *Globe and Mail,* May 21, 2020, https://www.theglobeandmail.com/opinion/article-in-canada-the-tide-of-opinion-is-turning-on-china/; Robyn Urback, "Canadians Have Been Gaslit on China," *Globe and Mail,* April 30, 2020, https://www.theglobeandmail.com/opinion/article-canadians-have-been-gaslit-on-china/; Robert Fife and Steven Chase, "Brian Mulroney Urges 'Immediate and Urgent Rethink' of Relations with China," *Globe and Mail,* June 30, 2020, https://www.theglobeandmail.com/politics/article-mulroney-urges-immediate-and-urgent-rethink-of-relations-with-china/; Charles Burton, "Joe Biden Is Coming – and Beijing Should Be Worried," *Globe and Mail,* December 4, 2020, https://www.theglobeandmail.com/opinion/article-joe-biden-is-coming-and-beijing-should-be-worried/.

29 Shada Islam, "Biden's 'Summit of Democracies' Won't Work," POLITICO, December 8, 2020, https://www.politico.eu/article/bidens-summit-of-democracies-wont-work/.
30 Ramachandra Guha, "India Was a Miracle Democracy. But It's Time to Downgrade Its Credentials," *Washington Post,* August 14, 2019, https://www.washingtonpost.com/opinions/2019/08/14/india-was-miracle-democracy-its-time-downgrade-its-credentials/.
31 Michael Vatikiotis, "With Western Democracy in Retreat, Asia May Have to Forge Its Own Path," *South China Morning Post,* March 15, 2020, https://www.scmp.com/week-asia/opinion/article/3075162/western-democracy-retreat-asia-may-have-forge-its-own-path.
32 Kevin G. Cai, "Constructing an Analytical Framework for Explaining Chinese Foreign Policy," *Chinese Political Science Review* 5, 3 (2020): 355–73, https://doi.org/10.1007/s41111-020-00150-5.
33 Cheng-Chwee Kuik, "Asymmetry and Authority: Theorizing Southeast Asian Responses to China's Belt and Road Initiative," *Asian Perspective* 45, 2 (2021): 255–76, https://doi.org/10.1353/apr.2021.0000.
34 John Geddie, "China's Growing Influence Rattles Southeast Asia as U.S. Retreats, Survey Shows," *Reuters,* January 15, 2020, https://www.reuters.com/article/us-china-southeast-asia-idUSKBN1ZE255.
35 Western narratives on Asia's order uniformly ignore the fact that all the Indo-Pacific Western states were at one time or another colonial powers in Asia. Australia, France, Germany, the Netherlands, the United Kingdom, and the United States have all used military power and economic coercion within Asia to establish sovereign control over regional states. Indeed, France's modern-day claim to its "Pacific" identify is only the most glaring example of Western colonialism's enduring legacy in Asia. For Canada – a state without a colonial history in Asia – alignment with these states becomes even more problematic when one considers how post-colonialism is increasingly prominent in Asian states' national identity discourse.
36 Asia Pacific Foundation of Canada, *Canadian Views on the Importance of Values and Economic Interests in Foreign Policy Approaches* (Vancouver: Asia Pacific Foundation of Canada, June 2021), 16.

37 I worked directly with Mandarin, Japanese, and Korean texts and used translation software for Indonesian, Malaysian, Thai, and Vietnamese.

Chapter 1: The Basics: A Critical Examination of Western Narratives on Asia

1 Berit Bliesemann de Guevara, *Myth and Narrative in International Politics: Interpretative Approaches to the Study of IR* (London: Palgrave Macmillan, 2016), 10.
2 Andrew Linklater, "Grand Narratives and International Relations," *Global Change, Peace and Security* 21, 1 (2009): 3–17, https://doi.org/10.1080/14781150802659234.
3 Leslie E. Wehner and Cameron G. Thies, "Role Theory, Narratives, and Interpretation: The Domestic Contestation of Roles," *International Studies Review* 16, 3 (2014): 411–36, https://doi.org/10.1111/misr.12149.
4 Alister Miskimmon, Ben O'Loughlin, and Laura Roselle, *Strategic Narratives: Communication Power and the New World Order* (London: Taylor and Francis, 2014), 44.
5 C. William Walldorf, *To Shape Our World for Good: Master Narratives and Regime Change in US Foreign Policy, 1900–2011* (Ithaca, NY: Cornell University Press, 2019), 15.
6 Alister Miskimmon, Ben O'Loughlin, and Laura Roselle, *Forging the World: Strategic Narratives and International Relations* (Ann Arbor, MI: University of Michigan Press, 2018), 22.
7 William Wohlforth, "Rethinking Cold War Historical Materialism," *International Studies Review* 4, 3 (2002): 186–88, http://www.jstor.org/stable/3186471.
8 Jae-Jung Suh, *Origins of North Korea's Juche: Colonialism, War, and Development* (New York: Lexington Books, 2013), 5.
9 Ronald R. Krebs, *Narrative and the Making of US National Security* (Cambridge: Cambridge University Press, 2015), 196.
10 See, for instance, Ivor Goodson et al., eds., *The Routledge International Handbook on Narrative and Life History* (London: Taylor and Francis, 2016), 11.
11 Milan Babik, *Poetics of International Politics: Fact and Fiction in Narrative Representations of World Affairs* (London: Taylor and Francis, 2018), 95.
12 Riikka Kuusisto, *International Relations Narratives: Plotting World Politics* (London: Routledge, 2019), https://doi.org/10.4324/9780429397721.
13 Walter L. Adamson, *Hegemony and Revolution: A Study of Antonio Gramsci's Political and Cultural Theory* (Berkeley University of California Press, 1980), 43.
14 Crystal Bartolovich, Neil Lazarus, and Timothy Brennan, eds., *Marxism, Modernity and Postcolonial Studies* (Cambridge: Cambridge University Press, 2002), 9.
15 Nancy Fraser and Rachel Jaeggi, *Capitalism: A Conversation in Critical Theory* (Oxford: Polity Press, 2018), 13.
16 John S. Dryzek, "Discursive Designs: Critical Theory and Political Institutions," *American Journal of Political Science* 31, 3 (1987): 656, https://doi.org/10.2307/2111287.
17 Hayden V. White, *The Content of the Form: Narrative Discourse and Historical Representation* (Baltimore: Johns Hopkins University Press, 1990), 58.

18 Edward S. Herman and Noam Chomsky, *Manufacturing Consent: Political Economy of the Mass Media* (New York: Knopf Doubleday, 2011), 20.
19 Frank Ninkovich, *Modernity and Power: A History of the Domino Theory in the Twentieth Century* (Chicago: University of Chicago Press, 1994), 292.
20 John Schwarzmantel and Mark McNally, eds., *Gramsci and Global Politics: Hegemony and Resistance* (London: Taylor and Francis, 2009), 124; G. John Ikenberry and Charles A. Kupchan, "Socialization and Hegemonic Power," *International Organization* 44, 3 (1990): 283–315, https://doi.org/10.1017/s002081830003530x; Michel Foucault, *Power/Knowledge: Selected Interviews and Other Writings, 1972–1977*, ed. Colin Gordon (New York: Pantheon Books, 1980), 246.
21 Robert W. Cox and Timothy J. Sinclair, *Approaches to World Order* (New York: Cambridge University Press, 1996), 124; Daniel H. Nexon and Iver B. Neumann, "Hegemonic-Order Theory: A Field-Theoretic Account," *European Journal of International Relations* 24, 3 (April 2017): 662–86, https://doi.org/10.1177/1354066117716524.
22 Richard Howson and Kylie Smith, eds., *Hegemony: Studies in Consensus and Coercion* (New York: Routledge, 2008), 121.
23 See, for instance, Amitav Acharya and Barry Buzan, eds., *Non-Western International Relations Theory: Perspectives on and beyond Asia* (New York: Routledge, 2009); Stephen Chan, Peter G. Mandaville, and Roland Bleiker, eds., *The Zen of International Relations* (Hampshire: Palgrave, 2001); Amitav Acharya, "Dialogue and Discovery: In Search of International Relations Theories beyond the West," *Millennium: Journal of International Studies* 39, 3 (2011): 619–37, https://doi.org/10.1177/0305829811406574.
24 Arlene B. Tickner, "Core, Periphery and (Neo)Imperialist International Relations," *European Journal of International Relations* 19, 3 (2013): 627–46, https://doi.org/10.1177/1354066113494323.
25 David C. Kang, *East Asia before the West: Five Centuries of Trade and Tribute* (New York: Columbia University Press, 2012), 89.
26 Michael N. Barnett and Raymond Duvall, *Power in Global Governance* (Cambridge: Cambridge University Press, 2011), 282.
27 Cemal Burak Tansel, "Deafening Silence? Marxism, International Historical Sociology and the Spectre of Eurocentrism," *European Journal of International Relations* 21, 1 (2014): 76–100, https://doi.org/10.1177/1354066113514779.
28 William Easterly, *The White Man's Burden: Why the West's Efforts to Aid the Rest Have Done So Much Ill and So Little Good* (London: Penguin, 2006), 145.
29 Kosuke Shimizu, ed., *Critical International Relations Theories in East Asia: Relationality, Subjectivity, and Pragmatism* (New York: Routledge, 2019), 11.
30 Daniel A. Bell and Wang Pei, *Just Hierarchy: Why Social Hierarchies Matter in China and the Rest of the World* (Princeton, NJ: Princeton University Press, 2020), 117.
31 Branwen Gruffydd Jones, *Decolonizing International Relations* (Lanham, MD: Rowman and Littlefield, 2006), 24.
32 Barry Buzan and Yongjin Zhang, eds., *Contesting International Society in East Asia* (Cambridge: Cambridge University Press, 2014), 207.

33 Benjamin de Carvalho, Halvard Leira, and John M. Hobson, "The Big Bangs of IR: The Myths That Your Teachers Still Tell You about 1648 and 1919," *Millennium: Journal of International Studies* 39, 3 (2011): 735–58, https://doi.org/10.1177/0305829811401459.

34 John M. Hobson, "Global Dialogical History and the Challenge of Neo-Eurocentrism," in *Asia, Europe, and the Emergence of Modern Science*, ed. Arun Bala (New York: Palgrave Macmillan, 2012), 13–33, https://doi.org/10.1057/9781137031730_2.

35 Yong-Soo Eun, "Opening Up the Debate over 'Non-Western' International Relations," *Politics* 39, 1 (2018): 4–17, https://doi.org/10.1177/0263395718805401.

36 David C. Kang, "Getting Asia Wrong: The Need for New Analytical Frameworks," *International Security* 27, 4 (2003): 57–85, https://doi.org/10.1162/016228803321951090.

37 Wiebke Wemheuer-Vogelaar et al., "The IR of the Beholder: Examining Global IR Using the 2014 TRIP Survey," *International Studies Review* 18, 1 (2016): 16–32, https://doi.org/10.1093/isr/viv032.

38 Emanuel Adler and Steven Bernstein, "Knowledge in Power: The Epistemic Construction of Global Governance," in *Power in Global Governance*, ed. Michael N. Barnett and Raymond Duvall (Cambridge: Cambridge University Press, 2011), 294–319.

39 Peter Beinart, "The Vacuous Phrase at the Core of Biden's Foreign Policy," *New York Times*, June 22, 2021, https://www.nytimes.com/2021/06/22/opinion/biden-foreign-policy.html.

40 Norah O'Donnell, "Secretary of State Antony Blinken on the Threat Posed by China," *CBS News*, May 2, 2021, https://www.cbsnews.com/news/antony-blinken-60-minutes-2021-05-02/.

41 Patrick Porter, "Wrestling with Fog: On the Elusiveness of Liberal Order," War on the Rocks, July 15, 2020, http://warontherocks.com/2020/07/wrestling-with-fog-on-the-elusiveness-of-liberal-order/.

42 "Forging a World of Liberty under Law: U.S. National Security in the 21st Century – Final Report of the Princeton Project on National Security," Council on Foreign Relations, October 3, 2006, https://www.cfr.org/event/forging-world-liberty-under-law-us-national-security-21st-century-final-report-princeton.

43 G. John Ikenberry and Anne-Marie Slaughter, *Forging a World of Liberty under Law: U.S. National Security In the 21st Century: Final Report of the Princeton Project on National Security* (Princeton, NJ: Woodrow Wilson School of Public and International Affairs, Princeton University, 2006), 23, https://www2.world-governance.org/IMG/pdf_0080_Forging_a_World_of_Liberty_Under_Law-2.pdf.

44 Stephen Wertheim, *Tomorrow, the World: The Birth of U.S. Global Supremacy* (Cambridge, MA: Harvard University Press, 2020), 101.

45 Ivo H. Daalder and James M. Lindsay, *The Empty Throne: America's Abdication of Global Leadership* (New York: Public Affairs, 2018), 42; Paul D. Miller, *American Power and Liberal Order: A Conservative Internationalist Grand Strategy* (Washington, DC: Georgetown University Press, 2016), 15.

46 Malcolm Jorgensen, "China Is Overturning the Rules-Based Order from Within," *The Interpreter*, August 12, 2020, https://www.lowyinstitute.org/the-interpreter/china-overturning-rules-based-order-within.

47 Hugh White, "Defend the 'Rules-Based Order' in Asia at Any Cost?" *The Strategist*, Australian Strategic Policy Institute, April 26, 2018, https://www.aspistrategist.org.au/defend-rules-based-order-asia-cost/.

48 Caitlin Byrne, "Securing the 'Rules-Based Order' in the Indo-Pacific: The Significance of Strategic Narrative," *Security Challenges* 16, 3 (2020): 10–15, https://www.jstor.org/stable/26924333.

49 Paul Poast (@ProfPaulPoast), "But as the Ngram shows, usage of 'rules-based order' took off starting in the early-to-mid 2000s," Twitter, May 4, 2021, https://twitter.com/ProfPaulPoast/status/1389555546756366338; Anne-Marie Slaughter, "Good Reasons for Going around the U.N.," *New York Times*, March 18, 2003, https://www.nytimes.com/2003/03/18/opinion/good-reasons-for-going-around-the-un.html.

50 US Department of Defense, *Indo-Pacific Strategy Report: Preparedness, Partnerships, and Promoting a Networked Region* (Washington, DC: US Department of Defense, 2019), 2, https://media.defense.gov/2019/jul/01/2002152311/-1/-1/1/department-of-defense-indo-pacific-strategy-report-2019.pdf.

51 White House, "Carbis Bay G7 Summit Communiqué," news release, June 13, 2021, https://www.whitehouse.gov/briefing-room/statements-releases/2021/06/13/carbis-bay-g7-summit-communique/; White House, "U.S.-EU Summit Statement," news release, June 15, 2021, https://www.whitehouse.gov/briefing-room/statements-releases/2021/06/15/u-s-eu-summit-statement/; NATO, "Brussels Summit Communiqué Issued by the Heads of State and Government Participating in the Meeting of the North Atlantic Council in Brussels 14 June 2021," news release, June 14, 2021, http://www.nato.int/cps/en/natohq/news_185000.htm.

52 Adam Breuer and Alastair Iain Johnston, "Memes, Narratives and the Emergent US-China Security Dilemma," *Cambridge Review of International Affairs* 32, 4 (2019): 429–55, https://doi.org/10.1080/09557571.2019.1622083.

53 Office of the Under Secretary of Defense (Comptroller), *Pacific Deterrence Initiative*, Department of Defense Budget Fiscal Year (FY) 2022 (Washington, DC: US Department of Defense, 2021), https://comptroller.defense.gov/Portals/45/Documents/defbudget/FY2022/fy2022_Pacific_Deterrence_Initiative.pdf.

54 "Free and Open Indo-Pacific," Ministry of Foreign Affairs of Japan, April 1, 2021, https://www.mofa.go.jp/policy/page25e_000278.html.

55 White House, "U.S.-Japan Joint Leaders' Statement: 'U.S.-Japan Global Partnership for a New Era,'" news release, April 16, 2021, https://www.whitehouse.gov/briefing-room/statements-releases/2021/04/16/u-s-japan-joint-leaders-statement-u-s-japan-global-partnership-for-a-new-era/.

56 Council of the European Union, *Council Conclusions on an EU Strategy for Cooperation in the Indo-Pacific* (Brussels: Council of the European Union, 2021), 2, https://data.consilium.europa.eu/doc/document/ST-7914-2021-INIT/en/pdf#:~:text=The%20EU's%20Indo%2DPacific%20strategy,principles%2C%20values%20or%20mutual%20interest.

57 Ministry for Europe and Foreign Affairs of France, "The Indo-Pacific Region: A Priority for France," Ministry for Europe and Foreign Affairs of France, 2018, https://www.diplomatie.gouv.fr/en/country-files/asia-and-oceania/the-indo-pacific-region-a-priority-for-france/; Government of the Netherlands, *Indo-Pacific: Guidelines for Strengthening Dutch and EU Cooperation with Partners in Asia* (The Hague: Government of the Netherlands, 2020), https://www.government.nl/documents/publications/2020/11/13/indo-pacific-guidelines; Federal Government of Germany, *Policy Guidelines for the Indo-Pacific Region: Germany – Europe – Asia: Shaping the 21st Century Together (Preliminary Translation of the Executive Summary)* (Berlin: Federal Government of Germany, 2020), https://rangun.diplo.de/blob/2380824/a27b62057f2d2675ce2bbfc5be01099a/policy-guidelines-summary-data.pdf.

58 Dan Sabbagh and Helen Davidson, "UK Says It Has No Plans for South China Sea Confrontation after Beijing Warning," *The Guardian*, July 30, 2021, https://www.theguardian.com/world/2021/jul/30/china-royal-navy-south-china-sea-warning-beijing; Martin Manaranche, "German Navy to Deploy a Frigate in Indo-Pacific Region for the First Time since 2016," *Naval News*, July 30, 2021, https://www.navalnews.com/naval-news/2021/07/german-navy-to-deploy-a-frigate-in-indo-pacific-region-for-the-first-time-since-2016/.

59 Australian Government, *Overview: 2017 Foreign Policy White Paper* (Barton: Australian Government, Department of Foreign Affairs and Trade, 2017), https://www.dfat.gov.au/sites/default/files/minisite/static/4ca0813c-585e-4fe1-86eb-de665e65001a/fpwhitepaper/foreign-policy-white-paper/overview.html.

60 Australian Government, *Shaping Rules and Institutions: 2017 Foreign Policy White Paper* (Barton: Australian Government, Department of Foreign Affairs and Trade, 2017), https://www.dfat.gov.au/sites/default/files/minisite/static/4ca0813c-585e-4fe1-86eb-de665e65001a/fpwhitepaper/foreign-policy-white-paper/chapter-six-global-cooperation/shaping-rules-and-institutions.html; Nick Bisley and Benjamin Schreer, "Will Australia Defend the 'Rules-Based Order' in Asia?" *The Strategist*, Australian Strategic Policy Institute, April 18, 2018, https://www.aspistrategist.org.au/will-australia-defend-rules-based-order-asia/.

61 Bec Strating, "Perspectives: Preserving the 'Rules-Based Order,'" *Asialink*, University of Melbourne, February 5, 2021, https://asialink.unimelb.edu.au/insights/perspectives-preserving-the-rules-based-order.

62 Andreas Bieler et al., *Global Restructuring, State, Capital and Labour: Contesting Neo-Gramscian Perspectives* (New York: Palgrave Macmillan, 2006), 9.

63 G. John Ikenberry, *Liberal Leviathan: The Origins, Crisis, and Transformation of the American World Order* (Princeton, NJ: Princeton University Press, 2012), 159.

64 Charles-Philippe David and David Grondin, eds., *Hegemony or Empire? The Redefinition of US Power under George W. Bush* (New York: Routledge, 2016), 84.

65 Demetrios James Caraley, ed., *American Hegemony: Preventive War, Iraq, and Imposing Democracy* (New York: Academy of Political Science, 2004), 101.

66 Van Jackson, *On the Brink: Trump, Kim, and the Threat of Nuclear War* (New York: Cambridge University Press, 2018), 161.
67 Evelyn Goh, "Contesting Hegemonic Order: China in East Asia," *Security Studies* 28, 3 (2019): 614–44, https://doi.org/10.1080/09636412.2019.1604989.
68 Amitav Acharya, "After Liberal Hegemony: The Advent of a Multiplex World Order*," *Ethics and International Affairs* 31, 3 (2017): 271–85, https://doi.org/10.1017/S089267941700020X.
69 Alexander Cooley and Daniel Nexon, *Exit from Hegemony: The Unraveling of the American Global Order* (New York: Oxford University Press, 2020), 54.
70 Randolph B. Persaud, *Counter-Hegemony and Foreign Policy: The Dialectics of Marginalized and Global Forces in Jamaica* (Albany: SUNY Press, 2001), 5.
71 Owen Worth, *Rethinking Hegemony* (London: Palgrave Macmillan, 2015), 12.
72 Elke Krahmann, "American Hegemony or Global Governance? Competing Visions of International Security," *International Studies Review* 7, 4 (2005): 531–45, https://doi.org/10.1111/j.1468-2486.2005.00531.x.
73 Michael Byers and Georg Nolte, eds., *United States Hegemony and the Foundations of International Law* (New York: Cambridge University Press, 2003), 10.
74 Prabhakar Singh and Benoît Mayer, eds., *Critical International Law: Postrealism, Postcolonialism, and Transnationalism* (Oxford: Oxford University Press, 2014), 53.
75 Armin von Bogdandy and Ingo Venzke, *In Whose Name? A Public Law Theory of International Adjudication* (New York: Oxford University Press, 2014), 26.
76 *National Security Strategy of the United States of America* (Washington, DC: White House, 2017), 19, https://trumpwhitehouse.archives.gov/wp-content/uploads/2017/12/NSS-Final-12-18-2017-0905.pdf; *National Security Strategy* (Washington, DC: White House, 2015), 1, https://obamawhitehouse.archives.gov/sites/default/files/docs/2015_national_security_strategy_2.pdf.
77 US Department of State, *A Free and Open Indo-Pacific: Advancing a Shared Vision* (Washington, DC: US Department of State, 2019), 11, https://www.state.gov/wp-content/uploads/2019/11/Free-and-Open-Indo-Pacific-4Nov2019.pdf; US Department of Defense, *Indo-Pacific Strategy Report,* 32.
78 White House, "US Strategic Framework for the Indo-Pacific" (declassified, January 2021), 4, https://trumpwhitehouse.archives.gov/wp-content/uploads/2021/01/IPS-Final-Declass.pdf.
79 Ned Price, "Department Press Briefing – February 2, 2021," US Department of State, February 2, 2021, https://www.state.gov/briefings/department-press-briefing-february-2-2021/.
80 Ned Price, "Department Press Briefing – February 25, 2021," US Department of State, February 25, 2021, https://www.state.gov/briefings/department-press-briefing-february-25-2021/.
81 Mark T. Esper, "Defense Secretary Addresses Free and Open Indo-Pacific at APCSS" (speech, Honolulu, August 26, 2020), US Department of Defense, https://www.defense.gov/Newsroom/Transcripts/Transcript/Article/2328124/defense-secretary-addresses-free-and-open-indo-pacific-at-apcss-courtesy-transc/; Ankit Panda, "Survey: China Gaining Influence over US in

Southeast Asia, with Likely Long-Term Consequences," *The Diplomat,* June 16, 2020, https://thediplomat.com/2020/06/survey-china-gaining-influence-over-us-in-southeast-asia-with-likely-long-term-consequences/.

82 Ned Price, "Secretary Blinken's Call with Australian Foreign Minister Payne," US Department of State, January 27, 2021, https://www.state.gov/secretary-blinkens-call-with-australian-foreign-minister-payne/; "Advancing US Engagement and Countering China in the Indo-Pacific and Beyond, before the Senate Committee on Foreign Relations" (testimony of David R. Stilwell, Assistant Secretary of State, Bureau of East Asian and Pacific Affairs, US Department of State, September 17, 2020), https://www.foreign.senate.gov/imo/media/doc/091720_Stilwell_Testimony.pdf; Joe Biden, "Remarks by President Biden on America's Place in the World" (remarks, Washington, DC, February 4, 2021), White House, https://www.whitehouse.gov/briefing-room/speeches-remarks/2021/02/04/remarks-by-president-biden-on-americas-place-in-the-world/.

83 Scott Morrison, "Address, Aspen Security Forum – 'Tomorrow in the Indo-Pacific'" (address, Aspen Security Forum, August 5, 2020), Parliament of Australia, https://parlinfo.aph.gov.au/parlInfo/download/media/pressrel/7486844/upload_binary/7486844.pdf;fileType=application%2Fpdf#search=%22media/pressrel/7486844%22; George Brandis, "Defending Liberal Democracies in an Increasingly Contested World" (lecture, Gallipoli Memorial Lecture, Australian High Commission, United Kingdom, June 25, 2020), https://uk.embassy.gov.au/lhlh/20200625.html.

84 Andrew Tillett, "PM Hails New Subs Deal as 'Forever Partnership,'" *Financial Review,* September 16, 2021, https://www.afr.com/politics/federal/pm-hails-new-subs-deal-as-forever-partnership-20210916-p58s3t.

85 "Press Conference by Foreign Minister MOTEGI Toshimitsu," Ministry of Foreign Affairs of Japan, October 6, 2020, https://www.mofa.go.jp/press/kaiken/kaiken4e_000852.html; Satoshi Suzuki, "India-Japan-France Workshop on the Indo-Pacific" (speech, India-Japan-France Workshop on the Indo-Pacific, New Delhi, January 19, 2021), Embassy of Japan in India, https://www.in.emb-japan.go.jp/Japan-India-Relations/20210119-Ambassador_Suzuki_speech_India-Japan-France_workshop_on_Indo-Pacific.pdf.

86 Céline Pajon, "France's Indo-Pacific Strategy and the Quad Plus," *Journal of Indo-Pacific Affairs* 3, 5 (Winter 2020/2021): 165–78; Abhijnan Rej, "German Defense Minister Continues Her Indo-Pacific Campaign," *The Diplomat,* November 5, 2020, https://thediplomat.com/2020/11/german-defense-minister-continues-her-indo-pacific-campaign/; Dipanjan Roy Chaudhury, "Netherlands Seeks to Align Its Indo-Pacific Vision with India: Envoy," *Economic Times,* February 24, 2021, https://economictimes.indiatimes.com/news/politics-and-nation/netherlands-seeks-to-align-its-indo-pacific-vision-with-india-envoy/articleshow/81185617.cms.

87 Zhang Bei, "Britain's Tilt to the Indo-Pacific," China-US Focus, January 22, 2021, https://www.chinausfocus.com/foreign-policy/britains-tilt-to-the-indo-pacific.

88 Wen-Qing Ngoei, *Arc of Containment: Britain, the United States, and Anticommunism in Southeast Asia* (Ithaca, NY: Cornell University Press, 2019), 48;

Notes to pages 34–35

Pankaj Mishra, *From the Ruins of Empire: The Revolt Against the West and the Remaking of Asia* (Toronto: Doubleday Canada, 2012), 124; Vincent Bevins, *The Jakarta Method: Washington's Anticommunist Crusade and the Mass Murder Program That Shaped Our World* (New York: Public Affairs, 2020), 210.

89 Jonathan Berkshire Miller, "It's Time for Ottawa to Rethink How It Sees Asia," *Globe and Mail*, April 18, 2019, https://www.theglobeandmail.com/opinion/article-its-time-for-ottawa-to-rethink-how-it-sees-asia/; Preston Lim, "Now Is the Time for a Canadian Pivot to the Indo-Pacific: Preston Lim for Inside Policy," Macdonald-Laurier Institute, November 17, 2020, https://www.macdonaldlaurier.ca/now-is-the-time-for-a-canadian-pivot-to-the-indo-pacific-preston-lim-for-inside-policy/.

90 Brett Byers, "What Canada Can Do about Chinese Aggression in the Indo-Pacific Region: Brett Byers in the Hill Times," Macdonald-Laurier Institute, November 20, 2019, https://www.macdonaldlaurier.ca/canada-can-chinese-aggression-indo-pacific-region-brett-byers-hill-times/; Scott Simon, "Canada Needs Likeminded Partners in the Indo-Pacific Region. It's Time to Consider Taiwan," *Vancouver Sun*, December 18, 2020, https://vancouversun.com/opinion/scott-simon-canada-needs-likeminded-partners-in-the-indo-pacific-region-its-time-to-consider-taiwan.

91 Stephen Nagy, "Japan's Indo-Pacific Vision Is a Template for Canada," *Japan Times*, February 25, 2021, https://www.japantimes.co.jp/opinion/2021/02/25/commentary/japan-commentary/covid-19-indo-pacific-china-canada-foip/; Edward Fishman and Siddharth Mohandas, "A Council of Democracies Can Save Multilateralism: Boris Johnson's 'D-10' Is the Club the World Desperately Needs," *Foreign Affairs*, August 3, 2020, https://www.foreignaffairs.com/articles/asia/2020-08-03/council-democracies-can-save-multilateralism.

92 Øystein Tunsjø, *The Return of Bipolarity in World Politics: China, the United States, and Geostructural Realism* (New York: Columbia University Press, 2018), 32; Arnau Busquets Guàrdia, "Europe on the Wane," *POLITICO*, December 26, 2019, https://www.politico.eu/article/europe-on-the-wane-global-economics-demographics-gdp/.

93 Federal Government of Germany, *Policy Guidelines for the Indo-Pacific Region;* Ministry for Europe and Foreign Affairs of France, "The Indo-Pacific Region: A Priority for France."

94 Ministry of Foreign Affairs of Japan 外務省, *Jiyūde hirakareta Indotaiheiyō* 自由で開かれたインド太平洋 [Free and open Indo-Pacific] (Tokyo: Ministry of Foreign Affairs of Japan), https://www.mofa.go.jp/files/000430632.pdf.

95 Frances Adamson, "The Indo-Pacific: Australia's Perspective" (speech, Kuala Lumpur, April 29, 2019), Australian Government, Department of Foreign Affairs and Trade, https://www.dfat.gov.au/news/speeches/Pages/the-indo-pacific-australias-perspective; Australian Government, Department of Foreign Affairs and Trade, *DFAT 2018–19 Annual Report* (Barton: Department of Foreign Affairs and Trade, 2019), https://www.dfat.gov.au/about-us/publications/corporate/annual-reports/Pages/department-of-foreign-affairs-and-trade-annual-report-2018-19.aspx/annual-report-2018-19/home/section-2/promote-a-stable-and-prosperous-indo-pacific/index.html.

96 US Department of State, *A Free and Open Indo-Pacific*, 12.
97 Esper, "Defense Secretary Addresses Free and Open Indo-Pacific at APCSS."
98 Bruce Vaughn et al., *The Trump Administration's "Free and Open Indo-Pacific": Issues for Congress* (Washington, DC: Congressional Research Service, 2018), 1, https://crsreports.congress.gov/product/pdf/R/R45396.
99 Lavina Lee, *Democracy Promotion: ANZUS and the Free and Open Indo-Pacific Strategy* (Sydney: United States Studies Centre at the University of Sydney, July 2019), https://www.ussc.edu.au/analysis/democracy-promotion-anzus-and-the-free-and-open-indo-pacific-strategy.
100 Lindsey Ford, *The Trump Administration and the "Free and Open Indo-Pacific"* (Washington, DC: Brookings Institution, 2020), 3, https://www.brookings.edu/wp-content/uploads/2020/05/fp_20200505_free_open_indo_pacific.pdf.
101 Matthew P. Goodman et al., *Delivering Prosperity in the Indo-Pacific: An Agenda for Australia and the United States* (Washington, DC: Center for Strategic and International Studies, 2019), 4, https://www.csis.org/analysis/delivering-prosperity-indo-pacific-agenda-australia-and-united-states.
102 Daniel A. Bell, *Beyond Liberal Democracy: Political Thinking for an East Asian Context* (Princeton, NJ: Princeton University Press, 2006), 3.
103 "Explore the Map," Freedom House, https://freedomhouse.org/explore-the-map.
104 Bell, *Beyond Liberal Democracy*, 82.
105 Kishore Mahbubani, "An Asian Perspective on Human Rights and Freedom of the Press," *Media Asia* 20, 3 (1993): 159–66, https://doi.org/10.1080/01296612.1993.11726418.
106 Kevin Tze-wai Wong and Victor Zheng, "Democratic Support and Cultural Values: An Empirical Study of Hong Kong and East Asian Societies," *China: An International Journal* 16, 2 (May 2018): 111-132, doi:10.1353/chn.2018.0016.
107 Natalie Sambhi, "Generals Gaining Ground: Civil-Military Relations and Democracy in Indonesia," Brookings Institution, January 22, 2021, 4, https://www.brookings.edu/articles/generals-gaining-ground-civil-military-relations-and-democracy-in-indonesia/.
108 Ibid.
109 Robert Wade, *Governing the Market: Economic Theory and the Role of Government in East Asian Industrialization* (Princeton, NJ: Princeton University Press, 2004), 347.
110 Jesus Felipe, ed., *Development and Modern Industrial Policy in Practice: Issues and Country Experiences* (Northampton, MA: Asian Development Bank/Edward Elgar Publishing, 2015), 109.
111 T.J. Pempel, ed., *The Politics of the Asian Economic Crisis* (Ithaca, NY: Cornell University Press, 1999), 10.
112 Lindsey W. Ford, "Sustaining the Future of Indo-Pacific Defense Strategy," Brookings Institution, September 28, 2020, https://www.brookings.edu/articles/sustaining-the-future-of-indo-pacific-defense-strategy/.
113 Tsuyoshi Minami, "Will the Quad Alliance Take Off?" Australian Institute of International Affairs, November 5, 2020, https://www.internationalaffairs.org.au/australianoutlook/will-the-quad-alliance-take-off/.

114 White House, "US Strategic Framework for the Indo-Pacific."
115 Hal Brands, "US Needs to Deny, Not Dominate, China in the Indo-Pacific," *Bloomberg*, January 31, 2021, https://www.bloomberg.com/opinion/articles/2021-02-01/u-s-needs-to-deny-not-dominate-china-in-the-indo-pacific.
116 David Scott, "The Indo-Pacific in US Strategy: Responding to Power Shifts," *Rising Powers Quarterly* 3, 2 (August 2018): 19–43.
117 Evelyn Goh, "Southeast Asian Strategies toward the Great Powers: Still Hedging after All These Years?" Asan Forum, February 22, 2016, http://www.theasanforum.org/southeast-asian-strategies-toward-the-great-powers-still-hedging-after-all-these-years/.
118 David R. Stilwell, "The South China Sea, Southeast Asia's Patrimony, and Everybody's Own Backyard" (remarks, Center for Strategic and International Studies [virtual], July 14, 2020), US Mission to ASEAN, https://asean.usmission.gov/the-south-china-sea-southeast-asias-patrimony-and-everybodys-own-backyard/.
119 Sung Chul Jung, Jaehyon Lee, and Ji-Yong Lee, "The Indo-Pacific Strategy and US Alliance Network Expandability: Asian Middle Powers' Positions on Sino-US Geostrategic Competition in Indo-Pacific Region," *Journal of Contemporary China* 30, 127 (2021): 53–68, https://doi.org/10.1080/10670564.2020.1766909.
120 Robert W. Cox, "Gramsci, Hegemony and International Relations: An Essay in Method," *Millennium: Journal of International Studies* 12, 2 (1983), https://doi.org/10.1177/03058298830120020701.
121 Ken Booth, ed., *Critical Security Studies and World Politics* (Boulder, CO: Lynne Rienner, 2005), 235.

Chapter 2: Asian Counter-Narratives: Indo-Pacific, Rules-Based Order, and Freedom and Openness

1 Joe Biden and Yoshihide Suga, "Remarks by President Biden and Prime Minister Suga of Japan at Press Conference" (remarks, Washington, DC, April 16, 2021), White House, https://www.whitehouse.gov/briefing-room/speeches-remarks/2021/04/16/remarks-by-president-biden-and-prime-minister-suga-of-japan-at-press-conference/.
2 Frédéric Grare and Manisha Reuter, "Moving Closer: European Views of the Indo-Pacific," European Council on Foreign Relations, September 13, 2021, https://ecfr.eu/special/moving-closer-european-views-of-the-indo-pacific/.
3 Anthony Galloway, "What's the Indo-Pacific – and How Does the Quad Work?" *Sydney Morning Herald*, September 16, 2021, https://www.smh.com.au/national/forget-asia-pacific-it-s-the-indo-pacific-we-live-in-now-where-is-that-exactly-20210810-p58hku.html.
4 Caitlin Byrne, "Securing the 'Rules-Based Order' in the Indo-Pacific: The Significance of Strategic Narrative," *Security Challenges* 16, 3 (2020): 10–15, https://www.jstor.org/stable/26924333?seq=1#metadata_info_tab_contents.
5 Kai He, "Three Faces of the Indo-Pacific: Understanding the 'Indo-Pacific' from an IR Theory Perspective," *East Asia* 35 (2018): 149–61, https://doi.org/10.1007/s12140-018-9286-5.

6 Pramod Jaiswal and Deepak Prakash Bhatt, eds., *Rebalancing Asia: The Belt and Road Initiative and Indo-Pacific Strategy* (Singapore: Springer, 2021), 223.
7 Peter Greste, Justin Stevens, and Alex McDonald, "'Misunderstanding' May Lead to Conflict between US and China over South China Sea, Expert Warns," *ABC [Australian Broadcasting Corporation] News,* October 2, 2016, https://www.abc.net.au/news/2016-10-03/south-china-sea-us-china-misunderstandings-may-cause-conflict/7893012.
8 Jun Sakurada 櫻田淳, "Go iken boshū: dōmei no nettowāku Beikoku igai no dare to kumubeki ka" ご意見募集＞同盟のネットワーク 米国以外の誰と組むべきか [Opinion solicitation: alliance network who should we partner with outside the United States?], *Mainichi Newspapers* 毎日新聞, February 12, 2020, https://mainichi.jp/premier/politics/articles/20200210/pol/00m/010/002000c; "Chōsa kenkyū: Nichibei no Indotaiheiyō senryaku o tou" 調査研究: 日米のインド太平洋戦略を問う [Research: questioning the US-Japan Indo-Pacific strategy], *Yomiuri Shimbun Online* 読売新聞オンライン, October 20, 2020, https://www.yomiuri.co.jp/choken/kijironko/ckworld/20210312-OYT8T50023/; Takeyuki Hasegawa 長谷川雄之, *Roshia to 'Ajiataiheiyō'/'Indotaiheiyō'* ロシアと「アジア太平洋」/「インド太平洋」 [Russia and "Asia Pacific"/"Indo Pacific"], NIDS Commentary [NIDS コメンタリー] 147 (Tokyo: National Institute for Defense Studies 防衛研究所, 2020), http://www.nids.mod.go.jp/publication/commentary/pdf/commentary147.pdf.
9 Hitoshi Tanaka 田中均, "'Ajiataiheiyō' kara 'Indotaiheiyō' e: Nihon gaikō no henka o dō miru no ka"「アジア太平洋」から「インド太平洋」へ～日本外交の変化をどう見るのか [From "Asia-Pacific" to "Indo-Pacific": how do you see the changes in Japanese diplomacy?]," *Ronza, Asahi Shimbun* 朝日新聞論座, April 28, 2021, https://webronza.asahi.com/politics/articles/2021042700005.html.
10 Hitoshi Tanaka 田中均, "Asahi Shimbun Ronza: 'Ajiataiheiyō' kara Indotaiheiyō e, Nihon no taigai shisei no henka o dō miru no ka" 朝日新聞 論座:「アジア太平洋」から「インド太平洋」へ—日本の対外姿勢の変化をどう見るのか [Asahi Shimbun Ronza: from "Asia-Pacific" to "Indo-Pacific" – how to see the changes in Japan's attitude toward foreign affairs], Japan Research Institute 国際戦略研究所, April 28, 2021, https://www.jri.co.jp/page.jsp?id=38824; Institute for Peace Policies 平和政策研究所, *Chūgoku no kyōi bunseki to Nihon no taichūgoku kihon senryaku* 中国の脅威分析と日本の対中国基本戦略 [Analysis of China's threat and Japan's basic strategy for China], Seisaku teigen 政策提言 [Policy proposal] 16 (Tokyo: Institute for Peace Policies 平和政策研究所, 2019), https://ippjapan.org/archives/1530.
11 Kumiko Haba 羽場久美子, "Yōroppa no tōgō, Ajia no bundan wa, Amerika no sekai senryaku – Ajia no kyōdō o ikani tsukuru ka? Ajia kinrin shokoku to no tairitsu o koete – Gakujutsu nettowāku no kōchiku" ヨーロッパの統合、アジアの分断は、アメリカの世界戦略 —アジアの共同をいかに作るか？アジア近隣諸国との対立をこえて—学術ネットワークの構築— [The integration of Europe and the division of Asia are America's global strategy – how to create collaboration in Asia? Beyond conflicts with neighbouring Asian countries – building academic networks], *Gakujutsu No Dōkō* 学術の動向 [Academic trends] 25, 9 (2020): 49–54, https://doi.org/10.5363/tits.25.9_49.

12 "Jimin Nikai kanjicho Intabyū chūgoku shuseki kokuhin 'kokueki chūshin ni kangaerubeki'" 自民・二階幹事長インタビュー 中国主席国賓「国益中心に考えるべき」 [Interview with Liberal Democratic Party secretary-general Nikai: inviting the president of China as a state guest 'should be considered based on Japan's national interest], *Sankei News* 産経ニュース, September 30, 2020, https://www.sankei.com/article/20200930-ZWLPFMLJPFNADKNVJ23HL5O32I/.

13 Choe Wongi, *"New Southern Policy": Korea's Newfound Ambition in Search of Strategic Autonomy*, Asie.Visions 118 (Paris: Ifri [French Institute of International Relations], January 2021): 15, https://www.ifri.org/sites/default/files/atoms/files/choe_new_southern_policy_korea_2021.pdf.

14 Jeju Peace Institute, *New Southern Policy, Achievements and Challenges over the Past Two Years: In the Aspect of Foreign and Security Policy* (Jeju: Jeju Peace Institute, August 9, 2019), http://jpi.or.kr/?p=979; Kang Gye-man and Lim Young-shin 강계만 임영신, "6eog-ingu Asean-eun beulluosyeon ... gieob-i ttwige jeongbuga majchumjiwon-eul" 6억인구 아세안은 블루오션 ... 기업이 뛰게 정부가 맞춤지원을 [With 600 million people, ASEAN is a blue ocean ... the government provides customized support for businesses to thrive]," *Maeil Economic Daily* 매일경제, September 12, 2018, https://www.mk.co.kr/news/economy/view/2018/09/576411/.

15 Jeju Peace Institute, *New Southern Policy*.

16 Yeongkwan Song, "Baideun sidae gugjetongsanghwangyeong-gwa Hangug-ui daeeungjeonlyag" 바이든 시대 국제통상환경과 한국의 대응전략 [The global trade environment in the Biden era and response strategies for Korea], *KDI FOCUS*, 104(kor) (February 24, 2021), https://papers.ssrn.com/sol3/papers.cfm?abstract_id=3790301; Choi Yoon-Young and Bae Jaeng Saeng 최윤영 배정생, "Choegeun a·Taejiyeog-ui Mega FTA chujingwa daeeung-gwaje: pogwaljeog·jeomjinjeog hwantaepyeong-yang-gyeongjedongbanjahyeobjeong(CPTPP)ui wisaeng mich geom-yeog chaebteoleul jungsim-eulo" 최근 아·태지역의 Mega FTA 추진과 대응과제 : 포괄적·점진적 환태평양경제동반자협정(CPTPP)의 위생 및 검역 챕터를 중심으로 [A study on the mega FTA in the Asia-Pacific region and key issues: focusing on the CPTPP SPS chapter], *Beobhag-yeongu* 법학연구 [Journal of Law] 60 (2019): 211–35, https://www.dbpia.co.kr/Journal/articleDetail?nodeId=NODE09227751.

17 Suwarti Sari and Mariane Delanova, "Strategi kebijakan luar negeri Indonesia dalam meningkatkan daya tawar di kawasan Indo-Pasifik" [Indonesian foreign policy strategies in increasing bargaining power in the Indo-Pacific region], *Jurnal Dinamika Global* [Journal of Global Dynamics] 6, 1 (2021), https://doi.org/10.36859/jdg.v6i01.415.

18 Ahmad Zaky Haidir, Panji Suwarno, and Surya Wiranto, "Sikap Indonesia dalam merespon konsep Indo Pasifik serta relasinya dengan kondisi pandemi COVID-19" [Indonesia's attitude in responding to the Indo-Pacific concept and its relationship with the conditions of the COVID-19 pandemic], *Jurnal Education and Development* 9, 3 (2021): 37–39, http://journal.ipts.ac.id/index.php/ED/article/view/2626/1778.

19 Rizki Roza, "Indian Ocean Rim Association (IORA) dan kepentingan Indonesia di Samudera Hindia" [Indian Ocean Rim Association (IORA) and Indonesia's

interests in the Indian Ocean], *Info Singkat: Hubungan Internasional* [Brief Info: International Relations] 7, 06/II/P3DI (March 2015), https://berkas.dpr.go.id/puslit/files/info_singkat/Info%20Singkat-VII-6-II-P3DI-Maret-2015-75.pdf.

20 Wan Zain, "Indo-Pasifik: strategi tersirat Amerika di rantau ini" [Indo-Pacific: America's implicit strategy in the region], *Astro Awani,* July 22, 2020, https://de-awani-web-portal-stg.eco.astro.com.my/berita-dunia/indo-pasifik-strategi-tersirat-amerika-di-rantau-ini-252275?amp=1.

21 "Muhyiddin tetap perkukuh hubungan antarabangsa" [Muhyiddin continues to strengthen international relations], *Sinar Harian,* [The daily light] February 28, 2021, https://www.sinarharian.com.my/article/126183/BERITA/Nasional/Muhyiddin-tetap-perkukuh-hubungan-antarabangsa.

22 Ministry of Foreign Affairs, Malaysia, "Dasar luar negara" [Foreign policy], Prime Minister's Office of Malaysia, 2019, https://www.pmo.gov.my/wp-content/uploads/2019/07/Dasar-Luar-Malaysia.pdf.

23 Dulyapak Preecharush ดุลยภาค ปรีชารัชช, "Cāk 'so meīy' t̄hụng "xī t̩ xī lū̀" læa "xin do-pæsifik" kār prạb rūp phūmiṣ̄āṣ̄tr̒ h̄ım̀ k̄hxng xecheīy" จาก 'โซเมีย' ถึง "ฮีใต้ อีลู่" และ "อินโด-แปซิฟิก" การปรับรูปภูมิศาสตร์ใหม่ของเอเชีย [From "Zomia" to "One Belt One Road" and "Indo-Pacific": the new geographic adjustment of Asia], *Thai Journal of East Asian Studies* 25, 1 (2021): 82–102, https://so02.tci-thaijo.org/index.php/easttu/article/view/247178.

24 Therdsak Paijuntuek เทอดศักดิ์ ไปจันทึก, "Khwām mạ̀nkhng k̄hxng xāseīyn kạb kār cạdkār khwām s̄ạmphạnṭh̒ prathes̄ p̄hāynxk" ความมั่นคงของอาเซียนกับการจัดการความสัมพันธ์ประเทศภายนอก [ASEAN security and the managing of the relations with the outside countries], *Governance Journal* วารสารการบริหารปกครอง 9, 1 (2020): 216–61, https://so01.tci-thaijo.org/index.php/gjournal-ksu/article/view/242512.

25 Duy Hoàng, "Chiến lược Ấn Độ Dương – Thái Bình Dương: Tầm nhìn và thực tiễn" [Indo-Pacific strategy: vision and practice], *Tạp chí Cộng sản* [Communist Magazine], December 15, 2020, https://www.tapchicongsan.org.vn/web/guest/the-gioi-van-de-su-kien/-/2018/820763/chien-luoc-an-do-duong---thai-binh-duong--tam-nhin-va-thuc-tien.aspx.

26 Đinh Hoàng Thắng, "Quan điểm của ASEAN về khu vực Ấn Thái Dương" [ASEAN's view of the Indo-Pacific region], *Văn hóa Nghệ An* [Nghe An Culture], August 2, 2019, http://www.vanhoanghean.com.vn/component/k2/nhin/13254-quan-diem-cua-asean-ve-khu-vuc-an-thai-duong.

27 Indri Yanuarti, Makarim Wibisono, and I Wayan Midhio, "Strategi kerja sama Indo-Pasifik untuk mendukung pertahanan negara: perspektif Indonesia" [Indo-Pacific cooperation strategy to support state defence: Indonesian perspective], *Strategi Perang Semesta* [Total war strategy] 6, 1 (2020), http://jurnalprodi.idu.ac.id/index.php/SPS/article/view/538; Hadis Tian, Panji Suwarno, and Supriyadi, "Konsep Lebensraum: perebutan hegemoni laut China Selatan Antara China dengan Amerika serikat" [The Lebensraum concept: the struggle for South China Sea hegemony between China and the United States], *Jurnal Education and Development* 9, 2 (2021): 127–36, http://journal.ipts.ac.id/index.php/ED/article/view/2501.

28 Sharon Seah et al., *The State of Southeast Asia: 2021 Survey Report* (Singapore: ASEAN Studies Centre at ISEAS–Yusof Ishak Institute, 2021), https://www.iseas.edu.sg/wp-content/uploads/2021/01/The-State-of-SEA-2021-v2.pdf.
29 Akio Mori 森 彰夫, "Semegi au minshu shugi to ken'i shugi-riberaruna sekai chitsujo no 'tasogare'-ron ni taisuru hihanteki kōsatsu" せめぎあう民主主義と権威主義—リベラルな世界秩序の「黄昏」論に対する批判的考察— [Democracy on the brink of authoritarianism: criticism of "The Twilight of the Liberal World Order"], *Yamato Daigaku Kenkyū Kiyō* 大和大学研究紀要 [Bulletin of Yamato University] 7 (March 2021): 51–71, https://yamato-u.repo.nii.ac.jp/?action=repository_action_common_download&item_id=222&item_no=1&attribute_id=22&file_no=1.
30 Mitsubishi Research Institute 三菱総合研究所, *Torendo 2: haken-koku no inai kokusai chitsujo* トレンド 2：覇権国のいない国際秩序 [Trend 2: international order without hegemons] (Tokyo: Mitsubishi Research Institute 三菱総合研究所, 2019), https://www.mri.co.jp/knowledge/insight/ecovision/dia6ou000001mwnz-att/ei20191025_mirai2050-1-2.pdf.
31 Shin Kawashima 川島真, "Shūkan Keidanren Taimusu: Chūgoku to kokusai chitsujo" 週刊 経団連タイムス：中国と国際秩序 [Weekly Keidanren Times: China and the international order], *Keidanren* 日本経済団体連合会, January 17, 2019, https://www.keidanren.or.jp/journal/times/2019/0117_10.html.
32 Kang Seon-ju 강선주, "Migug judoui jayujuui gugjejilseo: gwageo, hyeonjae, geuligo milae" 미국 주도의 자유주의 국제질서: 과거, 현재, 그리고 미래 [The American-led liberal international order: past, present and future], *Gugjejeongchinonchong* 국제정치논총 [Korean Journal of International Relations] 60, 2 (June 2020): 301–30, https://doi.org/10.14731/kjir.2020.06.60.2.301.
33 Kim Dong-eun 김동은, "Migug-ui Indo-Taepyeong-yang Jeonlyag-eun sin bongswaejeonlyag-inga?-Mi jeonlyagmunseoe natanan wihyeob-insiggwa daeso bongswaejeonlyaggwaui bigyo" 미국의 인도-태평양 전략은 신 봉쇄전략인가? -美 전략문서에 나타난 위협인식과 대소 봉쇄전략과의 비교- [Is the US Indo-Pacific strategy a containment strategy for China in the 21st century? Analysis of threat awareness in US strategic documents and comparison of containment strategy for the Soviet Union], *Hanguggunsa* 한국군사 [Korean military], 7 (June 2020): 71–112, https://doi.org/10.33528/kjma.2020.6.7.71.
34 Hyun In-taek 현인택, "Dong-Asia hegemoni yeogsawa Hangug-ui milae" 동아시아 헤게모니 역사와 한국의 미래 [The history of hegemony in East Asia and South Korea's future], *Gugjegwangyeyeongu* 국제관계연구 [Journal of International Politics] 22, 2 (2017): 5–51, https://doi.org/10.18031/jip.2017.12.22.2.5.
35 Airlangga Pribadi, "Hegemoni ideologi neoliberalisme dan diskursus demokrasi di Indonesia" [The ideological hegemony of neoliberalism and discourse on democracy in Indonesia], *Jurnal Politik* [Political Journal] 1, 1 (2010): 23–35, http://www.jurnalpolitik.ui.ac.id/index.php/jp/article/view/100.
36 Muhamad Lukman Arifianto, "Menyoal konsep demokrasi Amerika serikat: promosi dan trajektorinya" [Questioning the United States' concept of democracy: its promotion and trajectory], *Jurnal Keamanan Nasional* [National Security Journal] 3, 2 (November 2017): 189–231, https://doi.org/10.31599/jkn.v3i2.140.

37 Ahmad Dzaky, "Pemberdayaan pendidikan Islam dalam merespon tantangan globalisasi (telaah pengembangan profesionalitas pendidik dan penguatan sekolah berkualitas)" [Empowerment of Islamic education in responding to the challenges of globalization (a study of professional development of educators and strengthening quality schools)], *Darul Ulum: Jurnal Ilmiah Keagamaan, Pendidikan dan Kemasyarakatan* [Darul Ulum: Scientific Journal of Religion, Education and Society] 11, 1 (2020): 1–27, http://stitdukotabaru.ac.id/ejournal/index.php/darululum/article/view/43.

38 Asmady Idris, "Analisis teori hubungan antarabangsa dari perspektif Islam [Theory analysis of international relations from an Islamic perspective]," *International Journal of West Asian Studies* 11 (2019): 1–18, http://journalarticle.ukm.my/17086/1/36883-116344-1-SM%20%281%29.pdf.

39 Mansor Mohd Noor, "Naratif Bangsa Malaysia: ilmu, kewatanan dan negara bangsa dalam masyarakat kepelbagaian" [Bangsa Malaysia Narrative: knowledge, indigeneity and nation-state in a diverse society], *International Online Journal of Language, Communication, and Humanities* 3, 2 (2020): 33–49, http://insaniah.umk.edu.my/journal/index.php/insaniah/article/view/122.

40 Muhamad Takiyuddin Ismail, "Doktrin Bush: satu analisis hegemoni berideologi Gramsci" [The Bush doctrine: an analysis of Gramsci's ideological hegemony], *e-Bangi* 2, 2 (2007): 1–24, https://ejournal.ukm.my/ebangi/article/viewFile/22051/6862.

41 Werayut Kanchuchat วีระยุทธ กาญจน์ชูฉัตร, "Cāk s̄erīniym kèā s̄ū̀ s̄erīniym h̄ım̀ – Raṭ̄h thịy xyū̀ trng h̄ịn" จากเสรีนิยมเก่าสู่เสรีนิยมใหม่ – รัฐไทยอยู่ตรงไหน [From old liberalism to new liberalism – where is the Thai state?], The 101 World, July 17, 2017, https://www.the101.world/the-liberal-thai-state/.

42 Jarunee Mum Ban Sao จารุณี มุมบ้านเซ่า, "M̄h̄āwithyālạy ni kảkạb k̄hxng raṭ̄h ni bribth k̄hxng s̄erīniym h̄ım̀" มหาวิทยาลัยในกำกับของรัฐในบริบทของเสรีนิยมใหม่ [Autonomous university in the context of neoliberalism], *Wārs̄ār Kārmeụ̄xng Kār Brih̄ār Læa Kṭ H̄māy* วารสารการเมือง การบริหารและกฎหมาย [Journal of politics, administration and law] 12, 2 (2020): 55–78, http://ojslib3.buu.in.th/index.php/law/article/view/7168; Bongkochmas Ek-Iem บงกชมาศ เอกเอี่ยม, "Næwkhid h̄lạng kār phạṭ̄h̄nā: s̄ênthāngkār phạṭ̄h̄nā ni yukh h̄lạng kār phạṭ̄h̄nā" แนวคิดหลังการพัฒนา: เส้นทางการพัฒนาในยุคหลังการพัฒนา [Post-development thinking: path of development in the post-development era], *Wārs̄ār wichākār withyālạy brih̄ār ṣ̄ās̄tr̒* วารสารวิชาการวิทยาลัยบริหารศาสตร์ [Academic journal of the College of Administration] 4, 1 (2021): 159–80, https://so05.tci-thaijo.org/index.php/SASAJ/article/view/248320.

43 Nguyễn Phú Trọng, "Chúng ta cần một hệ thống chính trị mà quyền lực thực sự thuộc về nhân dân, do nhân dân và phục vụ lợi ích của nhân dân" [We need a political system where real power belongs to the people, by the people and serves the interests of the people], *Mặt trận Tổ quốc Việt Nam*, [Vietnam Fatherland Front] May 17, 2021, http://mattran.org.vn/tin-tuc/chung-ta-can-mot-he-thong-chinh-tri-ma-quyen-luc-thuc-su-thuoc-ve-nhan-dan-do-nhan-dan-va-phuc-vu-loi-ich-cua-nhan-dan-37644.html.

44 Tô Huy Rứa, "Cuộc khủng hoảng tài chính toàn cầu và những vấn đề đặt ra đối với Việt Nam" [Global financial crisis and problems for Vietnam]," *Báo Nhân*

Dân, [People Newspaper] December 13, 2009, https://nhandan.vn/tin-tuc-su-kien/Cuộc-khủng-hoảng-tài-chính-toàn-cầu-và-những-vấn-đề-đặt-ra-đối-với-Việt-Nam-559908/.

45 Nguyễn Thái Giao Thủy, "Ngoại giao văn hóa trong chính sách đối ngoại Việt Nam" [Cultural difference in Vietnam's foreign policy], *Tạp chí Khoa học* [Journal of science] 17, 4 (2020): 646–55, https://journal.hcmue.edu.vn/index.php/hcmuejos/article/view/2668.

46 Hitoshi Tanaka 田中均, "Asahi Shimbun Ronza: 2021-nen no gaikō kōsō, hōkatsu-teki tasō-teki kinō shugi (CMF) no susume" 朝日新聞 論座: 2021年の外交構想 – 包括的多層的機能主義 （CMF）のすすめ [Asahi Shimbun Ronza: 2021 diplomatic initiative: recommendation of comprehensive multi-layered functionalism (CMF)]," Institute for International Strategy 国際戦略研究所, December 23, 2020, https://www.jri.co.jp/page.jsp?id=37949.

47 Park Min-hee 박민희 기자, "Migugpyeon, Jung-gugpyeon anin 'Hangug-ui jwapyo' seontaeghae yeogdongjeog oegyoleul" 미국편, 중국편 아닌 '한국의 좌표' 선택해 역동적 외교를 [Choose "Korea's coordinates" rather than the US side and China side for dynamic diplomacy], *Hankyoreh* 한겨레 [The Hankyoreh], December 30, 2020, https://www.hani.co.kr/arti/politics/diplomacy/976485.html.

48 Choi Jae-Duck 최재덕, "Mijungpaegwongyeongjaeng-ui jeonmang-gwa Hangug-ui oegyojeonlyag – Aseangwa Sinnambangjeongchaeg-ui hyeoblyeog-eul jungsim-eulo" 미중패권경쟁의 전망과 한국의 외교전략 - 아세안과 신남방정책의 협력을 중심으로 [Prospects of the US-China hegemonic competition and Korea's diplomatic strategy – focused on cooperation between ASEAN and the New Southern Policy]," *Seullabeuhagbo* 슬라브학보 [Slavic gazette] 35, 2 (2020): 173–204, https://www.dbpia.co.kr/Journal/articleDetail?nodeId=NODE09361913.

49 Ade M. Wirasenjaya, "Regionalisme baru Asia Tenggara dan agenda revitalisasi kepemimpinan Indonesia di kawasan" [New Southeast Asia regionalism and Indonesian leadership revitalization agenda in the region], *Jurnal Majelis* [Journal assembly] 6, Arah Kebijakan Politik Luar Negeri (September 2020): 99–118, https://www.researchgate.net/profile/Ade-Wirasenjaya/publication/352261984_JURNAL_MAJELIS_Media_Aspirasi_Konstitusi/data/60c1326ba6f dcc2e612bfb49/ARAH-POLITIK-LUAR-NEGERI-INDONESIA-JURNAL-MPR.pdf#page=108.

50 Apinan Thasuthorn อภินันท์ ทะสุนทร, "Kār thūt cheing waṭʹhnṭhrrm: Nyobāy t̀āng prathes̄ʹ k̄hxng Thịy tx prathes̄ʹ pheụ̄̂xnb̂ān Xin do cīn" การทูตเชิงวัฒนธรรม : นโยบายต่างประเทศของไทย ต่อประเทศเพื่อนบ้านอินโดจีน [Cultural diplomacy : Thailand's foreign policy to Indochina, the neighbouring countries], *Journal of Politics and Governance* วารสารการเมืองการปกครอง 8, 3 (2018): 192–206, https://so03.tci-thaijo.org/index.php/jopag/article/view/162265; Hoa Nguyễn, "Vị thế Việt Nam trong cục diện mới của khu vực – bình luận – tạp chí cộng sản" [Vietnam's position in the new regional situation], *Tạp chí Cộng sản*, [Communist Magazine], December 12, 2020, https://www.tapchicongsan.org.vn/web/guest/tin-binh-luan/-/asset_publisher/DLIYi5AJyFzY/content/vi-the-viet-nam-trong-cuc-dien-moi-cua-khu-vuc.

51 Masahiko Aoki, Hyung-Ki Kim, and Masahiro Okuno-Fujiwara, eds., *The Role of Government in East Asian Economic Development: Comparative Institutional*

Analysis (New York: Clarendon Press, 1997), 267; Frederic C. Deyo, *The Political Economy of the New Asian Industrialism* (Ithaca, NY: Cornell University Press, 2018), 235; Ha-Joon Chang, *The East Asian Development Experience: The Miracle, the Crisis and the Future* (New York: Zed Books, 2006), 51; Kenichi Ohno and Izumi Ohno, eds., *Japanese Views on Economic Development: Diverse Paths to the Market* (New York: Routledge, 1998), 67; Indermit Gill and Homi Kharas, *An East Asian Renaissance: Ideas for Economic Growth* (Washington, DC: World Bank, 2007), 179.

52 Yun-han Chu and Wen-Chin Wu, *Sources of Regime Legitimacy in East Asian Societies*, Working Paper Series 135 (Taipei: Asian Barometer/Globalbarometer, 2017), http://www.asianbarometer.org/publications/4e2c990b4f87892dc872da06b640aac5.pdf.

53 Deepak Nayyar, *Resurgent Asia: Diversity in Development* (New York: Oxford University Press, 2019), 167; Ajit Singh, "'Asian Capitalism' and the Financial Crisis," *Munich Personal RePEc Archive* 54932 (1998): 1–22, https://mpra.ub.uni-muenchen.de/54932/1/MPRA_paper_54932.pdf.

54 Suk Hyun and James F. Paradise, "Toward an Asian Monetary Fund: Ideas for Transition," *Asian Economic Papers* 19, 2 (2020): 65–77, https://doi.org/10.1162/asep_a_00757.

55 Edelman, *Edelman Trust Barometer 2020* (Edelman, 2020), https://www.edelman.com/sites/g/files/aatuss191/files/2020-01/2020%20Edelman%20Trust%20Barometer%20Global%20Report.pdf.

56 Ministry of Economy, Trade and Industry of Japan 経済産業省, *Handōtai dejitaru sangyō senryaku* 半導体 デジタル産業戦略 [Semiconductor, digital industry strategy] (Tokyo: Ministry of Economy, Trade and Industry of Japan 経済産業省, 2021), https://www.meti.go.jp/press/2021/06/20210604008/20210603008-1.pdf; Ministry of Economy and Finance of the Republic of Korea, "Government Releases an English Booklet on the Korean New Deal," news release, Ministry of Economy and Finance of the Republic of Korea, 2020, https://english.moef.go.kr/pc/selectTbPressCenterDtl.do?boardCd=N0001&seq=4948#fn_download; Ministry of National Development Planning/National Development Planning Agency, Republic of Indonesia [Kantor Menteri Negara Perencanaan Pembangunan Nasional/Badan Perencanaan Pembangunan Nasional] *Visi dan arah pembangunan jangka panjang (PJP): tahun 2005–2025* [Long-term development vision and direction (PJP): 2005–2025] (Jakarta: Ministry of National Development Planning/National Development Planning Agency, Republic of Indonesia [Kantor Menteri Negara Perencanaan Pembangunan Nasional/Badan Perencanaan Pembangunan Nasional], 2005), https://policy.asiapacificenergy.org/sites/default/files/RPJP_2005-2025.pdf.

57 Doh Chull Shin and Hannah June Kim, *Do People in East Asia Truly Prefer Democracy to Its Alternatives? Western Theories versus East Asian Realities*, Working Paper Series 117 (Taipei: Asian Barometer/Globalbarometer, 2016), http://www.asianbarometer.org/publications/9300e4063f025f9bff862f506a22285d.pdf.

58 Ting-Yan Wang and Hong Liu, "An Emerging Asian Model of Governance and Transnational Knowledge Transfer: An Introduction," *Journal of Asian Public Policy* 11, 2 (2018): 121–35, https://doi.org/10.1080/17516234.2018.1477030.

59 Kevin Tze-wai Wong and Victor Zheng, "Democratic Support and Cultural Values: An Empirical Study of Hong Kong and East Asian Societies," *China: An International Journal* 16, 2 (May 2018): 111–32, doi:10.1353/chn.2018.0016; Hsin-Hsin Pan and Wen-Chin Wu, *Quality of Governance and Political Legitimacy: Governance-Based Legitimacy in East Asia*, Working Paper Series 121 (Taipei: Asian Barometer/Globalbarometer, 2016), http://www.asianbarometer.org/publications//96047634fd37cd9b360485a62ea44a56.pdf.

60 Ed Yong, "How the Pandemic Defeated America," *The Atlantic*, August 4, 2020, https://www.theatlantic.com/magazine/archive/2020/09/coronavirus-american-failure/614191/; "COVID Data Tracker," Centers for Disease Control and Prevention (CDC), https://covid.cdc.gov/covid-data-tracker/#datatracker-home.

61 Kishore Mahbubani, "East Asia's New Edge," *Project Syndicate*, July 22, 2020, https://www.project-syndicate.org/commentary/three-reasons-for-better-east-asian-covid19-response-by-kishore-mahbubani-2020-07.

62 Tanaka, "Asahi Shimbun Ronza: 'Ajiataiheiyō' Kara Indotaiheiyō e."

63 Haba, "Yōroppa no tōgō, Ajia no bundan."

64 Asia Pacific Initiative アジア・パシフィック・イニシアティブ, "Nihon ga kokusaitekina haisha ni naranai tame ni hitsuyōna koto (Funabashi Yōichi, Hosoya Yūichi, Jimbo Ken)" 日本が国際的な敗者にならない為に必要なこと（船橋洋一・細谷雄一・神保謙） [What Japan needs to do to avoid becoming an international loser (Yoichi Funabashi, Yuichi Hosoya, Ken Jimbo)], Asia Pacific Initiative アジア・パシフィック・イニシアティブ, May 3, 2021, https://apinitiative.org/2021/05/03/20984/.

65 Park Yong-soo 박용수, "Mijung paegwonyeongjaeng-gwa Mun Jaein jeongbuui daeeungjeonlyag" 미중 패권경쟁과 문재인 정부의 대응전략 [US-China rivalry and the Moon Jae-in administration's strategy], *Hangugdongbug-anonchong* 한국동북아논총 [*Journal of Northeast Asian Studies*] 25, 1 (2020): 5–27, https://doi.org/10.21807/JNAS.2020.03.94.005.

66 Eunmi Choi and Jeonghun Min 최은미 민정훈, "Abe jeong-gwon ha minjogjeongcheseong-gwa jayulobgo gaebangdoen Indo-Taepyeong-Yang jeonlyag-e gwanhan yeongu" 아베 정권 하 민족정체성과 자유롭고 개방된 인도-태평양 전략에 관한 연구 [National identity, free and open Indo-Pacific, and Abe government's foreign policy], *Gugjejeongchiyeongu* 국제정치연구 [The journal of international relations] 22, 3 (September 2019): 313–33, https://doi.org/10.15235/jir.2019.09.22.3.313.

67 Kim Taehwan 김태환, "Gachioegyoui busang-gwa gachiui 'jin-yeonghwa' gangdaegug salyewa Hangug gong-gong-oegyoui banghyangseong" 가치외교의 부상과 가치의 '진영화' 강대국 사례와 한국 공공외교의 방향성 [Values diplomacy driving global "blocization" of values : implications of great power cases for

Korea's public diplomacy], *Munhwawa Jeongchi* 문화와 정치 [Culture and politics] 6, 1 (March 2019): 5–32, https://www.dbpia.co.kr/Journal/article Detail?nodeId=NODE08002136.
68 Association of Southeast Asian Nations (ASEAN), "ASEAN Outlook on the Indo-Pacific," 2019, https://www.asean2019.go.th/wp-content/uploads/2019/06/11c49cba41666e4b9e5d4255186f2923-1.pdf.
69 Hoang Thi Ha, *ASEAN Navigates between Indo-Pacific Polemics and Potentials*, Perspective 49 (Singapore: ISEAS–Yusof Ishak Institute, 2021), https://www.iseas.edu.sg/wp-content/uploads/2021/03/ISEAS_Perspective_2021_49.pdf.
70 Indri Yanuarti et al., "Strategi kerja sama Indo-Pasifik untuk mendukung pertahanan negara: perspektif Indonesia" [Indo-Pacific cooperation as a strategy to enhance state defense: Indonesia's perspective], *Jurnal Strategi Pertahanan Semesta* [Journal of universal defense strategy] 6, 1 (2020): 41–70, https://jurnalprodi.idu.ac.id/index.php/SPS/article/download/538/519; Marcheilla Ariesta, "Indonesia gunakan Indo-Pasifik sebagai geopolitik kolaborasi" [Indonesia uses Indo-Pacific as collaborative geopolitics], *Medcom.Id*, October 24, 2018, https://www.medcom.id/internasional/asia/0k8Yvo0K-indonesia-gunakan-indo-pasifik-sebagai-geopolitik-kolaborasi.
71 Indri Yanuarti, Makarim Wibisono, and I Wayan Midhio, "Strategi kerja sama Indo-Pasifik untuk mendukung pertahanan negara: perspektif Indonesia" [Indo-Pacific cooperation strategy to support state defence: Indonesian perspective], *Strategi Perang Semesta* [Total war strategy] 6, 1 (2020), http://jurnalprodi.idu.ac.id/index.php/SPS/article/view/538; Rodon Pedrason, "Analisis kebijakan keamanan Indonesia di tengah persaingan China dan Amerika serikat di Laut Cina Selatan" [Analysis of Indonesia's security policy amid competition between China and the United States in the South China Sea]," *Jurnal Sains Sosio Humaniora* 4, 2 (December 2020): 997–1008, https://online-journal.unja.ac.id/JSSH/article/view/14407.
72 Kuik Cheng-Chwee and Ruhanie Ahmad, "'Hedging' di Laut China Selatan: analisis tindakan negara-negara Asia Tenggara" [Hedging in the South China Sea: analyzing Southeast Asian states' policy actions]," *Malaysian Journal of History, Politics and Strategic Studies* 47, 3 (December 2020): 58–86, http://journalarticle.ukm.my/17095/1/44773-144087-1-SM.pdf.
73 Piti Srisaengnam ปิติ ศรีแสงนาม, "Xāseīyn ṇ cudṣ̄ūnỳklāng k̄hxng yuthṭhṣ̄āsṭr̒ Xin Do-Pæsifik" อาเซียน ณ จุดศูนย์กลางของยุทธศาสตร์อินโด-แปซิฟิก [ASEAN at the centre of the Indo-Pacific strategy], 101.World, September 23, 2019, https://www.the101.world/asean-in-the-indo-pacific-strategy/; Rosli Jaya, "Mencatur sengketa di Laut China Selatan" [Arranging disputes in the South China Sea], *Suara Sarawak*, July 28, 2020, https://suarasarawak.my/2020/07/mencatur-sengketa-di-laut-china-selatan/.
74 "'Yuthṭhṣ̄āsṭr̒ Xin Do-Pæsifik' t̄ĥāthāy khwām pĕnklāng Xāseīyn" 'ยุทธศาสตร์อินโด-แปซิฟิก'ท้าทายความเป็นกลางอาเซียน ["Indo-Pacific strategy" challenges ASEAN neutrality], *Krungtheph Ṭhurkic* กรุงเทพธุรกิจ, [Bangkok business] June 22, 2021, https://www.bangkokbiznews.com/news/944913.
75 Nguyễn Tuấn Anh and Trần Thế Tuấn, "Đông nam á trong chiến lược Ấn Độ Dương – Thái Bình Dương tự do và rộng mở Của Mỹ" [Southeast Asia in

America's free and open Indo-Pacific strategy], *Tạp chí Nghiên cứu Đông Nam Á* [Journal of Southeast Asian studies] 7, 244 (2020), https://thuvienso.quochoi.vn/handle/11742/58556.

76 Phạm Hoàng Tú Linh, "Chiến lược ấn độ dương – Thái Bình Dương và tác động đối với Asean trong bối cảnh hiện nay (phần 2)" [The Indo-Pacific strategy and its impact on ASEAN in the current context (part 2)], Center for Indian Study, Ho Chi Minh National Academy of Politics [Trung tâm Nghiên cứu Ấn Độ, Học viện Chính trị quốc gia Hồ Chí Minh], October 31, 2018, http://cis.org.vn/article/3302/chien-luoc-an-do-duong-thai-binh-duong-va-tac-dong-doi-voi-asean-trong-boi-canh-hien-nay-phan-2.html.

77 Li Wan Tao, Suyono Thamrin, and Surryanto Djoko Waluyo, "Kerjasama keamanan China-Indonesia guna menangkal ancaman keamanan maritim kedua negara" [China-Indonesia security cooperation to determine the second country's maritime security threats], *Strategi Pertahanan Laut* [Sea defense strategy] 5, 3 (December 2019), http://jurnalprodi.idu.ac.id/index.php/SPL/article/view/586.

78 Mohd Mizan Aslam, "Konflik di Laut China Selatan makin genting" [The conflict in the South China Sea is getting more serious], *Harian Metro,* August 11, 2021, https://www.hmetro.com.my/rencana/2021/08/741467/konflik-di-laut-china-selatan-makin-genting; Mohd Fadhli Mohd Sulaiman, "Elak Malaysia terhimpit konflik kuasa besar di Laut China Selatan" [Avoid Malaysia being squeezed by a superpower conflict in the South China Sea], *Utusan Malaysia,* March 16, 2021, http://www.utusan.com.my/berita/2021/03/elak-malaysia-terhimpit-konflik-kuasa-besar-di-laut-china-selatan/.

79 Paijuntuek, "Khwām mạ̄nkhng k̄hxng xāseīyn kạb kār cạdkār khwām s̄ạmp̄hạnṭh̒ prathes̄ p̄hāynxk."

80 Trần Tuấn Sơn and Vũ Đức Tho, "Về sáng kiến an ninh hàng hải (MSI) của Mỹ ở khu vực Đông Nam Á" [On the US Maritime Security Initiative (MSI) in Southeast Asia], *Bộ đội Biên phòng Việt Nam* [Vietnam Border Guard], January 18, 2021, http://lyluanchinhtri.vn/home/index.php/thuc-tien/item/3390-ve-sang-kien-an-ninh-hang-hai-msi-cua-my-o-khu-vuc-dong-nam-a.html.

81 Association of Southeast Asian Nations (ASEAN), "ASEAN Outlook on the Indo-Pacific."

82 Narendra Modi, "Prime Minister's Keynote Address at Shangri-La Dialogue" (speech, Shangri-La Dialogue, Singapore, June 1, 2018), Government of India, Ministry of External Affairs, https://www.mea.gov.in/Speeches-Statements.htm?dtl/29943/Prime+Ministers+Keynote+Address+at+Shangri+La+Dialogue+June+01+2018.

83 Association of Southeast Asian Nations (ASEAN), "ASEAN Outlook on the Indo-Pacific."

84 Government of India, Ministry of External Affairs, "Indo-Pacific Division Briefs" [2020], https://mea.gov.in/Portal/ForeignRelation/Indo_Feb_07_2020.pdf.

85 Lee Hsien Loong, "The Endangered Asian Century: America, China, and the Perils of Confrontation," *Foreign Affairs* 99, 4 (July/August 2020): 52–64.

86 Natalie Sambhi, "Indonesia's Indo-Pacific Vision: Staying the Course in a Covid-19 World," *Asia Policy* 15, 4 (October 2020): 37–50.

87 Jürgen Haacke, "The Concept of Hedging and Its Application to Southeast Asia: A Critique and a Proposal for a Modified Conceptual and Methodological Framework," *International Relations of the Asia-Pacific* 19, 3 (2019): 375–417, https://doi.org/10.1093/irap/lcz010.

88 Lee Hsien Loong, "PM Lee Hsien Loong at the IISS Shangri-La Dialogue 2019" (speech, Shangri-La Dialogue, Sngapore, May 31, 2019), Prime Minister's Office Singapore, https://www.pmo.gov.sg/Newsroom/PM-Lee-Hsien-Loong-at-the-IISS-Shangri-La-Dialogue-2019; Lee, "The Endangered Asian Century."

Chapter 3: Asian Counter-Narratives: Western State Identity in the Asia-Pacific

1 See, for instance, "The Power of America's Example: The Biden Plan for Leading the Democratic World to Meet the Challenges of the 21st Century," Biden Harris Democrats, Democratic National Committee, https://joebiden.com/americanleadership/; Melissa Conley Tyler, "Will the Next President Restore American Leadership in Asia?" Pursuit, University of Melbourne, October 20, 2020, https://pursuit.unimelb.edu.au/articles/will-the-next-president-restore-american-leadership-in-asia; Bradley Wood, "Australia's Vision of Leadership in the Indo-Pacific," East Asia Forum, July 15, 2020, https://www.eastasiaforum.org/2020/07/15/australias-vision-of-leadership-in-the-indo-pacific/; Ashley Townshend and Brendan Thomas-Noone, "Australia Steps Up in Defense of the Indo-Pacific Order," *The Diplomat*, September 1, 2020, https://thediplomat.com/2020/08/australia-steps-up-in-defense-of-the-indo-pacific-order/.

2 European Commission, *Questions and Answers: EU Strategy for Cooperation in the Indo-Pacific* (Brussels: European Commission, 2021), https://ec.europa.eu/commission/presscorner/detail/en/QANDA_21_4709; White House, "Joint Leaders Statement on AUKUS," news release, September 15, 2021, https://www.whitehouse.gov/briefing-room/statements-releases/2021/09/15/joint-leaders-statement-on-aukus/.

3 Veerle Nouwens and Garima Mohan, "Europe Eyes the Indo-Pacific, but Now It's Time to Act," War on the Rocks, June 24, 2021, https://warontherocks.com/2021/06/europe-eyes-the-indo-pacific-but-now-its-time-to-act/; "New Aukus Alliance yet Another Threat to Peace and Stability," *South China Morning Post*, September 17, 2021, https://www.scmp.com/comment/opinion/article/3149212/new-aukus-alliance-yet-another-threat-peace-and-stability.

4 White House, "President Biden to Convene Leaders' Summit for Democracy," news release, August 11, 2021, https://www.whitehouse.gov/briefing-room/statements-releases/2021/08/11/president-biden-to-convene-leaders-summit-for-democracy/; Andrew Latham, "The G7 and NATO Won't Cut It: Why a New Alliance Is Needed," *The Hill*, April 12, 2021, https://thehill.com/opinion/international/547742-the-g7-and-nato-wont-cut-it-why-a-new-alliance-is-needed.

5 "U.S. and 'Like-Minded' Partners Will Keep Security in Asia: Admiral," *Reuters*, December 12, 2019, https://www.reuters.com/article/us-southchinasea-usa

-idUSKBN1YH0OI; "New Aukus Alliance yet Another Threat to Peace and Stability."
6 Nahal Toosi, "Are You on the List? Biden's Democracy Summit Spurs Anxieties – and Skepticism," *POLITICO,* November 28, 2020, https://www.politico.com/news/2020/11/28/biden-democracy-summit-440819; Jeffrey Cimmino and Matthew Kroenig, "Strengthen Likeminded Allies and Partners and the Rules-Based International System," Atlantic Council Strategy Paper Series, Atlantic Council, December 16, 2020, https://www.atlanticcouncil.org/content-series/atlantic-council-strategy-paper-series/strengthen-likeminded-allies-and-partners-and-the-rules-based-international-system/.
7 Yee-Kuang Heng, "Enabling NATO's Engagements with Like-Minded Partners in the Asia-Pacific," in *NATO and the Asia-Pacific,* ed. Joseph McQuaide (Toronto: NATO Association of Canada, 2020), https://www.researchgate.net/publication/347397605_Enabling_NATO's_engagements_with_like-minded_partners_in_the_Asia-Pacific_in_NATO_and_the_Asia-Pacific_The_NATO_Association_of_Canada_Fall_2020.
8 Michael J. Green, "An Alliance of Democracies Is Essential: The Only Question Is – What Kind?" *The Interpreter,* June 16, 2021, https://www.lowyinstitute.org/the-interpreter/alliance-democracies-essential.
9 Andrew Erskine, "Special Report: NATO's Indo-Pacific Strategy Needs Japan," NATO Association of Canada, September 2, 2021, https://natoassociation.ca/special-report-natos-indo-pacific-strategy-needs-japan/.
10 Ishaan Tharoor, "An Emerging New Alliance of Democracies," *Washington Post,* December 18, 2020, https://www.washingtonpost.com/world/2020/12/18/an-emerging-new-alliance-democracies/.
11 Michael A. Peters et al., "The China-Threat Discourse, Trade, and the Future of Asia. A Symposium," *Educational Philosophy and Theory* 54 (2022): 1531–49, https://doi.org/10.1080/00131857.2021.1897573.
12 See, for example, Ryan Hass, "The Case for Continued American Leadership in Asia," Brookings Institution, December 29, 2017, https://www.brookings.edu/opinions/the-case-for-continued-american-leadership-in-asia/.
13 See, for instance, US Department of State, *A Free and Open Indo-Pacific: Advancing a Shared Vision* (Washington, DC: US Department of State, 2019), https://www.state.gov/wp-content/uploads/2019/11/Free-and-Open-Indo-Pacific-4Nov2019.pdf.
14 John Lee, "Joe Biden Shows He Is No Barack Obama and Is Up for the Fight," *Weekend Australian,* February 8, 2021, https://www.theaustralian.com.au/commentary/joe-biden-shows-he-is-no-barack-obama-and-is-up-for-the-fight/news-story/30f2953a4cc561bcac53995e8efab4f1; Jorge Castañeda, "Jorge Castañeda on Why America's Civilisation Will Prevail," *The Economist,* August 31, 2021, https://www.economist.com/by-invitation/2021/08/31/jorge-castaneda-on-why-americas-civilisation-will-prevail; Robert Kagan, "A Superpower, Like It or Not: Why Americans Must Accept Their Global Role," *Foreign Affairs,* March/April 2021, https://www.foreignaffairs.com/articles/united-states/2021-02-16/superpower-it-or-not.

15 See, for instance, Susumu Nishibe 西部邁, *America no taizai* アメリカの大罪 [America's deadly sins] (Tokyo: Shogakukan 小学館, 2003).

16 Takamichi Takahashi 高橋孝途, "Taiwan sōtō-sen ni omou: Chūgoku ni yoru Taiwan no buryoku tōitsu no kanōsei to Nihon no sonae" 台湾総統選に想う：中国による台湾の武力統一の可能性と日本の備え [Thinking about Taiwan's presidential election: a possibility of China's unification of Taiwan's armed forces and Japan's preparation], *Mainichi Newspapers* 毎日新聞, December 27, 2019, https://mainichi.jp/premier/politics/articles/20191224/pol/00m/010/008000c.

17 Shigeru Ishiba 石破茂, "Anpo kaitei 60-nen sono kōzai to kongo" 安保改定60年その功罪と今後 [60 years of the security treaty revision: its merits and demerits and the future] (press conference, Japan National Press Club 日本記者クラブ, Tokyo, February 25, 2020), https://s3-us-west-2.amazonaws.com/jnpc-prd-public-oregon/files/2021/03/0f603fab-1dd9-42de-a6fc-80a403241716.pdf; Oki Nagai 永井央紀, "Ishiba-shi ga Hōchū, kankei kyōka o uttae" 石破氏が訪中、関係強化を訴え [Mr. Ishiba appeals for strengthening relations during his visit to China], *Nikkei* 日本経済新聞, December 28, 2018, https://www.nikkei.com/article/DGXMZO39495690Y8A221C1EA3000/.

18 Katsuhisa Saito 斉藤 勝久, "Beichu zenmen taiketsu, Taiwan yūji wa ariuru ka: Miyamoto Yūji moto Chūgoku taishi ga yomitoku kaikeihō mondai" 米中全面対決、台湾有事はあり得るか：宮本雄二・元中国大使が読み解く「海警法」問題 [US-China full-scale confrontation, is Taiwan contingency possible: Yuji Miyamoto, former Chinese ambassador interprets the "Coast Guard Law" issue], Nippon.com, April 7, 2021, https://www.nippon.com/ja/in-depth/d00702/.

19 Kim Kwanok 김관옥, "Teuleompeujeongbuui Daejung-gug anbojeongchaeg: Baideunjeongbuwaui bigyoyeongu" 트럼프정부의 대중국 안보정책: 바이든정부와의 비교연구 [The Trump administration's security policy toward China: a comparative study with the Biden administration's policy], *Gugjejeongchiyeongu* 국제정치연구 [The journal of international relations] 24, 2 (2021): 53–74, https://www.dbpia.co.kr/Journal/articleDetail?nodeId=NODE10573185.

20 Lee Hyobin, Son Wonbae, and Park Mun Su 이효빈 손원배 박문수, "Mi·Jung galdeung-eulo bon gisulpaegwon jeonjaeng: Teuleompeuneun wae Hwaweileul gong-gyeoghaessneunga?" 미·중 갈등으로 본 기술패권 전쟁 : 트럼프는 왜 화웨이를 공격했는가? [A technology hegemony war between the United States and China : why did Trump attack Huawei?], *Jeongchijeongboyeongu* 정치정보연구 [Political Information Research] 23, 2 (2020): 349–74, https://www.dbpia.co.kr/Journal/articleDetail?nodeId=NODE09370030.

21 Park Hwee-rhak 박휘락, "Migug 'Indo-Taepyeong-yang jeonlyag'gwa Hangug-e daehan ham-ui bunseog: 'Tukidideseu hamjeong'ui wiheom" 미국 "인도-태평양 전략" 과 한국에 대한 함의 분석: "투키디데스 함정"의 위험 [An analysis of the "US Indo-Pacific strategy" and implications for South Korea: risks of "Thucydides' trap"], *Gugjejeongchiyeongu* 국제정치연구 [The journal of international relations] 23, 2 (2020): 105–29, https://doi.org/10.15235/jir.2020.06.23.2.105.

22 Cabinet Office, Government of Japan 内閣府政府広報室, "*Gaikō ni kansuru yoron-chōsa" no gaiyō* 「外交に関する世論調査」の概要 [Overview of "public opinion

poll on diplomacy"] (Tokyo: Cabinet Office, Government of Japan 内閣府政府広報室, 2021), https://survey.gov-online.go.jp/r02/r02-gaiko/gairyaku.pdf.
23 NHK, *"Nihon to Amerika ni kansuru yoronchōsa" tanjun shūkei kekka* 「日本とアメリカに関する世論調査」単純集計結果 ["Public opinion survey on Japan and the United States" simple aggregation results] (Tokyo: NHK, 2020), https://www.nhk.or.jp/senkyo/opinion-polls/01/opinion-polls.pdf.
24 Ibid.
25 Richard Wike, Janell Fetterolf, and Mara Mordecai, "U.S. Image Plummets Internationally as Most Say Country Has Handled Coronavirus Badly," Pew Research Center, September 15, 2020, https://www.pewresearch.org/global/2020/09/15/us-image-plummets-internationally-as-most-say-country-has-handled-coronavirus-badly/.
26 Korea Institute for National Unification 통일연구원, 「*Mi daeseon ihu Han-Migwangye jeonmang-e daehan yeolonjosa*」 *josagyeolgwa balpyo* 「미 대선 이후 한미관계 전망에 대한 여론조사」 조사결과 발표 [Public opinion survey on the prospects of Korea-US relations after the US election] (Seoul: Korea Institute for National Unification 통일연구원, 2020), https://www.kinu.or.kr/brd/board/630/L/menu/399?brdType=R&thisPage=1&bbIdx=59459&searchField=&searchText=.
27 Gallup International, *4dae gang-gug gugje jeongchaeg insiggwa 2030nyeon cho-gangdaegug jeonmang 4* 대 강국 국제 정책 인식과 2030년 초강대국 전망 [Awareness of the international policy of the four major powers and the prospect of super-powers in 2030], Gallup International End of Year Survey 다국가 비교 조사 (Seoul: Gallup International, 2000), 12, https://www.gallup.co.kr/dir/Gallup Report/GallupReport(20210304)_Superpower_GIA.pdf.
28 Korea Institute for National Unification, 「*Mi daeseon ihu HanMigwangye jeonmang-e daehan yeolonjosa*」 *josagyeolgwa balpyo*.
29 Choi Ji-sun 최지선, "Choeuseon oegyogwaje ... 'Hanmidongmaeng ganghwa' 50.2% 'Nambuggwangye bog-won' 17.5%" 최우선 외교과제 ... '한미동맹 강화' 50.2% '남북관계 복원' 17.5% [A top priority for diplomacy ... "strengthening the Republic of Korea–US alliance" 50.2% "restoring inter-Korean relations" 17.5%], *dongA.com*, January 2, 2021, https://www.donga.com/news/Politics/article/all/20210102/104734352/1.
30 Ary Arseno, "Containment Amerika serikat terhadap fenomena rise of China dalam perspektif hegemoni realisme" [United States containment of the rise of China phenomenon in the perspective of hegemony realism], *Indonesian Journal of Global Discourse* 12, 1 (January-June 2019): 167–82, https://doi.org/10.31219/osf.io/unbfy.
31 Lalu Azhar Rafsanjani, Lalu Puttrawandi Karjaya, and Khairur Rizki, "Rivalitas Amerika Serikat (AS) dan China dalam menjadi security orderer di Asia Timur" [The rivalry of the United States (US) and China in the security order in East Asia], *Indonesian Journal of Global Discourse* 2, 1 (January-June 2020): 27–44, http://ijgd.unram.ac.id/index.php/ijgd/article/view/6.
32 Ahmad Sahide, "Proteksionisme Trump dan masa depan supremasi politik AS" [Trump's protectionism and America's global political supremacy], *Jurnal*

Ilmiah Hubungan Internasional [Scientific journal of international relations] 17, 1 (2021): 1–16, https://doi.org/10.26593/jihi.v17i1.3570.1-16.

33 Rais Hussin, "Malaysia mesti bijak pilih tawaran dua kuasa besar" [Malaysia must wisely choose the offer of the two great powers], *Berita Harian*, [Daily news] May 25, 2020, https://www.bharian.com.my/kolumnis/2020/05/692922/malaysia-mesti-bijak-pilih-tawaran-dua-kuasa-besar.

34 Kuik Cheng-Chwee and Ruhanie Ahmad, "'Hedging' di Laut China Selatan: analisis tindakan negara-negara Asia Tenggara" ["Hedging" in the South China Sea: analyzing Southeast Asian states' policy actions], *Malaysian Journal of History, Politics and Strategic Studies* 47, 3 (December 2020): 58–86, https://ejournal.ukm.my/jebat/article/view/44773.

35 Chittipat Poonkham จิตติภัทร พูนขำ, "C̄hāk thas̄ʹn̂ nyobāy t̀āng pra thes̄ʹ k̄hxng Bị Den: meụ̄x Xmerikā t̂xng nả lok" ฉากทัศน์นโยบายต่างประเทศของไบเดน : เมื่ออเมริกาต้องนำโลก [Biden's foreign policy scene: when America leads the world], The 101 World, November 9, 2020, https://www.the101.world/bidens-foreign-policy/.

36 Piti Srisaengnam ปิติ ศรีแสงนาม, "The 1st QUAD summit: Cīn k̄hùxs̄ʹ p̄hạy s̀xn rên" The 1st QUAD Summit: จีนคือภัยซ่อนเร้น [The 1st QUAD summit: China is a hidden threat], The 101 World, March 16, 2021, https://www.the101.world/the-1st-quad-summit/.

37 Piti Srisaengnam ปิติ ศรีแสงนาม, "53 pī X̄āseīyn: keid cāk S̄ngkhrāmyĕn 1.0 p̄hechiy h̄n̂ā S̄ngkhrāmyĕn 2.0" 53 ปีอาเซียน: เกิดจากสงครามเย็น 1.0 เผชิญหน้าสงครามเย็น 2.0 [53 years ASEAN: born of the Cold War 1.0, facing the Cold War 2.0], The 101 World, August 7, 2020, https://www.the101.world/53-years-of-asean/; Kantheera Phuriwikrai กานต์ธีรา ภูริวิกรัย, "Mxng s̄mrp̣hūmi X̄āseīyn læa Xin Do-Pæsifik 2021" มองสมรภูมิอาเซียนและอินโด-แปซิฟิก 2021 [Looking at the ASEAN and Indo-Pacific battlefield 2021], The 101 World, February 5, 2021, https://www.the101.world/asean-and-indo-pacific-2021/.

38 Trần Minh, "Châu Á – Thái Bình Dương: tâm điểm bất ổn mới (kỳ 2)" [Asia-Pacific: the new focus of instability (part 2)], *Vietnam Times Tạp Chí Thời Đại*, [Vietnam Times] December 11, 2020, https://thoidai.com.vn/chau-a-thai-binh-duong-tam-diem-bat-on-moi-ky-2-123173.html.

39 Phạm Thị Thanh Bình, "'Chiến lược Ấn Độ Dương – Thái Bình Dương tự do và rộng mở' của Mỹ: vai trò và cách thức triển khai" [America's "Free and Open Indo-Pacific Strategy": role and implementation], *Tạp chí Cộng sản*, [Communist Magazine], April 4, 2020, https://www.tapchicongsan.org.vn/web/guest/the-gioi-van-de-su-kien/-/2018/816028/%E2%80%9Cchien-luoc-an-do-duong---thai-binh-duong-tu-do-va-rong-mo%E2%80%9D-cua-my--vai-tro-va-cach-thuc-trien-khai.aspx.

40 Trần Việt Thái, "Chiến lược Ấn Độ Dương – Thái Bình Dương tự do, rộng mở và vấn đề đặt ra đối với Asean" [Free and open Indo-Pacific strategy and problems for ASEAN], *National Defence Journal Tạp Chí Quốc Phòng Toàn Dân*, October 12, 2018, http://tapchiqptd.vn/vi/quoc-phong-quan-su-nuoc-ngoai/chien-luoc-an-do-duong-thai-binh-duong-tu-do-rong-mo-va-van-de-dat-ra-doi-voi-asean/12930.html.

41 Siew Mum Tang et al., *The State of Southeast Asia: 2020 Survey Report* (Singapore: ISEAS–Yusof Ishak Institute, 2020), 32, https://www.iseas.edu.sg/images/pdf/TheStateofSEASurveyReport_2020.pdf.
42 Ibid., 40.
43 Ibid., 29.
44 Hsin-Hsin Pan, "Is the USA the Only Role Model in Town? Empirical Evidence from the Asian Barometer Survey," *Journal of Asian and African Studies* 55, 5 (February 2020): 733–49.
45 Laura Silver, Kat Devlin, and Christine Huang, "Unfavorable Views of China Reach Historic Highs in Many Countries," Pew Research Center, May 10, 2021, https://www.pewresearch.org/global/2020/10/06/unfavorable-views-of-china-reach-historic-highs-in-many-countries/.
46 Ministry for Europe and Foreign Affairs of France, "The Indo-Pacific Region: A Priority for France," Ministry for Europe and Foreign Affairs of France, https://www.diplomatie.gouv.fr/en/country-files/asia-and-oceania/the-indo-pacific-region-a-priority-for-france/.
47 Cristina Gallardo, "Global Britain Pivots to Asia," *POLITICO,* March 15, 2021, https://www.politico.eu/article/boris-johnson-walks-on-a-tightrope-in-uks-foreign-policy-reset-asia/.
48 Jürgen Haacke, "The United Kingdom's 'Tilt' toward the Indo-Pacific," East Asia Forum, June 18, 2021, https://www.eastasiaforum.org/2021/06/18/the-united-kingdoms-tilt-toward-the-indo-pacific/.
49 Fraser Cameron, "Asia Wants a Stronger Global Role for Europe," EURACTIV, February 16, 2017, https://www.euractiv.com/section/trade-society/opinion/asia-wants-a-stronger-global-role-for-europe/.
50 Kumiko Haba 羽場久美子, "Yōroppa no tōgō, Ajia no bundan wa, Amerika no sekai senryaku – Ajia no kyōdō o ikani tsukuru ka? Ajia kinrin shokoku to no tairitsu o koete – gakujutsu nettowāku no kōchiku" ヨーロッパの統合、アジアの分断は、 アメリカの世界戦略 ―アジアの共同をいかに作るか？ アジア近隣諸国との対立をこえて ―学術ネットワークの構築― [The integration of Europe and the division of Asia are America's global strategy – how to create collaboration in Asia: beyond conflicts with neighbouring Asian countries – building academic networks," *Gakujutsu No Dōkō* 学術の動向 [Academic trends] 25, 9 (2020): 49–54, https://doi.org/10.5363/tits.25.9_49.
51 Hirotaka Watanabe 渡邊啓貴, "Ōshū no Ajia no renketsu-sei senryaku to sekai senryaku to shite no senryaku-teki jiritsu" 欧州のアジアの連結性戦略と世界戦略としての戦略的自立 [Europe's Asian connectivity strategy and strategic independence as a global strategy], Japan Forum on International Relations 日本国際フォーラム, March 31, 2021, https://www.jfir.or.jp/wp/wp-content/uploads/2021/03/e2a51fc73ede55830fe12a62e4592f93.pdf.
52 Michito Tsuruoka 鶴岡路人, "Ōshū wa 'Indotaiheiyō' ni naze, doko made kan'yo suru ka" 欧州は「インド太平洋」になぜ、どこまで関与するか [Why and how much Europe is involved in the "Indo-Pacific"], *Foresight,* July 21, 2021, https://www.fsight.jp/articles/-/48110.

53 Yuichiro Miyashita 宮下雄一郎, "Kenkyū repōto: kaiyō kokka to shite no Furansu: Indotaiheiyō pawā ga kakaeru mondai"〔研究レポート〕海洋国家としてのフランス:「インド太平洋パワー」が抱える問題 [Research report: France as a maritime nation: problems of "Indo-Pacific power"], Japan Institute of International Affairs 日本国際問題研究所, March 23, 2021, https://www.jiia.or.jp/column/post-71.html.

54 Shim Sung Eun 심성은, "Yuleob-ui Indo-Taepyeong-yang jeonlyag: Peulangseuui yeoghal-eul jungsim-eulo" 유럽의 인도-태평양 전략: 프랑스의 역할을 중심으로 [Europe and Indo-Pacific strategy: France's role and contribution], *Jeongchijeongboyeongu* 정치정보연구 [Political Information Research] 24, 2 (2021): 119–49, https://doi.org/10.15617/psc.2021.6.30.2.119.

55 Son Jinseok 손진석, "'In·taeeseo milae jilseo gyeoljeongdoenda' Asialo dongjinhaneun Yeong·Bul·Dog" '인·태에서 미래 질서 결정된다' 아시아로 동진하는 英·佛·獨 ["The future order is determined by the human race" British, French, and Germany moving eastward to Asia], *Chosunilbo* 조선일보 [Chosun Media], August 3, 2021, https://www.chosun.com/international/international_general/2021/08/03/3ZRWDKLVMJHL7OH6DA6ATMZO34/; Jeon Jeong-yoon 전정윤, "'Jung-gug gyeonje' Indo·Taepyeong-yang hyeoblyeog, Yuleob-eulo hwagdae" '중국 견제' 인도·태평양 협력, 유럽으로 확대 [Indo-Pacific cooperation to "check in China" expands to Europe], *Hankyoreh* 한겨레 [The Hankyoreh], April 6, 2021, https://www.hani.co.kr/arti/international/international_general/989721.html; Yoo Yong-won 유용원 and Kim Jin-myung 김진명, "Nato·Kwodeu Taepyeong-yangseo yeonhabhunlyeon ... Jung powijeonseon guchughanda" 나토·쿼드 태평양서 연합훈련 ... 中 포위전선 구축한다 [NATO-Quad joint exercises in the Pacific ... China builds a siege line], *Chosunilbo* 조선일보 [Chosun Media], June 15, 2021, https://www.chosun.com/international/international_general/2021/06/15/3GVOI2LPZNAUJMVCXLGLJB2UMQ/.

56 Lee Jaeseung 이재승, "Indo·Taepyeong-yang 'saepanjjagi' ttwieodeuneun Yuleob ... Han, 'aus-saideo'ui sigan kkeutnaganda" 인도·태평양 '새판짜기' 뛰어드는 유럽 ... 韓, '아웃사이더'의 시간 끝나간다 [Europe jumping into the Indo-Pacific "new game." The time of "the outsider" is ending in Korea], *Chosunilbo* 조선일보 [Chosun Media], May 31, 2021, https://www.chosun.com/opinion/specialist_column/2021/05/31/X43JJ7TSSBGS7J4OIIQNXK2GFE/.

57 AFP, "Jerman kirim kapal perang ke Indo-Pasifik, klaim bela mitra" [Germany sends warships to Indo-Pacific, claims defending partners], CNN Indonesia, March 8, 2021, https://www.cnnindonesia.com/internasional/20210802213824-134-675503/jerman-kirim-kapal-perang-ke-indo-pasifik-klaim-bela-mitra; Arsito Hidayatullah, "Jerman kirim kapal perangnya ke Laut Cina Selatan dan Pasifik" [Germany sends warships to the South China Sea and the Pacific], suara.com, August 4, 2021, https://www.suara.com/news/2021/08/04/173408/jerman-kirim-kapal-perangnya-ke-laut-cina-selatan-dan-pasifik.

58 Adlinahani Binti Khalil, "Britain mahu jadi kuasa tentera utama dunia" [Britain wants to be the world's leading military power], *Utusan Malaysia,* [Malaysian envoy] August 2, 2021, https://www.utusan.com.my/luar-negara/2021/08/britain-mahu-jadi-kuasa-tentera-utama-dunia/; AFP, "Perancis cabar Beijing di

Laut China Selatan" [France challenges Beijing in the South China Sea], *Berita Harian* [Daily news], June 12, 2018, https://www.bharian.com.my/dunia/eropah/2018/06/437300/perancis-cabar-beijing-di-laut-china-selatan.

59 "'Xāseīyn' s̄mrphūmi h̄ım̀ tawạntk thæ̆k thīm ngạdk̄hx Cīn – S̄h̄rạṭh̄‡ cı̂ khelīyṙ pạyh̄ā Phm̀ā" 'อาเซียน' สมรภูมิใหม่ ตะวันตกแท็กทีมงัดข้อจีน - สหรัฐฯ จี้เคลียร์ปัญหาพม่า ["ASEAN" new battleground, the west tag team to break the China-US deal to clear the Burma problem], Voice Online, August 4, 2021, https://www.voicetv.co.th/read/-bnRSnwue.

60 Lục Minh Tuấn, "Cường quốc biển Châu Âu nhìn về Châu Á" [European maritime power looks to Asia], *Tuổi Trẻ*, July 24, 2021, https://tuoitre.vn/news-20210724122810896.htm.

61 Tang Siew Mun et al., *The State of Southeast Asia: 2020 Survey Report* (Singapore: ASEAN Studies Centre at ISEAS–Yusof Ishak Institute, 2020), 41, 25, https://www.iseas.edu.sg/wp-content/uploads/pdfs/TheStateofSEASurveyReport_2020.pdf, 15, 17.

62 Tang et al., *The State of Southeast Asia: 2020*, 23.

63 Tang et al., *The State of Southeast Asia: 2020*, 45-47.

64 Sharon Seah et al., *The State of Southeast Asia: 2021 Survey Report* (Singapore: ASEAN Studies Centre at ISEAS–Yusof Ishak Institute, 2021), 41, 25, https://www.iseas.edu.sg/wp-content/uploads/2021/01/The-State-of-SEA-2021-v2.pdf.

65 William Bratton, "'Global' Britain's Pretensions of Relevance in Asia Pale amid China's Rise," *South China Morning Post*, May 10, 2021, https://www.scmp.com/comment/opinion/article/3132444/global-britains-pretensions-relevance-asia-pale-amid-chinas-rise.

66 Jeremy Shapiro and Nick Witney, "The Delusions of Global Britain: London Will Have to Get Used to Life as a Middle Power," *Foreign Affairs*, March 23, 2021, https://www.foreignaffairs.com/articles/europe/2021-03-23/delusions-global-britain; Simon Jenkins, "Boris Johnson's Military Alliance in the Pacific Is Reckless Post-Imperial Nostalgia," *The Guardian*, September 20, 2021, https://www.theguardian.com/commentisfree/2021/sep/20/boris-johnson-military-alliance-pacific-reckless-post-imperial-nostalgia-aukus.

67 Nobuyuki Yamaoka 山岡信幸, *Gekihen suru sekai no henka o yomitoku: kyōyō to shite no chiri* 激変する世界の変化を読み解く：教養としての地理 [Geography as a culture: understanding the drastic changes in the world] (Tokyo: PHP kenkyūjo PHP 研究所, 2021); Tomohiko Satake 佐竹知彦, *Ōsutoraria no aratana gaikō seisaku hakusho ga shisa suru koto* オーストラリアの新たな外交政策白書が示唆すること [What Australia's new foreign policy white paper suggests], NIDS Commentary [NIDS コメンタリー] 67 (Tokyo: National Institute for Defense Studies 防衛研究所, 2017), http://www.nids.mod.go.jp/publication/commentary/pdf/commentary067.pdf; Tsutomu Kikuchi 菊池努, *Ōsutoraria to 'Indotaiheiyō': keizai sōgoizon, chikara no kōzō, chiiki seido* オーストラリアと「インド太平洋」：経済相互依存、力の構造、地域制度 [Australia and "Indo-Pacific": economic interdependence, power structure, regional system], Heisei 25-nendo gaimushō gaikō anzen hoshō chōsa kenkyū jigyō (sōgō jigyō) 'indotaiheiyō Jidai' No Nihon Gaikō –

Secondary Powers/Suingu States e No Taiō 平成25年度外務省外交・安全保障調査研究事業 (総合事業)「インド太平洋時代」の日本外交 –Secondary Powers/Swing States への対応 [2013 Ministry of Foreign Affairs, Foreign Affairs and Security Research Project (Comprehensive Project) Japan's Diplomacy in the "Indo-Pacific Era": Correspondence to Secondary Powers/Swing States] (Tokyo: Japan Institute of International Affairs 日本国際問題研究所, 2014), https://www2.jiia.or.jp/pdf/resarch/H25_Indo-Pacific/05-kikuchi.pdf.

68 Akemi Kobayashi 小林明美, "Ōsutoraria no Ajia Taiheiyō kyōryoku: Hōku Kītingu Rōdōtō seiken ni okeru seisaku keisei o chūshin ni" オーストラリアのアジア・太平洋協力 ―ホーク＝キーティング労働党政権における政策形成を中心に [Australia's Asia-Pacific cooperation: from the point of view of policy making of the Hawke-Keating Labor governments], *Bulletin of the Graduate School, Soka University* 創価大学大学院紀要 32 (2010): 101–18, https://soka.repo.nii.ac.jp/?action=repository_action_common_download&item_id=35101&item_no=1&attribute_id=15&file_no=1.

69 Kazuhiro Namao 生尾和弘, "Ōsutoraria to Komon Werusu no hen'yō: Minamiafurika dattai no shōgeki" オーストラリアとコモンウェルスの変容 ―南アフリカ脱退の衝撃 [Australia and change in the Commonwealth of Nations: the impact of South Africa's departure], *Dokkyo Working Papers* 獨協大学英語文化研究 49 (2016): 77–114, https://dokkyo.repo.nii.ac.jp/?action=repository_uri&item_id=970&file_id=68&file_no=1; Yoshihiro Toyama 遠山嘉博, "Haku Gōshugi kara tabunkashugi e" 白豪主義から多文化主義へ [From white Australia to multiculturalism]," *Otemon Economic Review* 追手門経済論集 38, 1 (2003): 1–18, https://www.i-repository.net/contents/outemon/ir/102/102030905.pdf.

70 Hwang Jun-beom 황준범, "'Banjung yeondae' bongyeoghwa ... Mi·Il·Indo·Hoju 12il cheos Kwodeu jeongsanghoeui" '반중 연대' 본격화 ... 미·일·인도·호주 12일 첫 쿼드 정상회의 ["Anti-Chinese solidarity" begins in earnest ... the first Quad summit meeting on the 12th of the United States, Japan, India, and Australia], *Hankyoreh* 한겨레 [The Hankyoreh], March 10, 2021, https://www.hani.co.kr/arti/international/international_general/986124.html.

71 Ra Mi-ryeong, Shin Min-geum, and Shin Min-yi 라미령 신민금 신민이, "Hoju Nyujillaendeuui Daeasia gyeongjehyeoblyeog hyeonhwang-gwa sisajeom" 호주·뉴질랜드의 대아시아 경제협력 현황과 시사점 [Status and implications of Australia–New Zealand's economic cooperation with Asia], *Yeongujalyo* 연구자료 [Research data] 18, 1 (2018), https://www.dbpia.co.kr/Journal/articleDetail?nodeId=NODE07438627; La Meeryung, Shin Mingeum, and Shin Minlee 라미령 신민금 신민이, "Hoju·Nyujillaendeuui Daeasia gyeongjehyeoblyeog hyeonhwang-gwa sisajeom" 호주·뉴질랜드의 대아시아 경제협력 현황과 시사점 [Australia and New Zealand's ties with Asia and their implications], *KIEP Research Paper, Policy References* 18, 1 (2018), https://doi.org/10.2139/ssrn.3181834.

72 Song Seongjong 송승종, "Baideun haengjeongbuui Indo-Taepyeong-yang jeonlyag" 바이든 행정부의 인도·태평양 전략 [Indo-Pacific strategy of the Biden administration], *Han-ilgunsamunhwayeongu* 한일군사문화연구 [Korea-Japan military culture research] 31 (2021): 81–112, https://www.kci.go.kr/kciportal/ci/sereArticleSearch/ciSereArtiView.kci?sereArticleSearchBean.artiId=ART002713336.

Notes to pages 64–65

73 Aleksius Jemadu, "Kebijakan politik dan keamanan Australia di kawasan Asia Pasifik" [Australian political and security policy in the Asia-Pacific region], *Jurnal Ilmu Sosial Dan Ilmu Politik* [Journal of social and political sciences] 10, 2 (2006): 143–63, https://journal.ugm.ac.id/index.php/jsp/article/view/11016.

74 Rio Akbar Pramanta et al., "Kemitraan strategis non-zero sum game: hubungan ASEAN-Australia dalam konteks geopolitik" [Non-zero-sum game strategic partnership: ASEAN-Australia relations in a geopolitical context], *Indonesian Perspective* 3, 2 (March 2019): 111–26, https://doi.org/10.14710/ip.v3i2.22347.

75 Mulyadi Mulyadi, "Analisa kebijakan politik luar negeri pada konflik Laut China Selatan dari perspektif Australia" [Analysis of foreign political policy on the South China Sea conflict from Australian perspective], *Jurnal Inovasi Penelitian* [Journal of research innovation] 2, 4 (2021): 1121–32, https://stp-mataram.e-journal.id/JIP/article/view/832.

76 Ronna Nirmala, "Bakamla: AUKUS berpotensi munculkan ketidakstabilan Laut China Selatan" [Bakamla: AUKUS has the potential to cause instability in the South China Sea], BeritaBenar, September 20, 2021, https://www.benarnews.org/indonesian/berita/aukus-laut-china-selatan-09202021163242.html; "AUKUS: Malaysia, negara ASEAN perlu sentiasa nyatakan kegusaran" [AUKUS: Malaysia, ASEAN countries must always express their concerns], *Astro Awani*, September 19, 2021, https://www.astroawani.com/berita-malaysia/aukus-malaysia-negara-asean-perlu-sentiasa-nyatakan-kegusaran-320657; Norawazni Yusof, "AUKUS: Malaysia, menteri Asean akan buat kenyataan bersama" [AUKUS: Malaysia, ASEAN ministers will make a joint statement], *Sinar Harian* [The daily light], September 18, 2021, https://www.sinarharian.com.my/article/162139/BERITA/Nasional/AUKUS-Malaysia-Menteri-Asean-akan-buat-kenyataan-bersama.

77 Ismail Hashim Yahaya, "Aukus atau rakus?" [Steamy or greedy?], Malaysian Insight, September 21, 2021, https://www.themalaysianinsight.com/bahasa/s/340512.

78 Kantheera Phuriwikrai กานต์ธีรา ภูริวิกรัย, "X̄ān Thiy Xāseīyn læa Xin do-Pæsifik kạb Duly p̣hākh Prīchā rach ch" อ่านไทย อาเซียน และอินโด-แปซิฟิก กับ ดุลยภาค ปรีชารัชช [Read Thai, ASEAN and Indo-Pacific with Dulyapak Preecharach]," The 101 World, August 26, 2020, https://www.the101.world/dulyapak-asean-indopacific-interview/.

79 "'Cingcô'lô s̄ūk's̄ngkhrāmyĕn yukh h̄ım̀'" 'จิงโจ้'โล้สึก'สงครามเย็นยุคใหม่' ["Kangaroo" fights in the "new era of Cold War"], S̄yāmrạṭ̄h สยามรัฐ, August 2, 2019, https://siamrath.co.th/n/94279; "S̄h̄rạṭ̄h bīb p̣hanṭhmitr prachāṭhiptịy leụ̄xk k̄ĥāng t̂ān Cīn" สหรัฐบีบพันธมิตรประชาธิปไตย เลือกข้างต้านจีน [US presses democratic alliance choose a side against China], NEW18, 2020, https://www.newtv.co.th/news/61096.

80 Treenut Ingkutanon ตรีนุช อิงคุทานนท์, "Cīn vs S̄h̄rạṭ̄h‡ S̄ngkhrāmyĕn khrậng h̄ım̀ nxk s̄mrp̣hūmi kārmeụ̄xng" จีน vs สหรัฐฯ สงครามเย็นครั้งใหม่นอกสมรภูมิการเมือง [China vs US: a new Cold War outside the political battlefield], *Thịyrạṭ̄h Xxnlịn̒* ไทยรัฐออนไลน์ [Thairath online], April 22, 2021, https://www.thairath.co.th/news/2074448.

81 Kiều Anh, "Liên minh chống Trung Quốc của Mỹ ở châu Á: 9 người 10 ý" [America's anti-China coalition in Asia: 9 people 10 ideas], *VOV,* March 28, 2021, https://vov.vn/the-gioi/quan-sat/lien-minh-chong-trung-quoc-cua-my-o-chau-a-9-nguoi-10-y-846242.vov; Vũ Hợp, "Mỹ lôi kéo phương Tây đối phó Trung Quốc: Liệu có châm ngòi cho Chiến tranh Lạnh mới?" [US entices the west to deal with China: will it spark a new Cold War?], *VOV,* June 15, 2021, https://vov.vn/the-gioi/my-loi-keo-phuong-tay-doi-pho-trung-quoc-lieu-co-cham-ngoi-cho-chien-tranh-lanh-moi-866379.vov.

82 "Căng thẳng Australia–Trung Quốc: thêm dầu vào lửa!" [Australia-China tension: adding fuel to the fire!], *Công an Nhân dân* [*Public Security News*] May 6, 2021, https://cand.com.vn/Binh-luan-quoc-te/Cang-thang-Australia-Trung-Quoc-Them-dau-vao-lua-i604610/; Tiệp Nguyễn, "Mỹ, Nhật, Ấn, Úc lập 'NATO châu Á' đối phó Trung Quốc?" [US, Japan, India, Australia form "NATO Asia" to deal with China?], *VietTimes,* November 28, 2017, https://viettimes.vn/post-64830.html.

83 Seah et al., *The State of Southeast Asia: 2021,* 21–22.

84 Ibid., 25, 38.

85 Florence W. Yang 楊雯婷, "Taichu shisei no ondo-sa? Nichibei no Indotaiheiyō senryaku oyobi Taichu seisaku no hikaku" 対中姿勢の温度差？日米のインド太平洋戦略及び対中政策の比較 [A different vision toward China? Comparing the Indo-Pacific strategy and China policy of the US and Japan], *Mondai to Kenkyū* 問題と研究 [Issues and research] 50, 1 (March 2021): 127–78, http://iirj.nccu.edu.tw/data/50_1/05-50(1)-4%20%E6%A5%8A%E9%9B%AF%E5%A9%B7.pdf.

86 Satoshi Shirai 白井 聡 "Nihon wa 'Ten'nō no ue' ni Amerika o itadaite iru 'anpo taisei ga sengo no kokutai ni natta'" 日本は「天皇の上」にアメリカを戴いている「安保体制が戦後の国体になった」 [Japan places the United States "above the Emperor" "The security framework became the structure of the state after the war] PRESIDENT Online, May 14, 2018, https://president.jp/articles/-/25080.

87 Takashi Okada 岡田 充, "Nihon to amerikano 'Chūgoku-kan' wa sekai hyōjun'na no ka: Nihon to Amerika no taichu-kan ni wa henken ga aru" 日本とアメリカの「中国観」は世界標準なのか: 日本とアメリカの対中観には偏見がある [Is the "view of China" of Japan and the United States the world standard? There is prejudice in Japan and the United States' view of China], *Toyo Keizai Online* 東洋経済オンライン, March 21, 2021, https://toyokeizai.net/articles/amp/417862?page=3.

88 Takaehiko Nakao and Taizo Miyagi 中尾武彦 宮城大蔵, "'Seichō suru Ajia' to Nihon wa dō mukiaubeki ka: zen Ajiakaihatsuginkō sōsai no Nakao Takehiko-shi ni kiku" 「成長するアジア」と日本はどう向き合うべきか: 前アジア開発銀行総裁の中尾武彦氏に訊く [How Japan should face "growing Asia": interview with Takehiko Nakao, former president of the Asian Development Bank], *Toyo Keizai Online* 東洋経済オンライン, June 11, 2021, https://toyokeizai.net/articles/-/430195.

89 Lee Kitae 이기태, "Abe jeongbuui Daeyeong-gug · Daepeulangseu anbo hyeoblyeog – Indotaepyeong-yang jiyeog-ui anboneteuwokeu hwagdae" 아베 정부의 대영국 · 대프랑스 안보 협력 - 인도태평양 지역의 안보네트워크 확대 [Abe government's security cooperation with Britain and France: expansion of Japan's

security networks in the Indo-Pacific], *Jeongchijeongboyeongu* 정치정보연구 [Political Information Research 22, 3 (2019): 243–69, https://doi.org/10.15617/psc.2019.10.31.3.243; Choi Heesik 최희식, "Abe jeong-gwon-ui oegyoanbojeongchaeg: haeyang-anjeonbojang-eul jungsim-eulo" 아베 정권의 외교안보정책: 해양안전보장을 중심으로 [Abe's foreign policy and security policy: focusing on maritime security], *Gugbang-Yeongu* 국방연구 [National Defence Research] 61, 4 (2018): 117–39, https://papersearch.net/thesis/article.asp?key=3651675; Lee Ki-wan and Yeo Hyeon-cheol 이기완 여현철, "Baideun haengjeongbu ihu Ilbon-ui daeoejeongchaeggwa jubyeongug gwangye: jisogseong-gwa hangyeleul jungsim-eulo" 바이든 행정부 이후 일본의 대외정책과 주변국 관계: 지속성과 한계를 중심으로 [Japan's foreign policy and diplomatic relations since the Biden administration: persistence and limitations], *Hanguggwa Gugjesahoe* 한국과 국제사회 [Korea and global affairs] 5, 3 (2021): 101–27, https://db.koreascholar.com/article?code=408485.

90 Choi Eunmi 최은미, "Ilbon-eun yeojeonhi 'ban-eunghyeong gugga' inga? : Abe naegag-eseo natanan Ilbon-oegyoui byeonhwawa yeonsogseong" 일본은 여전히 '반응형 국가'인가? : 아베 내각에서 나타난 일본외교의 변화와 연속성 [Is Japan still a "reactive state"? Changes and continuities of Japan's diplomacy in the Abe government], *Ilbon-yeongunonchong* 일본연구논총 [The Korea journal of Japanese studies] 49 (2019): 110–41, https://papersearch.net/thesis/article.asp?key=3690449; Jeon Seong-gon 전성곤, "Ilbon jegugjuuiui geulimjaloseo 'pawo-epegteu' ui yogmang" 일본 제국주의의 그림자로서 '파워-에펙트'의 욕망 [The desire of "power-effect" as the shadow of Japanese imperialism], *Il-eoilmunhag* 일어일문학 [Japanese and Japanese literature] 86 (2020): 239–56, https://www.dbpia.co.kr/Journal/articleDetail?nodeId=NODE09351575.

91 Kwon Tae Whan 권태환, "Ilbon-ui gunsajeonlyaggwa uliui daeeung" 일본의 군사전략과 우리의 대응 [Japan's military strategy and our response], *Gunsanondan* 군사논단 [Military journal] 100, 1 (2020): 221–91, https://papersearch.net/thesis/article.asp?key=3819913.

92 Ade Priangani, "Yoshihide Suga policy dalam melanjutkan Abenomics di Kawasan Asia Timur dan tenggara" [Yoshihide Suga policy to continue Abenomics in East and Southeast Asia], *Jurnal Dinamika Global* [Journal of global dynamics] 6, 1 (2021): 1–19, https://doi.org/10.36859/jdg.v6i01.389.

93 Michelle Natalia, "China dan Jepang berebut dominasi di Indo-Pasifik" [China and Japan fight for dominance in the Indo-Pacific], IDX Channel TV, July 9, 2021, https://www.idxchannel.com/economics/china-dan-jepang-berebut-dominasi-di-indo-pasifik.

94 Kurniadi, "Rivalitas Indonesia, China, Jepang, dan India di Indo-Pasifik" [Rivalry of Indonesia, China, Japan, and India in the Indo-Pacific], Universitas Tanjungpura, March 11, 2020, https://www.untan.ac.id/rivalitas-indonesia-china-jepang-dan-india-di-indo-pasifik/.

95 Jompol, "Yīpùn kạb yuthṭhṣ̄ās̄tr̒ t̂ān Cīn mùng h̄n̂ā Weīydnām-Xindonīseīy" ญี่ปุ่นกับยุทธศาสตร์ต้านจีน มุ่งหน้าเวียดนาม-อินโดนีเซีย [Japan and its anti-China strategy heading to Vietnam-Indonesia], workpointTODAY, October 22, 2020, https://workpointtoday.com/japan-visit-vietnam-indonesia-analysis/; Pridi Boonsue ปรีดี บุญซื่อ, "Yīpùn nı yukh nāykrạṭ̄hmntrī Yo chi h̄i dea Sūka bthbāth

thī̀ pkpxng rabeīyb s̄erīnīym Xecheīy" ญี่ปุ่นในยุคนายกรัฐมนตรี โยชิฮิเดะ ซูกะ บทบาทที่ปกป้องระเบียบเสรีนิยมเอเซีย [Japan during Prime Minister Yoshihide Suga's role in defending the liberal order of Asia], ThaiPublica, April 21, 2021, https://thaipublica.org/2021/04/pridi241/.

96 "Thảmị nā yk‡ Ỵ̀ipùn leụ̄xk yeụ̄xn Weīydnām pĕn prathes̄̒ræk h̄ịlạng rạb tảh̄æǹng" ทำไมนายกฯ ญี่ปุ่น เลือกเยือนเวียดนามเป็นประเทศแรกหลังรับตำแหน่ง [Why did the Japanese prime minister choose to visit Vietnam as the first country after taking office?], Voice Online, October 2, 2020, https://www.voicetv.co.th/read/BkTUBFxl1.

97 "Bị Den peid kem ruk chumnum Xxs̄terleīy-Xindeīy-Ỵ̀ipùn t̂ān Cīn khrậng ræk" ไบเดนเปิดเกมรุก ชุมนุมออสเตรเลีย-อินเดีย-ญี่ปุ่นต้านจีนครั้งแรก [Biden opened the attack. Australia-India-Japan rally against China for the first time], Post Today, March 10, 2021, https://www.posttoday.com/world/647487; "Nā yk‡ Ỵ̀ipùn khn h̄ım̀ terīym yeụ̄xn Xāseīyn s̄ædng cudyụ̄n s̄nạbs̄nun S̄h̄rạṭh‡" นายกฯ ญี่ปุ่น คนใหม่เตรียมเยือนอาเซียนแสดงจุดยืนสนับสนุนสหรัฐฯ [New Japanese prime minister to visit ASEAN to show support for US], VOA, October 13, 2020, https://www.voathai.com/a/new-japan-pm-plans-asia-trip/5618703.html.

98 "Một Số nhận định về chính sách đối ngoại Nhật Bản" [Some comments on Japanese foreign policy], IRYS CLUB, November 18, 2020, https://irysclub.com/2020/11/18/mot-so-nhan-dinh-ve-chinh-sach-doi-ngoai-nhat-ban/.

99 Ngô Minh Trí, "Tân thủ tướng Nhật có thay đổi chính sách về Biển Đông?" [Will the new Japanese prime minister change policy on the East Sea?], Thanh Niên, [Youth] September 18, 2020, https://thanhnien.vn/the-gioi/tan-thu-tuong-nhat-co-thay-doi-chinh-sach-ve-bien-dong-1280469.html; Duy Hoàng, "Chiến lược ấn độ dương – Thái Bình Dương: tầm nhìn và thực tiễn" [Indo-Pacific strategy: vision and practice], Tạp chí Cộng sản, [Communist Magazine], December 15, 2020, https://www.tapchicongsan.org.vn/vi_VN/web/guest/thuc-tien-kinh-nghiem1/-/2018/820763/view_content.

100 Toru Ito 伊藤融, Indo gaikō no naka no "modi gaikō," dentō-teki gaikō kara no dappi ka, keizoku ka? インド外交のなかの「モディ外交」—伝統的外交からの脱皮か、継続か？ ["Modi diplomacy" in Indian diplomacy: is it a break from traditional diplomacy or a continuation?] (Kajima Institute of International Peace 鹿島平和研究所, 2019), http://www.kiip.or.jp/taskforce/doc/anzen20190312_T_Ito.pdf.

101 Mari Izuyama 伊豆山真理, "Suriranka, Morudibu ni okeru Indo to Chūgoku no kyōsō: Indo no kinrin shokoku seisaku no shiten kara" スリランカ、モルディブにおけるインドと中国の競争—インドの近隣諸国政策の視点から— [India-China competition in Sri Lanka and Maldives: from the perspective of India's neighbouring countries policy], Bōeikenkyūsho Kiyō 防衛研究所紀要 [Bulletin of the National Institute for Defense Studies] 22, 2 (January 2020): 1–20, http://www.nids.mod.go.jp/publication/kiyo/pdf/bulletin_j22_2_2.pdf.

102 Takenori Horimoto 堀本武功, "Dai 2-ki Modi gaikō to Nichiinkankei: Tōmen wa missetsuna kankei no keizoku ka" 第2期モディ外交と日印関係：当面は密接な関係の継続か [Phase 2 Modi diplomacy and Japan-India relations: will close relationships continue for the time being?], Nippon.com, April 13, 2020, https://www.nippon.com/ja/in-depth/a06701/.

103 Manabu Shimizu 清水学, "Indo Modi seiken to tai Chūtō seisaku" インド・モディ政権と対中東政策 [Modi government and the Middle East: a paradigm change in the political concept], *Chūtō Rebyū* 中東レビュー [Middle East review] 7 (2020): 115–37, https://doi.org/10.24765/merev.Vol.7_J-Art03; "(Shasetsu) Nihon to Indo iki nagaku gokei kankei mezase"（社説）日本とインド 息長く互恵関係めざせ [(Editorial) Japan and India aim for a long-lasting reciprocal relationship]," *Asahi Shimbun* 朝日新聞, December 3, 2019, https://www.asahi.com/articles/DA3S14279913.html.

104 Kim Chanwahn 김찬완, "Modijeongbu oegyojeongchaeg-ui gyeoljeong-yoin: jisoggwa byeonhwaleul jungsim-eulo" 모디정부 외교정책의 결정요인 :지속과 변화를 중심으로 [Determinants of India's foreign policy under Modi government – with special reference to continuity and change], *Nam-asiayeongu* 남아시아연구 [South Asian studies] 24, 2 (2018): 29–49, https://www.dbpia.co.kr/journal/articleDetail?nodeId = NODE07534205&nodeId = NODE07534205&medaTypeCode = 185005&language = ko_KR.

105 Kim Youcheer 김유철, "Budong-gugga(Swing State)loseoui Indo: oegyonoseon-ui jinhwa gyeonglowa Miguggwaui ihaegwangye sulyeom-e daehan nonjaeng-eul jungsim-eulo" 부동국가 (Swing State) 로서의 인도: 외교노선의 진화 경로와 미국과의 이해관계 수렴에 대한 논쟁을 중심으로 [India as a global swing state: demystifying its foreign policy doctrine and examining the convergence of strategic interests with the United States], *Gugjejeongchinonchong* 국제정치논총 [Korean Journal of International Relations] 60, 1 (2020): 155–92, https://doi.org/10.14731/kjir.2020.03.60.1.155.

106 Cho Won-deuk 조원득, *MiJung gyeongjaeng gudo ha Indo oegyojeongchaeg-ui byeonhwa yangsang-gwa Sinnambangjeongchaeg* 미중 경쟁 구도 하 인도 외교정책의 변화 양상과 신남방정책 [India's foreign policy in the competitive landscape between the US and China changes and the New Southern Policy], Policy Research Series 2020–26 (Seoul: Institute of Foreign Affairs and National Security 국립외교원 외교안보연구소, 2020), http://www.ifans.go.kr/knda/com/fileupload/FileDownloadView.do;jsessionid = 3j0HSU + EkrTMi6vgfkgcLHs + .public21?storgeId = c61b04e5-0182-4c75-ad21-828ecacfb855&uploadId = 11477868109615316&fileSn = 1.

107 Pratama Khalik, "Pengaruh nilai Hindutva dalam kebijakan luar negeri India terhadap status Kashmir era kepemimpinan Narendra Modi" [The influence of Hindutva values in Indian foreign policy on the status of Kashmir under the leadership of Narendra Modi] (Yogyakarta: Universitas Gadjah Mada, 2021), http://etd.repository.ugm.ac.id/penelitian/detail/197932; Nurul Itsna Rosdiana, "Analisis pencabutan pemberlakuan otonomi khusus Kashmir dan Jammu oleh pemerintah India" [Analysis of the revocation of the implementation of the special autonomy of Kashmir and Jammu by the government of India]," *Jurnal Ilmu Sosial dan Humaniora* [Journal of social sciences and humanities] 9, 2 (2020): 347–55, https://doi.org/10.23887/jish-undiksha.v9i2.23051; Ani Nursalikah, "Laporan: di bawah Modi, India tempat berbahaya bagi Muslim" [Report: under Modi, India is a dangerous place for Muslims], *Republika Online*, December 17, 2020, https://www.republika.co.id/berita/qlfszu366/laporandi-bawah-modi-india-tempat-berbahaya-bagi-muslim.

108 "Umat Islam di India terancam, semuanya gara-gara parti politik ni ..." [Muslims in India are threatened, all because of this political party ...], Orangkata.my, June 11, 2019, https://orangkata.my/politik/umat-islam-di-india-terancam-semuanya-gara-gara-parti-politik-ni/; "Henti keganasan kepada minoriti Islam di India" [Stop the violence against the Muslim minority in India], *Perak Today*, November 8, 2015, https://peraktoday.com.my/2015/11/henti-keganasan-kepada-minoriti-islam-di-india/.

109 A.A. Gede Agung Baskara Kepakisan, "Respon kebijakan luar negeri 'Neighborhood First' India terhadap kerjasama bilateral China Pakistan economic corridor 2015" [India's "neighbourhood first" foreign policy response to China Pakistan economic corridor 2015 bilateral cooperation], *Jurnal Analisis Hubungan Internasional* [Journal of international relations analysis] 7, 3 (December 2018): 12–30, http://journal.unair.ac.id/download-fullpapers-jahi87e63b5d7afull.pdf.

110 Noudy Naufal and Shofwan Al-Banna Choiruzzad, "Dinamika domestik dalam kebijakan luar negeri: mundurnya India dari Regional Comprehensive Economic Partnership (RCEP)" [Domestic dynamics in foreign policy country: withdrawal of India from Regional Comprehensive Economic Partnership (RCEP)], *Jurnal Hubungan Internasional* [Journal of international relations] 14, 1 (January–June 2021), https://e-journal.unair.ac.id/JHI/article/download/21043/14634.

111 Ravichandran Moorthy and Kavaramma Subramaniam, "Pemikiran strategik dasar luar India: dari dasar pandang timur ke dasar tindak timur" [Basic strategic thinking outside India: from an eastern viewpoint to an eastern base of action], *Jebat: Malaysian Journal of History, Politics and Strategic Studies* 44, 2 (2017): 51–72, http://journalarticle.ukm.my/13359/.

112 "Wabak berganda ancam India" [Multiple epidemics threaten India], *Sinar Harian* [The daily light], May 24, 2021, https://www.sinarharian.com.my/article/140300/GLOBAL/Wabak-berganda-ancam-India; Mohd Farhan Md Ariffin and Nurul Syahadah Mohd Riza, "Jadikan tsunami COVID-19 di India iktibar menginsafkan" [Make the COVID-19 tsunami in India a convincing lesson], *Berita Harian,* [Daily news] April 29, 2021, https://www.bharian.com.my/rencana/lain-lain/2021/04/812256/jadikan-tsunami-covid-19-di-india-iktibar-menginsafkan.

113 Supawit Kaewkunok ศุภวิชญ์ แก้วคูนอก, "Meụ̄̀x Xindeīy mị̀ xyāk pĕn pheīyng mhāxảnāc k̄hxng Xecheīy Tı̂" เมื่ออินเดียไม่อยากเป็นเพียงมหาอำนาจของเอเชียใต้ [When India does not want to be just the superpower of South Asia], The 101 World, June 27, 2019, https://www.the101.world/india-dominant-power-beyond-south-asia/; Phansart Jenraumjit พันธุ์ศาสตร์ เจนร่วมจิต, "P̣hạy khukkhām miti d̂ān khwām mạ̀n khngthī̀ s̄̀ng p̣hl t̀x kār dảnein nyobāy t̀āng pratheṣ̄ k̄hxng Xindeīy: bribth d̂ān khwām mạ̀nkhng læa kār thh̄ār ni pī kh.ṣ̄.2000–2014" ภัยคุกคามมิติด้านความมั่นคงที่ส่งผลต่อการดำเนินนโยบายต่างประเทศ ของอินเดีย: บริบทด้านความมั่นคงและการทหารในปี ค.ศ.2000–2014 [Dimension of security threats that affect the foreign policy of India: the context of security and military in 2000–2014], *Wārs̄ār ṣ̄h̄ withyākār wicạy: C̄hbạb bạṇthit ṣ̄ụkṣ̄ā* วารสาร

สหวิทยาการวิจัย: ฉบับบัณฑิตศึกษา [Journal of interdisciplinary research: graduate studies] 4, 3 (2015): 75–84, https://so03.tci-thaijo.org/index.php/JIRGS/article/view/228823.

114 Kantheera Phuriwikrai กานต์ธีรา ภูริวิกรัย, "X̒ān Xindeīy nı rabeīyb lok h̄ım̀ kạb Ṣ̄uph wichỵ̒ Kæ̂w khūn xk" อ่านอินเดียในระเบียบโลกใหม่ กับ ศุภวิชญ์ แก้วคูนอก [Read India in the new world order with Supawit Kaewkunok], The 101 World, August 4, 2020, https://today.line.me/th/v2/article/g8Lo2p; Supawit Kaewkunok ศุภวิชญ์ แก้วคูนอก, "Xindeīy: cāk prathes̄ʹ p̄hū̂ p̄hlit wạkhsīn s̄ū̀ wikvt kho wid-19 ralxk h̄ım̀" อินเดีย: จากประเทศผู้ผลิตวัคซีน สู่วิกฤตโควิด-19 ระลอกใหม่ [India: from vaccine-producing country into a new wave of COVID-19 crisis], The 101 World, May 17, 2021, https://www.the101.world/covid-19-in-india-2021/.

115 Nguyễn Trần Xuân Sơn, "Sự điều chỉnh chính sách đối ngoại của Ấn Độ từ sau năm 1991 đến nay" [The adjustment of India's foreign policy from 1991 to the present], Tạp chí Cộng sản [Communist Magazine], March 10, 2021, https://www.tapchicongsan.org.vn/web/guest/tin-binh-luan/-/asset_publisher/DLIYi5AJyFzY/content/su-dieu-chinh-chinh-sach-doi-ngoai-cua-an-do-tu-sau-nam-1991-den-nay#.

116 Lê Văn Toan, "Chính sách đối ngoại của Ấn Độ hiện nay và tác động đến an ninh chính trị của Việt Nam" [India's current foreign policy and its impact on Vietnam's political security], Lý luận chính trị [Political theory], March 25, 2019, http://lyluanchinhtri.vn/home/index.php/quoc-te/item/2781-chinh-sach-doi-ngoai-cua-an-do-hien-nay-va-tac-dong-den-an-ninh-chinh-tri-cua-viet-nam.html.

117 Ellina P. Shavlay, "Cách tiếp cận của Ấn Độ và Nga tới khu vực ấn độ dương – Thái Bình Dương (phần 3)" [India and Russia's approaches to the Indo-Pacific (part 3)], Ho Chi Minh National Academy of Politics, Center for Indian Study [Trung tâm Nghiên cứu Ấn Độ, Học viện Chính trị quốc gia Hồ Chí Minh], January 7, 2021, http://cis.org.vn/article/4556/cach-tiep-can-cua-an-do-va-nga-toi-khu-vuc-an-do-duong-thai-binh-duong-phan-3.html.

118 Seah et al., *The State of Southeast Asia: 2021*, 20, 22.
119 Yun-han Chu and Yu-tzung Chang, "Battle for Influence: Perceptions in Asia of China and the US," *Global Asia* 12, 1 (2017): 107, http://asianbarometer.org/publications//38bd8798df38c115ef8a76646fd41fb4.pdf.
120 Ibid.
121 Tang et al., *The State of Southeast Asia: 2020*, 19.
122 Seah et al., *The State of Southeast Asia: 2021*, 29.
123 Ibid., 13.
124 Ibid., 16.
125 Ibid., 19.
126 Liu Jie 劉傑, "Chūgoku no 'ittai ichiro' seisaku to Ajiano 'chi no kyōdōtai' Ajia kinrin shokoku to no tairitsu o koete: gakujutsu nettowāku no kōchiku" 中国の「一帯一路」政策と アジアの「知の共同体」アジア近隣諸国との対立をこえて ――学術ネットワークの構築―― [Beyond the conflict between China's "One Belt, One Road" policy and Asia's "knowledge community" Asian neighbours: building

academic networks], *Gakujutsu No Dōkō* 学術の動向 [Academic trends] 25, 9 (2020): 18–21, https://www.jstage.jst.go.jp/article/tits/25/9/25_9_18/_pdf/-char/ja; Kunio Takahashi 高橋邦夫, "Chūgoku jōsei geppō: 'Chūgoku no tokushoku aru' takokukanshugi" 中国情勢月報：'中国の特色ある'多国間主義 [China situation monthly report: "China's characteristic multilateralism"], Japan Research Institute 日本総研, May 28, 2021, https://www.jri.co.jp/page.jsp?id=38976; Rumi Aoyama 青山瑠妙, "Kenkyū repōto: kokunai seiji to rendō suru Chūgoku no gaikō"〔研究レポート〕国内政治と連動する中国の外交 [Research report: China's diplomacy linked to domestic politics], Japan Institute of International Affairs 日本国際問題研究所, March 12, 2021, https://www.jiia.or.jp/column/post-57.html.

127 *Chūgoku no taigai seisaku to sho gaikoku no Taichu seisaku* 中国の対外政策と諸外国の対中政策 [China's foreign policy and foreign policies toward China], Senryaku nenji hōkoku 戦略年次報告 [Strategic annual report] 2019 (Tokyo: Japan Institute of International Affairs 日本国際問題研究所, 2019), https://www.jiia.or.jp/strategic_comment/2020/02/pdf/f37bf46e5ea62960ff72ee74332bc26478109e1a.pdf; Tomohiko Uyama 宇山智彦, "Roshia to Chūgoku no chiiki shugi kara saikō suru seiryoku-ken eikyō-ken: kokuryoku kan'yo kyōkan" ロシアと中国の地域主義から再考する勢力圏・影響圏―国力・関与・共感― [Reconsidering the spheres of power and influence from regionalism of Russia and China: national power, involvement, empathy], Japan Forum on International Relations 日本国際フォーラム, 2021, https://www.jfir.or.jp/studygroup_article/5684/.

128 Junya Sano 佐野淳也, "Sūchi kara mita Chūgoku no ittai ichiro koso no jitsuzō ―: 'Shinchū' koku o fuyasu tame ni suishin" 数値からみた中国の一帯一路構想の実像―「親中」国を増やすために推進 [Real image of China's Belt and Road Initiative from the numerical value: promoting to increase the number of "pro-Chinese" countries], *Kantaiheiyō Bijinesu Jōhō RIM* 環太平洋ビジネス情報 RIM [Pacific Rim business information RIM] 21, 80 (2021): 66–86, https://www.jri.co.jp/page.jsp?id=38255; Juichi Inada 稲田十一, "Kenkyū repōto: kyū kakudai suru Chūgoku no taigai keizai kyōryoku to sono 'kihan'"〔研究レポート〕急拡大する中国の対外経済協力とその「規範」[Research report: China's rapidly expanding foreign economic cooperation and its "norms"], Japan Institute of International Affairs 日本国際問題研究所, January 8, 2021, https://www.jiia.or.jp/column/post-29.html.

129 IDE-JETRO, *Chūgoku Shakai kagaku-in – Jetoro Ajiakeizaikenkyūsho kyōsai kokusai gakujutsu shinpojiumu 'posutokorona jidai no nitchū keizai kyōryoku'* 中国社会科学院 － ジェトロ・アジア経済研究所 共催 国際学術シンポジウム「ポストコロナ時代の日中経済協力」 [Chinese Academy of Social Sciences and JETRO Asia Keizai Institute co-sponsored international academic symposium "Japan-China economic cooperation in the post-corona era"] (IDE-JETRO, 2020), https://www.ide.go.jp/library/Japanese/Event/Reports/pdf/20201027.pdf.

130 Lee Joo-hyung 이주형, "Jung-gug-ui dajajuui oegyowa Ildaeillo jeonlyag" 중국의 다자주의 외교와 일대일로 전략 [The multilateral diplomacy and "One Belt, One Road" strategy of China], *Daehanjeongchihaghoebo* 대한정치학회보 [Journal of the Korean Political Science Association] 24, 1 (2016): 131–50, https://www.kci.

go.kr/kciportal/ci/sereArticleSearch/ciSereArtiView.kci?sereArticleSearch Bean.artiId=ART002083474; Lee Wang-hwi 이왕휘, *(Ataejiyeog-yeongusilijeu) Baideun sigi Jung-gug-ui dajaoegyo jeonmang* (아태지역연구시리즈) 바이든 시기 중국의 다자외교 전망 [(Asia-Pacific Research Series) multilateral diplomacy prospects of China in the Biden era] (Seoul: Institute of Foreign Affairs and National Security 국립외교원 외교안보연구소, 2021), http://www.ifans.go.kr/knda/ifans/kor/act/ActivityView.do?ctgrySe=15&sn=13789&boardSe=pbl&korean EngSe=KOR; Choo Jaewoo 주재우, "Mijung jeonlyaggyeongjaeng sidaee Migug-ui dae Jung-gug baetajeog dajajuuiwa Jung-gug-ui daeeung" 미중 전략경쟁 시대에 미국의 대 중국 배타적 다자주의와 중국의 대응 [China's response to America's China-exclusive multilateralism], *Jeonlyag-yeongu* 전략연구 [Strategic Studies] 28, 1 (2021): 7–35, https://doi.org/10.46226/jss.2021.03.28.1.7.

131 Kim Sung-Han and Kim Min-sung 김성한 김민성, "Indo·Taepyeong-yangjeonlyag dae Ildaeilloui chungdol donghyang-gwa Hangug-ui oegyoanbojeonlyag" 인도·태평양전략 대 일대일로의 충돌 동향과 한국의 외교안보전략 [Indo-Pacific strategy versus Belt and Road Initiative: strategic implications for South Korea], *Jeonlyag-yeongu* 전략연구 [Strategic Studies] 28, 2 (2021): 7–44, https://doi.org/10.46226/jss.2021.07.28.2.7.

132 Chung Kuyoun 정구연, "Asean(ASEAN) guggadeul-ui hejing-gwa Dong-Asia anboakitegcheoui byeonhwa jeonmang: Daemi · Daejung gunsaoegyoleul jungsim-eulo" 아세안(ASEAN) 국가들의 헤징과 동아시아 안보아키텍처의 변화 전망: 대미·대중 군사외교를 중심으로 [ASEAN's hedging and East Asian security architecture: focusing on military diplomacy toward the US and China], *Hangug-dongbug-anonchong* 한국동북아논총 [*Journal of Northeast Asian Studies*] 25, 2 (2020): 27–51, https://doi.org/10.21807/JNAS.2020.06.95.027.

133 Lee Ji-yong 이지용, "Jung-gug-ui haeoegaebaltujamodel teugjing bunseog: Ildaeillo salyeleul jungsim-eulo" 중국의 해외개발투자모델 특징 분석: 일대일로 사례를 중심으로 [Analysis of China's overseas investment model: centred on cases of One Belt, One Road], *Guggajeongchaeg-yeongu* 국가정책연구 [Public policy review] 34, 2 (2020): 33–59, https://papersearch.net/thesis/article.asp?key=3798513; Lee Changju 이창주, "Kolona-19 gugmyeon haui Jung-gug Ildaeillo bunseog" 코로나-19 국면 하의 중국 일대일로 분석 [Analysis on the Belt and Road Initiative under the COVID-19], *Jung-gugjisigneteuwokeu* 중국지식네트워크 [China knowledge network] (2020): 139–81, https://www.dbpia.co.kr/Journal/article Detail?nodeId=NODE09407417.

134 Dino Patti Djalal, "Hubungan Indonesia-China, pilar stabilitas kawasan" [Indonesia-China relations, pillars of regional stability], KOMPAS.com, December 31, 2020, https://nasional.kompas.com/read/2020/12/31/16172591/hubungan-indonesia-china-pilar-stabilitas-kawasan?page=all; "Babak baru hubungan China-RI di tengah pandemi Corona" [A new chapter of China-Indonesia relations amid the corona pandemic], detiknews, February 10, 2021, https://news.detik.com/internasional/d-5368308/babak-baru-hubungan-china-ri-di-tengah-pandemi-corona.

135 Elba Damhuri, "Ambisi melipattigakan hubungan dagang Indonesia China" [Ambition to triple Indonesia-China trade relations]," *Republika Online,* April 3, 2021, https://www.republika.co.id/berita/qqz2ym440/ambisi-melipattigakan

-hubungan-dagang-indonesia-china; Nur Aini, "China: hubungan ekonomi dengan Indonesia kuat meski pandemi" [China: strong economic relations with Indonesia despite the pandemic], *Republika Online,* May 6, 2020, https://www.republika.co.id/berita/q9v61q382/china-hubungan-ekonomi-dengan-indonesia-kuat-meski-pandemi.

136 Vincent Jansen, "Dampak kompetisi AS-China di Laut China Selatan terhadap kebijakan luar negeri Indonesia" [The impact of US-China competition in the South China Sea on Indonesia's foreign policy] (Bandung: Universitas Katolik Parahyangan, 2017), http://repository.unpar.ac.id/handle/123456789/5614.

137 Luki aulia, "Indonesia-China perkuat kerja sama vaksin Covid-19" [Indonesia-China strengthen cooperation on COVID-19 vaccines], *Kompas,* April 3, 2021, https://www.kompas.id/baca/internasional/2021/04/03/indonesia-china-perkuat-kerja-sama-vaksin-covid-19/.

138 "Hubungan, persahabatan Malaysia-China diharap meningkat secara signifikan" [Malaysia-China relations and friendship are expected to increase significantly], *Berita Harian* [Daily news], January 19, 2020, https://www.bharian.com.my/berita/nasional/2020/01/648249/hubungan-persahabatan-malaysia-china-diharap-meningkat-secara.

139 "Malaysia, China ibarat sebuah keluarga" [Malaysia, China are like a family]," *Sinar Harian* [The daily light], April 2, 2021, https://www.sinarharian.com.my/article/131655/BERITA/Nasional/Malaysia-China-ibarat-sebuah-keluarga; "Ungkapan 'abang besar' sebagai tanda hormat – Hishammuddin" [The expression "big brother" as a sign of respect – Hishammuddin], *Berita Harian* [Daily news], April 3, 2021, https://www.bharian.com.my/berita/nasional/2021/04/803229/ungkapan-abang-besar-sebagai-tanda-hormat-hishammuddin.

140 Roy Anthony Rogers, "Ciri-ciri unik dasar luar Malaysia" [Basic unique characteristics outside Malaysia], *Sinar Premium,* September 2, 2021, https://premium.sinarharian.com.my/article/153328/mediasi-kritis/cetusan/ciri-ciri-unik-dasar-luar-malaysia.

141 Mohammad Ikhram Mohammad Ridzuan, Mohd Ikbal Mohd Huda, and Sity Daud, "Enam dekad grand strategyMalaysia terhadap China (1957–2018): dasar luar negaramembangun terhadap negara kuat" [Malaysia's six decades of grand strategy against China (1957–2018): the foreign policy building against a strong country], *International Journal of East Asian Studies* 8, 1 (2019): 31–44, https://ejournal.um.edu.my/index.php/IJEAS/article/view/22583/11213; "Kerajaan Komited Kukuhkan Hubungan Malaysia-China – PM" [The government is committed to strengthening Malaysia-China relations – PM], *Berita Harian* [Daily news], May 25, 2019, https://www.bharian.com.my/berita/nasional/2019/05/568161/kerajaan-komited-kukuhkan-hubungan-malaysia-china-pm.

142 "Khos̄'k kt.Ȳā khwām s̄amphanṭh̄ Thịy – Cīn næ̀nfæ̀n rxb d̂ān mị̄mī khwām k̄hạdyæ̂ng" โฆษก กต.ย้ำความสัมพันธ์ไทย - จีนแน่นแฟ้นรอบด้าน ไม่มีความขัดแย้ง [A spokesman for the Ministry of Foreign Affairs reiterated that the relationship between Thailand and China was close in all aspects. No conflict], *S̄yāmrạṭh*

สยามรัฐ [Siam Rath], June 15, 2021, https://siamrath.co.th/n/253147; Sukjai Wongwaisiriwat, Suphit Suwannik, and Chonnitis Chaisingthong นางสาวสุขใจ ว่องไวศิริวัฒน์ นายสุพริศร์ สุวรรณิก นายชนม์นิธิศ ไชยสิงห์ทอง, "S̄hrạt̄hṭ vs Cīn: s̄xng mh̄āxảnāc h̄nụ̀ng cud pelī̀yn s̄ảkhạỵ læa s̄ìng thī̀ Thịy khwr thả" สหรัฐฯ VS จีน: สองมหาอำนาจ หนึ่งจุดเปลี่ยนสำคัญ และสิ่งที่ไทยควรทำ [US versus China: two superpowers, one key turning point and what Thailand should do], Bank of Thailand ธนาคารแห่งประเทศไทย, 2020, https://www.bot.or.th:443/Thai/ResearchAndPublications/articles/Pages/Article_29Oct2020.aspx.

143 Kriengsak Charoenwongsak เกรียงศักดิ์ เจริญวงศ์ศักดิ์, "Khwām r̀wmmụ̄x 'Cīn-Xāseīyn' yukh h̄lạng Kho wid-19" ความร่วมมือ 'จีน-อาเซียน' ยุคหลังโควิด-19 [China-ASEAN cooperation in the post-COVID-19 era], Krungtheph T̄hurkic Mīdeīy กรุงเทพธุรกิจ มีเดีย [Bangkok business media], January 2, 2021, https://www.bangkokbiznews.com/news/915262; Piti Srisaengnam ปีติ ศรีแสงนาม, "6 Praděn kār kh̄ā kār lngthun khwām s̄ạmphạnṭh̄ rah̄ẁāng prathes̄ thī̀ Thịy t̂xng cạbtā nı pī 2021" 6 ประเด็นการค้า การลงทุน ความสัมพันธ์ระหว่างประเทศ ที่ไทยต้องจับตาในปี 2021 [6 issues of trade, investment, international relations that Thailand must keep an eye on in 2021], The Standard, December 29, 2020, https://thestandard.co/6-issues-that-thailand-must-keep-an-eye-on-in-2021/.

144 Thanaphon Kongjieng, "Khwām s̄ạmphạnṭh̄ k̄hxngkxng thạph Thịy kạb kxng-thạph Cīn nı yukh khṇa rạks̄ʹā khwām s̄ngb h̄æ̀ng chāti (khs̄ch.)" ความสัมพันธ์ของกองทัพไทยกับกองทัพจีนในยุคคณะรักษาความสงบแห่งชาติ (คสช.) [The relationship between the Thai army and the Chinese army in the time of the National Council for Peace and Order (NCPO)], Wārs̄ār kār wicạy kār brih̄ār kār phạt̄'hnā วารสารการวิจัยการบริหารการพัฒนา [Journal of development management research] 10, 2 (2020): 97–108, https://so01.tci-thaijo.org/index.php/JDAR/article/view/244074; Porntip Tunpasert, "S̄t̄hānkārṇ̒ khwām mạ̀nkhng rah̄ẁāng prathes̄ p̣hāyh̄lạng kār rabād k̄hxng wịrạs̄ COVID-19" สถานการณ์ความมั่นคงระหว่างประเทศภายหลังการระบาดของไวรัส COVID-19 – สำนักงานสภาความมั่นคงแห่งชาติ [International security situation after the COVID-19 outbreak], Office of the National Security Council สำนักงานสภาความมั่นคงแห่งชาติ, July 20, 2020, https://www.nsc.go.th/%E0%B8%AA%E0%B8%96%E0%B8%B2%E0%B8%99%E0%B8%81%E0%B8%B2%E0%B8%A3%E0%B8%93%E0%B9%8C%E0%B8%84%E0%B8%A7%E0%B8%B2%E0%B8%A1%E0%B8%A1%E0%B8%B1%E0%B9%88%E0%B8%99%E0%B8%84%E0%B8%87%E0%B8%A3%E0%B8%B0%E0%B8%AB/.

145 Nguyễn Hữu Cát and Vũ Quang Đức, "Trung Quốc thực hiện chính sách đối ngoại và các tác động đến khu vực châu Á - Thái Bình Dương" [China's foreign policy implementation and impacts on the Asia-Pacific region], Lý luận chính trị [Political theory], December 31, 2018, http://lyluanchinhtri.vn/home/index.php/quoc-te/item/2768-trung-quoc-thuc-hien-chinh-sach-doi-ngoai-va-cac-tac-dong-den-khu-vuc-chau-a-thai-binh-duong.html.

146 "Giữ gìn, phát triển tình hữu nghị Việt-Trung luôn là trọng tâm trong chính sách đối ngoại của Việt Nam" [Preserving and developing the Vietnam-China friendship has always been the focus of Vietnam's foreign policy], VTV News [Báo điện tử], June 4, 2021, https://vtv.vn/news-20210604191644261.htm.

Chapter 4: Asian Narratives on Asia's Security Order: Western Hegemony as a Source of Instability

1. Stephen M. Walt, *The Hell of Good Intentions: America's Foreign Policy Elite and the Decline of U.S. Primacy* (New York: Farrar, Straus and Giroux, 2018), 53.
2. Henry W. Brands, *Bound to Empire: The United States and the Philippines* (New York: Oxford University Press, 1992), 13.
3. Samir Puri, *The Shadows of Empire: How Imperial History Shapes Our World* (New York: Pegasus Books, 2021), 197.
4. Harry S. Truman, "Statement by the President, Truman on Korea," History and Public Policy Program Digital Archive, Public Papers of the Presidents, Harry S. Truman, 1945–1953, June 27, 1950, http://digitalarchive.wilsoncenter.org/document/116192.
5. Bruce Cumings, *The Korean War: A History* (New York: Modern Library, 2011), xvii.
6. Robert Jervis and Jack Snyder, eds., *Dominoes and Bandwagons: Strategic Beliefs and Great Power Competition in the Eurasian Rimland* (Oxford: Oxford University Press, 1991), 12.
7. Mark Lawrence and Fredrick Logevall eds., *The First Vietnam War: Colonial Conflict and Cold War Crisis* (Cambridge, MA: Harvard University Press, 2007), 131.
8. Vincent Bevins, *The Jakarta Method: Washington's Anticommunist Crusade and the Mass Murder Program That Shaped Our World* (New York: Public Affairs, 2020), 123.
9. Victor D. Cha, *Powerplay: The Origins of the American Alliance System in Asia* (Princeton, NJ: Princeton University Press, 2018), 9–10.
10. Amitav Acharya, *Whose Ideas Matter? Agency and Power in Asian Regionalism* (Ithaca, NY: Cornell University Press, 2011), 65–66.
11. "Diaoyu" is the Chinese name for the islands and "Senkaku" is the Japanese name.
12. David Asher, "North Korea's Criminal Activities: A Growing Proliferation Challenge," Wilson Center, October 21, 2005, https://www.wilsoncenter.org/event/north-koreas-criminal-activities-growing-proliferation-challenge.
13. *North Korea's Criminal Activities: Financing the Regime: Hearing before the Committee on Foreign Affairs, House of Representatives, One Hundred Thirteenth Congress, First Session, March 5, 2013* (Washington, DC: US Government Printing Office, 2013); Robert E. Kelly, "North Korea as a 'Mafia State,'" *The Interpreter*, February 27, 2017, https://www.lowyinstitute.org/the-interpreter/north-korea-mafia-state.
14. David E. Sanger and William J. Broad, "Once 'No Longer a Nuclear Threat,' North Korea Now in Standoff with U.S.," *New York Times*, August 10, 2018, https://www.nytimes.com/2018/08/10/us/politics/north-korea-denuclearize-peace-treaty.html.
15. Evans Revere, "North Korea's New Nuclear Gambit and the Fate of Denuclearization," Brookings Institution, March 26, 2021, https://www.brookings.edu/blog/order-from-chaos/2021/03/26/north-koreas-new-nuclear-gambit-and-the-fate-of-denuclearization/.

Notes to pages 79–81   203

16 Aaron Blake, "Why Trump's Threat to 'Totally Destroy' North Korea Is Extraordinary – Even for Him," *Washington Post*, September 19, 2017, https://www.washingtonpost.com/news/the-fix/wp/2017/09/19/why-trumps-threat-to-totally-destroy-north-korea-is-extraordinary-even-for-him/.
17 Euan Graham, "Back in Focus: The United Nations Command in South Korea," *The Interpreter*, June 18, 2017, https://www.lowyinstitute.org/the-interpreter/back-focus-united-nations-command-south-korea.
18 Jim Garamone, "U.S.-Korean Alliance Is Key to Peace, Stability in Northeast Asia," US Department of Defense, March 18, 2021, https://www.defense.gov/Explore/News/Article/Article/2541273/us-korean-alliance-is-key-to-peace-stability-in-northeast-asia/.
19 James L. Schoff, "Strengthening U.S. Alliances in Northeast Asia," Carnegie Endowment for International Peace, July 16, 2015, https://carnegieendowment.org/2015/07/16/strengthening-u.s.-alliances-in-northeast-asia-pub-60750.
20 Caitlin Doornbos, "Ships from the US, Japan, South Korea, Australia Sail Together to Guam after RIMPAC," *Stars and Stripes*, September 9, 2020, https://www.stripes.com/news/pacific/ships-from-the-us-japan-south-korea-australia-sail-together-to-guam-after-rimpac-1.644340.
21 Van Jackson, *On the Brink: Trump, Kim, and the Threat of Nuclear War* (New York: Cambridge University Press, 2018), 13.
22 See, for instance, Jung Iljun 정일준, "Hanbando 'haeg-wigi' ui gyebohag: haegwigi damlon-ui sahoejeog guseong-gwa Bughan-ui haegmujang" 한반도 '핵위기'의 계보학 : 핵위기 담론의 사회적 구성과 북한의 핵무장 [The genealogy of "nuclear crisis" over Korean Peninsula: the social construction of nuclear crisis discourse and North Korea's nuclear weapons], *Gyeongjewasahoe* 경제와사회 [*Journal of Economics and Social Sciences*] 115 (2017): 40–71, https://www.dbpia.co.kr/Journal/articleDetail?nodeId=NODE07245679; Park Hyung-jun 박형준, "Nodongsinmun-eul tonghae bon Bughan-ui Daemi insig: bihaeghwa hyeobsang-eul jungsim-eulo" 노동신문을 통해 본 북한의 대미 인식 : 비핵화 협상을 중심으로 [North Korea's perception of the US through the Rodong Sinmun: focusing on the denuclearization negotiations], *Dongbug-ayeongu* 동북아연구 [*Northeast Asian Studies*] 34, 2 (2019): 107–36, https://oak.chosun.ac.kr/handle/2020.oak/16067; Noh Jin-cheol 노진철, "Hanbandoui jeonjaeng/pyeonghwa-jeongchiwa dongmaeng, geuligo Bughaeg wigi: jagijungeojeog chegyeilon-ui gwanjeom-eseo" 한반도의 전쟁/평화-정치와 동맹, 그리고 북핵 위기 : 자기준거적 체계이론의 관점에서 [Korean War/peace-politics and alliances, North Korean nuclear crisis: from a viewpoint of self-referential system theory]," *Gyeongjewasahoe* 경제와사회 [*Journal of Economics and Social Sciences*] 126 (2020): 563–99, https://doi.org/10.18207/criso.2020..126.563.
23 See, for instance, Jung Il-sung and Go Woon 정일성 고운, "Bughan-ui haegmujanglyeoggwa guggahaengdong byeonhwa bunseog" 북한의 핵무장력과 국가행동 변화 분석 [Analysis of North Korea's nuclear weapon capacity and state behaviour change], *Hangugdongbug-anonchong* 한국동북아논총 [*Journal of Northeast Asian Studies*] 82 (2017): 191–212, https://www.dbpia.co.kr/Journal/articleDetail?nodeId=NODE07433258; Kim Chang-hee 김창희, "Bughan-ui

jaganglyeogjeiljuuiwa inminnolyeogdong-won-e gwanhan yeongu" 북한의 자강력제일주의와 인민노력동원에 관한 연구 [A study on the principle of self-help and mobilization of people's efforts in North Korea], *Hangugdongbug-anonchong* 한국동북아논총 [*Journal of Northeast Asian Studies*], 85 (2017): 99–121, https://doi.org/10.21807/JNAS.2017.12.85.99; Hong Woo-taek 홍우택, "Bughan-ui guggaseonghyang bunseoggwa moui bunseog-eul tonghan haegjeonlyag geomjeung" 북한의 국가성향 분석과 모의 분석을 통한 핵전략 검증 [Analysis on the national character of North Korea and verification of the nuclear strategy by means of simulation analysis], *Gugbangjeongchaeg-yeongu* 국방정책연구 [*Defence Policy Research*] 32, 4 (2017): 83–114, https://www.dbpia.co.kr/Journal/articleDetail?nodeId=NODE08828018.

24 Kang Ho-seok 강호석, "Migug-ui haeg-wihyeob-i Hanbando haegmunje-ui bonjil" 미국의 핵위협이 한반도 핵문제의 본질 [The US nuclear threat is the essence of the nuclear issue on the Korean Peninsula], *Minpeulleoseu* 민플러스 [Minplus], May 30, 2018, https://www.minplusnews.com/news/articleView.html?idxno=5210; Lee Sang-hwan 이상환, "Bughan haegmugi gaebalgwa Hangug-ui oegyojeonlyag :Migug sinhaengjeongbuui daeoejeongchaeg-e daehan daeeung-eul jungsim-eulo" 북한 핵무기 개발과 한국의 외교전략 :미국 신행정부의 대외정책에 대한 대응을 중심으로 [North Korean nuclear weapons development and South Korean diplomatic strategies – focusing on South Korean countermeasures to the new US administration foreign policies], *Jeongchijeongboyeongu* 정치정보연구 [*Political Information Research*] 20, 1 (2017): 121–41, https://doi.org/10.15617/psc.2017.02.20.1.121.

25 Na Hoseon and Cha Changhoo 나호선 차창훈, "Jejaeilongwa Daebugjejae hyogwa-e daehan bipanjeog geomto: pijejaegug-ui daeeung-eul jungsim-eulo" 제재이론과 대북제재 효과에 대한 비판적 검토: 피제재국의 대응을 중심으로 [A critical review of sanctions theory and its effectiveness on North Korea: focused on reaction of targeted state], *Dongbug-ayeongu* 동북아연구 [*Northeast Asian Studies*] 35, 1 (2020): 43–85; Lee Hyouk Hui and Kim Yong Hyun 이혁희 김용현, "Migug-ui Naengjeongi bongswaewa Talnaengjeongi bongswae bigyo: Daebugjejaee juneun sisajeom" 미국의 냉전기 봉쇄와 탈냉전기 봉쇄 비교 : 대북제재에 주는 시사점 [A comparison of the Cold War–era containment and post-Cold War–era blockade of the US: implications of sanctions on North Korea], *Bughanhag-yeongu* 북한학연구 [*North Korean Studies*] 16, 2 (2020): 43–74, https://papersearch.net/thesis/article.asp?key=3847635.

26 Lee Heon-kyung 이헌경, "Migug-ui daebugjeongchaeg gyeoljeong-yoin bunseog" 미국의 대북정책 결정요인 분석 [An analysis of the US policy determinants to North Korea], *Hangugdongbug-anonchong* 한국동북아논총 [*Journal of Northeast Asian Studies*] 24, 2 (2019): 117–36, https://doi.org/10.21807/JNAS.2019.06.91.117.

27 Kim Joo-sam 김주삼, "Yuen-ui bughaeg Daebugjejaejochiui silhyoseong-gwa Bughan-ui chejesaengjonjeonlyag" 유엔의 북핵 대북제재조치의 실효성과 북한의 체제생존전략 [Efficacy of UN's sanctions on North Korea's nuclear and regime survival strategy], *Hanguggwa Gugjesahoe* 한국과 국제사회 [Korea and global affairs] 2, 1 (2018): 69–92, https://www.dbpia.co.kr/Journal/articleDetail?

nodeId = NODE10132693; Im So-jeong 임소정, "Gugjesahoeui Daebugjejae hyeonhwang-gwa jeonmang" 국제사회의 대북제재 현황과 전망 [Current status and prospects of international sanctions against North Korea], *KIEP] Gichojalyo* [KIEP] 기초자료 [*Basic Data*] 18, 1 (2018), https://www.dbpia.co.kr/Journal/articleDetail?nodeId = NODE07369420.

28 Ha Sang-sik 하상식, "Migug-ui Bughan bihaeghwa jeongchaeg silpaewa Han-migongjo gwaje" 미국의 북한 비핵화 정책 실패와 한미공조 과제 [The US failure in denuclearization of North Korea and tasks for policy coordination between South Korea and the US], *Gugjejeongchiyeongu* 국제정치연구 [The journal of international relations] 19, 2 (2016): 1–33.

29 Haba Kumiko 羽場久美子, "Yōroppa no tōgō, Ajia no bundan wa, Amerika no sekai senryaku – Ajia no kyōdō o ikani tsukuru ka?, Ajia kinrin shokoku to no tairitsu o koete – gakujutsu nettowāku no kōchiku –" ヨーロッパの統合、アジアの分断は、アメリカの世界戦略 ―アジアの共同をいかに作るか？，アジア近隣諸国との対立をこえて ―学術ネットワークの構築― [The integration of Europe and the division of Asia are America's global strategy – how to create a joint venture in Asia – beyond conflicts with neighbouring Asian countries – building academic networks –], *Gakujutsu No Dōkō* 学術の動向 [Academic trends] 25, 9 (2020): 49–54.

30 Akiyama Masahiro 秋山昌廣, "Kitachōsen mondai e no torikumi wa minaoshi no toki" 北朝鮮問題への取り組みは見直しのとき [Reviewing Japan's foreign policy toward North Korea], *Asahi Shimbun* 論座, January 23, 2018, https://webronza.asahi.com/politics/articles/2018011900003.html.

31 Japan Institute of International Affairs 日本国際問題研究所, "'Fukakujitsusei no jidai' no Chōsenhantō to Nihon no gaikō anzen hoshō' kenkyūkai chūkan hōkoku repōto" 「『不確実性の時代』の朝鮮半島と日本の外交・安全保障」研究会中間報告レポート ["Diplomacy and security between Korean peninsula and Japan in the age of uncertainty" conference interim report], October 30, 2019, http://www2.jiia.or.jp/RESR/column_page.php?id = 369 https://core.ac.uk/download/pdf/328112019.pdf.

32 Hirayiwa Junji 平岩俊司, "Kimu Jon'un seiken no Kitachōsen to kokusai shakai" 金正恩政権の北朝鮮と国際社会 [North Korea and the international community under the Kim Jong-un regime], *Mitahyōron* 三田評論, February 14, 2019, https://www.mita-hyoron.keio.ac.jp/other/201902-1.html.

33 Wang Fan 王帆, "Meiduichao zhengce, hululi maide shenmeyao" 美对朝政策，葫芦里卖的什么药 [US policy toward North Korea: what can we learn from it?], *Huanqiu shibao* 环球时报 [Global times], June 4, 2021, https://opinion.huanqiu.com/article/43OPwea33aT.

34 Li Ruochuan 李若川, "Meihan tongmeng shiyuxia de 'Sade' Ruhan chengyin yanjiu" 美韩同盟视域下的 "萨德" 入韩成因研究 [A study on causes of "THAAD" entering South Korea from the perspective of the US-Korea alliance] (master's thesis, Xiangtan University 湘潭大学, 2018).

35 Wang Junsheng 王俊生, "Zhimian Meiguo xinyilun 'Zhongguo weixielun'" 直面美国新一轮 "中国威胁论" [Preparing for a new round of US "China threat theory"], *Shijie zhishi* 世界知识 [World knowledge] 16 (2018): 58–59.

36 Li Li and Zhan Debin 李丽 詹德斌, "Telangpu zhengfu Duichao zhengce de tiaozheng" 特朗普政府对朝政策的调整 [The Trump administration's adjusted North Korea policy], *Guoji luntan* 国际论坛 23, 2 (2021): 34–52.
37 Yang Yueru and Wang Yubo 杨岳儒 王钰博, "Suzhu 'jingzhun jinrong zhicai' – lijie meiguo 'jixian shiya' zhengce" 诉诸"精准金融制裁" – – 理解美国"极限施压"政策 [US "maximum pressure" policy resorts to economic sanctions], *Jiangnan shehui xueyuan xuebao* 江南社会学院学报 [Journal of Jiangnan Institute of Sociology] 22, 2 (2020): 67–73.
38 "US Warns Beijing against Using Force in South China Sea," *The Guardian*, February 20, 2021, https://www.theguardian.com/world/2021/feb/20/us-warns-beijing-against-using-force-in-south-china-sea; Liu Zhen, "EU Hits Out at Beijing's Actions in South China Sea," *South China Morning Post*, April 25, 2021, https://www.scmp.com/news/china/diplomacy/article/3131016/eu-hits-out-beijings-actions-south-china-sea.
39 Ralph Jennings, "Western Countries Send Ships to South China Sea in Pushback against Beijing," *Voice of America*, February 22, 2021, https://www.voanews.com/east-asia-pacific/voa-news-china/western-countries-send-ships-south-china-sea-pushback-against.
40 Hannah Beech, "China's Sea Control Is a Done Deal, 'Short of War with the U.S.,'" *New York Times*, September 20, 2018, https://www.nytimes.com/2018/09/20/world/asia/south-china-sea-navy.html.
41 Steven Stashwick, "China's South China Sea Militarization Has Peaked," *Foreign Policy*, August 19, 2019, https://foreignpolicy.com/2019/08/19/chinas-south-china-sea-militarization-has-peaked/.
42 House Armed Services Committee, "Full Committee Hearing: 'National Security Challenges and U.S. Military Activities in the Indo-Pacific,'" March 10, 2021, https://armedservices.house.gov/2021/3/full-committee-hearing-national-security-challenges-and-u-s-military-activities-in-the-indo-pacific.
43 US Department of State, *A Free and Open Indo-Pacific: Advancing a Shared Vision* (Wasington, DC: US Department of State, November 4, 2019), 11, https://www.state.gov/wp-content/uploads/2019/11/Free-and-Open-Indo-Pacific-4Nov2019.pdf.
44 See, for example, "Rapid Construction at Cambodia's Ream Points to China," *Asia Maritime Transparency Initiative*, May 21, 2021, https://amti.csis.org/.
45 White House, "Carbis Bay G7 Summit Communiqué," news release, June 13, 2021, https://www.whitehouse.gov/briefing-room/statements-releases/2021/06/13/carbis-bay-g7-summit-communique/.
46 Frédéric Grare, "The EU's Indo-Pacific Strategy: A Chance for a Clear Message to China and Europe's Allies," European Council on Foreign Relations, April 22, 2021, https://ecfr.eu/article/the-eus-indo-pacific-strategy-a-chance-for-a-clear-message-to-china-and-europes-allies/.
47 Mike Mochizuki and Jiaxiu Han, "Is China Escalating Tensions with Japan in the East China Sea?" *The Diplomat*, September 16, 2020, https://thediplomat.com/2020/09/is-china-escalating-tensions-with-japan-in-the-east-china-sea/.
48 White House, "U.S.-Japan Joint Leaders' Statement: 'U.S.-Japan Global Partnership for a New Era,'" April 16, 2021, https://www.whitehouse.gov/briefing

-room/statements-releases/2021/04/16/u-s-japan-joint-leaders-statement-u-s-japan-global-partnership-for-a-new-era/.
49. Edmund J. Burke and Astrid Stuth Cevallos, *In Line or Out of Order: China's Approach to ADIZ in Theory and Practice* (Santa Monica, CA: RAND Corporation, 2017), 1.
50. Adam P. Liff, *China, Japan, and the East China Sea: Beijing's "Gray Zone" Coercion and Tokyo's Response* (Washington, DC: Brookings Institution, 2019), https://www.brookings.edu/wp-content/uploads/2019/12/FP_20191202_east_china_sea_liff.pdf.
51. Michael O'Hanlon, *China, the Gray Zone, and Contingency Planning at the Department of Defense and Beyond* (Washington, DC: Brookings Institution, 2019), https://www.brookings.edu/wp-content/uploads/2019/09/FP_20190930_china_gray_zone_ohanlon.pdf.
52. Shin Sang-jin 신상진, "Daemanmunjewa Bughaegmunjeleul dulleossan Jungmigwangye: Dongbug-a anbowigiui hyeoblyeogjeog gwanli" 대만문제와 북핵문제를 둘러싼 중미관계: 동북아 안보위기의 협력적 관리 [Sino-US relations over the Taiwan issue and North Korean nuclear issue: cooperative management of the security crisis in Northeast Asia], *Guggajeonlyag* 국가전략 [National strategy] 13, 3 (2007): 55–88.
53. Syaiful Hakim, "Sesjen Wantannas: konflik AS-China potensi ancaman stabilitas keamanan" [Secretary General Wantannas: US-China conflict potential threat to security stability], *Antara*, June 7, 2021, https://www.antaranews.com/berita/2197986/sesjen-wantannas-konflik-as-china-potensi-ancaman-stabilitas-keamanan.
54. Mochammad Ade Pamungkas, "Konflik AS vs China Memanas di Laut China Selatan" [US vs China conflict heats up in the South China Sea], *Tirto*, July 16, 2020, https://tirto.id/konflik-as-vs-china-memanas-di-laut-china-selatan-fQ9U.
55. Fitriyan Zamzami, "Narasi perang di Laut China Selatan" [Narrative of war in the South China Sea], *Republika*, May 7, 2020, https://www.republika.co.id/berita/q9yc4e393/narasi-perang-di-laut-china-selatan.
56. "Ketegangan di Laut China Selatan menuju perang?" [Tensions in the South China Sea may lead to war], Kuseman.com, April 25, 2020, https://kuseman.com/2020/04/25/ketegangan-di-laut-china-selatan-menuju-perang/.
57. "Laut China Selatan bukan tempat hegemoni AS" [The South China Sea is not a place of US hegemony], CRI Online, April 10, 2021, http://malay.cri.cn/20210410/1b7c4525-1e00-e7cb-361d-2836a0a79179.html.
58. Nattarin Rattanaphiboon ณัฐรินทร์ รัตนะพิบูลย์, "Meụ̂x khwām pạ̀np̀wn nı Thalecīntı̂ krathb kịl t̄hụng S̄h̄rạṭ̄hxmerikā" เมื่อความปั่นป่วนในทะเลจีนใต้กระทบไกลถึงสหรัฐอเมริกา [When the turbulence in the South China Sea hits as far as the United States], The 101 World, July 22, 2020, https://www.the101.world/south-china-sea-conflict-affects-usa/.
59. Thiwin Suputtikul ธิวินท์ สุพุทธิกุล, "Khwām ǹā cheụ̀xt̄hụ̄x læa chụ̀xs̄eīyng nı Thalecīntı̂: H̄māk s̄ảkhạỵ nı kem mh̄ạāxảnāc Cīn-S̄h̄rạṭ̄h‡" ความน่าเชื่อถือและชื่อเสียงในทะเลจีนใต้: หมากสำคัญในเกมมหาอำนาจ จีน-สหรัฐฯ [Trust and reputation in the South China Sea: key pieces in China-US superpower games], The 101

World, September 17, 2019, https://www.the101.world/credibility-and-reputation-on-south-china-sea/.
60 Hiếu Chân, "Mỹ cần công nhận chủ quyền của các nước ven Biển Đông" [The US needs to recognize the sovereignty of the countries along the East Sea], *Saigonnho News,* April 25, 2020, https://saigonnhonews.com/hoa-ky/my-can-cong-nhan-chu-quyen-cua-cac-nuoc-ven-bien-dong/.
61 Nguyễn Ngọc Chu, "Hoa Kỳ đã không còn đứng ngoài các tranh chấp chủ quyền ở Biển Đông Nam Á" [The United States has no longer been left out of the sovereignty disputes in the Southeast Asia Sea], *Saigon Post,* July 15, 2020, https://www.thesaigonpost.com/2020/07/hoa-ky-khong-con-ung-ngoai-cac-tranh.html.
62 Chu Jingtao 褚静涛, "Zhongguo jindaishi Diaoyudao yu Liuqiu guishu" 中国近代史钓鱼岛与琉球归属 [The ownership of the Diaoyu Islands and Ryukyu in modern Chinese history], *Jianghai xuekan* 江海学刊 6 (2012), https://www.aisixiang.com/data/125228.html.
63 Zhang Haipeng 张海鹏, "Diaoyudao zhuquan zhengyi yu baodiao qiantu" 钓鱼岛主权争议与保钓前途 [The sovereignty dispute of Diaoyu Islands and the future of Diaoyu Islands security] (speech, Taiwan, April 9, 2021), https://www.aisixiang.com/data/126717.html.
64 Tao Xinfei 陶新菲, "Meiguo 'Yatai zaipingheng' zhanluedui Zhongri Diaoyudao zhengduan de yingxiang" 美国 "亚太再平衡"战略对中日钓鱼岛争端的影响 [The impact of the US "Asia-Pacific rebalancing" strategy on the Sino-Japanese Diaoyu Islands dispute], *"Juece luntan - qiye jingxihua guanli yu juece yanjiu xueshu yantaohui" lunwenji* "决策论坛－－企业精细化管理与决策研究学术研讨会"论文集 [Proceedings of "decision forum - - academic seminar on enterprise refinement management and decision-making"] (Beijing, Shehui kexue wenxian chuban she 社会科学文献出版社 [Social science literature press], 2015), 37–38.
65 "Kiyoshi Takenaka and Sui-Lee Wee, "Japan infuriates China by agreeing to buy disputed isles," *Reuters,* September 10, 2012, https://www.reuters.com/article/us-china-japan-idUSBRE8890AU20120910.
66 Republic of China (Taiwan) Ministry of Foreign Affairs, "Regarding the Full Text of Our Government's Refutation of the Sixteen Questions and Answers on the Diaoyutai Island's Sixteen Questions," Republic of China (Taiwan) Ministry of Foreign Affairs, https://www.mofa.gov.tw/cp.aspx?n=445.
67 Ch'en Yung-feng and Ishii Nozomi 陳永峰 石井望, "Tiao yü t'ai feng yün T'ai Jih hsüeh che kuan tien" 釣魚台風雲台日學者觀點 [Viewpoints of Taiwan and Japanese scholars on Diaoyu Islands disputes], *Duli p'inglun* 獨立評論 [Independent review], August 13, 2015, https://opinion.cw.com.tw/blog/profile/52/article/3197; Chang Yü-ming 張育銘, "Pao Tiao hsien ch'ü i shuang (Ch'en Mei Hsia) k'an cheng fu shih wang ta yü ch'i tai" 保釣先驅遺孀(陳美霞)看政府失望大於期待 [Widow of the former Diaoyu Islands defender frustrated with the government], Diaoyutai Education Association 釣魚台教育協會, July 26, 2016, https://diaoyutai.tw/2016/07/26/%E4%BF%9D%E9%87%A3%E5%85%88%E9%A9%85%E9%81%BA%E5%AD%80%E9%99%B3%E7%BE%8E%E9%9C%9E%E7%9C%8B%E6%94%BF%E5%BA%9C-%E5%A4%B1%E6%9C%9B%E5%A4%A7.

Notes to pages 87–88

68 "Hanguo Fanri shiwei xian 'diaoyudao shi Zhongguode' kouhao" 韩国反日示威现 "钓鱼岛是中国的" 口号 [Slogan "Diaoyu Islands belong to China" appeared in South Korea's anti-Japanese demonstration], *Wangyi* 网易 [Net Ease], July 3, 2014, https://news.163.com/photoview/00AO0001/68559.html#p = A07KESI 400AO0001.
69 Kang Hyo-baek 강효백, "Ilbon-i Senkakuleul gug-yuhwahan jinjja iyu" 일본이 센카쿠를 국유화한 진짜 이유 [The real reason Japan nationalized Senkaku], *Jugan Joseon* 주간조선 [Weekly Chosun], September 17, 2012, http://weekly.chosun.com/client/news/viw.asp?ctcd = c02&nNewsNumb = 002224100014.
70 Lee Chung-won 이충원, "Yeogsa sog oneul 'beoljib-eul geondeulida' Ilbon, Senkaku yeoldo gug-yuhwa" 역사속 오늘 > '벌집을 건드리다' ... 일본, 센카쿠 열도 국유화 [Today in history "touching the beehive" ... Japan nationalizes the Senkaku Islands], *Yonhap News* 연합뉴스, September 11, 2015, https://www.yna.co.kr/view/AKR20150909066600039.
71 Michael Green, "What Is the U.S. 'One China' Policy, and Why Does It Matter?" Center for Strategic and International Studies, May 25, 2021, https://www.csis.org/analysis/what-us-one-china-policy-and-why-does-it-matter.
72 Chris Horton, "Taiwan's Status Is a Geopolitical Absurdity," *The Atlantic*, July 22, 2019, https://www.theatlantic.com/international/archive/2019/07/taiwans-status-geopolitical-absurdity/593371/.
73 Richard Bush, *From Persuasion to Coercion: Beijing's Approach to Taiwan and Taiwan's Response* (Washington, DC: Brookings Institution, 2019), https://www.brookings.edu/wp-content/uploads/2019/11/FP_20191120_beijing_taiwan_bush.pdf.
74 Kharis Templeman, "How Taiwan Stands Up to China," *Journal of Democracy* 31, 3 (2020): 85–99, https://doi.org/10.1353/jod.2020.0047.
75 Michael Hunzeker and Dennis Weng, "The Painful, but Necessary, Next Steps in the U.S.-Taiwanese Relationship," War on the Rocks, September 24, 2020, https://warontherocks.com/2020/09/the-painful-but-necessary-next-steps-in-the-u-s-taiwanese-relationship/.
76 Huang Tzu-ti, "Australia Mulls Military Options in Event China Invades Taiwan," *Taiwan News*, April 19, 2021, https://www.taiwannews.com.tw/en/news/4180942.
77 Teddy Ng, "British Navy Vessel Passes through Taiwan Strait," *South China Morning Post*, December 7, 2019, https://www.scmp.com/news/china/diplomacy/article/3041076/british-navy-vessel-passes-through-taiwan-strait; Idrees Ali and Phil Stewart, "Exclusive: In Rare Move, French Warship Passes through Taiwan Strait," *Reuters*, April 25, 2019, https://www.reuters.com/article/us-taiwan-france-warship-china-exclusive-idUSKCN1S10Q7.
78 Philip Anstrén, "Why Europe's Future Is on the Line in the Taiwan Strait," Atlantic Council, March 24, 2021, https://www.atlanticcouncil.org/blogs/new-atlanticist/why-europes-future-is-on-the-line-in-the-taiwan-strait/.
79 Helen Davidson, "'Stronger Together': Taiwan Foreign Minister Urges New Alliance against China," *The Guardian*, December 7, 2020, https://www.theguardian.com/world/2020/dec/07/stronger-together-taiwan-foreign-minister-urges-new-alliance-against-china.

80 Loren Thompson, "Why Sell Weapons to Taiwan? Because Washington's China Strategy Won't Work without It," *Forbes,* October 18, 2019, https://www.forbes.com/sites/lorenthompson/2019/10/18/why-sell-weapons-to-taiwan-because-washingtons-china-strategy-wont-work-without-it/?sh=1f21b184263c.

81 Joshua Espena and Chelsea Bomping, "The Taiwan Frontier and the Chinese Dominance for the Second Island Chain," Australian Institute of International Affairs, August 13, 2020, https://www.internationalaffairs.org.au/australian outlook/taiwan-frontier-chinese-dominance-for-second-island-chain/.

82 J. Michael Cole, "Is China Preparing for War in the Taiwan Strait," *The National Interest,* November 16, 2020, https://nationalinterest.org/blog/buzz/china-preparing-war-taiwan-strait-171079.

83 Eugene Gholz, Benjamin Friedman, and Enea Gjoza, "Defensive Defense: A Better Way to Protect US Allies in Asia," *Washington Quarterly* 42, 4 (February 2019): 171–89, https://doi.org/10.1080/0163660x.2019.1693103.

84 Michele Lowe and Alice Cho, "Ambiguity Doesn't Work: Taiwan Needs Strategic Clarity," Real Clear Defense, March 18, 2021, https://www.realcleardefense.com/articles/2021/03/18/ambiguity_doesnt_work_taiwan_needs_strategic_clarity_768765.html.

85 Secretary of State Michael R. Pompeo, "Lifting Self-Imposed Restrictions on the U.S.-Taiwan Relationship," press statement, January 9, 2021, https://2017-2021.state.gov/lifting-self-imposed-restrictions-on-the-u-s-taiwan-relationship/index.html.

86 Chao Deng and Chun Han Wong, "Biden Sends Important Foreign-Policy Signal with Taiwan Inauguration Invite," *Wall Street Journal,* January 21, 2021, https://www.wsj.com/articles/biden-sends-important-foreign-policy-signal-with-taiwan-inauguration-invite-11611230623.

87 Jason Scott, "U.S. in Talks with Australia on Responses to War over Taiwan, Diplomat Says," *Bloomberg,* March 31, 2021, https://www.bloomberg.com/news/articles/2021-04-01/u-s-in-talks-with-australia-on-taiwan-response-diplomat-says; Chang Sue-chung, "France's Pivotal Support of Taiwan," *Taipei Times,* May 16, 2021, https://www.taipeitimes.com/News/editorials/archives/2021/05/17/2003757522; David Green, "Taiwan Needs to Be a Part of the UK's China Strategy," *The Diplomat,* January 1, 2021, https://thediplomat.com/2020/12/taiwan-needs-to-be-a-part-of-the-uks-china-strategy/; Finbarr Bermingham, "Europe's Biggest Party to Take Tougher Line on China, Push Taiwan Investment Deal," *South China Morning Post,* March 9, 2021, https://www.scmp.com/news/china/diplomacy/article/3124748/europes-biggest-party-set-take-tougher-line-china-push-taiwan.

88 "Abaikan amarah China, Amerika tetap kirim kapal perang ke Selat Taiwan" [Ignoring China's anger, America continues to send warships to the Taiwan Strait], JPNN, May 19, 2021, https://www.jpnn.com/news/abaikan-amarah-china-amerika-tetap-kirim-kapal-perang-ke-selat-taiwan.

89 Ary Arseno, "Containment Amerika Serikat terhadap fenomena rise of China dalam perspektif hegemoni realisme" [United States containment strategy toward China's rise in perspective hegemony realism], *Jurnal Hubungan Internasional* [Journal of international relations] 12, 9 (2019): 167–82.

90 "Cīn woy S̄ʹhrạṭ̄h mị̀ h̄yud k̀xkwn Ch̀xngkhæb Tị̂h̄wạn" จีนโวยสหรัฐ ไม่หยุดก่อกวนช่องแคบไต้หวัน [China urges US not to stop harassing Taiwan Strait], *K̄h̀āw Pracả Wạn* ข่าวประจำวัน [Daily news], April 8, 2021, https://www.dailynews.co.th/foreign/835964; Thiwin Suputtikul ธีวินท์ สุพุทธิกุล, "Kem kār bạ̀n khlxn s̄t̄hāna: Xīk h̄nụ̀ng næw patha s̄xng f̄ạ̀ng f̄āk Ch̀xngkhæb Tị̂h̄wạn" เกมการบั่นคลอนสถานะ : อีกหนึ่งแนวปะทะสองฝั่งฝากช่องแคบไต้หวัน [Status deterioration game: another frontline on both sides of the Taiwan Strait], The 101 World, Febrauary 18, 2020, https://www.the101.world/taiwan-territorial-dispute/.

91 "Khi 2 bờ Eo Biển Đài Loan căng thẳng, Pháp, Mỹ 'song kiếm hợp bích'" [When the two sides of the Taiwan Strait are tense, France and the United States "match swords"] *Tuổi Trẻ* [Youth], May 15, 2020, https://tuoitre.vn/khi-2-bo-eo-bien-dai-loan-cang-thang-phap-my-song-kiem-hop-bich-20200515093639192.htm; Bich Thuan, "Tàu chiến Mỹ qua Eo Biển Đài Loan, Trung Quốc tuyên bố sẵn sàng đối phó mọi đe dọa" [US warship passes through Taiwan Strait, China declares readiness to deal with any threats], *VOV*, May 19, 2021, https://vov.vn/the-gioi/tau-chien-my-qua-eo-bien-dai-loan-trung-quoc-tuyen-bo-san-sang-doi-pho-moi-de-doa-859033.vov.

92 Shin Sang-jin, "Daemanmunjewa Bughaegmunjeleul dulleossan Jungmigwangye: Dongbug-a anbowigiui hyeoblyeogjeog gwanli."

93 Shin Beom-cheol 신범철 "[milaegil] mijung paegwongyeongjaeng-gwa daemanui milae" 미래길] 美中패권경쟁과 대만의 미래 [Future road the US-China hegemonic competition and Taiwan's future], *Milae Hanggug* 미래한국 [Future Korea], March 4, 2021, https://www.futurekorea.co.kr/news/articleView.html?idxno=145832.

94 Shin Sang-jin, "Daemanmunjewa Bughaegmunjeleul dulleossan Jungmigwangye: Dongbug-a anbowigiui hyeoblyeogjeog gwanli."

95 Fumino Niwa 丹羽文生, "Abe gaikō to Taiwan – sono seidjiteki keifu –" 安倍外交と台湾 —その政治的系譜— [Abe diplomacy and Taiwan – its political genealogy –], *Mondai To Kenkyū* 問題と研究 [Issues and research] 47, 2 (2018): 141–72.

96 Kurashige tokurō 倉重篤郎, "Anpo kaitei 60-nen sono kōzai to kongo' (3) Shigeru Ishiba, Shūgiin giin" 「安保改定 60 年 その功罪と今後」(3)石破茂・衆議院議員 ["60 years of the revision of the security treaty, its merits and demerits, and the future" (3) Shigeru Ishiba, member of the House of Representatives], *Nihonkishakurabu* 日本記者クラブ, [Japan National Press Club] February 25, 2020, https://s3-us-west-2.amazonaws.com/jnpc-prd-public-oregon/files/2021/03/0f603fab-1dd9-42de-a6fc-80a403241716.pdf.

97 "Nichibei shunō kaidan dō miru, yanagisawa kyōji-shi, nakayama toshihiro-shi, Ako Tomoko-shi" 日米首脳会談どう見る 柳沢協二氏、中山俊宏氏、阿古智子氏 [How do you see the Japan-US summit meeting], *Asahi Shimbun* 朝日新聞, April 19, 2021, https://digital.asahi.com/articles/DA3S14875342.html?_requesturl=articles/DA3S14875342.html&pn=4.

98 "Nichibei shunō kaidan, takeuchi yukio-shi, zakku kūpā-shi, Ki Yontao-shi" 日米首脳会談 竹内行夫氏、ザック・クーパー氏、帰泳濤氏 [Discussion on Japan-US summit meeting], *Asahi Shimbun* 朝日新聞, April 18, 2021, https://www.asahi.com/articles/DA3S14875111.html.

99 Mie Oba, "Dai 204-kai kokkai Sangiin yosan iinkai kōchōkai daiyichiban Reiwa 3-nen 3-katsu 16 nichi" 第204回国会 参議院 予算委員会公聴会第1号 令和3年3月16日 [The budget committee of the lower house of the Diet public hearing no. 1 on March 16, 2021], National Diet Library 国立国会図書館, March 16, 2021, https://kokkai.ndl.go.jp/#/detail?minId=120415262X00120210316&spkNum=147&single.

100 Wang Hsiao-po 王曉波, "Meikuo Tuit'ai chengts'e ti yenpien ho liangan chengchih" 美國對台政策的演變和兩岸政治 [The evolution of US policy toward Taiwan and China –Taiwan politics], *Haihsia p'inglun* 海峽評論 [Strait review] 328, 4 (2018): 71–75.

101 Ci-Ze Li 李其澤, "Bai Deng zhengfu dui Zhong zhengce zhuzhou yu taihai jushi fenxi" 拜登政府對中政策主軸與台海局勢分析 [The main axis of The Biden Administration's China Policy and an Analysis of the Cross-Strait Situation], *Quanqiu zhengzhi pinglun* 全球政治評論 [Review of Global Politics], Special Issue 7 (2022): 77–92, http://140.120.40.139/File/Userfiles/0000000033/files/5%E6%9D%8E%E5%85%B6%E6%BE%A4.pdf; Heng-Chung Hsiao 蕭衡鍾, "Taiwan zai dangdai Meiguo duiwai zhanlue bushu zhong de dingwei: Huoban huo qizi" 台灣在當代美國對外戰略部署中的定位: 夥伴或棋子 [Contemporary Taiwan' Position under Foreign Strategy Deploy for US.: Partner or Chessman], *Taiwan guoji yanjiu jikan* 臺灣國際研究季刊 [Taiwan international studies quarterly] 17, 3 (2021): 121–39.

102 Hsieh Hsien-ching 謝賢璟, "Ts'ung mi te mo shih t'an t'ao ch'uan p'u wai chiao ssu wei chi ch'i tui liang an kuan hsi chih ying hsiang" 從米德模式探討川普外交思維及其對兩岸關係之影響 [Examining Trump's diplomatic thinking based on the Mead model and its influence on cross-strait relations], *Chan wang yü t'an so yüeh k'an* 展望與探索月刊 [Outlook and discovery monthly] 17, 9 (2019): 64–93.

103 Jie Dalei 节大磊, "Meitai 'qiexiangchang' de xiandu he weixianxing" 美台"切香肠"的限度和危险性 [Limits and risks of US-Taiwan's close interaction], *Huanqiu shibao* 环球时报 [Global times], September 14, 2020, https://www.aisixiang.com/data/122878.html.

104 Qiu Chaobing 仇朝兵, "Zhongmei guanxi xintaishi xiade taiwan wenti: zouxiang yu pinggu" 中美关系新态势下的台湾问题: 走向与评估 [Analysis of Taiwan issue under the recent Sino-U.S. relation circumstance]. *Tongyi zhanxianxue yanjiu* 统一战线学研究 [United front studies] 5, 1 (2021): 53–76.

105 Xinqiang 信强, "'Zhanlue gaowei zichan': quanli geju, Zhongmei guanxi yu Taiwan zhanlue jiaose de shanbian" "战略高危资产":权力格局、中美关系与台湾战略角色的嬗变 [Strategic high-risk assets: power structure, Sino-US relations and the evolution of Taiwan's strategic role], *Taiwan yanjiu jikan* 台湾研究集刊 4 (2020): 72–83.

106 Chenfeng 晨枫, "Zhanlue mohu vs zhanlue qingxi: Meiguo zai Taiwan wentishang de liangnan xuanze" 战略模糊vs战略清晰: 美国在台湾问题上的两难选择 [America's dilemma on Taiwan issue: strategic ambiguity or strategic clarity], *Guangchazhewang* 观察者网 [Observer network], May 9, 2021, https://www.guancha.cn/ChenFeng3/2021_05_09_590111.shtml.

107 Bruce Jones and Adam Twardowski, "Bolstering Democracies in a Changing International Order: The Case for Democratic Multilateralism," Brookings

Institution, March 23, 2021, https://www.brookings.edu/research/bolstering-democracies-in-a-changing-international-order-the-case-for-democratic-multilateralism/.
108 Kiyoteru Tsutsui, "Let's Keep It the 'Free and Open' Indo-Pacific," Freeman Spogli Institute for International Studies, Stanford University, January 4, 2021, https://fsi.stanford.edu/news/lets-keep-it-free-and-open-indo-pacific.
109 "How to Secure a Free and Open Indo-Pacific," *Washington Post,* March 15, 2021, https://www.washingtonpost.com/brand-studio/wp/2021/03/15/feature/how-to-secure-a-free-and-open-indo-pacific/.
110 Thomas Wilkins, *An Indo-Pacific Regional Order? Frameworks for Cooperation and the Future of Geopolitical Competition* (Ottawa: Macdonald-Laurier Institute, 2021), https://macdonaldlaurier.ca/files/pdf/20210203_An_Indo-Pacific_regional_order_Wilkins_COMMENTARY_FWeb.pdf?mc_cid=48f35c919e&mc_eid=9b2c01864a.
111 Brahma Chellaney, "A Concert of Indo-Pacific Democracies," *The Strategist,* November 14, 2018, https://www.aspistrategist.org.au/a-concert-of-indo-pacific-democracies/; Andrew Erskine and Emilio Angeles, "The Luring of the Indo-Pacific: Can NATO Formulate a Collective Regional Strategy for Its Members," NATO Association of Canada, June 1, 2021, https://natoassociation.cathe-luring-of-the-indo-pacific-can-nato-formulate-a-collective-regional-strategy-for-its-members/.
112 Caitlin Byrne, "Securing the 'Rules-Based Order' in the Indo-Pacific: The Significance of Strategic Narrative," *Security Challenges* 16, 3 (2020): 10–15.
113 "How Western Democracies Can Help Taiwan," *Financial Times,* September 1, 2020, https://www.ft.com/content/db635f87-8cce-4c4e-bb13-4b03b37cfb2e.
114 Maiko Ichihara, "Expanding Multilateral Frameworks for Democracy in Asia and the Necessity of Track 1.5 Approaches," Brookings Institution, March 22, 2021, https://www.brookings.edu/articles/expanding-multilateral-frameworks-for-democracy-in-asia-and-the-necessity-of-track-1-5-approaches/.
115 NATO, "Brussels Summit Communiqué Issued by the Heads of State and Government Participating in the Meeting of the North Atlantic Council in Brussels 14 June 2021," news release, June 14, 2021, https://www.nato.int/cps/en/natohq/news_185000.htm?selectedLocale=en.
116 White House, "Carbis Bay G7 Summit Communiqué."
117 Irawan Soni, "Diskursus Indo-Pasifik: Hegemoni Amerika, persaingan strategis, hingga transformasi geopolitik kawasan" [Indo-Pacific discourse: american hegemony, strategic competition, until regional geopolitical transformation], *Mandala: Jurnal hubungan international* 1, 2 (2018): 282–310.
118 Lalu Azhar Rafsanjani, "Rivalitas Amerika Serikat (AS) dan China dalam menjadi security orderer di Asia Timur" [The rivalry of the United States (US) and China in being a security orderer in East Asia], *Indonesian Journal of Global Discourse* 2, 1 (2020): 27–44.
119 Wan Zain, "Indo-Pasifik: strategi tersirat Amerika di rantau ini" [Indo-Pacific: America's implicit strategy in the region], *Astro Awani,* July 22, 2020, https://de-awani-web-portal-stg.eco.astro.com.my/berita-dunia/indo-pasifik-strategi-tersirat-amerika-di-rantau-ini-252275?amp=1.

120 Abdul Abadi, "Biden, geopolitik Islam dan Asia" [Biden, Islamic Geopolitics and Asia], *Sinar Harian* [The daily light], November 12, 2020, https://www.sinarharian.com.my/article/109761/KOLUMNIS/Biden-geopolitik-Islam-dan-Asia.

121 Piti Srisaengnam ปีติ ศรีแสงนาม, "53 Pī xāseīyn: Keid cāk s̄ngkhrāmyĕn 1.0 P̄hechiyh̄n̂ā s̄ngkhrāmyĕn 2.0" 53 ปีอาเซียน: เกิดจากสงครามเย็น 1.0 เผชิญหน้าสงครามเย็น 2.0 [53 years of ASEAN: born of the Cold War 1.0, facing the Cold War 2.0], The 101 World, August 7, 2020, https://www.the101.world/53-years-of-asean/.

122 Chittipat Poonkham จิตติภัทร พูนขำ, "C̄hāk thas̄ʹn̒ nyobāy t̀āng pra thes̄ʹ k̄hxng Bị Den: Meụ̄̂x Xmerikā t̂xng nả lok" ฉากทัศน์นโยบายต่างประเทศของไบเดน : เมื่ออเมริกาต้องนำโลก [Biden's foreign policy scene: when America leads the world], The 101 World, November 9, 2020, https://www.the101.world/bidens-foreign-policy/; Kantheera Phuriwikrai กานต์ธีรา ภูริวิกรัย, "X̀ān Thịy Xāseīyn læa Xin Do-Pæsifik kạb Duly P̄hākh Prīchā Rạch Ch" อ่านไทย อาเซียน และอินโด-แปซิฟิก กับ ดุลยภาค ปรีชารัชช [Read Thai, ASEAN, and Indo-Pacific with Dulyapak Preecharach], The 101 World, August 26, 2020, https://www.the101.world/dulyapak-asean-indopacific-interview.

123 Pham Thi Thanh Binh, "'Chiến lược Ấn Độ Dương-Thái Bình Dương tự do và rộng mở' của Mỹ: Vai trò và cách thức triển khai" [America's "Free and Open Indo-Pacific Strategy": role and implementation], *Tạp chí Cộng sản* [Communist Magazine], April 4, 2020, https://tapchicongsan.org.vn/web/guest/the-gioi-van-de-su-kien/-/2018/816028/%E2%80%9Cchien-luoc-an-do-duong---thai-binh-duong-tu-do-va-rong-mo%E2%80%9D-cua-my--vai-tro-va-cach-thuc-trien-khai.aspx#; Tuan Anh, "Hải quân Châu Âu tăng hiện diện ở Ấn Độ-Thái Bình Dương đối phó Trung Quốc" [European navy increases presence in Indo-Pacific to deal with China], *Vietnam Net*, March 5, 2021, https://vietnamnet.vn/vn/the-gioi/hai-quan-chau-au-tang-hien-dien-o-an-do-thai-binh-duong-doi-pho-trung-quoc-717435.html.

124 "Đối sách của Việt Nam trước chiến lược Châu Á-Thái Bình Dương của Hoa Kỳ: tiếp cận theo biến đổi mới của tình hình" [Vietnam's countermeasures to the US's Asia-Pacific strategy: a new transformative approach], *Tạp Chí Khoa Học Công Nghệ* [Science and technology magazine], March 2, 2021, https://vjst.vn/vn/tin-tuc/4520/doi-sach-cua-viet-nam-truoc-chien-luoc-chau-a---thai-binh-duong-cua-hoa-ky--tiep-can-theo-bien-doi-moi-cua-tinh-hinh.aspx.

125 "Jimintō sōsai kōho Ishiba moto kanji-chō ni kiku! Dokuji intabyū kara mieru seisaku to wa" 自民党総裁候補・石破元幹事長に聞く！独自インタビューから見える政策とは [Conversation with the Liberal Democratic Party presidential candidate], YouTube video, posted by "テレ東BIZ," September 7, 2020, https://www.youtube.com/watch?v=8BAG_PAqZao; Fujimoto Kinya 藤本 欣也, "Nikai kanji-chō, Shuseki to no kaidan-go 'Beikoku no kaoiro o ukagaubekidenai'" 二階幹事長、習主席との会談後「米国の顔色をうかがうべきでない」 [Japan secretary-general supports the success of BRI], *Sankei News* 産経ニュース, January 22, 2021, https://www.sankei.com/article/20190424-REWIVYKZDFKCDI3A53CCLS6QCI/; Tanaka Kin 田中均, "Ajiataiheiyō' kara 'indotaiheiyō' e – Nihon no

taigai shisei no henka o dō miru no ka"「アジア太平洋」から「インド太平洋」へ——日本の対外姿勢の変化をどう見るのか [Japan's foreign policy variation: from "Asia-Pacific" to "Indo-Pacific"], Institute for International Strategy 国際戦略研究所, April 28, 2021, https://www.jri.co.jp/page.jsp?id=38824.

126 "Suga-shi, Ajia-ban Natō 'Hanchū hōi-mō ni narazaru o ezu' Jimintōsōsaisen kōho ga kōkai tōronkai" 菅氏、アジア版ＮＡＴＯ「反中包囲網にならざるを得ず」自民党総裁選候補が公開討論会 *Sankei News* 産経ニュース, January 11, 2021, https://www.sankei.com/article/20200912-DOR66IYW2RMGZMUWDFVBKOVMDI/.

127 "Nitchū ryōkoku ga shinrai kankei o kōchiku shi, sōgo ni sonchō shi au pātonā ni -seiji・gaikō bunka-kai hōkoku-" 日中両国が信頼関係を構築し、相互に尊重しあうパートナーに～政治・外交分科会報告～ [To partners who build a relationship of trust and respect between Japan and China – politics and diplomacy subcommittee report], Genron NPO言論NPO, October 27, 2019, https://www.genron-npo.net/world/archives/7389.html.

128 Kim Duk-ki 김덕기, "Migug-ui gongsejeog Indo·Taepyeong-yang jeonlyag gwanjeom-eseo bon Mi·Jung paegwongyeongjaeng-gwa Hangug-ui daeeung-jeonlyag" 미국의 공세적 인도·태평양 전략 관점에서 본 미·중 패권경쟁과 한국의 대응전략 [A study on US-China hegemony competition based on US offensive Indo-Pacific strategy and Republic of Korea's response strategy], *Military Journal* 군사논단100, 1 (2020): 75–167.

129 Yoo Sang-beom 유상범, "Teuleompeu haengjeongbuui Indo-Taepyeong-yang jeongchaeg: hyeonsang jindangwa jeonmang" 트럼프 행정부의 인도-태평양 정책: 현상 진단과 전망 [The Trump administration's Indo-Pacific policy: diagnosis and prospects], *National Defence Research* 국방연구62, 2 (2019): 53–75.

130 Kim Jaekwan Kim, "Miguggwa Jung-gug-ui 'Indo-Taepyeong-yang jeonlyag' gwa paegwon gyeongjaeng" 미국과 중국의"인도-태평양 전략"과 패권 경쟁 [The US and China's Indo-Pacific strategy and their hegemonic competition over this region], *Dongbug-ayeongu* 동북아연구 [*Northeast Asian Studies*] 33, 2 (2018): 265–300.

131 Lin Yongxin and He Xianqing 林勇新 贺先青, "'Yintai' diyuan zhengzhi jiangou jiqi dui Zhongguo zhoubian waijiao huanjing de yingxiang" "印太" 地缘政治建构及其对中国周边外交环境的影响 ["Indo-Pacific" geopolitical construction and its impact on China's neighbouring diplomatic environment], *Nanhai xuekan* 南海学刊 [South China Sea Journal] 6, 3 (2020): 100–11.

132 Ge Tengfei 葛腾飞, "'Yintai' diqu anquan zhixu fenzheng yu Zhongguo de diqu zhixu yuanjing" "印太" 地区安全秩序纷争与中国的地区秩序愿景 ["Indo-Pacific" regional security order disputes and China's vision of regional order], *Waijiao pinglun* 外交评论 [Diplomatic review] 38, 3 (2021): 73–100.

133 Wu Tong and Zhang Cong 吴彤 张聪, "Chongsu jianzhipai: Baideng zhinang de Meiguo fangan" 重塑建制派：拜登智囊的美国方案 [Reshaping the establishment: Biden regime's plan on America's future], *Wenhua zongheng* 文化纵横 [Cultural aspect] 1 (2021): 10–13.

134 Sun Yunfei and Liu Changming 孙云飞, 刘昌明, "'Yintai' diqu anquan fuheti de xingcheng yu Meiguo baquan huchi" "印太" 地区安全复合体的形成与美国霸权护持

[The formation of the "Indo-Pacific" regional security complex and the continuation of US hegemony], *Jiaoxue yu yanjiu* 教学与研究 [Teaching and research] 12 (2019): 36–47.

Chapter 5: Chinese Counter-Narratives: The Chinese Communist Party, Hong Kong, Xinjiang, and Foreign Affairs

1 "President Xi Jinping's Speech at Davos Agenda Is Historic Opportunity for Collaboration," World Economic Forum, January 25, 2021, https://www.weforum.org/press/2021/01/president-xi-jinping-s-speech-at-davos-agenda-is-historic-opportunity-for-collaboration/.
2 Xi Jinping, "Let the Torch of Multilateralism Light up Humanity's Way Forward" (special address, World Economic Forum Virtual Event of the Davos Agenda, January 25, 2021), Ministry of Foreign Affairs of the People's Republic of China, https://www.fmprc.gov.cn/mfa_eng/zxxx_662805/t1848323.shtml.
3 See, for example, Takashi Funakoshi 冨名腰隆, "'Shin reisen wa sekai o bunretsu e mukawa seru' Shūshi, Beikoku o kensei" 「新冷戦は世界を分裂へ向かわせる」習氏、米国を牽制 ["The new Cold War will drive the world into division," Mr. Xi restrains the United States], *Asahi Shimbun* 朝日新聞, January 25, 2021, https://www.asahi.com/articles/ASP1T7KVQP1TUHBI027.html; Seon Han-gyeol 선한결, "Sijinping 'Jung dogjanoseon' sisa ... 'tagug sahoejedo gang-yo malla'" 시진핑 中 독자노선 시사 ... 타국 사회제도 강요 말라 | 한경닷컴 [Xi Jinping's "Chinese reader route" preview ... "don't force the social system of other countries"], *Hangyeong Geullobeolmakes* 한경 글로벌마켓 [Hankyung global market], January 25, 2021, https://www.hankyung.com/international/article/202101251198i; Lintar Satria, "Xi Jinping ingatkan as risiko Perang Dingin" [Xi Jinping reminds US of Cold War risk], *Republika Online,* January 26, 2021, https://www.republika.co.id/berita/qnj3m5377/xi-jinping-ingatkan-as-risiko-perang-dingin; Kompatit Sakulhuang คมปทิต สกุลหวง, "DAVOS 2021: Sī cîn p̄hing teụ̄xn 's̄ngkhrāmyĕn khrậng h̄ım̀' h̄āk s̄h̄rạṭ̄h‡ yạng dein h̄n̂ā pkp̂xng kār kĥā bæ bth rạm p̄̀" DAVOS 2021: สีจีนผิง เตือน 'สงครามเย็นครั้งใหม่' หาก สหรัฐฯ ยังเดินหน้าปกป้องการค้าแบบทรัมป์ [DAVOS 2021: Xi Jinping warns of "a new Cold War" if US continues to protect trade like Trump], *The Standard,* January 26, 2021, https://thestandard.co/xi-jinping-say-will-be-another-cold-war-for-united-states/.
4 See, for example, "Xi Jinping Wows Them at Davos: China's President Sweet-Talks Liberal Leaders as He Threatens Taiwan," *Wall Street Journal,* January 25, 2021, https://www.wsj.com/articles/xi-jinping-wows-them-at-davos-11611617879; Hung Tran, "Xi Jinping at the Virtual Davos: Multilateralism with Chinese Characteristics," Atlantic Council, January 26, 2021, https://www.atlanticcouncil.org/blogs/new-atlanticist/xi-jinping-at-the-virtual-davos-multilateralism-with-chinese-characteristics/.
5 Eryk Bagshaw, "Two-Track Xi Reveals China Is in No Mood for Reconciliation," *Sydney Morning Herald,* January 26, 2021, https://www.smh.com.au/world/asia/two-track-xi-reveals-china-is-in-no-mood-for-reconciliation-20210126-p56wvm.html; Bloomberg, "Signaling No Change in China's Course, Xi Warns against New Cold War," *Japan Times,* January 26, 2021, https://www.japantimes.

co.jp/news/2021/01/26/asia-pacific/china-xi-cold-war-us/; Ambrose Evans-Pritchard, "Xi Jinping's Davos Magic Wears Thin as China Flexes Its Muscles," *Telegraph*, January 25, 2021, https://www.telegraph.co.uk/business/2021/01/25/xi-jinpings-davos-magic-wears-thin-china-flexes-muscles/; Dave Lawler, "Xi Jinping Warns against 'New Cold War' in Davos Speech," *Axios*, January 25, 2021, https://www.axios.com/xi-jinping-joe-biden-davos-new-cold-war-speech-4f5cbf8d-4e95-44e3-9bc4-5a9c581fefef.html.

6 Charles Parton, "Reacting to Xi Jinping's Davos Speech," China Institute, SOAS University of London, January 28, 2021, https://blogs.soas.ac.uk/china-institute/2021/01/28/reacting-to-xi-jinpings-davos-speech/; James Bloodworth, "Why Are Progressives Still Defending China's Brutal Dictatorship?" *New Statesman*, June 15, 2021, https://www.newstatesman.com/comment/2021/06/why-are-progressives-still-defending-china-s-brutal-dictatorship; "CHINA: Beijing's Foreign 'Useful Idiots' Support Its Xinjiang Propaganda," Human Rights Without Frontiers, May 6, 2021, https://hrwf.eu/china-beijings-foreign-useful-idiots-support-chinas-propaganda-about-uyghur-muslims-who-are-they/.

7 Michael D. Swaine et al., "The Overreach of the China Hawks" *Foreign Affairs*, October 26, 2020, https://www.foreignaffairs.com/articles/china/2020-10-23/overreach-china-hawks; Herbert Yee and Ian Storey, *The China Threat: Perceptions, Myths and Reality* (Abingdon-on-Thames, UK: Taylor and Francis, 2004).

8 Michael Auslin, "Remaking Our World Order," *Wall Street Journal*, April 4, 2017, https://www.wsj.com/articles/remaking-our-world-order-1491347321/; David Dollar and Ryan Hass, "Getting the China Challenge Right," Brookings Institution, March 23, 2021, https://www.brookings.edu/research/getting-the-china-challenge-right/; Lindsey W. Ford and James Goldgeier, "Retooling America's Alliances to Manage the China Challenge," Brookings Institution, March 23, 2021, https://www.brookings.edu/research/retooling-americas-alliances-to-manage-the-china-challenge/; Jake Sullivan and Hal Brands, "China Has Two Paths to Global Domination," *Foreign Policy*, July 3, 2020, https://foreignpolicy.com/2020/05/22/china-superpower-two-paths-global-domination-cold-war/.

9 Chas Freeman et al., "Washington Is Playing a Losing Game with China," East Asia Forum, May 17, 2021, https://www.eastasiaforum.org/2021/05/09/washington-is-playing-a-losing-game-with-china/.

10 Thomas C. Schelling, *Arms and Influence* (New Haven, CT: Yale University Press, 2020), 262.

11 Paul Evans and Yuen Pao Woo, "Anti-China Sentiment Is Becoming Anti-Chinese Prejudice in Canada," *Globe and Mail*, June 21, 2021, https://www.theglobeandmail.com/opinion/article-anti-china-sentiment-is-becoming-anti-chinese-prejudice-in-canada/; Yuen Pao Woo, "Sen. Yuen Pau Woo: Debates in Canada about China Are Toxic – a Reply to Derek Burney," *National Post*, July 13, 2021, https://nationalpost.com/opinion/sen-yuen-pau-woo-debates-in-canada-about-china-are-toxic-a-reply-to-derek-burney.

12 Roger Garside, "Regime Change in China Is Not Only Possible, It Is Imperative," *Globe and Mail*, May 1, 2021, https://www.theglobeandmail.com/opinion/article-the-us-and-its-allies-must-pursue-regime-change-in-china/;

Nathan VanderKlippe, "Canada's Approach to China Has Hit a Wall – Which Is the Perfect Time to Take a New Path," *Globe and Mail*, September 25, 2020, https://www.theglobeandmail.com/world/article-canadas-approach-to-china-has-hit-a-wall-which-is-the-perfect-time/; Nathan VanderKlippe, "As China Moves Away from Communist Regime, Cracks Appear," *Globe and Mail*, March 20, 2015, https://www.theglobeandmail.com/news/world/as-china-moves-away-from-communist-regime-cracks-appear/article23548297/.

13 Christopher Voss, *Never Split the Difference: Negotiating as if Your Life Depended on It* (New York: Harper Business, 2016), 15.

14 Owen Churchill and Robert Delaney, "US Vice-President Mike Pence Steps Up Attacks on China by Backing Donald Trump's Claim It's Trying to Sabotage Elections," by Owen Churchill and Robert Delaney," *South China Morning Post*, October 5, 2018, https://www.scmp.com/news/china/politics/article/2167050/us-vice-president-mike-pence-increases-jabs-china-says-it-wants; Kate O'Keeffe and William Mauldin, "Mike Pompeo Urges Chinese People to Change Communist Party," *Wall Street Journal*, July 24, 2020, https://www.wsj.com/articles/secretary-of-state-pompeo-to-urge-chinese-people-to-change-the-communist-party-11595517729; Peter Martin, "Top White House Official Criticizes 'Totalitarian' Xi in Chinese," *Bloomberg*, October 23, 2020, https://www.bloomberg.com/news/articles/2020-10-23/top-white-house-official-criticizes-totalitarian-xi-in-chinese.

15 Sadanand Dhume, "It's Not Bigotry to Tell the Truth about China," *Wall Street Journal*, April 1, 2021, https://www.wsj.com/articles/its-not-bigotry-to-tell-the-truth-about-china-11617294842.

16 Ibid.; Joseph Bosco, "We Can Help the Chinese People Change Their Communist Regime," *The Hill*, December 22, 2020, https://thehill.com/opinion/international/531184-we-can-help-the-chinese-people-change-their-communist-regime; Zack Cooper and Hal Brands, "America Will Only Win When China's Regime Fails," *Foreign Policy*, March 11, 2021, https://foreignpolicy.com/2021/03/11/america-chinas-regime-fails/.

17 Ann Scott Tyson, "Vilified Abroad, Popular at Home: China's Communist Party at 100," *Christian Science Monitor*, February 18, 2021, https://www.csmonitor.com/World/Asia-Pacific/2021/0218/Vilified-abroad-popular-at-home-China-s-Communist-Party-at-100.

18 US Senate Committee on Foreign Relations, "Full Committee Hearing: Nominations," Foreign Relations Committee, January 19, 2021, https://www.foreign.senate.gov/hearings/nominations-011921.

19 Peter Mattis, "Yes, the Atrocities in Xinjiang Constitute a Genocide," *Foreign Policy*, April 15, 2021, https://foreignpolicy.com/2021/04/15/xinjiang-uyghurs-intentional-genocide-china/; Carlie Porterfield, "Pelosi Calls for 'Diplomatic Boycott' of 2022 Beijing Olympics over China's Human Rights Violations," *Forbes*, May 18, 2021, https://www.forbes.com/sites/carlieporterfield/2021/05/18/pelosi-calls-for-diplomatic-boycott-of-2022-china-olympics-over-human-rights-violations/?sh=3981f9ab52ba.

20 Elliott Zaagman, "China's Own 'Great Delusion,'" *The Interpreter*, October 23, 2019, https://www.lowyinstitute.org/the-interpreter/china-s-own-great

-delusion; Bruce Newsome, "Is China Heading for Global Empire or Soviet Collapse?" *The Critic,* February 12, 2021, https://thecritic.co.uk/is-china-heading-for-global-empire-or-soviet-collapse/; Alex Joske, *The Party Speaks for You: Foreign Interference and the Chinese Communist Party's United Front System,* Report No. 32/2020 (Barton: Australian Strategic Policy Institute, 2020), https://www.aspi.org.au/report/party-speaks-you; Garside, "Regime Change in China Is Not Only Possible, It Is Imperative"; Theresa Fallon, "China Shoots Itself in the Foot on EU-US Relations," Observer Research Foundation, May 24, 2021, https://www.orfonline.org/expert-speak/china-shoots-itself-in-the-foot-on-eu-us-relations/; Irwin Cotler and Judith Abitan, "The Chinese Communist Party's Culture of Corruption and Repression Has Cost Lives around the World," *Globe and Mail,* April 14, 2020, https://www.theglobeandmail.com/opinion/article-the-chinese-communist-partys-culture-of-corruption-and-repression-has/; Youngmin Kim, *A History of Chinese Political Thought* (Germany: Wiley, 2017).

21 Charles Burton, "The Chinese Communist Party Is Not Really Very Chinese at All," *Globe and Mail,* July 3, 2020, https://www.theglobeandmail.com/opinion/article-the-chinese-communist-party-is-not-really-very-chinese-at-all/.

22 Qu Qingshan 曲青山, "Zhongguo gongchandang bai nian guang hui" 中国共产党百年光辉" [CPC: 100 years of glory], *Xinhua Net* 新华网, February 3, 2020, http://www.xinhuanet.com/politics/2021-02/03/c_1127057915.htm.

23 Zheng Yongnian 郑永年, "Zhongguo Gongchandang yu Zhongguo xiandaihua" 中国共产党与中国现代化 [CPC and the modernization of China], Huanan li gong da xue hua yuan jiang tan di 48 jiang 华南理工大学华园讲坛第48讲 [South China University of Technology Huayuan Forum Lecture 48] (speech, Guangzhou, 2021), https://www.aisixiang.com/data/126610.html.

24 Jiang Jinquan 江金全, "Zhongguo Gongchandang de fenggong weiji" 中国共产党的丰功伟绩 [Great achievements of CPC], *Renmin ribao* 人民日报 [People's daily], April 14, 2021; Li Chunhua 李春华, "Zhongguo Gongchandang weishenme neng dedao renmin de yonghu he zhichi" 中国共产党为什么能得到人民的拥护和支持 [Reasons why CPC can win people's advocacy and support], *Xinhua Net* 新华网, September 26, 2016, http://www.xinhuanet.com//politics/2016-09/26/c_129299742.htm.

25 Zhang Weiwei 张维为, "Zhongguo Gongchandang he xiandai Zhongguo de xingcheng" 中共产党和现代中国的形成 [CPC and the formation of contemporary China] (speech, Shanghai, May 4, 2021), https://www.guancha.cn/Zhang WeiWei/2021_05_04_589651.shtml.

26 Qu Qingshan, "Zhongguo gongchandang bai nian guang hui."

27 Pan Wei 潘维, "Zhongguo de shehui zhuyi daolu yu Zhongguo Gongchandang de sige sanshinian" 中国的社会主义道路与中国共产党的四个三十年 [China's path of socialism and the fourth thirty years of CPC], *Jing ji daokan* 经济导刊 [Economic Herald], April 2017, https://www.jingjidaokan.com/icms/null/null/ns:LHQ6LGY6LGM6MmM5Yzg2ODg1ZGVhNTVlODAxNWRlYmE4YzFmZ DAwMTMscDosYTosbTo=/show.vsml.

28 Shi Zhongquan 石仲泉, "Zhongguo daolu de bainian tansuo jiqi xianshi qishi" 中国道路的百年探索及其现实启示 [The exploration and inspiration of China's

hundred-year path], *Xuexi yuekan* 学习月刊 [Learning monthly] 3 (2021): 12–14.
29 Li Zhongjie 李忠杰, "Zhongguo Gongchandang zhiguo lizheng de zhongyao fangshi" 中国共产党治国理政的重要方式 [Essential factors of CPC's governing], *Jingji ribao*经济日报 [Economic daily], November 12, 2020, http://paper.ce.cn/jjrb/html/2020-11/12/content_431915.htm.
30 Li Zhongjie 李忠杰, "Zhongguo Gongchandang fuyou tese de shehui zhengzhi gongneng" 中国共产党富有特色的社会政治功能 [CPC's unique socio-political function], *Renmin luntan* 人民论坛 July 3, 2020, http://www.rmlt.com.cn/2020/0703/585641.shtml; Kong Yuan 孔元, "Meiguo dangdai baozhou zhuyi de minzu zhuyi zhuanxiang" 美国当代保守主义的民族主义转向 [Modern America's nationalized conservatism], *Guowai lilun dongtai* 国外理论动态 [Theoretical dynamics abroad] 1 (2020): 124–32.
31 Tian Xianhong 田先红, "Zhengdang ruhe yinling shehui?" 政党如何引领社会? [How does CPC lead a society?], *Kaifang shidai* 开放时代 [Open Times] 2 (2020): 118–44; "Zhongguo zhengfu heyi huode gao manyidu? zhechang fabuhui geichu daan" 中国政府何以获得高满意度？这场发布会给出答案 [How Chinese government won high satisfaction], *CCTV News* 央视新闻, March 13, 2021, http://m.news.cctv.com/2021/03/12/ARTIPwgjQ8XxvUkkqNQD9p4Z210312.shtml.
32 Yang Yingjie 杨英杰, "Zhongguo Gongchandang weishenme 'neng'" 中国共产党为什么"能" [Why CPC has high capacity], *Hongqi wengao* 红旗文稿 [Red flag manuscript] 13 (2019): 40.
33 Bei Danning, Cui Jiahui, and Wang Shengzhang 贝淡宁 崔佳慧 王生章, "Bijiao Zhongguo he Xifang de zhengzhi jiazhiguan: neng xuedao shenme, weishenme zhongyao" 比较中国和西方的政治价值观：能学到什么，为什么重要 [A comparison between Chinese and Western political values: what we can learn and why it is important], *Jishou daxue xuebao* 吉首大学学报 [Journal of Jishou University] 39 (2018): 1–10.
34 Liu Hui, Shi Yucen, Wang Youling, and Wang Bingyang 刘慧 施雨岑 王优玲 王秉阳, "Manzu renmin xinqidai zai fazhanzhong baozhang he gaishan minsheng" 满足人民新期待在发展中保障和改善民生 [Meet people's demands, guarantee and improve people's lives during development], *Xinhua Net* 新华网, September 26, 2019, http://www.xinhuanet.com/politics/70zn/2019-09/26/c_1125045674.htm.
35 Lihui 李慧, "Juli minsheng nuan minxin – 2020 nian woguo minsheng gaishan lueying," 聚力民生暖民心 – – 2020年我国民生改善掠影 [Highlights of Chinese government's 2020 enhancement of living standards], *Xinhua Net* 新华网, December 17, 2020, http://www.xinhuanet.com/politics/2020-12/17/c_1126870055.htm.
36 Jiang Jinquan 江金权, "Fanfu changlian de Zhongguo daan" 反腐倡廉的中国答案 [China's responses to fight corruption and advocate probity], *Zhongguo jijian jianchabao* 中国纪检监察报 [China discipline inspection and supervision news], May 20, 2021; Jin Bei 金碚, "Huanbao yu fupin shi Zhongguo jingji zengzhang xinmifang" 环保与扶贫是中国经济增长新秘 [Environmental protection and poverty reduction: new keys to China's economic development], *Renmin ribao* 人民日报 [People's daily], January 24, 2018; Li Xiaoyun 李小云, "Shenke lijie he

Notes to page 105

bawo Zhongguo tese fanpinkun lilun," 深刻理解和把握中国特色反贫困理论 [Understand China's special anti-poverty theory], *Guangming ribao* 光明日报 [Guang Ming Daily], March 22, 2021, https://epaper.gmw.cn/gmrb/html/2021-03/22/nw.D110000gmrb_20210322_2-15.htm.

37. (@Shenghuo zhong de huayang yuansu) (@生活中的花樣元素), "Zaoshang shangban kandao tushu dasha duiguo you 10 laige nongmingong" 早上上班看到图书大厦对过有10来个农民工 [Saw about ten migrant workers across that bookstore building], Weibo, December 21, 2020, https://weibo.com/6043541876/Jzs6HCPHn?from=page_1005056043541876_profile&wvr=6&mod=weibotime&ssl_rnd=1622049723.0266&type=comment#_rnd1622049895924; (@Fengyu tongxing xiang wang you wo) (@风雨同行相望有我), "Heimodi fanlan chengzai, quancheng dige dijie tingyun kongsu: women yao liangquan heyi!" 黑摩的泛滥成灾，全城的哥的姐停运控诉：我们要两权合一! [Taxi drivers on strike, asked for regulations of illegal motor taxi], Weixin gongzhong hao, 2021, accessed June 1, 2021, https://mp.weixin.qq.com/s/xyy-YNngGfb02xDsaeS1IA; (@A_uncleChau), "Jintian quanti yuangong bagong taoxin wuguo" 今天全体员工罢工讨薪无果 [Staff failed to get their salary paid], Weibo, May 15, 2021, https://weibo.com/2622323931/KfxsDobGE?from=page_1005052622323931_profile&wvr=6&mod=weibotime&ssl_rnd=1622050014.6917&type=comment.

38. Fu Xiaojing 付筱菁, "Zai tuopin gongjian zhong lüzhi buli nongxu zuojia banqian buzu sancheng que huangbao 100%" 在脱贫攻坚中履职不力弄虚作假 搬迁不足三成却谎报100% [Falsification and dereliction found: relocation mission reported done, less than 30 percent in fact], Central Committee for Discipline Inspection 中央纪委国家监委, May 11, 2020, https://www.ccdi.gov.cn/special/jdbg3/gz_bgt/sfjds_jdbg3/202005/t20200511_217017.html; Jiang zhen 江真, "Xi Jinping tiewan zhangkong, jundui fanfu fengbao haizaigua" 习近平铁腕掌控军队反腐风暴还在刮 [Anti-corruption mission in the army continues, thanks to Xi Jinping's harsh acts], VOA Chinese, May 19, 2021, https://www.voachinese.com/a/Xi-Jinping-consolidates-his-control-of-military-through-anti-corruption-campaign-20210519/5896224.html.

39. Shi Zhongquan, "Zhongguo daolu de bainian tansuo jiqi xianshi qishi."

40. "Ai de Man: 2021 nian Ai de Man xinren du tiao cha Zhongguo baogao" 爱德曼：2021年爱德曼信任度调查中国报告 [Edelman: 2021 Edelman Trust survey China report], *Xinlang caijing* 新浪财经 [Sina finance], April 8, 2021, https://finance.sina.com.cn/tech/2021-04-08/doc-ikmyaawa8417811.shtml.

41. China Daily 中国日报网, "Diaocha: Zhongguo minzhong dui Zhongguo Gongchandang de manyi du he xinren du shangsheng" 调查：中国民众对中国共产党的满意度和信任度上升 [Survey: Chinese people's satisfaction with and trust in the Communist Party of China has risen], *Guangming* 光明网 [Bright net], June 15, 2021, https://politics.gmw.cn/2021-06/15/content_34924310.htm; Sha Xueliang 沙雪良, "Zhongguo She Ke Yuan zhengfu toumingdu zhishu baogao fabu butong danwei zhengwu gongkai chaju jiao da" 中国社科院政府透明度指数报告发布 不同单位政务公开差距较大 [Chinese Academy of Social Sciences government transparency index report released], *Xinlang* 新浪 [Sina], May 19, 2021, https://news.sina.com.cn/c/2021-05-19/doc-ikmyaawc6213033.shtml.

42 Edward Cunningham, Tony Saich, and Jesse Turiel, *Understanding CCP Resilience: Surveying Chinese Public Opinion through Time* (Cambridge, MA: Harvard Kennedy School, Ash Center for Democratic Governance and Innovation, 2020), https://ash.harvard.edu/files/ash/files/final_policy_brief_7.6.2020.pdf.
43 Global Times 环球时报, "Huanqiu Yuqing Diaocha Zhongxin Zuixin min diao: guoban Zhongguo qingnian 'Xifang guan' yin yiqing gaibian" 环球舆情调查中心最新民调: 过半中国青年'西方观'因疫情改变 [Global Public Opinion Survey Center's latest poll: more than half of Chinese youths' "Western outlook" has changed due to the epidemic], *Huanqiu wang* 环球网 [World wide web], April 20, 2021, https://world.huanqiu.com/article/42nD6YLz7ve.
44 Kaxton Siu, "Hong Kong's War against Authoritarianism: How Did It Start and What Is at Stake for the World?" *Global Asia*, September 2019, https://www.globalasia.org/v14no3/feature/hong-kongs-war-against-authoritarianism-how-did-it-start-and-what-is-at-stake-for-the-world_kaxton-siu.
45 Rebecca Joseph, "Hong Kong Extradition Bill: What Is It and Why Are People Protesting," *Global News*, June 10, 2019, https://globalnews.ca/news/5373041/hong-kong-extradition-bill/.
46 Mike Ives and Ezra Cheung, "Protesters Start Three Days of Civil Disobedience in Hong Kong," *New York Times*, August 3, 2019, https://www.nytimes.com/2019/08/03/world/asia/hong-kong-protest.html.
47 Javier C. Hernández, "Harsh Penalties, Vaguely Defined Crimes: Hong Kong's Security Law Explained," *New York Times*, July 1, 2020, https://www.nytimes.com/2020/06/30/world/asia/hong-kong-security-law-explain.html.
48 Lindsay Maizland and Eleanor Albert, "Hong Kong's Freedoms: What China Promised and How It's Cracking Down," Council on Foreign Relations, February 17, 2021, https://www.cfr.org/backgrounder/hong-kong-freedoms-democracy-protests-china-crackdown; Andreas Illmer, "China Is 'Trampling on Hong Kong's Democracy,'" *BBC News*, April 3, 2021, https://www.bbc.com/news/world-asia-china-56585731.
49 David Brunnstrom, "U.S. Senators Revive Bill to Make Refugee Status Easier for Hong Kong Protesters," *Reuters*, February 9, 2021, https://www.reuters.com/article/us-usa-hongkong-refugees-idUSKBN2A935W; Angus Watson and James Griffiths, "Australia Suspends Extradition with Hong Kong and Offers Path to Citizenship for City's Residents," *CNN*, July 9, 2020, https://www.cnn.com/2020/07/09/asia/australia-hong-kong-extradition-intl-hnk/index.html; "Hong Kong: UK Makes Citizenship Offer to Residents," *BBC News*, July 1, 2020, https://www.bbc.com/news/uk-politics-53246899; Immigration, Refugees and Citizenship Canada, *Canada Launches Hong Kong Pathway That Will Attract Recent Graduates and Skilled Workers with Faster Permanent Residency*, Government of Canada, February 3, 2021, https://www.canada.ca/en/immigration-refugees-citizenship/news/2021/02/canada-launches-hong-kong-pathway-that-will-attract-recent-graduates-and-skilled-workers-with-faster-permanent-residency.html.
50 Jessie Lau, "Hong Kong Police Arrest 53 Pro-Democrats on Subversion Charges," *The Diplomat*, January 6, 2021, https://thediplomat.com/2021/01/hong-kong-police-arrest-53-pro-democrats-on-subversion-charges/.

51 "EU Calls for Immediate Release of Over 50 Detained Hong Kong Activists," *EuroNews,* January 6, 2021, https://www.euronews.com/2021/01/06/about-50-hong-kong-activists-arrested-under-new-security-law; Nathan VanderKlippe, "China Drops 'Political Guillotine' on Hong Kong with Arrest of 53 Pro-Democracy Politicians, Scholars," *Globe and Mail,* January 6, 2021, https://www.theglobeandmail.com/world/article-china-drops-political-guillotine-on-hong-kong-with-arrest-of-53-pro/.

52 Steven Chase, "Canadian MPs Call for Sanctions against Chinese Officials behind Beijing's Crackdown in Hong Kong," *Globe and Mail,* February 26, 2021, https://www.theglobeandmail.com/politics/article-canadian-mps-call-for-sanctions-against-chinese-officials-behind/.

53 Li Zhexian 李哲贤, ed., "Guowuyuan Gangaoban fayanren: qianglie fandui dihui Quanguo Renda youguan jueding de ganshe xingjing" 国务院港澳办发言人：强烈反对诋毁全国人大有关决定的干涉行径" [Hong Kong and Macau Affairs Office of the State Council spokesman: China strongly disagrees with interference in the decisions made by National People's Congress], *Xinhua Net* 新华网, March 14, 2021, http://www.xinhuanet.com/2021-03/14/c_1127209846.htm; Lu Cheng 鹿铖, "Xifang guojia zai Xianggang wentishang zhishou huajiao zhichi baotu" 西方国家在香港问题上指手画脚支持暴徒 [Western countries support terrorists in Hong Kong protests], *Guangming ribao* 光明日报 [Guang Ming Daily], December 25, 2019, https://epaper.gmw.cn/gmrb/html/2019-11/25/nw.D110000gmrb_20191125_5-12.htm.

54 "Kanmingbai Xianggang de xianzhuang, bixu xiangaodong zhe 6 ge wenti" 看明白香港的现状，必须先搞懂这6个问题 [What happened to Hong Kong in six points], *China Daily* 中国日报, August 21, 2019, http://cn.chinadaily.com.cn/a/201908/21/WS5d6e216da31099ab995ddb94.html.

55 Chi Kuen Lau, *Hong Kong's Colonial Legacy* (Hong Kong: Chinese University Press, 1997).

56 "Zhichi baotu de ren jile: Yingguo zhejianzhi shizai gei Xianggang guanfang he beijing songlian" 支持暴徒的人急了：英国这简直是在给香港官方和北京"送脸 [UK brought shame on itself, thanks to those who support terrorists in Hong Kong], *Global Times* 环球时报, October 16, 2019, https://baijiahao.baidu.com/s?id=1647527013477395376&wfr=spider&for=pc.

57 Ministry of Foreign Affairs of China, "2021nian 1 yue 7 ri waijiaobu fayanren Hua Chunying zhuchi lixing jizhehui 2021" 2021年1月7日外交部发言人华春莹主持例行记者会 [Press conference hosted by Ministry of Foreign Affairs spokesman Hua Chunying on January 7, 2021], January 7, 2021, https://www.fmprc.gov.cn/web/fyrbt_673021/jzhsl_673025/202101/t20210107_5419713.shtml.

58 Sina (@Xian rongyi) (@宪容易), "Dawanqu zhenghe shi Xianggang shehui jingji fanzhan de xinqidian" 大湾区整合是香港社会经济发展的新起点 [Integration of Guangdong–Hong Kong–Macau big bay area: a new start for Hong Kong's economic development], Sina.com, March 1, 2019, http://blog.sina.com.cn/s/blog_8db3ce3d01030lce.html?tj=fina.

59 Huang Yuexi and Xu Haibo 黄月细 徐海波, "'Yiguo liangzhi' xia Xianggang gongmin jiaoyu de fansi yu jiangou" "一国两制"下香港公民教育的反思与建构 [Rethink and examine Hong Kong citizens' education under the "one country,

two systems"], *Dangdai gangao yanjiu* 当代港澳研究 [Contemporary Hong Kong and Macau studies] 4 (2017); Wen Xuepeng 温学鹏, "Xianggang de 'gaodu zizhi' yu weilai zhengzhi fazhan" 香港的"高度自治"与未来政策发展 [High degree of autonomy and future policy-making in Hong Kong], *Suzhou daxue xuebao* 苏州大学学报[Journal of Soochow University] 4 (2017): 56–66.

60 Yan Xiaojun 阎小骏, "Jiujing shenme caishi yiguo liangzhi de chuzhong?" 究竟什么才是一国两制的初衷? [What is the original intention of "one country, two systems"?], *Mingpao* 明报, July 20, 2019, https://www.aisixiang.com/data/117273.html.

61 Han Dayuan 韩大元, "Xiugai wanshan Xianggang xuanju zhidu shi jianchi he wanshan 'yiguo liangzhi' zhidu tixi de biran yaoqiu" 修改完善香港选举制度是坚持和完善"一国两制"制度体系的必然要求 [Refining Hong Kong's election system a prerequisite for "one country, two systems"], *Renmin ribao* 人民日报 [People's daily], February 25, 2021, A16.

62 Guo Shuqing 郭树清, "Zhongguo qingji de xinjieduan yu Xianggang tequ de xinjiyu" 中国经济的新阶段与香港特区的新机遇 [New phase of China's economics, and opportunities for Hong Kong], (speech at the 14th Asian Financial Forum, 2021), People's Bank of China 中国人民银行, January 18, 2021, http://www.pbc.gov.cn/goutongjiaoliu/113456/113469/4164110/index.html.

63 "Xifang zhichi Xianggang baoli yishishuang" 西方支持香港暴力一时爽 [Western societies lacking foresight for supporting violence in Hong Kong], *Global Times* 环球时报, October 21, 2019, https://baijiahao.baidu.com/s?id=1647981337984407744&wfr=spider&for=pc.

64 Rao Geping 饶戈平, "Xianggang Tebie Xingzhengqu weihu guojia anquanfa: xuexi yu jiedu" 香港特别行政区维护国家安全法: 学习与解读 [Law of the People's Republic of China on Safeguarding National Security in the Hong Kong Special Administrative Region: a study and interpretation], *Gangao yanjiu* 港澳研究 [Hong Kong and Macau studies] 3 (2020).

65 Li Xiaojia 李小加, "Guanyu Xianggang guoji jinrong zhongxin diwei de yixie qianjian" 关于香港国际金融中心地位的一些浅见 [Some thoughts on Hong Kong, an international financial centre], HKEx Pulse, *Weixin gongzhonghao*, June 5, 2020, https://mp.weixin.qq.com/s?_biz=MzA4ODAxMzAyMA%3D%3D&mid=2664960811&idx=1&sn=d5654175a12185042b5a43bebf532678&scene=45#wechat_redirect.

66 Chen Duanhong 陈端洪, "Guojia anquan yu xianfa" 国家安全与宪法 [National security and the constitution], (speech keynotes, Hong Kong, December 5, 2020), Aisixiang 爱思想, https://www.aisixiang.com/data/123800.html.

67 Lam Cheng Yuet-ngor 林郑月娥, "Guojia anquan he zhengquan anquan buke fenge" 国家安全和政权安全不可割 [National security is inseparable from regime security] (speech keynotes, Hong Kong, April 15, 2021), Aisixiang 爱思想, https://www.aisixiang.com/data/126067.html.

68 Tian Feilong 田飞龙, "Xuanju anquan yu Xianggang minzhu de xinzhixu" 选举安全与香港民主的新秩序 [Election security and new orders of Hong Kong democracy], March 2021, https://www.aisixiang.com/data/125732.html.

69 Natalie Wong, Danny Lee, Chris Lau, and Phila Siu, "Hong Kong National Security Law: 53 Held for Subversion in Biggest Crackdown Yet," *South China*

Morning Post, January 6, 2021, https://www.scmp.com/news/hong-kong/law-and-crime/article/3116573/dozens-hong-kong-opposition-lawmakers-activists.

70 Colm Quinn, "Blinken Names and Shames Human Rights Abusers," *Foreign Policy,* March 31, 2021, https://foreignpolicy.com/2021/03/31/blinen-uyghur-china-human-rights-report/.

71 "Australia Parliament Debates Motion on Uighur Abuses in Xinjiang," *Al Jazeera,* March 22, 2021, https://www.aljazeera.com/news/2021/3/22/australia-parliament-debates-motion-on-uighur-abuses-in-xinjiang; Patrick Wintour, "UK MPs Declare China Is Committing Genocide against Uyghurs in Xinjiang," *The Guardian,* April 22, 2021, https://www.theguardian.com/world/2021/apr/22/uk-mps-declare-china-is-committing-genocide-against-uyghurs-in-xinjiang; "Canada's Parliament Declares China's Treatment of Uighurs 'Genocide,'" *BBC News,* February 23, 2021, https://www.bbc.com/news/world-us-canada-56163220.

72 Olivia Enos, "Religious Persecution in China Must Be Called Out," Heritage Foundation, October 14, 2020, https://www.heritage.org/religious-liberty/commentary/religious-persecution-china-must-be-called-out.

73 "China Uighurs: Xinjiang Ban on Long Beards and Veils," *BBC News,* April 1, 2017, https://www.bbc.com/news/world-asia-china-39460538.

74 "China Forcing Birth Control on Uighurs to Suppress Population, Report Says," *BBC News,* June 29, 2020, https://www.bbc.com/news/world-asia-china-53220713.

75 Helen Davidson, "US 'Deeply Disturbed' by Reports of Systematic Rape in China's Xinjiang Camps," *The Guardian,* February 4, 2021, https://www.theguardian.com/world/2021/feb/04/us-is-deeply-disturbed-by-reports-of-systematic-in-chinas-uighurxinjiang-camps.

76 Associated Press, "Full-Blown Boycott Pushed for 2022 Winter Olympics in Beijing," *ESPN,* May 17, 2021, https://www.espn.com/olympics/story/_/id/31459936/full-blown-boycott-pushed-2022-winter-olympics-beijing.

77 Adrian Zenz, "Xinjiang's New Slavery," *Foreign Policy,* December 11, 2019, https://foreignpolicy.com/2019/12/11/cotton-china-uighur-labor-xinjiang-new-slavery/.

78 "Uighurs: Western Countries Sanction China over Rights Abuses," *BBC News,* March 22, 2021, https://www.bbc.com/news/world-europe-56487162.

79 Sun Yan 孙琰, "Xi Jinping chuancheng fazhan Zhonghua youxiu chuantong wenhua sixiang yanjiu" 习近平传承发展中华优秀传统文化思想研究 [Xi Jinping thought on heritage and promotion of Chinese cultures and traditions] (master's thesis, Changsha University of Science and Technology 长沙理工大学, 2018); "Xinjiang ge minzu pingdeng quanli de baozhang" 新疆各民族平等权利的保障 [Guarantee of equal rights of all ethnic groups in Xinjiang], Aisixiang 爱思想, July 17, 2021, https://www.aisixiang.com/data/127567.html.

80 Li Ziyuan 李资源, "Shaoshu minzu chuantong wenhua chuancheng jiaoyu yingzhuyi de jige wenti" 少数民族传统文化传承教育应注意的几个问题 [Several key points in the education of minority cultural heritage], *Zhongnan minzu daxue xuebao* 中南民族大学学报 [Journal of South-Central Minzu University] 2 (2018): 58–62.

81 Guo Song 郭松, "Mao Zedong minzu jingji sixiang jidui minzu quyu xiandaihua qishi" 毛泽东民族经济思想及对民族区域现代化启示 [Mao Zedong thought on ethnic groups and economics, and its inspiration on the modernization of regional autonomy], *Guizhou minzu yanjiu* 贵州民族研究 [Guizhou ethnic studies] 11 (2015): 10–13.

82 Ye Xiaoqing and Xu Juan 叶小青 徐娟, "Renkou jiegou, jiaoyu yu shaoshuminzu diqu pinkunlü" 人口结构、教育与少数民族地区贫困率 [Population structure, education, and poverty rate in ethnic minority regions], *Tongji yu juece* 统计与决策 [Statistics and decision] 4 (2021): 86–90.

83 Wang Hongli 王宏丽, "Xinjiang 70 nian fanpinkun licheng: chengxiao, jingyan, zhanwang" 新疆70年反贫困历程：成效、经验、展望 [70 years of anti-poverty process in Xinjiang: impacts, experience, and expectation], *Journal of Karamay* 克拉玛依学刊 5 (2019): 3–12.

84 Qi Fangfang, Xie Dawei, and Su Ying 齐放芳 谢大伟 苏颖, "Yidi fupin banqian yimin fanqian yiyuan fenxi – jiyu Xinjiang nanjiang shendu pinkun diqu diaocha shuju de shizheng fenxi" 易地扶贫搬迁移民返迁意愿分析——基于新疆南疆深度贫困地区调查数据的实证分析 [Analysis of migrants' willingness to return and relocate based on surveys conducted in areas of extreme poverty in Xinjiang], *Xinjiang shehui kexue* 新疆社会科学 [Xinjiang social sciences] 2 (March 2021): 133–38.

85 Yang Rui and Liu Huihong 杨芮 刘会红, "Yidaiyilu xia Xinjiang kaifangshi jingji fazhan wenti ji duice yanjiu" 一带一路下新疆开放式经济发展问题及对策研究 [Xinjiang's open-ended economic development and strategy studies under the BRI policy], *Jingmao shijian* 经贸实践 [Economic and trade practice] 18 (2018): 81–82.

86 Zheng Ziqing and Zheng Gongcheng 郑子青 郑成功, "Xiaochu pinkun: Zhongguo qiji yu zhongguo jingyan" 消除贫困：中国奇迹与中国经验 [Eliminating poverty: China's miracle and experience], *Journal of the Party School of the Central Committee of the CPC (Chinese Academy of Governance)* 中共中央党校（国家行政学院）学报 2 (2021): 39–48.

87 Li Xuejun 李学军, "Nanjiang sidizhou tuopin gongjian chengxiao fenxi" 南疆四地州脱贫攻坚成效分析 [Analysis of the effect of poverty alleviation in four prefectures of southern Xinjiang], *Journal of the Party School of Xinjiang Production and Construction Corps (XPCC) of CPC* 兵团党校学报 4 (2020): 74–79.

88 Zhang Guofeng 张国峰, "Xinjiang weiwuer zizhiqu jiaoyu jingzhun fupin moshi tanjiu" 新疆维吾尔自治区教育精准扶贫模式探究 [Targeted poverty alleviation model in Xinjiang autonomous region] (master's thesis, North China Electric Power University 华北电力大学, 2020).

89 Dai Jicheng and Jiang Limeng 戴继诚 姜李萌, "Jingwai 'Dongtu' kongbu shili de wangluo xushi yu yingdui" 境外"东突"恐怖势力的网络叙事与应对 [Online narrative structure and corresponding countermeasures of overseas "East Turkistan" terrorism], *Gonganxue yanjiu* 公安学研究 [Public security studies] 2 (2021): 110–22.

90 Wang Lin 王林, "Dui Meiguo kongbu zhuyi guobie baogao de jiedu yu sikao" 对美国《恐怖主义国别报告》的解读与思考 [Interpretation and thoughts on US

"country reports on terrorism"], *Changjiang luntan* 长江论坛 [Yangtze River forum] 167, 2 (2021): 58–64.

91 Gu Huaxiang 顾华详, "Yi Xi Jinping fazhi sixiang weizhidao de yifa Zhijianglun" 以习近平法治思想为指导的依法治疆论 [Ruling Xinjiang by law theory corresponding to Xi Jinping thought on the rule of law], *Tongyi zhanxianxue yanjiu* 统一战线学研究 [United front studies] 2 (2021): 53–66.

92 Yang Chaoyue 杨超越, "Xinzhongguo chenglihou Zhongguo bianjiang anquan wenti de bianqian ji yingxiang – yi Xinjiang wei anli" 新中国成立后中国边疆安全问题的变迁及影响 – 以新疆为案例 [Evolution and influences of frontier security in China – a case study of Xinjiang], *Xinjiang sheke luntan* 新疆社科论坛 [Xinjiang Social Science Forum] 5 (2020): 50–58.

93 Ren Bingqing 任炳清, "Exploration and Experience of Anti-Terrorism in China," *China Religion* 1 (2020): 36–37; Wang Lin, "Twenty Years' Rule of Law for Chinese Anti-terrorism: Review and Prospect," *Tiedao jingguan gaodeng zhuanke xuexiao xuebao* 铁道警官高等专科学校学报 [Journal of Railway Police College] 1 (2021): 43–53.

94 Ren Yantao and Zhu Xiaoyan 任延涛 朱小艳, "Xifang kongbu zhuyi jijinhua de zhuyao lilun pingshu" 西方激进化的主要理论评述 [Western radicalized mainstream theories review], *Zhongguo xingjing xueyuan xuebao* 中国刑警学院学报 [Journal of China Criminal Police Academy] 5 (2017): 25–29.

95 Chang An 常安, "Yiji duren de zhongzu miejue pai: renquan jiekou yu baquan xingjing" 以己度人的"种族灭绝"牌:人权借口与霸权行径 [So-called "genocide" is an excuse of human rights and western hegemony of human rights], April 16, 2021, http://m.aisixiang.com/data/126073.html.

96 "China 'Indefinitely' Suspends Key Economic Dialogue with Australia," *BBC News*, May 6, 2021, https://www.bbc.com/news/business-57004797.

97 Audrye Wong, "How Not to Win Allies and Influence Geopolitics: China's Self-Defeating Economic Statecraft," *Foreign Affairs* 100, 3 (May/June 2021): 44–53, https://www.foreignaffairs.com/articles/china/2021-04-20/how-not-win-allies-and-influence-geopolitics.

98 Maria Abi-Habib, "How China Got Sri Lanka to Cough Up a Port," *New York Times*, June 25, 2018, https://www.nytimes.com/2018/06/25/world/asia/china-sri-lanka-port.html.

99 Rush Doshi, *The Long Game: China's Grand Strategy to Displace American Order* (Oxford: Oxford University Press, 2021), 235.

100 Charles Edel and David O. Shullman, "How China Exports Authoritarianism: Beijing's Money and Technology Is Fueling Repression Worldwide," *Foreign Affairs*, September 16, 2021, https://www.foreignaffairs.com/articles/china/2021-09-16/how-china-exports-authoritarianism.

101 Jessica Chen Weiss and Jeremy L. Wallace, "Domestic Politics, China's Rise, and the Future of the Liberal International Order: International Organization," *International Organization* 75, 2 (2021): 635–64.

102 Michael J. Mazarr, Timothy R. Heath, and Astrid Stuth Cevallos, *China and the International Order* (Santa Monica, CA: RAND Corporation, 2018), https://www.

rand.org/content/dam/rand/pubs/research_reports/RR2400/RR2423/RAND_RR2423.pdf.

103 Hal Brands, "To Compete with China, We Need the Liberal International Order," American Enterprise Institute, October 30, 2020, https://www.aei.org/op-eds/to-compete-with-china-we-need-the-liberal-international-order/.

104 Wang Yongzhou and Zhang Jiangang 王永周 张建岗, "Xi Jinping Zhongguo tese shehuizhuyi waijiao sixiang yanjiu" 习近平新时代中国特色社会主义外交思想研究 [Xi Jinping thought on diplomacy with Chinese characteristics for a new era], *Juece tansuo* 决策探索 [Policy Research & Exploration] 3 (2021): 11–12.

105 Liu Jianwei 刘建伟, "Meiou jingji zhicai yanjiu: fazhan mailuo yu qianyan yiti" 美欧经济制裁研究: 发展脉络与前沿议题 [US-Europe economic sanctions: development context and frontier issues], *Hubei shehui kexue* 湖北社会科学 [Hubei social sciences] 3 (2020): 42–48.

106 Yong Sub Choi, "Keeping the Americans in: The THAAD Deployment on the Korean Peninsula in the Context of Sino-American Rivalry," *Contemporary Security Policy* 41, 4 (2020): 632–52.

107 Xiao Huan 肖欢, "Aodaliya guofang zhanlue de tiaozheng jidui Yintai anquan xingshi de yingxiang" 澳大利亚国防战略的调整及对印太安全形势的影响 [The adjustment of Australia's national defence strategy and its impact on the Indo-Pacific security situation], *Waiyu xuekan* 外语学刊 [Foreign Language Research] 1 (2021): 52–58.

108 Shi Yunxia, "On the Major Country Diplomatic Strategies with Chinese Characteristics in the New Era," *Journal of Guizhou Provincial Party School* 2 (2021): 23–33; Tian Ge 田革, "Lunlengzhan hou Zhongguo waijiao zhanlue de tiaozheng yu fazhan" 论冷战后中国外交战略的调整与发展 [Adjustment and development of China's diplomatic strategy after the Cold War], *Qiqihar daxue xuebao* 齐齐哈尔大学学报 [Journal of Qiqihar University] 7 (2019): 111–13.

109 Wang Da 王达, "Meiguo duihua yishi xingtai ezhi shengji de shizhi" 美国对华意识形态遏制升级的实质 [The essence of the escalation of US ideological containment toward China], *Makesi zhuyi yanjiu* 马克思主义研究 [Marxist studies] 4 (2020): 148–57; Zhou Lingni 周玲妮, "Xifang wuminghua Zhongguo duiwai yuanzhu he touzi fenxi" 西方污名化中国对外援助和投资分析 [The stigmatization of China's rescue assistance and investments by western countries], *Jiangnan shehui xueyuan xuebao* 江南社会学院学报 [Journal of Jiangnan Institute of Sociology] 4 (2019): 43–49.

110 Liu Feitao 刘飞涛, "Xieposhi waijiao: zhanlue jingzheng shidai Meiguo duiwai zhanlue de zhuanxing" 胁迫式外交:战略竞争时代美国对外战略的转型 [Coercive diplomacy: the transformation of US foreign strategy in the era of strategic competition], *Heping yu fazhan* 和平与发展 [Peace and development] 2 (2020): 17–39; "Meiyuan wuqihua: Telangpu zhengshi jiekai xinlengzhan shidai de huobi zhanlue" 美元武器化: 特朗普正式揭开新冷战时代的货币战争 [Weaponization of US dollar: Trump led the currency cold war], *Qiaoke zonghe zixun* 樵客综合资讯 [Comprehensive information on woodcutter], September 6, 2019, https://baijiahao.baidu.com/s?id=1643900455365185571&wfr=spider&for=pc.

111 Xu Shaomin and Li Jiang 徐少民 李江, "'Zhongguo zhaiwu xianjing waijiaolun' de fazhan jiqi miuwu" 中国债务陷阱外交论的发展及其谬误 [The emergence and fallacy of "China's debt-trap diplomacy"], *Guoji wenti yanjiu* 国际问题教育 [International issues education] 1 (2020): 40–53.

112 Zhang Henglong and Zhang Lingyan 张恒龙 张玲燕, "'Yidai yilu'changyi dui yanxian guojia zhaiwu wenti yingxiang de shizheng yanjiu" "一带一路"倡议对沿线国家债务问题影响的实证研究 [Study of debt repayment issues in BRI countries], *Shanghai daxue xuebao (shehui kexue ban)* 上海大学学报（社会科学版）[Journal of Shanghai University (Social Science Edition)] 2 (2021): 88–104.

113 Wang Liwei 王力为, "Zhou Xiaochuan: Zhongguo wei zui pinkun guojia huan zhai yu 13 yi Meiyuan wei G20 guojia zhong zuiduo" 周小川：中国为最贫困国家缓债逾13亿美元 为G20国家中最多 [Zhou Xiaochuan: China has eased the debt of the poorest country by more than US\$1.3 billion, which is the most among the G20 countries], *Caixin* 财新, May 29, 2021, http://finance.caixin.com/2021-05-29/101719969.html.

114 "Suowei 'zhaiwu xianjing' shi meishi 'sahuang waijiao' youyi lizheng" 所谓"债务陷阱"是美式"撒谎外交"又一例证 ["Debt trap": another example of American diplomacy lies], *Beijing ribao* 北京日报, [Beijing daily] October 13, 2020, https://baijiahao.baidu.com/s?id=16804336779664 76612&wfr=spider&for=pc.

115 Wei Hao, Guo Ye, and Wu Jun 魏浩 郭也 巫俊, "Zhongguo shichang, jinkou maoyi yu shijie jingji zengzhang" 中国市场、进口贸易与世界经济增长 [Chinese market, import trade, and world economic growth], *Forum of World Economics and Politics* 世界政治经济论坛 3 (2021): 26–53.

116 Hu Zhiding, Ge Yuejing, Du Debin, and Liu Yuli 胡志丁 葛岳静 杜德斌 刘玉立, "Zouxiang weida fuxing de Zhongguo diyuan zhanlue: guojia zhoubianlun" 走向伟大复兴的中国地缘战略：国家周边论 [China's geostrategic theory of neighbouring areas], *Shijie dili yanjiu* 世界地理研究 [World regional studies] 3 (2021): 443–53.

117 Gong Piping and Jiang Chao 公丕萍 姜超, "'Yidai yilu' jianshe dui yanxian guojia jingji zengzhang de yingxiang xiaoguo yu zhongjie lujing" "一带一路"建设对沿线国家经济增长的影响效果与中介路径 [BRI's impact on the economic growth of other BRI countries and intermediate routes], *Shijie dili yanjiu* 世界地理研究 [World regional studies] 3 (2021): 465–47.

118 Zhu Feng 朱锋, "Zhongmei zhanluexia de guoji quanli jiegou: zouxiang junheng haishi baquan gonggu?" 中美战略下的国际权力结构:走向均衡还是霸权巩固？[International power structure under the China-US strategy: balance or hegemony?], October 5, 2020, https://www.aisixiang.com/data/123092.html.

119 Dawei 达巍, "Xianxing guoji zhixu yanbian de fangxiang yu Zhongguo de xuanze" 现行国际秩序演变的方向与中国的选择 [The evolution of international order and China's choice], *Guoji wenti yanjiu* 国际问题研究 [International studies] 1 (2021): 100–11.

120 Jin Canrong and Liu Ruobing 金灿荣 刘若冰, "Zhongguo guoji zhixuguan de yanbian yu fazhan" 中国国际秩序观的演变与发展 [The evolution and development of China's view on international order], *Xibei daxue xuebao* 西北大学学报 [Journal of the Northwest University] 1 (2021): 5–13.

121 Liang Yabin 梁亚滨, "Meiguo jianli he weichi" 美国建立和维持霸权的偏好与方式变化: 从接纳到排斥 [Establishing and maintaining American hegemony: from adoption to exclusion], *Yatai anquan yu Haiyang yanjiu* 亚太安全与海洋研究 [Asia Pacific security and ocean studies] May 22, 2021, https://www.aisixiang.com/data/126658.html.

122 Li Ze 李泽, "Dongya diqu zhixu zhuanxing de fuza dongtai – jiyu juese lilun de fenxi" 东亚地区秩序转型的复杂动态 – – 基于角色理论的分析 [The complex dynamics of order transformation in East Asia: an analysis based on the role theory], *Dangdai yatai* 当代亚太 [Contemporary Asia Pacific] 4 (2020): 18–42.

Chapter 6: Mapping a Canadian Policy Approach to Asia: National Interests, Asian Narratives, and Network Analysis

1 Kenneth Waltz and Stephen M. Walt, *Man, the State, and War: A Theoretical Analysis* (New York: Columbia University), 37.

2 Martha Finnemore, *National Interests in International Society* (Ithaca, NY: Cornell University Press, 1996), 3.

3 "Canada and the Asia-Pacific," Global Affairs Canada, December 22, 2021, https://www.international.gc.ca/world-monde/international_relations-relations_internationales/asia_pacific-asie_pacifique/index.aspx?lang=eng; "Canada and the Association of Southeast Asian Nations (ASEAN)," Global Affairs Canada, September 26, 2022, https://www.international.gc.ca/world-monde/international_relations-relations_internationales/asean/index.aspx?lang=eng.

4 "Canada's Defence Relations in the Asia Pacific Region," Government of Canada, May 2015, https://www.canada.ca/en/news/archive/2015/05/canada-defence-relations-asia-pacific-region.html; Marius Grinius, "Canada's Security Role in Asia-Pacific," Canadian Global Affairs Institute, July 2016, https://www.cgai.ca/canada_s_security_role_in_asia_pacific.

5 "Current Operations and Joint Military Exercises List," Government of Canada, January 13, 2022, https://www.canada.ca/en/department-national-defence/services/operations/military-operations/current-operations/list.html.

6 Paul Evans, "Elements of a Canadian Strategy for Southeast Asia: The Strategic Relevance of ASEAN," in *Southeast Asia in an Evolving Global Landscape: Prospects for an Integrated Region and Implications for Canada* (Vancouver: University of British Columbia, 2017), 73–78, https://sppga.ubc.ca/wp-content/uploads/sites/5/2017/10/19-Paul-Evans.pdf.

7 Peter G. Hall, "Canada's Diversification in Asia," Export Development Canada, August 16, 2018, https://www.edc.ca/en/weekly-commentary/canada-diversification-in-asia.html.

8 Global Affairs Canada, *The Canada-Asia Trade and Investment for Growth Program* (Ottawa: Global Affairs Canada, n.d.), https://www.international.gc.ca/development-developpement/assets/pdfs/countries-pays/TRIGR_Information_Brochure_Asia.pdf.

9 "Comprehensive and Progressive Agreement for Trans-Pacific Partnership (CPTPP)," Global Affairs Canada, December 31, 2020, https://www.

international.gc.ca/trade-commerce/trade-agreements-accords-commerciaux/agr-acc/cptpp-ptpgp/index.aspx?lang=eng.
10 Tom Alton, "Canada-China Trade: 2020 Year in Review," China Institute, University of Alberta, February 22, 2021, https://www.ualberta.ca/china-institute/research/analysis-briefs/2021/canada-china-2020-yearinreview.html.
11 Marc Frenette, Youjin Choi, and April Doreleyers, "International Student Enrolment in Postsecondary Education Programs Prior to COVID-19," Statistics Canada, June 15, 2020, https://www150.statcan.gc.ca/n1/pub/11-626-x/11-626-x2020003-eng.htm.
12 "Canada and the Asia-Pacific Economic Cooperation (APEC)," Government of Canada, September 12, 2022, https://www.international.gc.ca/world-monde/international_relations-relations_internationales/apec/index.aspx?lang=eng.
13 "Comprehensive and Progressive Agreement for Trans-Pacific Partnership (CPTPP)," Government of Canada, December 31, 2020, https://www.international.gc.ca/trade-commerce/trade-agreements-accords-commerciaux/agr-acc/cptpp-ptpgp/index.aspx?lang=eng.
14 Maan Alhmidi, "Conservatives Call on Liberals to Stop Payments to the Asian Infrastructure Investment Bank," *Globe and Mail*, March 25, 2021, https://www.theglobeandmail.com/politics/article-conservatives-call-on-liberals-to-stop-payments-to-the-asian/.
15 "ASEAN Secretariat Organisational Structure," ASEAN, January 2016, https://asean.org/the-asean-secretariat-basic-mandate-functions-and-composition/organizational-structure-of-the-asean-secretariat-2/.
16 Overview of ASEAN-Canada Dialogue Relations," ASEAN, October 2021, https://asean.org/wp-content/uploads/2021/10/Overview-of-ASEAN-Canada-Dialogue-Relations-as-of-October-2021-ERD2.pdf.
17 Hoang Thi Ha, "ISEAS 2021/13 'Repositioning the ADMM-Plus in a Contested Region,'" ISEAS–Yusof Ishak Institute, February 2021, https://www.iseas.edu.sg/articles-commentaries/iseas-perspective/iseas-2021-13-repositioning-the-admm-plus-in-a-contested-region-hoang-by-thi-ha/.
18 "16th ASEAN Ministerial Meeting on the Environment and the 16th Meeting of the Conference of the Parties to the ASEAN Agreement on Transboundary Haze Pollution" ASEAN, October 22, 2021, https://asean.org/16th-asean-ministerial-meeting-on-the-environment-and-the-16th-meeting-of-the-conference-of-the-parties-to-the-asean-agreement-on-transboundary-haze-pollution/.
19 Sharon Seah and Melinda Martinus, *Gaps and Opportunities in ASEAN's Climate Governance* (Singapore: ISEAS Publishing, May 2021), 23–24, https://www.iseas.edu.sg/wp-content/uploads/2021/03/TRS5_21.pdf.
20 Global Affairs Canada, "Minister Ng Co-chairs 9th Annual ASEAN Economic Ministers Meeting–Canada Consultations," news release, August 29, 2020, https://www.canada.ca/en/global-affairs/news/2020/08/minister-ng-co-chairs-9th-annual-asean-economic-ministers-meeting-canada-consultations.html.

21 Ministry of Economy, Trade and Industry of Japan, "ASEAN Economic Ministers Meeting and Related Meetings Held," news release, August 28, 2020, https://www.meti.go.jp/english/press/2020/0828_001.html.
22 Françoise Nicolas, *The Economic Pillar of Korea's New Southern Policy: Building on Existing Assets,* Asie.Visions 120 (Paris: Ifri [French Institute of International Relations], February 2021).
23 Shihong Bi, "Cooperation between China and ASEAN under the Building of ASEAN Economic Community," *Journal of Contemporary East Asia Studies* 10, 1 (February 2021): 83–107, doi:10.1080/24761028.2021.1888410.
24 Embassy of the People's Republic of China in the Republic of Kenya, "Wang Yi Reviews Five Successful Experiences of China-ASEAN Cooperation over the Past 30 Years," June 8, 2021, accessed July 19, 2021, http://ke.china-embassy.gov.cn/eng/zgyw/202106/t20210608_9112672.htm.
25 Kazushi Shimizu, "The ASEAN Economic Community and the RCEP in the World Economy," *Journal of Contemporary East Asia Studies* 10, 1 (2021): 1–2, doi:10.1080/24761028.2021.1907881.
26 "Overview of ASEAN-Canada Dialogue Relations."
27 "Overview of ASEAN-Japan Dialogue Relations," ASEAN, September 30, 2022, accessed November 5, 2022, https://asean.org/wp-content/uploads/2022/10/Overview-ASEAN-Japan-Relations-full-version-as-of-30-September-2022.pdf.
28 "Overview of ASEAN-Republic of Korea Dialogue Relations," ASEAN, November 26, 2021, accessed November 5, 2022, https://asean.org/wp-content/uploads/2021/12/Overview-of-ASEAN-ROK-Dialogue-Relations-as-of-26-Nov-2021.pdf.
29 "Overview of ASEAN-China Dialogue Relations," ASEAN, April 2020, accessed July 19, 2021, https://asean.org/storage/2012/05/Overview-of-ASEAN-China-Relations-22-Apr-2020-00000002.pdf https://asean.org/wp-content/uploads/2012/05/Overview-of-ASEAN-China-Relations-22-Apr-2020-00000002.pdf.
30 "Overview of ASEAN-Japan Dialogue Relations"; "Overview of ASEAN-Canada Dialogue Relations."
31 "Overview of ASEAN-Australia Dialogue Relations," ASEAN, September 2022, accessed November 5, 2022, https://asean.org/wp-content/uploads/2022/09/Overview-of-ASEAN-Australia-DR_as-of-23-September-2022.pdf.
32 "ASEAN, Republic of Korea Promote Closer Cooperation on Labour and Employment," ASEAN, March 26, 2021, accessed July 19, 2021, https://asean.org/asean-republic-of-korea-promote-closer-cooperation-on-labour-and-employment/.
33 Ministry of Foreign Affairs of the People's Republic of China, "Wang Yi Reviews Five Successful Experiences."
34 "Plan of Action to Implement the ASEAN-China Strategic Partnership for Peace and Prosperity (2021–2025)," ASEAN, 2021, accessed November 5, 2022, https://asean.org/storage/2012/05/ASEAN-China-POA-2021-2025.pdf- https://asean.org/wp-content/uploads/2012/05/ASEAN-China-POA-2021-2025.pdf.

Notes to pages 138–42   233

35 Amitav Acharya, "9 Contingent Socialization in Asian Regionalism: Possibilities and Limits," in *Integrating Regions*, ed. Miles Kahler and Andrew Macintyre (Redwood City, CA: Stanford University Press, 2020), 222–42.
36 "Brief Introduction of LMC China Secretariat," Lancang-Mekong Cooperation, http://www.lmcchina.org/eng/node_1009541.html.
37 Shannon Tiezzi, "China, Southeast Asian Leaders Meet to Discuss the Mekong's Plight," *The Diplomat*, August 25, 2020, https://thediplomat.com/2020/08/china-southeast-asian-leaders-meet-to-discuss-the-mekongs-plight/.
38 Sovinda Po and Christopher B. Primiano, "Explaining China's Lancang-Mekong Cooperation as an Institutional Balancing Strategy: Dragon Guarding the Water," *Australian Journal of International Affairs* 75, 3 (2021): 323–40, https://doi.org/10.1080/10357718.2021.1893266.
39 "About BIMSTEC," Bay of Bengal Initiative for Multi-Sectoral Technical and Economic Cooperation, accessed July 19, 2021, https://bimstec.org/?page_id=189 https://bimstec.org/about-bimstec/.
40 "BIMSTEC Centers," Bay of Bengal Initiative for Multi-Sectoral Technical and Economic Cooperation, August 6, 2018, accessed July 19, 2021, https://bimstec.org/?page_id=1292 https://bimstec.org/bimstec-centres/.
41 "Member States" Conference on Interaction and Confidence Building Measures in Asia (CICA), accessed November 5, 2022, https://www.s-cica.org/index.php?view=page&t=member_states.
42 "About CICA," Conference on Interaction and Confidence Building Measures in Asia (CICA), July 19, 2021, accessed July 19, 2021, https://www.s-cica.org/index.php?view=page&t=about.
43 Xi Jinping, "New Asian Security Concept for New Progress in Security Cooperation," Ministry of Foreign Affairs of the People's Republic of China, May 21, 2014, accessed November 5, 2022, https://www.fmprc.gov.cn/mfa_eng/zxxx_662805/t1159951.shtmlhttps://www.fmprc.gov.cn/mfa_eng/wjdt_665385/zyjh_665391/201405/t20140527_678163.html#:~:text=No%20country%20should%20attempt%20to,force%20for%20regional%20security%20cooperation.
44 "Member States for CICA Delegates."
45 "The Meeting of the Advisory Council of the Belt and Road Forum for International Cooperation 2021 is Held via Video Link," Ministry of Foreign Affairs of the People's Republic of China, December 18, 2021, https://www.fmprc.gov.cn/mfa_eng/wjb_663304/zygy_663314/gyhd_663338/202112/t20211218_10471545.html.
46 Jessie Gammon, "Second 'Silk Road NGO Cooperation Network Forum' Held in Beijing," China Development Brief, April 30, 2019, https://chinadevelopmentbrief.cn/reports/second-silk-road-ngo-cooperation-network-forum-held-in-beijing/.
47 Li Qing, "A People's Network: NGO Cooperation Gathers Momentum in Belt and Road Members," *Beijing Review*, April 30, 2019, http://www.bjreview.com/World/201904/t20190430_800166743.html.

48 "Strategies," Greater Tumen Initiative, http://www.tumenprogramme.org/?list-1525.html.
49 "About BFA," Boao Forum, https://english.boaoforum.org/about.html.
50 "Introduction," Beijing Xiangshan Forum, http://www.xiangshanforum.cn/forum_info_EN.

Conclusion: Toward Omnidirectional Diplomacy and Strategic Integration

1 White House, "Readout of President Joe Biden's Participation in the APEC Virtual Leaders' Retreat," news release, July 16, 2021, https://www.whitehouse.gov/briefing-room/statements-releases/2021/07/16/readout-of-president-joe-bidens-participation-in-the-apec-virtual-leaders-retreat/.
2 Gregory W. Meeks, "The Build Back Better World Partnership Could Finally Break the Belt and Road," *Foreign Policy*, June 28, 2021, https://foreignpolicy.com/2021/06/28/the-build-back-better-world-partnership-could-finally-break-the-belt-and-road/#:~:text=It%20creates%20a%20whole%2Dof,in%20the%20Indo%2DPacific%20and.
3 Zhang Hui and Zhang Dan, "China Urges Unity, Announces $3b Aid at APEC; US Eyes Splitting Region," *Global Times*, July 16, 2021, https://www.globaltimes.cn/page/202107/1228840.shtml.
4 Xi Jinping 习近平, "Tuanjie hezuo kang yi yinling jingji fisu" 团结合作抗疫引领经济复苏 [Unite and cooperate to fight the epidemic, lead the economic recovery] (speech, APEC Informal Economic Leaders' Retreat, Wellington, New Zealand, July 16, 2021), *Xinhua Net* 新华网, http://www.xinhuanet.com/politics/leaders/2021-07/16/c_1127663536.htm.
5 William Mauldin and Alex Leary, "U.S. Warns Businesses over Rising Risks in Hong Kong under China Crackdown," *Wall Street Journal*, July 16, 2021, https://www.wsj.com/articles/u-s-warns-businesses-over-rising-risks-in-hong-kong-under-china-crackdown-11626429600.
6 Evelyn Goh, "Great Powers and Hierarchical Order in Southeast Asia: Analyzing Regional Security Strategies," *International Security* 32, 3 (2008): 120, https://doi.org/10.1162/isec.2008.32.3.113.
7 Takashi Inoguchi, ed., *The SAGE Handbook of Asian Foreign Policy* (London: SAGE, 2021); Michael D. Barr, *Cultural Politics and Asian Values* (New York: Routledge, 2002), 53.
8 Takashi Inoguchi, *Japan's Foreign Policy in an Era of Global Change* (New York: Bloomsbury, 2012), 17; Amiko Nobori 昇亜美子, "Wakatsuki Hidekazu-cho 'zenhōigaikō' no jidai – Reisen henyō-ki no Nihon to Ajia, 1971–80" 若月秀和著『「全方位外交」の時代-冷戦変容期の日本とアジア・一九七一~八〇年』 [Authored by Hidekazu Wakatsuki, the age of "omnidirectional diplomacy": Japan and Asia during the Cold War transformation, 1971–80]," *Kokusai Seiji* 国際政治 2007, 148 (2007): 150–53, https://doi.org/10.11375/kokusaiseiji1957.148_150.
9 M. Taylor Fravel, *Testimony before the US-China Economic and Security Review Commission: Hearing on "US-China Relations at the Chinese Communist Party's Centennial"* (Washington, DC: US-China Economic and Security Review Commission, 2021), 8, https://www.uscc.gov/sites/default/files/2021-01/M_Taylor_Fravel_Testimony.pdf.

10 Suh Bo-hyuk, "Surviving in the Face of Hegemony: North Korea's Post–Cold War American Policy," in *Understanding North Korea: Indigenous Perspectives*, ed. Han Jongwoo and Jung Tae-hern (New York: Lexington Books, 2014), 156.
11 Goh, "Great Powers and Hierarchical Order in Southeast Asia," 127.
12 Eric Teo Chu Cheow, "New Omnidirectional Overtures in Thai Foreign Policy," *Asian Survey* 26, 7 (1986): 745, https://www.jstor.org/stable/2644209; Pongphisoot Busbarat, "'Bamboo Swirling in the Wind': Thailand's Foreign Policy Imbalance between China and the United States," *Contemporary Southeast Asia* 38, 2 (2016): 240, https://www.jstor.org/stable/24916631.
13 Evan A. Laksmana, "Pragmatic Equidistance: How Indonesia Manages Its Great Power Relations," in *China, the United States, and the Future of Southeast Asia*, ed. David B.H. Denoon (New York: New York University Press, 2017), 113–35, https://static1.squarespace.com/static/57e3c9e1d1758e2877e03ba5/t/5bcf79f70d9297b3ea87f50b/1540323832548/Chp+-+Pragmatic+equidistance+-+NYU.pdf.
14 Adam Mount and Van Jackson, "Biden, You Should Be Aware That Your Submarine Deal Has Costs," *New York Times*, September 30, 2021, https://www.nytimes.com/2021/09/30/opinion/aukus-china-us-australia-competition.html; Ravil Shirodkar, "Malaysia Says AUKUS Alliance May Lead to Arms Race, Provocation," *Bloomberg*, September 18, 2021, https://www.bloomberg.com/news/articles/2021-09-18/malaysia-says-aukus-alliance-may-lead-to-arms-race-provocation; Chandran Nair, "A New Imperial Alliance Threatens Peace In Asia," *Noéma*, September 30, 2021, https://www.noemamag.com/aukus-new-imperial-alliance-threatens-peace-in-asia.
15 Iain Marlow and Philip Heijmans, "China Neighbors Worry Australia Sub Deal Will Disrupt Region," *Bloomberg*, September 20, 2021, https://www.bloomberg.com/news/articles/2021-09-20/china-neighbors-worry-australia-sub-deal-will-destabilize-region; "Aukus Could Trigger a 'Nuclear Arms Race,' Says North Korea," *BBC News*, September 20, 2021, https://www.bbc.com/news/world-asia-58621056; Elizabeth Law, "Aukus Security Agreement Will Spark Regional Arms Race, Says China," *Straits Times*, September 30, 2021, https://www.straitstimes.com/asia/east-asia/aukus-security-agreement-will-spark-regional-arms-race-says-china; Tom McTague, "Joe Biden's New World Order," *The Atlantic*, September 16, 2021, https://www.theatlantic.com/international/archive/2021/09/us-uk-australia-china/620094/.
16 Karolina Gawron-Tabor, "Between Cooperation and Competition: The Strategic Partnership between the European Union and the US," in *States, International Organizations and Strategic Partnerships*, ed. Lucyna Czechowska et al. (Cheltenham, UK: Edward Elgar Publishing, 2019), 244.
17 Anton Grizold and Vinko Vegiè, "Small States and Alliances: The Case of Slovenia," in *Small States and Alliances*, ed. Erich Reiter and Heinz Gärtner (New York: Springer-Verlag, 2001), 148.
18 For more on European integration, see, for instance, R. Daniel Kelemen, Anand Menon, and Jonathan Slapin, eds., *The European Union: Integration and Enlargement*, Journal of European Public Policy Series (New York: Routledge, 2015), 3–4; Brent F. Nelsen and Alexander Stubb, eds., *The European Union:*

Readings on the Theory and Practice of European Integration (Boulder, CO: Lynne Rienner, 2014), 45.
19 Association of Southeast Asian Nations, *ASEAN Community Vision 2025* (Jakarta: ASEAN, 2015), 13, https://www.asean.org/wp-content/uploads/images/2015/November/aec-page/ASEAN-Community-Vision-2025.pdf.
20 Department of Information Services 新聞傳播處, "Zhongyao zhengce" 重要政策 [Important policy], Executive Yuan, Republic of China (Taiwan) 行政院, September 26, 2016, https://www.ey.gov.tw/Page/5A8A0CB5B41DA11E/86f143fa-8441-4914-8349-c474afe0d44e; Ministry of Foreign Affairs of Japan 外務省, *Jiyūde hirakareta Indotaiheiyō* 自由で開かれたインド太平洋 [Free and open Indo-Pacific] (Tokyo: Ministry of Foreign Affairs of Japan), https://www.mofa.go.jp/files/000430632.pdf; "Sin (sin) nambangjeongchaeg" 신(新)남방정책 [New Southern Policy], Ministry of Culture, Sports and Tourism, Republic of Korea 문화체육관광부, September 6, 2021, https://www.korea.kr/special/policyCurationView.do?newsId=148853887.
21 See, for instance, "Zhongguo fazhan huiji zhoubian guojia Yazhou zhengti guoji xingxiang tisheng" 中国发展惠及周边国家 亚洲整体国际形象提升 [China's development benefits neighbouring countries and Asia's overall international image has improved], State Council Information Office of the People's Republic of China 中华人民共和国国务院新闻办公室, April 6, 2012, http://www.scio.gov.cn/zhzc/2/2/Document/1138339/1138339.htm; A. Muh. Ibnu Aqil, "Jokowi Attends ASEAN Summits, Encourages Cooperation for Economic Recovery," *Jakarta Post,* November 14, 2020, https://www.thejakartapost.com/seasia/2020/11/14/jokowi-attends-asean-summits-encourages-cooperation-for-economic-recovery.html.
22 See, for instance, Lee Hsien Loong, "PM Lee Hsien Loong at the Opening Ceremony of the 51st ASEAN Foreign Ministers' Meeting" (address, 51st ASEAN Foreign Ministers' Meeting, Singapore, August 2, 2018), Prime Minister's Office Singapore, https://www.pmo.gov.sg/Newsroom/pm-lee-hsien-loong-opening-ceremony-51st-asean-foreign-ministers-meeting.
23 Asia Pacific Foundation of Canada, *Asian Views on Economic Engagement with Canada: Perspectives from Business Leaders and Policy Experts in Asia* (Vancouver: Asia Pacific Foundation of Canada, 2020), 11, https://www.asiapacific.ca/sites/default/files/publication-pdf/Asian%20Views%20on%20Economic%20Engagement%20with%20Canada.pdf.
24 Vidya Nadkarni, *Strategic Partnerships in Asia: Balancing without Alliances* (New York: Routledge, 2010), 10.
25 See, for instance, Georg Strüver, "China's Partnership Diplomacy: International Alignment Based on Interests or Ideology," *Chinese Journal of International Politics* 10, 1 (Spring 2017): 31–65, https://doi.org/10.1093/cjip/pow015; Jeffrey Reeves, "China's Silk Road Economic Belt Initiative: Network and Influence Formation in Central Asia," *Journal of Contemporary China* 27, 112 (2018): 502–18, https://doi.org/10.1080/10670564.2018.1433480.
26 See, for instance, H.D.P. Envall and Ian Hall, "Asian Strategic Partnerships: New Practices and Regional Security Governance," *Asian Politics and Policy* 8, 1 (2016): 87–105, https://doi.org/10.1111/aspp.12241.

Notes to pages 152–55

27 Tassilo Herrschel and Peter Newman, *Cities as International Actors: Urban and Regional Governance beyond the Nation State* (London: Palgrave Macmillan, 2017), 101; Raffaele Marchetti, *City Diplomacy: From City-States to Global Cities* (Ann Arbor, MI: University of Michigan Press, 2021), 28.
28 "Asia Business Leaders Advisory Council," Asia Pacific Foundation of Canada, https://www.asiapacific.ca/networks/ablac.
29 "First Canadian Women-Only Virtual Business Mission to Taiwan – March 2021," Asia Pacific Foundation of Canada, https://www.asiapacific.ca/networks/womens-business-missions/taiwan.
30 Innovation, Science and Economic Development Canada, "Government of Canada Takes Action to Protect Canadian Research and Intellectual Property," news release, July 12, 2021, https://www.canada.ca/en/innovation-science-economic-development/news/2021/07/government-of-canada-takes-action-to-protect-canadian-research-and-intellectual-property.html.
31 Kait Bolongaro and Alberto Nardelli, "With Merkel Going, Trudeau Aspires to Be 'Dean' of G7," *Bloomberg*, June 13, 2021, https://www.bnnbloomberg.ca/with-merkel-going-canada-s-trudeau-aspires-to-be-dean-of-g-7-1.1616476; Leyland Cecco, "Canada's Failed UN Security Council Bid Exposes Trudeau's 'Dilettante' Foreign Policy," *The Guardian*, June 18, 2020, https://www.theguardian.com/world/2020/jun/18/canada-loses-bid-un-security-council-seat-justin-trudeau.
32 Rupa Subramanya, "Justin Trudeau's Botched Asia Policy Puts Canada at the Back of the Bus," *Nikkei Asia*, September 16, 2021, https://asia.nikkei.com/Opinion/Justin-Trudeau-s-botched-Asia-policy-puts-Canada-at-the-back-of-the-bus.
33 Jeffrey Reeves, *Canada and the "Indo-Pacific": "Diverse" and "Inclusive," Not "Free" and "Open"* (Vancouver: Asia Pacific Foundation of Canada, 2020), 75.

Selected Bibliography

Acharya, Amitav. "After Liberal Hegemony: The Advent of a Multiplex World Order*." *Ethics and International Affairs* 31, 3 (2017): 271–85.
–. "Dialogue and Discovery: In Search of International Relations Theories beyond the West." *Millennium: Journal of International Studies* 39, 3 (2011): 619–37.
–. *Whose Ideas Matter? Agency and Power in Asian Regionalism.* Ithaca, NY: Cornell University Press, 2011.
Acharya, Amitav, and Barry Buzan, eds. *Non-Western International Relations Theory: Perspectives on and beyond Asia.* New York: Routledge, 2009.
Adamson, Walter L. *Hegemony and Revolution: A Study of Antonio Gramsci's Political and Cultural Theory.* Berkeley: University of California Press, 1980.
Adler, Emanuel, and Steven Bernstein. "Knowledge in Power: The Epistemic Construction of Global Governance." In *Power in Global Governance,* edited by Michael N. Barnett and Raymond Duvall, 294–319. Cambridge: Cambridge University Press, 2011.
Aoki, Masahiko, Hyung-Ki Kim, and Masahiro Okuno-Fujiwara, eds., *The Role of Government in East Asian Economic Development: Comparative Institutional Analysis* (New York: Clarendon Press, 1997).
Babik, Milan. *Poetics of International Politics: Fact and Fiction in Narrative Representations of World Affairs.* London: Taylor and Francis, 2018.
Barnett, Michael N., and Raymond Duvall. *Power in Global Governance.* Cambridge: Cambridge University Press, 2011.
Barr, Michael D. *Cultural Politics and Asian Values.* New York: Routledge, 2002.
Bartolovich, Crystal, Neil Lazarus, and Timothy Brennan. *Marxism, Modernity and Postcolonial Studies.* Cambridge: Cambridge University Press, 2002.

Bell, Daniel A. *Beyond Liberal Democracy: Political Thinking for an East Asian Context.* Princeton, NJ: Princeton University Press, 2006.
Bell, Daniel A., and Wang Pei. *Just Hierarchy: Why Social Hierarchies Matter in China and the Rest of the World.* Princeton, NJ: Princeton University Press, 2020.
Bevins, Vincent. *The Jakarta Method: Washington's Anticommunist Crusade and the Mass Murder Program That Shaped Our World.* New York: Public Affairs, 2020.
Bieler, Andreas, et al. *Global Restructuring, State, Capital and Labour: Contesting Neo-Gramscian Perspectives.* New York: Palgrave Macmillan, 2006.
Bliesemann de Guevara, Berit. *Myth and Narrative in International Politics: Interpretative Approaches to the Study of IR.* London: Palgrave Macmillan, 2016.
Bogdandy, Armin von, and Ingo Venzke. *In Whose Name? A Public Law Theory of International Adjudication.* New York: Oxford University Press, 2014.
Booth, Ken, ed. *Critical Security Studies and World Politics.* Boulder, CO: Lynne Rienner, 2005.
Brands, Henry W. *Bound to Empire: The United States and the Philippines.* New York: Oxford University Press, 1992.
Breuer, Adam, and Alastair Iain Johnston. "Memes, Narratives and the Emergent US-China Security Dilemma." *Cambridge Review of International Affairs* 32, 4 (2019): 429–55.
Buzan, Barry, and Yongjin Zhang, eds. *Contesting International Society in East Asia.* Cambridge: Cambridge University Press, 2014.
Byers, Michael, and Georg Nolte, eds. *United States Hegemony and the Foundations of International Law.* New York: Cambridge University Press, 2003.
Byrne, Caitlin. "Securing the 'Rules-Based Order' in the Indo-Pacific: The Significance of Strategic Narrative." *Security Challenges* 16, 3 (2020): 10–15.
Caraley, Demetrios James, ed. *American Hegemony: Preventive War, Iraq, and Imposing Democracy.* New York: Academy of Political Science, 2004.
Cha, Victor D. *Powerplay: The Origins of the American Alliance System in Asia.* Princeton, NJ: Princeton University Press, 2018.
Chan, Stephen, Peter G. Mandaville, and Roland Bleiker, eds. *The Zen of International Relations.* Hampshire: Palgrave, 2001.
Chang, Ha-Joon. *The East Asian Development Experience: The Miracle, the Crisis and the Future.* New York: Zed Books, 2006.
Cooley, Alexander, and Daniel Nexon. *Exit from Hegemony: The Unraveling of the American Global Order.* New York: Oxford University Press, 2020.
Cox, Robert W. "Gramsci, Hegemony and International Relations: An Essay in Method." *Millennium: Journal of International Studies* 12, 2 (1983): 162–75.
Cox, Robert W., and Timothy J. Sinclair. *Approaches to World Order.* New York: Cambridge University Press, 1996.
Cumings, Bruce. *The Korean War: A History.* New York: Modern Library, 2011.
Daalder, Ivo H., and James M. Lindsay. *The Empty Throne: America's Abdication of Global Leadership.* New York: Public Affairs, 2018.
David, Charles-Philippe, and David Grondin, eds. *Hegemony or Empire? The Redefinition of US Power under George W. Bush.* New York: Routledge, 2016.

de Carvalho, Benjamin, Halvard Leira, and John M. Hobson. "The Big Bangs of IR: The Myths That Your Teachers Still Tell You about 1648 and 1919." *Millennium: Journal of International Studies* 39, 3 (2011): 735–58.

Deyo, Frederic C. *The Political Economy of the New Asian Industrialism, The Political Economy of the New Asian Industrialism.* Ithaca, NY: Cornell University Press, 2018.

Dryzek, John S. "Discursive Designs: Critical Theory and Political Institutions." *American Journal of Political Science* 31, 3 (1987): 656–79.

Easterly, William. *The White Man's Burden: Why the West's Efforts to Aid the Rest Have Done So Much Ill and So Little Good.* London: Penguin, 2006.

Eun, Yong-Soo. "Opening Up the Debate over 'Non-Western' International Relations." *Politics* 39, 1 (2018): 4–17.

Felipe, Jesus, ed. *Development and Modern Industrial Policy in Practice: Issues and Country Experiences* (Northampton, MA: Asian Development Bank/Edward Elgar Publishing, 2015.

Foucault, Michel. *Power/Knowledge: Selected Interviews and Other Writings, 1972–1977,* edited by Colin Gordon. New York: Pantheon Books, 1980.

Fraser, Nancy, and Rachel Jaeggi. *Capitalism: A Conversation in Critical Theory.* Oxford: Polity Press, 2018.

Gill, Indermit, and Homi Kharas. *An East Asian Renaissance: Ideas for Economic Growth* (Washington, DC: World Bank, 2007).

Goh, Evelyn. "Contesting Hegemonic Order: China in East Asia." *Security Studies* 28, 3 (2019): 614–44.

–. "Great Powers and Hierarchical Order in Southeast Asia: Analyzing Regional Security Strategies." *International Security* 32, 3 (2008): 113–57.

Goodman, Matthew P., et al. *Delivering Prosperity in the Indo-Pacific: An Agenda for Australia and the United States.* Washington, DC: Center for Strategic and International Studies, 2019.

Goodson, Ivor, et al., eds. *The Routledge International Handbook on Narrative and Life History.* London: Taylor and Francis, 2016.

Haacke, Jürgen. "The Concept of Hedging and Its Application to Southeast Asia: A Critique and a Proposal for a Modified Conceptual and Methodological Framework." *International Relations of the Asia-Pacific* 19, 3 (2019): 375–417.

Herman, Edward S., and Noam Chomsky. *Manufacturing Consent: Political Economy of the Mass Media.* New York: Knopf Doubleday, 2011.

Hobson, John M. "Global Dialogical History and the Challenge of Neo-Eurocentrism." In *Asia, Europe, and the Emergence of Modern Science,* edited by Arun Bala, 13–33. New York: Palgrave Macmillan, 2012.

Howson, Richard, and Kylie Smith, eds. *Hegemony: Studies in Consensus and Coercion.* New York: Routledge, 2008.

Hyun, Suk, and James F. Paradise. "Toward an Asian Monetary Fund: Ideas for Transition." *Asian Economic Papers* 19, 2 (2020): 65–77.

Ikenberry, G. John. *Liberal Leviathan: The Origins, Crisis, and Transformation of the American World Order.* Princeton, NJ: Princeton University Press, 2012.

Ikenberry, G. John, and Charles A. Kupchan. "Socialization and Hegemonic Power." *International Organization* 44, 3 (1990): 283–315.

Ikenberry, G. John, and Anne-Marie Slaughter. *Forging a World of Liberty under Law: U.S. National Security in the 21st Century: Final Report of the Princeton Project on National Security*. Princeton, NJ: Woodrow Wilson School of Public and International Affairs, Princeton University, 2006.

Inoguchi, Takashi, ed. *The SAGE Handbook of Asian Foreign Policy*. London: SAGE, 2021.

Jackson, Van. *On the Brink: Trump, Kim, and the Threat of Nuclear War*. New York: Cambridge University Press, 2018.

Jervis, Robert, and Jack Snyder, eds. *Dominoes and Bandwagons: Strategic Beliefs and Great Power Competition in the Eurasian Rimland*. Oxford: Oxford University Press, 1991.

Jones, Branwen Gruffydd. *Decolonizing International Relations* (Lanham, MD: Rowman and Littlefield, 2006).

Jung, Sung Chul, Jaehyon Lee, and Ji-Yong Lee. "The Indo-Pacific Strategy and US Alliance Network Expandability: Asian Middle Powers' Positions on Sino-US Geostrategic Competition in Indo-Pacific Region." *Journal of Contemporary China* 30, 127 (2021): 53–68.

Kang, David C. *East Asia before the West: Five Centuries of Trade and Tribute*. New York: Columbia University Press, 2012.

–. "Getting Asia Wrong: The Need for New Analytical Frameworks." *International Security* 27, 4 (2003): 57–85.

Krahmann, Elke. "American Hegemony or Global Governance? Competing Visions of International Security." *International Studies Review* 7, 4 (2005): 531–45.

Krebs, Ronald R. *Narrative and the Making of US National Security*. Cambridge: Cambridge University Press, 2015.

Lawrence, Mark, and Fredrick Logevall, eds. *The First Vietnam War: Colonial Conflict and Cold War Crisis*. Cambridge, MA: Harvard University Press, 2007.

Lee Hsien Loong. "The Endangered Asian Century: America, China, and the Perils of Confrontation." *Foreign Affairs* 99, 4 (July/August 2020): 52–64.

–. "In Full: PM Lee Hsien Loong's Speech at the 2019 Shangri-La Dialogue." Speech, Shangri-La Dialogue, Singapore, May 31, 2019.

Linklater, Andrew. "Grand Narratives and International Relations." *Global Change, Peace and Security* 21, 1 (2009): 3–17.

Mahbubani, Kishore. "An Asian Perspective on Human Rights and Freedom of the Press." *Media Asia* 20, 3 (1993): 159–66.

Miller, Paul D. *American Power and Liberal Order: A Conservative Internationalist Grand Strategy*. Washington, DC: Georgetown University Press, 2016.

Mishra, Pankaj. *From the Ruins of Empire: The Revolt Against the West and the Remaking of Asia*. Toronto: Doubleday Canada, 2012.

Miskimmon, Alister, Ben O'Loughlin, and Laura Roselle. *Forging the World: Strategic Narratives and International Relations*. Ann Arbor, MI: University of Michigan Press, 2018.

—. *Strategic Narratives: Communication Power and the New World Order.* London: Taylor and Francis, 2014.

Nayyar, Deepak. *Resurgent Asia: Diversity in Development.* New York: Oxford University Press, 2019.

Nexon, Daniel H., and Iver B. Neumann. "Hegemonic-Order Theory: A Field-Theoretic Account." *European Journal of International Relations* 24, 3 (April 2017): 662–86.

Ngoei, Wen-Qing. *Arc of Containment: Britain, the United States, and Anticommunism in Southeast Asia.* Ithaca, NY: Cornell University Press, 2019.

Ninkovich, Frank. *Modernity and Power: A History of the Domino Theory in the Twentieth Century.* Chicago: University of Chicago Press, 1994.

Ohno, Kenichi, and Izumi Ohno, eds. *Japanese Views on Economic Development: Diverse Paths to the Market* (New York: Routledge, 1998).

Pempel, T.J., ed. *The Politics of the Asian Economic Crisis.* Ithaca, NY: Cornell University Press, 1999.

Persaud, Randolph B. *Counter-Hegemony and Foreign Policy: The Dialectics of Marginalized and Global Forces in Jamaica.* Albany: SUNY Press, 2001.

Puri, Samir. *The Shadows of Empire: How Imperial History Shapes Our World.* New York: Pegasus Books, 2021.

Rapp-Hooper, Mira. *Shields of the Republic: The Triumph and Peril of America's Alliances.* Cambridge, MA: Harvard University Press, 2020.

Reeves, Jeffrey. *Canada and the "Indo-Pacific": "Diverse" and "Inclusive," Not "Free" and "Open."* Vancouver: Asia Pacific Foundation of Canada, 2020.

Sambhi, Natalie. "Indonesia's Indo-Pacific Vision: Staying the Course in a Covid-19 World." *Asia Policy* 15, 4 (October 2020): 37–50.

Schelling, Thomas C. *Arms and Influence.* New Haven, CT: Yale University Press, 2020.

Schwarzmantel, John, and Mark McNally, eds. *Gramsci and Global Politics: Hegemony and Resistance.* London: Taylor and Francis, 2009.

Shimizu, Kosuke, ed. *Critical International Relations Theories in East Asia: Relationality, Subjectivity, and Pragmatism.* New York: Routledge, 2019.

Singh, Ajit. "'Asian Capitalism' and the Financial Crisis." *Munich Personal RePEc Archive* 54932 (1998): 1–22.

Singh, Prabhakar, and Benoît Mayer, eds. *Critical International Law: Postrealism, Postcolonialism, and Transnationalism.* Oxford: Oxford University Press, 2014.

Suh, Jae-Jung. *Origins of North Korea's Juche: Colonialism, War, and Development.* New York: Lexington Books, 2013.

Tansel, Cemal Burak. "Deafening Silence? Marxism, International Historical Sociology and the Spectre of Eurocentrism." *European Journal of International Relations* 21, 1 (2014): 76–100.

Tickner, Arlene B. "Core, Periphery and (Neo)Imperialist International Relations." *European Journal of International Relations* 19, 3 (2013): 627–46.

Tunsjø, Øystein. *The Return of Bipolarity in World Politics: China, the United States, and Geostructural Realism.* New York: Columbia University Press, 2018.

Voss, Christopher. *Never Split the Difference: Negotiating as if Your Life Depended on It.* New York: Harper Business, 2016.

Wade, Robert. *Governing the Market: Economic Theory and the Role of Government in East Asian Industrialization.* Princeton, NJ: Princeton University Press, 2004.

Walldorf, C. William. *To Shape Our World for Good: Master Narratives and Regime Change in US Foreign Policy, 1900–2011.* Ithaca, NY: Cornell University Press, 2019.

Walt, Stephen M. *The Hell of Good Intentions: America's Foreign Policy Elite and the Decline of U.S. Primacy.* New York: Farrar, Straus and Giroux, 2018.

Wang, Ting-Yan, and Hong Liu. "An Emerging Asian Model of Governance and Transnational Knowledge Transfer: An Introduction." *Journal of Asian Public Policy* 11, 2 (2018): 121–35.

Wehner, Leslie E., and Cameron G. Thies. "Role Theory, Narratives, and Interpretation: The Domestic Contestation of Roles." *International Studies Review* 16, 3 (2014): 411–36.

Wemheuer-Vogelaar, Wiebke, et al. "The IR of the Beholder: Examining Global IR Using the 2014 TRIP Survey." *International Studies Review* 18, 1 (2016): 16–32.

Wertheim, Stephen. *Tomorrow, the World: The Birth of U.S. Global Supremacy.* Cambridge, MA: Harvard University Press, 2020.

White, Hayden V. *The Content of the Form: Narrative Discourse and Historical Representation.* Baltimore: Johns Hopkins University Press, 1990.

Wohlforth, William. "Rethinking Cold War Historical Materialism." *International Studies Review* 4, 3 (2002): 186–88.

Worth, Owen. *Rethinking Hegemony.* London: Palgrave Macmillan, 2015.

Index

Abe, Shinzo/Shinzo government: on Canadian-Japanese cooperation in Indo-Pacific, 3; cross-strait policy, 9–11; on Japan-China relations, 67; Japan-US relations and, 56; and like-minded state cooperation, 33; and rules-based order, 29; US alignment and, 57. *See also* Japan

Acharya, Amitav, 77

Adler, Emanuel, 27

ASEAN (Association of Southeast Asian Nations): about, 133–34; agreement with, 62; and Asia-Pacific regional integration, 150; Canadian understanding of institutions in, 11; Community Vision 2025, 149; dialogue mechanisms, 134; domination of Asia-Pacific institutionalism, 133; and EAS, 134; European Union and, 26, 62; free and open concept and, 50, 51; India and, 138; and Indo-Pacific concept, 42, 50, 52, 59, 128; like-minded state and, 32; Malaysia and, 43; and maritime freedom, 51; Master Plan on ASEAN Connectivity, 149; network analysis of, 133–39; neutrality, 50; New Zealand and, 138; omnidirectional diplomacy and, 148; + mechanisms/status, 15, 134, 138–39, 151; +3 Macroeconomic Research Office (AMRO), 48; +3 states, 134; +6 states, 134, 136; Political-Security Community, 136, 137; and RCEP, 136; Regional Forum (ARF), 124, 127, 134, 135, 138; and Russia, 59; Secretariat, 134; Senior Economic Officials Meeting (SEOM), 135; Senior Officials Meeting on Transnational Crime (SOMTC), 136; Senior Officials on Environment (ASOEN), 135; and South China Sea, 38, 85, 151; and strategic integration, 149, 150; supranational governance in national interests, 123; UK and, 60–61; US and, 32, 58, 59; US-China conflict and, 59; Vietnamese writers on, 44; Western critiques of, 25–26; Western

Index

leadership and, 84, 95; working groups, 134. *See also* non-ASEAN institutions
ASEAN Defence Ministers' Meeting-Plus (ADMM+), 134, 136, 137, 138; Expert Working Group (EWG), 135
ASEAN Economic Community, 14, 136
ASEAN Economic Ministers Meeting (AEMM), 135
ASEAN Ministerial Meetings on the Environment (AMME), 135
ASEAN Socio-Cultural Community (ASCC), 135; ROK-ASEAN Consultative Group in the Employment and Labour Sector, 137
ASEAN Working Group on Climate Change (AWGCC), 135
ASEAN-Australia relationship: ASEAN Australia Awards-Endeavour Scholarship and Fellowships, 137; ASEAN Post Ministerial Conference with Australia (PMC+1), 136; ASEAN-Australia Forum, 136; ASEAN-Australia Joint Cooperation Committee Meeting (JCC), 136; ASEAN-Australia Smart Cities initiative, 135; ASEAN-Australia Special Summit, 136; ASEAN-Australia-New Zealand Free Trade Area (AANZFTA), 136; and climate change, 135; Indonesian narratives on, 64; leveraging of strategic engagement in, 138; scholarship programs in, 137; as subject to shifts, 64
ASEAN-Canada relationship, 124, 133, 134–37, 138–39, 151–52; and ASEAN+ status, 138, 139; and bottom-up vs. top-down change, 138; Canada in ADMM+ Expert Working Group, 135; Canada in ASEAN Regional Forum, 124, 134, 135; Canada-ASEAN Post Ministerial Conference Plus One (PMC+1), 135; Canada's added value in, 138–39; China-Canada relationship and, 139; and climate change, 135; and economic issues, 125, 135–36; free trade agreements, 134, 138; and human rights, 138; participation in ASEAN's operational and tactical-level institutions, 138; "plus" status, 134; scholarship program in, 137; and security, 136–37, 138; socio-cultural engagement in, 137; in strategic integration, 134–37
ASEAN-China relationship: ASEAN and China Cooperative Operations in Response to Dangerous Drugs (ACCORD), 137; and ASEAN+1 dialogues, 137; ASEAN-China Customs Directors General Consultation Meeting, 136; ASEAN-China Health Ministers Meeting, 137; ASEAN-China Science, Technology and Innovation Cooperation Week, 137; ASEAN-China Senior Officials' Meeting on Health Development, 137; ASEAN-China Transport Ministers Meeting, 136; ASEAN-China Work Plan on Cooperation in Culture and Arts, 138; ASEAN-China Young Leaders Scholarship Program, 137–38; and BRI alignment with ASEAN Economic Community, 136; and climate change, 135; and free and open concept, 50; leveraging of strategic engagement in, 138; socio-cultural engagement in, 137–38; and South China Sea, 51; and stability, 71; US and, 59; working groups in, 137
ASEAN-Japan relationship, 135–36; ASEAN-Japan Defence Ministers' Informal Meeting, 136; ASEAN-Japan Economic Resilience Action Plan, 136; ASEAN-Japan Energy Efficiency Partnership (AJEEP),

135; and climate change, 135; economics in, 135–36; leveraging of strategic engagement in, 138; and security linkages, 136–37; socio-cultural engagement in, 137
ASEAN-South Korea relationship: ASEAN-Korea Network on Climate Change Adaptation in Aquaculture, 135; ASEAN-Republic of Korea Dialogue, 137; ASEAN-Republic of Korea Senior Officials Meeting, 137; ASEAN-Republic of Korea Summit, 137; as balanced engagement, 42; free trade agreement in, 136; leveraging of strategic engagement in, 138; New Southern Policy in ASEAN Economic Community, 136; and security linkages, 136–37; socio-cultural engagement in, 137; South Korea in ASEAN + 3, 134
Ash Center for Democratic Governance and Innovation, poll on CPC, 105–6
Asia Business Leaders Advisory Council (ABLAC), 153
Asia Pacific Foundation of Canada, 11, 150; Women-only Business Missions to Asia, 153
Asian Barometer Survey: attitudes toward China in, 70; and regional state attitudes toward US vs. regional governance, 59–60
Asian Development Bank (ADB), 133
Asian Financial Crisis (1997), 37, 46, 48
Asian Intrastructure Investment Bank (AIIB), 133
Asian narratives: on Australia, 55, 63, 64–66, 74, 129; on Canada, 150; and Canadian foreign policy, 74–75, 97, 148, 156; and Canadian national interests, 125, 156; and Canadian resources/efforts expenditure, 151; on China, 55, 70–73, 74; on China's activities in Asia, 127; critical analysis of, 7–8; critical theory and, 156; on democracy, 36, 126; and economic liberalism, 126; on economic systems, 126–27; on European states/European Union, 55, 60–63; on free and open concept, 36, 47–51, 126; on governance, 126–27; on India, 55, 64, 68–70, 74; on Indo-Pacific concept, 13, 17, 41–44, 52–53; interconnectivity in, 14; and international relations, 26–27; on Japan, 55, 63–64, 66–68, 74, 129; on natural equilibrium in Asia, 145; on North Korea, 80–83; and omnidirectional diplomacy, 10, 152; on rules-based order, 44–46; on security, 17–18, 97, 130–31; on South China Sea, 85–86; and stability, 156; in strategic integration, 150–51; on UK, 55, 62–63; on US, 55, 56–60, 70–71, 130–31; on Western foreign policy motivations, 130; on Western hegemony, 130; on Western leadership, 74, 94–97, 128, 130–31; on Western state involvement/leadership, 7, 17
Asia-Pacific Center for Security Studies (APCSS), 35
Asia-Pacific Economic Cooperation (APEC), 126, 133; Virtual Leaders' Retreat, 144–45
AUKUS trilateral: Australia in, 37, 40, 64, 113, 147; Australia-US relations and, 65; Canada and, 16, 147, 151; China and, 54; Chinese activities in the South China Sea and, 84; Chinese aggression as common enemy and, 113; Indo-Pacific concept and, 40, 54; Japan in, 37; like-minded state concept and, 55; rules-based order and, 33; security and establishment of, 54; UK and, 63, 113; US in, 6, 29, 54, 65, 113; Western alignment

Index 247

in, 7; Western leadership and, 96; Western revisionism and, 130; as Western-oriented, 11
Australia: and ASEAN, 64; in ASEAN + 6, 134, 136; Asian narratives on, 55, 63, 64–66, 74, 129; and AUKUS, 40, 54, 64, 65, 113, 147; Canadian policy-makers and, 130; on CPC, 103; in EAS, 134; on European involvement, 60–61; in Five Eyes, 40; and free and open concept, 35, 37; in G7, 40; Indonesian scholarship on, 64–65; and Indo-Pacific concept, 40, 65, 78, 145, 147, 155; Japanese narratives on, 64; as like-minded state, 8, 33; Malaysian scholarship on, 65; as model Asian democracy/state, 55, 74; in Quad, 40, 64, 113; as regional actor, 65–66; and rules-based order, 29–30; and South China Sea, 64–65, 85; South Korean narratives on, 64; and Taiwan, 88, 89, 118; Thai scholarship on, 65; troops in South Korea, 79–80; and US, 63, 64, 65, 147; Vietnamese narratives on, 65; and Western leadership, 65; Western narratives on, 55, 74, 129; as Western state, 64; and Xinjiang, 110. *See also* ASEAN-Australia relationship; China-Australia relationship
Australia for ASEAN Scholarships, 137

Bangladesh: in ASEAN Regional Forum, 134; in BIMSTEC, 140
Bay of Bengal Initiative for Multi-Sectoral Technical and Economic Cooperation (BIMSTEC), 16, 140–41; Myanmar and Thailand in, 69
Beijing Xiangshan Forum, 142
Belt and Road Forum for International Cooperation, 141

Belt and Road Initiative (BRI), 46; alignment with ASEAN Economic Community, 136; "Build Back Better World Partnership" alternative to, 144; Canadian foreign policy and, 119; Chinese analysts on, 115–16; Indo-Pacific concept and, 43, 72; and interconnectivity, 14; Japanese scholarship on, 72; Japan's Indo-Pacific concept compared, 67; purpose of, 115–16; and regional growth, 145; and Silk Road Fund, 116; South Korean scholarship on, 72; Western alternatives to, 97; Western narrative surrounding, 114, 115–16; Western opposition to, 50
Bernstein, Steven, 27
Bharatiya Janata Party (BJP): and COVID-19 crisis, 69; Hindutva agenda, 68–69
Biden, Joe/Biden administration: address to APEC Virtual Leaders' Retreat, 144–45; and ASEAN-US cooperation, 32; and Asia-Pacific, 6; and "Build Back Better World Partnership," 144; and Canadian alignment with US, 12; and China, 12, 71; and CPC, 93, 102; and free and open Indo-Pacific, 35; Indo-Pacific strategy, 28; and like-minded state, 32; Moon Jae-in and, 40; and Muslim states, 95; North Korean policy, 80; and rules-based order, 28, 29; and Taiwan, 87, 89, 91, 93; and US-China relations, 58; and Xingjiang, 110. *See also* United States
Blinken, Antony, 102
Boao Forum for Asia, 142
Booth, Kenneth, 39
"Build Back Better World Partnership," 144
Burton, Charles, 103

Cambodia: alignment with China vs. US, 59; and China, 10; in LMC forum, 140

Canada: Asian narratives on, 150; as Asia-Pacific state, 154–55; and AUKUS, 147; on CPC, 103; and democracy, 34, 120; and EAS, 134; engagement with Asian states, 8; free trade agreements, 125, 155; and G7, 34, 121, 147–48; as "global saviour," 120–21; and hegemonic narratives, 38; and human rights, 120; and Indo-Pacific concept, 3, 4, 5, 13, 148–49; Indo-Pacific strategies and, 121; and international law, 120; Japan and, 12; and like-minded state, 34, 120, 121; as middle power, 3, 34, 120, 124; and NATO, 121, 148; and non-ASEAN institutions, 140, 142–53, 148; and Quad, 147; relations with Western states/actors in Asia, 7; and rules-based order, 34; troops in South Korea, 79–80; in United Nations, 147–48; and US, 5–7, 9, 12–13; and Xinjiang, 110. *See also* ASEAN-Canada relationship; China-Canada relationship; foreign policy (Canada); national interests (Canada)

Cha, Victor, *Powerplay: The Origins of the American Alliance System in Asia*, 77

Champagne, François-Philippe, 107

Chiang Mai Initiative Multilateralization (CMIM), 48

China: aggression by, 55, 72, 113, 133; Asian narratives on, 55, 70–73, 74; Asian states on Western alignment vs. with China, 72; Asian states' wariness regarding, 10; assertion by, 72, 94; and AUKUS trilateral, 54; Belt and Road Initiative (BRI), 14, 41, 50, 114, 115–16; Cambodia and, 10; and Canada in ADMM+ Expert Working Group, 135; coercion by, 83, 84, 88, 113, 114; cognitive empathy toward, 111; Confucian heritage, 103; containment of, 45, 58, 59, 61, 72, 90, 92, 96, 130; and COVID-19, 71, 115, 144; "debt-trap diplomacy," 113–14, 115; defence, 89; diplomatic recognition of, vs. Taiwan, 88; in East China Sea, 84–85; and economics, 47, 72, 99, 103–4; European involvement in Asia and, 61; European Union and, 78; foreign policy, 71–72; France and, 78; free and open concept, and, 35, 37, 114; and free trade, 70–71; and genocide, 118; Germany and, 78; and governance, 8, 48, 59–60; in GTI, 142; and Hong Kong, 118, 145; and human rights, 8; illiberalism of, 41, 94, 99, 100; India and, 64, 69, 113, 130; in Indian Ocean, 51; Indonesia/Indonesian scholarship and, 10, 51, 72; Indo-Pacific concept and, 43; influence, 70; Japan-US relationship and, 56; Laos and, 10; like-minded state and, 32; in LMC forum, 140; "Made in China 2025," 48; Malaysia/Malaysian scholarship and, 10, 43, 73; Meng Wanzhou detention, 3–4; minority policies, 110–11; Myanmar and, 10; national development plans, 48; and natural equilibrium of Asia, 145; Netherlands and, 78; and new Asian order, 116–17; and North Korea, 83, 96; omnidirectional diplomacy, 146; and one-China policy, 87–88, 92; poverty eradication in, 111–12; protests in, 105; regime change, 101; regional support for, 127; and reunification, 108; revisionism by, 32, 41, 55, 70, 74, 83, 84, 96, 113, 114, 119, 127; and rules-based order, 28, 30, 38, 114, 116, 119;

Index

and security, 94; and South China Sea, 38, 51, 71, 72, 73, 83–84, 85, 137; South Korea/South Korean scholarship and, 42, 58, 72, 96, 113; Southeast Asian opinion on, 59; and stability, 9–10, 71, 74; strategic partnerships, 152; students in Canada, 125; terrorism in, 112; Thailand/Thai narratives and, 10, 73; trade restriction by, 114–15; in "two systems," 108; UK and, 78, 113; US and, 37–38; values, 8, 9–10; Vietnam/Vietnamese scholarship and, 10, 51, 59, 73, 128; and Western hegemony, 116; Western leadership, and competition with, 95; Western narratives on, 21, 26, 55, 71, 99–100; "win-win" relations with states, 123; and Xinjiang, 145; and Zambia, 114. See also ASEAN-China relationship; Belt and Road Initiative (BRI); Communist Party of China (CPC); cross-strait relations

China Development Bank, 115

China-ASEAN Clean Coal Conversion Technology Exchange and Promotion, 135

China-ASEAN Connectivity Cooperation Committee, 136

China-ASEAN Cultural Forum, 138

China-ASEAN Education Cooperation Week, 137

China-ASEAN Expo, 137

China-ASEAN Investment Cooperation Fund, 136

China-ASEAN Maritime Cooperation Fund, 136

China-Australia relationship, 63, 64, 65, 78, 113, 118, 119; Australian chauvinistic diplomacy and, 147; Australian US alignment and, 147; Chinese embargo, 113, 115

China-Canada relationship: ASEAN-Canada relationship vs., 139; Canadian policy and, 101, 117–19; Canadian public views and, 11–12; Chinese narratives on, 18, 100–1; Meng detention and, 3–4; strategic empathy in, 148

China-Japan relationship, 42, 49, 56, 63–64, 96, 113, 129; Asian narratives on, 66; and China-Taiwan relations, 91–92; competition in, 72; Japanese narratives on China, 129; Japanese relationship with European states, and, 67; Japanese scholarship on Chinese foreign policy, 71–72; US and, 56

China-Taiwan relationship. See cross-strait relations

China-US relationship, 37–38, 77–78, 82–83, 100, 102, 113, 115; Australia and, 64, 65; Biden administration re-engagement with China, 71; China-Taiwan relationship vs., 87–89; Chinese analysts on US-Taiwan relations, 92–93; competition within, 73; THAAD and, 115; Thai scholarship on, 58–59; Vietnamese scholarship on, 59

Chinese Communist Party (CCP). See Communist Party of China (CPC)

Chinese narratives: about, 100–1; on BRI, 115–16; and Canadian foreign policy, 128; on China, 100–1; on Chinese foreign policy, 114–17; on cross-strait relations, 128; on East China Sea, 86; on Hong Kong, 107–9, 128; on minority development, 128; on North Korea, 82–83; on poverty reduction, 128; on rules-based order, 97; and security, 128; on Taiwan, 92–93; on US-Taiwan relations, 92–93; on Western leadership, 96–97; on Western provocation of North Korea, 83; Western reaction to, 101; on Xinjiang, 110–13, 128

Chong, Michael, 107

climate change: and ASEAN-Canada relationship, 135; equidistance and, 13; strategic integration and, 11; Xi on, 99

Cold War: "2.0," 59, 95; Australia and US-China relations, and new, 65; and changes in Asia, 116; containment strategy, 45; European states, and new, 61; and Korean Peninsula, 81–82; and like-minded state, 34; values during, 20

colonialism: critical theory and postcolonial writing, 22; and European involvement in Asia, 60; Hong Kong and, 107; and Korean War, 77; and like-minded state, 10, 34; neocolonialism in Western narratives, 10; non-ASEAN institutions and, 139; and rules-based order, 45; US, 81; and Vietnam War, 77; Western narratives and, 25

communism, 77, 80

Communist Party of China (CPC): Biden administration and, 93, 102; Canadian foreign policy regarding, 5, 117–18; Canadian policy writers on, 5; Chinese Academy of Social Sciences poll on, 105; Cold War-era rhetoric regarding, 102; domestic support for, 18, 102–6, 127–28; "dual circulation" economic policy, 111; effectiveness of, 103–5; and genocide, 102, 110; in Hong Kong, 106; and human rights, 118; illegitimacy of, 100; internal metrics focus, 113; and internal stability, 113; leadership, 103–4; minority policies, 110–11; poverty eradication, 111–12; pragmatism of, 104–5; and protests in China, 105; Taiwan and, 91; Trump administration and, 93, 102; Western anti-CPC rhetoric, 103; Western narratives on, 25; and Xinjiang, 110, 118

Comprehensive and Progressive Agreement for Trans-Pacific Partnership (CPTPP), 125, 126; Canada in, 133, 153, 155; Japan and, 40; Japanese foreign policy and, 66; regional writing on, 46; South Korea and, 42

Conference on Interaction and Confidence Building Measures in Asia (CICA), 15, 141, 148, 151

Council for Security Cooperation in the Asia Pacific (CSCAP), 124

COVID-19 pandemic: China and, 71, 115; and democracy/democratic states, 9, 36; in Europe, 71; and free and open concept, 36; in India, 69, 130; Japan and, 71; origins of, 113; in Thailand, 73; in UK, 49; in US, 49, 60, 71; US vs. China as supplier of vaccine, 144; Western vaccine provision, 59; and Western vs. Asian state governance, 49

critical theory/analysis: about critical theory, 22–24; and alternative narrative on Asia, 24; and Asian narratives, 7–8, 156; and Asia's international relations, 25–27; and Canada's relations with Western states, 7–10; and Canada-US relations, 5–7; and Canadian foreign policy, 5–10; and free and open concept, 34–38; on global institutions, 31; and hegemony, 22, 23–24; and Indo-Pacific concept, 24, 41; on international law, 31; and like-minded state, 32–34; and power, 22, 24; and rules-based order, 28–32; and Western narratives, 23–24, 25–26; Western narratives/paradigms vs., 4–5

cross-strait relations, 87–93; Canadian foreign policy regarding, 118–19; China and, 118–19; Chinese narratives on, 92, 128; Indonesian writing on, 90;

Japanese narratives on, 91–92; South Korean analysts on, 91; Southeast Asian writing on, 90; Taiwanese narratives on, 92; US and, 91, 92; Western narrative on, 87–88. *See also* Taiwan

democracy: Asian narratives on, 36, 126; Australia as model Asian, 55; autocratic/mixed-model governance vs., 59–60; Canada and, 34, 120; Chinese culture and, 88; COVID-19 and, 9, 36; decline in Asia, 9; and free and open concept, 26, 35; Global Financial Crisis and, 104; and governance, 36, 126; Hong Kong and, 106, 107, 108, 109, 118; rules-based order and, 45; and security, 94; strategic integration and, 122; Taiwan and, 88; US hegemony and, 78; Western leadership and, 93, 94; Western narratives and, 120; and Western narratives on China, 26
democratic liberalism. *See* liberal democracy
Dialogue for Innovative and Sustainable Growth (DISG), 136
Diaoyu/Senkaku Islands, 78, 84, 86–87, 115
Dokdo/Senkaku Islands, 87

East Asia Summit (EAS), 134, 136, 137, 138
East China Sea: air defence identification zone (ADIZ) in, 84; Canadian foreign policy and, 97–98; China and, 84–85; Chinese literature on, 86; South Korean discourse on, 87; territorial disputes, 78; Western narratives on, 84–85
East Turkistan Islamic Movement (ETIM), 112
economics/economy systems, 46; ASEAN-Canada relationship and, 135–36; in ASEAN-China relationship, 136; in ASEAN-Japan relationship, 136; Asian narratives on, 126–27; Canada and advancement of growth, 124; and Canada as Asia-Pacific state, 154–55; Canadian institutional involvement in, 133; and Canadian national interests, 124–25; China and, 72, 99, 103–4; economic liberalism, 26, 35, 46, 126; and European engagement in Asia, 60; free and open concept in, 36–37, 47–48; modernization, 72, 103, 111, 112; North Korea, 81; state intervention/-directed development and, 47
Edelman poll on CPC, 105
Eight-Nation Alliance, 62
Esper, Mark, 4, 35
European states/European Union: ASEAN compared to, 26; in ASEAN Regional Forum, 134; Asian narratives on, 55, 60–63; and China, 78; colonialism and, 60; and COVID-19, 71; on CPC, 103; and disequilibrium between Asian states, 61; and Indo-Pacific concept, 40, 60, 78; Indo-Pacific strategy, 29; institutional support for involvement in Asia, 60–61; Japan and, 67; and like-minded state paradigm, 33; military activities, 61; strategic integration in, 149; supranational governance in national interests, 123; and Taiwan, 88, 89; US and rules-based order and, 29
Expert Development Canada (EDC), 153

Five Eyes intelligence alliance, 16, 40, 54
foreign policy (Canada): adaptive approach, 13–14, 127; Asian diaspora community and, 152–53; Asian institutionalism and, 151–52; Asian narratives and, 74–75;

Asian narratives toward China's activities and, 127; Asian region as afterthought in, 155; Asian vs. Western narratives and, 53, 74–75, 97, 148, 156; bilateral relations in, 152; and BRI, 119; on China, 101, 117–19; and Chinese foreign policy, 119; Chinese perspectives and, 128; on CPC, 5, 117–18; critical analysis in, 5; on cross-strait relations, 118–19; and East China Sea, 97–98; equal engagement with Asian states, 131; equidistance in, 13; and G7, 120; on Hong Kong, 118; humility in, 13, 98; Indo-Pacific concept and, 74, 131, 150–51; and Indo-Pacific strategy, 128–29; and like-minded state, 8–10; narratives and, 19; and NATO, 120; network analysis and, 131–32; and North Korea, 98; omnidirectional diplomacy in, 11–14, 145, 147–49, 152, 156; rules-based order and, 32, 74, 127; and security, 97–98; and South China Sea, 97–98; strategic integration in, 14–16, 122, 145, 150–54, 156; and Taiwan, 98; understanding of operational environment and, 97; value-free, 8; and Western alignment, 120–22; Western assumptions and, 26; on Xinjiang, 118
Foucault, Michel, 23, 156
France: Asian narratives on, 60; and China, 78; colonies, 61; and free and open concept, 34; and Indo-Pacific concept, 40, 60, 78, 145; Indo-Pacific strategy, 29; as like-minded state, 33; and Taiwan/Taiwan Strait, 88, 89, 90, 118; troops in South Korea, 79–80
free and open concept: ASEAN and, 50; Asian narratives on, 36, 47–51, 126; Australia and, 35, 37; China and, 35, 37, 99, 114; contradictions in, 36; COVID-19 and, 36; critical theory and, 34–38; and democracy, 26, 35; and economic liberalism, 35; in economics, 36–37, 47–48; France and, 34; Germany and, 34–35; and governance, 36, 48–49; Indonesia and, 36, 50; and Indo-Pacific concept, 35; and international law, 37; Japan and, 35, 37, 49, 66; like-minded state and, 55; Malaysian scholarship on, 50; in maritime security, 51; in politics, 48–49; protectionism vs., 36–37; rules-based order and, 41; and security, 36–37; South Korean scholarship on, 49; Thai scholarship on, 50; US and, 35, 38, 78, 144; uses of terms in, 35; Vietnamese scholarship on, 50–51; Western hegemony and, 35–36, 37, 78; Western leadership and, 26; Western narratives on, 26, 34–38, 47
A Free and Open Indo-Pacific (US State Department), 32, 35
Free and Open Indo-Pacific (FOIP) vision (Japan), 3, 29, 33
free trade/free trade agreements (FTAs): ASEAN-Canada relationship and, 134, 138; in ASEAN-South Korea relationship, 136; Asian narratives and, 47, 48; Canada and, 125, 155; China and, 70–71; in Indo-Pacific concept, 71; US and, 71; Western states advocating for, 34
Freedom House, freedom index, 36
Fukuda, Takeo/Fukuda Doctrine, 146

G7, 16; Australia in, 40; Canada in, 5, 13, 34, 120, 121, 131, 147–48, 155; Indo-Pacific concept and, 40, 54; and security against China, 94; US and rules-based order and, 29; as Western-oriented, 11
Gallup poll, on foreign policy toward Asia, 57–58

gender equality: ASEAN and, 138; Canada and advancement of, 124, 146, 148; CPC and, 112; equidistance and, 13; international order and, 148; strategic integration and, 11
genocide, 100, 102, 110, 113, 118
Germany: Asian narratives on, 60; and China, 78; and free and open concept, 34–35; and Indo-Pacific concept, 29, 40, 78, 145; as like-minded state, 33; and Taiwan, 118
Global Britain strategy, 60, 62–63
Global Financial Crisis (2008), 37, 46, 48, 104
Global Times Public Opinion Survey Center, on Chinese support for Western government models, 106
Globe and Mail, on Canada-China relations, 9
governance: Asian narratives on, 126–27; autocratic/mixed-model vs. democratic, 59–60; Canada in non-ASEAN institutions and, 142; China and, 8; during COVID-19 pandemic, 48; CPC and, 104–5; democracy and, 36, 126; democratic liberalism and, 48–49; free and open concept and, 36, 48–49; Western alignment and, 12; in Western states vs. China, 104
Gramsci, Antonio, 20, 22, 23, 38
Greater Tumen Initiative (GTI), 142, 151

hegemony: Canada and, 38; critical theory and, 22, 23–24; cultural, 23, 100, 156; and discursive power, 156; dissension from, 38; and international law, 31; narratives and, 22–23; order vs., 116; and power, 24; and rules-based order, 30; and strategic development, 38–39; US, 17, 76–78, 95, 96; Western leadership and, 95; and Western narratives, 17. *See also* Western hegemony
The Hell of Good Intentions (Walt), 76
Hong Kong: arrests in, 109; Asian attitudes regarding, 127; Basic Law Article 13, 109; Canadian policy regarding, 118; China and, 106–9, 118, 145; Chinese narratives on, 107–9, 128; CPC in, 106; and democracy, 106, 107, 108, 109, 118; Legislative Council, 109; Liaison Office, 109; national security law (NSL) and, 106, 109; Office for Safeguarding National Security, 109; Police Force, 108; post-colonial understanding of, 107; protests in, 106, 108; in "two systems," 108; UK and, 107–8; UK handover to China, 106; US companies in, 145; Western narratives regarding, 106–9
Huawei, 4, 56
human rights: ASEAN-Canada relationship and, 138; Canada and, 120; Canada and advancement of, 124; Canada in non-ASEAN institutions and, 142; China and, 8; CPC and, 118; equidistance and, 13; freedom and, 36; strategic integration and, 11, 15, 122; and Western alignment, 12; Western narratives and, 120; Western states and, 7

ideology: China and, 123; counter-narratives and, 24; CPC and, 105; dominant state and, 20; hegemony and, 23; and like-minded state, 9; narratives and, 20, 23; and networks, 15; and omnidirectional diplomacy, 10–11, 145, 146; process-based outcomes vs., 127; and strategic integration, 146. *See also* values
Ikenberry, G. John, 20, 23, 28

illiberalism: of China, 41, 94, 99, 100; of India, 129; narrative alignment and, 23; of US foreign policy, 9. *See also* liberalism
imperialism. *See* colonialism
India: "Acting East" policy, 69; alignment of, 68; and ASEAN, 138; in ASEAN + 6, 134; Asian narratives on, 55, 64, 68–70, 74; in BIMSTEC, 140; Canadian policymakers and, 130; and China, 64, 69, 113, 130; COVID-19 in, 69, 130; free market opposition in, 48; illiberalism of, 129; and Indo-Pacific concept, 52; instability of, 130; Japanese scholarship on, 68; and Kashmir, 69; as like-minded state, 55, 64, 129–30; "Look East" policies, 69; multidirectional relations, 130; Muslim population, 129; and Muslim world, 69; in Quad, 113; and RCEP, 68, 69; and security, 69; and South Asia, 69–70; South Korea/South Korean scholarship and, 42, 68; strategic partnerships, 152; students in Canada, 125; values, 9; Western narratives on, 55, 74, 129–30; as Western-aligned, 130
Indian Ocean, 42, 50
Indian Ocean Rim Association (IORA), 41
Indonesia: alignment with China vs. US, 59; and China, 10, 51; communism in, 77; and free and open concept, 36, 50; and Indo-Pacific concept, 41, 44, 50, 52–53; and institutions, 46; and IORA, 43; "National Long-Term Development Plan," 48; omnidirectional diplomacy, 147; and "two-oceans" approach, 43
Indonesian narratives: on alignment with China vs. US, 72; on Australia, 64–65; on European states, 62; on India, 69; on Indo-Pacific concept, 43; on Japan, 67; on maritime security, 51; on rules-based order, 45; on South China Sea, 65, 85; on Taiwan, 90; on US as benevolent leader, 58; on Western leadership, 95
Indo-Pacific concept: about, 40; ASEAN and, 44, 52, 128; Asian narratives on, 13, 17, 41–44, 52–53, 157; Asia-Pacific concept vs., 43; in AUKUS, 40; Australia and, 40, 65, 78, 145, 147, 155; and BRI, 43, 72; Canada and, 3, 4, 5, 13, 121, 148–49, 150–51, 155, 157; Canadian foreign policy and, 74, 128–29, 131; and Canadian national interests, 131; and China, 43; critical theory and, 24, 41; and dissonance between Western and Asian narratives, 41; European Union and, 40, 60, 78; in Five Eyes, 40; France and, 29, 40, 60, 78, 145; free and open concept and, 35; free trade in, 71; in G7, 40; as geographic construct, 41–44, 60; Germany and, 29, 40, 78, 145; India and, 52; Indonesia/Indonesian scholarship and, 41, 43, 44, 50, 52–53; Japan/Japanese scholarship and, 7, 40, 41, 42, 66, 145, 155; and liberalism, 41; Malaysian scholarship on, 43; and marginalization of Southeast Asia, 95; middle-power diplomacy and, 3; Netherlands and, 29, 40, 60, 78; non-alignment with, 13; omnidirectional diplomacy vs., 13; in Quad, 40; rules-based order and, 28, 29, 33, 40–41; Singapore and, 52; South Korea and, 41, 42; and stability/instability, 57, 93; and strategic integration, 151; Thailand/Thai scholarship and, 41, 43, 95; UK and, 60, 78, 145; US and, 3, 4, 35, 40, 43, 44, 45, 57, 77, 94, 145;

Vietnam/Vietnamese narratives and, 41, 43–44, 50–51, 95; Western hegemony and, 13; Western leadership and, 26, 74; Western narratives on, 21, 23, 54, 128; in Western vs. Asian narratives, 17, 41–42, 52–53
Initiative for ASEAN Integration (IAI), 149
instability. *See* stability/instability
Institute for Southeast Asian Studies (ISEAS) polls: on Australia as economic power, 65–66; on European Union, 62; on US, 59
institutions: Canada and, 15, 133, 151–52, 153; creation of opportunities for participation in, 152; critical theory and, 22, 31; engagement with like-minded states vs., 15; on European engagement in Asia, 60–61; Indonesia on, 46; and Indo-Pacific concept, 41; Japan on, 46; network analysis of Canadian involvement in, 18; and networks, 15, 132–33; South Korea on, 46; and strategic integration, 11, 14–15, 146, 151–53; understanding of, 146; Western narratives on, 31; Western standards for, 26
international law: Canada and, 120; critical theory on, 31; free and open concept and, 37; hegemony and, 31; strategic integration and, 122; US violations of, 97; Western narratives and, 21, 120; Western states and, 7; Xi on, 99
International Monetary Fund, 58
international relations (IR): Canada-US relations and, 6; critical theory and, 25–27; narratives and, 19; quantitative vs. qualitative analysis in scholarship on, 27; scholarship in English vs. non-Western languages, 27; strategic integration in IR theory, 149; Western vs. regional narratives and, 25–27

Iran: and CICA, 141; India and, 70, 130; US and, 30, 95
Iraq, 29, 30
Islamic states: Malaysia and, 43; rules-based order, and Islamic values, 45; US and, 95

Japan: in ASEAN + 3, 134; Asian narratives on, 55, 63–64, 66–68, 74, 129; and Asian NATO, 96; and Canada, 3, 130; colonialization, 77; and COVID-19, 71; and CPTPP, 42; and Diaoyu/Senkaku Islands, 84, 86–87, 115; and Dokdo/Takeshima Islands, 87; economics in, 47; and European states, 60–61, 67; and free and open concept, 35, 37, 49, 66; Free and Open Indo-Pacific vision, 3, 116, 149; governance in, 60; as GTI observer, 142; Imperial Defense Policy, 67; Indonesian scholarship on, 67; and Indo-Pacific concept, 40, 41, 66, 145, 155; on institutions, 46; and Korean War, 77; as like-minded state, 8, 33; Meiji Restoration, 45; national development plans, 48; omnidirectional diplomacy, 146; and one-China principle, 92; in Quad, 66, 67, 113; and RCEP, 42; as regional actor, 66; and rules-based order, 29; and South China Sea, 85; South Korea/South Korean scholarship and, 42, 67; strategic partnerships, 152; "Strategy for Semiconductors and the Digital Industry," 48; and Taiwan, 91–92, 118; Thai writing on, 67; values, 9; Vietnamese scholarship on, 67–68; Western alignment, 55, 63, 66, 68, 129, 130; Western narratives on, 55, 74, 129; Western troops in, 80. *See also* Abe, Shinzo/Shinzo government; China-Japan relationship

Japan Cabinet Office, poll on Japan-US relations, 57
Japan-ASEAN Dialogue on Defence Cooperation, 136
Japanese narratives: on Australia, 64; on China, 129; on Chinese foreign policy, 71–72; on cross-strait relations, 91–92; on European Union, 61; on India, 68; on Indo-Pacific concept, 7, 42; on Japanese status as Western vs. Asian partner, 129; on North Korea, 81–82; on rules-based order, 7, 44–45; on US as benevolent leader, 56; on Western engagement, 7; on Western leadership, 95–96
Japan-US relationship: Asian narratives on, 63, 66; and China-Japan relationship, 56; Indo-Pacific concept and, 43; Japanese opinion on, 57; Japanese reliance on US leadership in, 96; Japanese strategic dependency in, 67, 129; US forces in Japan, 83; and US-China relations, 91–92; US-Korea relations and, 82
Johnson, Boris government, 62–63
Joint Statement on Strengthening Media Exchanges and Cooperation between ASEAN and China, 138
Joko Widodo, 52–53

Kennan, George, 28
Kishi, Nobusuke government, cross-strait policy, 91
Kishida, Fumio/Kishida government: Japan-US relations and, 56; and like-minded state cooperation, 33; and rules-based order, 29
Korea Institute for National Unification, poll on South Korea-US relations, 57
Korean Peninsula: Canada and, 124; Cold War and, 81–82; US and, 22–23, 81–82. *See also* North Korea; South Korea

Korean War (1950), 22–23, 77, 82, 93
Kovrig, Michael, 4
Kunming rail station attack (2014), 112
Kupchan, Charles A., 20, 23

Lancang-Mekong Cooperation (LMC), 16, 140, 151
Laos: alignment with China vs. US, 59; and China, 10; in LMC forum, 140
Lee Hsien Loong, 52
liberal democracy: Confucianism and, 103; and governance, 48–49; and national interests, 123
liberalism: Canada and, 120; China in South China Sea and, 84; coalition of states, 9; Indo-Pacific concept and, 41; like-minded states and, 120; Malaysian scholarship on, 50; rules-based order and, 11, 45; US hegemony and, 78; Western narratives and, 25. *See also* economic liberalism; illiberalism
like-minded state(s): Australia as, 8, 33; Canada and, 34, 120, 121; and Canadian China policy, 9; Canadian foreign policy and, 8–10; Cold War and, 34; colonialism and, 10, 34; critical theory and, 32–34; engagement with regional states/actors/institutions vs., 15; France as, 33; and free and open concept, 55; Germany as, 33; India as, 55, 64, 129–30; and insider/outsider states, 55; and instability, 55; Japan as, 8, 33; and liberalism, 120; narratives and, 23; Netherlands as, 33; omni-directional diplomacy vs., 8; revisionism vs., 32; rules-based order and, 33; strategic integration vs., 8; and strategic value, 55; Taiwan as, 89; UK as, 33; US and, 9, 12, 32–33, 34; and US-ASEAN

cooperation, 32; values and, 12; Western narratives and, 21, 32, 54–55
Liu Xiaobo, 115

Mahan, Alfred, 76–77
Malaysia: alignment with China vs. US, 59; and ASEAN, 43; and Asia-Pacific concept, 43; and China, 10, 43; economics in, 47; and Indo-Pacific concept, 41; and Islamic world, 43; national development plans, 48
Malaysian narratives: on alignment with China vs. US, 73; on Australia, 65; on China-Malaysia relationship, 73; on free and open concept, 50; on French and English naval activities in South China Sea, 62; on India, 69; and Indo-Pacific concept, 43; on maritime security, 51; on rules-based order, 45; on South China Sea, 85; on Taiwan Strait, 90; on US as benevolent leader, 58; on US-China competition, 73; on Western leadership, 95; on Western liberal values, 50
Mao Zedong, 111
maritime security, 51, 85. *See also* East China Sea; South China Sea
Mekong River Commission (MRC), 140
Mekong-Japan Cooperation, 140
Mekong-US Partnership, 140
Meng Wanzhou, 3–4
middle power: Canada as, 3, 34, 120, 124; Canada's G7 membership and, 5; diplomacy, and Indo-Pacific strategy, 3
Modi, Narendra/Modi government, 52, 129; focus on South Asia, 69–70; and Hindu vs. Muslim relations, 69; and Kashmir, 68–69; and Myanmar and Thailand in BIMSTEC, 69; Vietnamese scholarship on, 69–70. *See also* India
Moon Jae-in administration, 40
Morrison, Scott/Morrison government, 115, 119; and like-minded state cooperation, 33; strategic approach to Asia, 147. *See also* Australia
Muhyiddin Yassin, 41
Muslim states. *See* Islamic states
Myanmar: alignment with China vs. US, 59; in BIMSTEC, 69, 140; and China, 10; in LMC forum, 140

narratives: about, 19–21; alignment of, 21; and cultural hegemony, 23; as defining features, 21; as dogmas/assumptions, 20; dominant states and, 20; and hegemonic control, 22–23; and like-minded states, 23; and national interests, 145; and omnidirectional diplomacy, 145; power dynamics and, 20; role in Asian affairs, 20–21; and strategic environment, 145; US, 21; and values/ideologies, 20
national interests: liberal democracy and, 123; narratives and, 145; power and, 123; security and, 123; supranational governance and, 123; Western involvement and, 128
national interests (Canada): ASEAN and, 138; in Asia, 122–25; Asian narratives and, 125, 156; Asia-Pacific strategic plans and, 155; bilateral/multilateral involvement and, 125; Canada in non-ASEAN institutions and, 143; economics and, 124–25; Indo-Pacific concept and, 131, 155, 157; institutions and, 146; international relations theory and, 123; narratives and, 145; and networks, 131, 145–46; power and, 124; rules-based order and, 123; security

and, 124; stability and, 124, 125; strategic integration and, 122; Western narratives vs., 10, 155
NATO, 16; Asian, 96; Canada in, 13, 121, 131, 148, 155; Canadian foreign policy and, 120; China on expansion of, 96; on Chinese influence, 94; Indo-Pacific concept and, 54; US and rules-based order and, 29; as Western-oriented, 11
Natural Sciences and Engineering Research Council of Canada (NSERC), 153–54
Netherlands: Asian narratives on, 60; and China, 78; and Indo-Pacific concept, 29, 40, 60, 78; as like-minded state, 33; and Taiwan Strait, 90
network analysis, 131–32; of ASEAN, 133–39; of Canadian involvement in Asian institutions, 18; and Canadian strategy toward Asia, 132–33; linkages, 132; nodes, 132; of non-ASEAN institutionalism, 139–43; and omnidirectional diplomacy, 132; and state engagement, 131–32; and strategic integration, 132
networks/networking: Asian institutions and, 15, 132–33; Canada in non-ASEAN institutions and, 142–43; Canadian national interests and, 131; Canadian participation in, 133; creation of opportunities for participation, 152; and national interests, 145–46; and strategic integration, 15, 149–50
Never Split the Difference (Voss), 102
New Colombo Plan Scholarship Program, 137
New National Security Guidelines for Research Partnerships (2021), 154
New Zealand: and ASEAN, 138; in ASEAN+6, 134, 136; in ASEAN-Australia-New Zealand Free Trade Area, 136; in EAS, 134; South Korean narratives on, 64; troops in South Korea, 79–80
NHK, poll on Japan-US relations, 57
non-ASEAN institutions, 11; Canada and, 140, 142–43, 148, 151–52; and colonialism, 139; dialogue groups, 140; network analysis of, 139–43; and Western leadership, 139; and Western narratives, 139; working groups, 140
North Korea: about, 79; in ASEAN Regional Forum, 134; Asian narratives regarding, 80–83; and Asian security, 96; behaviour of, 82; Canadian foreign policy on, 98; China and, 83, 96; Chinese narratives on, 82–83; economic growth, 81; as GTI observer, 142; Japanese counter-narratives on, 81–82; nuclear program, 78, 79, 81, 82; omnidirectional diplomacy, 146; peace with South Korea, 58; Russia and, 83, 96; sanctions against, 80, 81, 82; in Six-Party Talks (6PT), 146; South Korean scholarship on, 80–81; US and, 37, 79, 80, 81, 82–83; values, 20; Western provocation of, 83; Western scholarship on, 79–80

Obama, Barack/Obama administration: defence-dependency, 6; and Japanese nationalization of Diaoyu/Senkaku Islands, 86; like-minded state under, 32
omnidirectional diplomacy: about, 146; adaptivity and, 13–14; and ASEAN, 148; Asian foreign policy principles and, 146; Asian narratives and, 10, 152; Asian vs. Western narratives and, 53; Canada and, 147–49; Canada in non-ASEAN institutions and, 143; in Canadian foreign policy, 147–49, 152, 156; China and, 146; and

Index

CICA, 148; counter-narratives and, 24; critical evaluation of narratives and, 145; Indonesia and, 147; Indo-Pacific concept vs., 13; Japan and, 146; like-minded state vs., 8; network analysis and, 132; neutrality in, 152; North Korea and, 146; Singapore and, 146; and strategic approach, 18; strategic integration and, 16; strategic non-alignment and, 13; Thailand and, 147; Vietnam and, 146
Organisation for Economic Co-operation and Development (OECD), 45
Outlook on the Indo-Pacific (ASEAN), 50, 52

Pelosi, Nancy, 102
Pence, Mike, 102
People's Liberation Army (PLA), 91
Philippines: China and, 113; Philippine-American War, 76–77; students in Canada, 125
Pompeo, Mike, 89, 102, 109–10
post-colonialism. *See under* colonialism
Pottinger, Matthew, 102
power: and Canadian national interests, 124; critical theory and, 22, 24; hegemonic narratives and, 24; and narratives, 20; and national interests, 123; security and, 123
Powerplay: The Origins of the American Alliance System in Asia (Cha), 77

Quadrilateral Security (the Quad): Australia in, 37, 40, 64, 113; Canada and, 16, 147, 151; Chinese aggression as common enemy and, 113; growing activity, 50; India in, 113; Indo-Pacific concept and, 40, 54; Japan in, 37, 66, 67, 113; Japanese foreign policy and, 66–67; Japanese working with Australia and India in, 67; like-minded state concept and, 55; rules-based order and, 29, 33; Thai scholarship on, 58, 67; US and, 6, 29, 113; Western alignment in, 7; Western leadership and, 96; Western revisionism and, 130; as Western-oriented, 11

Regional Comprehensive Economic Partnership (RCEP), 46, 126; as ASEAN-driven, 136; EU involvement in, 62; India/Modi government and, 68, 69; Japan and, 40, 66; South Korea and, 42
revisionism: by China, 29, 32, 41, 74, 83, 84, 96, 113, 114, 119, 127; like-minded state vs., 32; rules-based order vs., 28, 29; by Russia, 32; by US, 96; Western states and, 130
Rim of the Pacific Exercise (RIMPAC), 80
ROK-ASEAN Consultative Group in the Employment and Labour Sector, 137
Roosevelt, Theodore, 76–77
rules-based order (RBO): about, 28, 40–41; adaptability of, 30; Asian narratives on, 44–46; attacks on, 30–31; Australia and, 29–30; Canada and, 32, 34, 74, 123, 127; China and, 28, 30, 38, 97, 114, 116, 119; Chinese revisionism vs., 28, 29; colonialization and, 45; critical theory and, 28–32; and democracy, 45; and free and open concept, 41; hegemony and, 30; Indonesian writers on, 45; Indo-Pacific concept and, 28, 29, 33, 40–41; and Islamic values, 45; Japan/Japanese narratives and, 7, 29, 44–45; liberalism and, 11, 45; and like-minded state, 33; Malaysian scholarship on, 45; protection of, 31; South Korean narratives on, 7, 45; Thai scholarship

on, 45, 46; and universal values, 45; US and, 28, 29, 30, 31, 33, 44, 45, 144; Vietnamese narratives on, 46; and Western alignment, 7, 11, 74; Western leadership and, 7, 54, 93, 97; Western narratives and, 21, 28, 44; Western vs. Asian narratives regarding, 46; Xi and, 99

Russia: in ADMM+, 134; ASEAN and, 50; in EAS, 134; in GTI, 142; India and, 130; like-minded state and, 32; and North Korea, 83, 96; revisionism by, 32; South Korea and, 42

Schelling, Thomas, 101

security: ASEAN-Canada relationship and, 136–37, 138; ASEAN-Japan relationship and, 136; ASEAN-South Korea relationship and, 136–37; Asian narratives on, 17–18, 97, 130–31; Canadian foreign policy and, 97–98; and Canadian national interests, 124; China/Chinese narratives on, 78, 92, 94, 128; cross-strait relations and, 90; democracy and, 94; in East China Sea, 84–85; free and open concept and, 36–37; India and, 69; and national interests, 123; North Korea and, 79, 96; and power, 123; in South China Sea, 83–84, 85–86; Taiwan and, 87–93; US and, 6–7, 37; US threat narratives and, 78–80; Western alignment and, 7, 12; Western hegemony and, 130; Western institutions and, 54; Western involvement and, 17–18, 78; Western leadership and, 93–97; Western narratives on, 21, 23, 26–27. *See also* United States: threat narratives

Shangri-La Dialogue (Singapore), 52

Silk Road Fund, 115, 116

Silk Road NGO Cooperation Network Forum, 141–42

Singapore: economics in, 47; governance in, 48, 59–60; and Indo-Pacific concept, 52; national development plans, 48; omnidirectional diplomacy, 146; polls on US, 59

Sino-British Joint Declaration (1984), 106, 107–8

Six-Party Talks (6PT), 79, 80, 146

Slaughter, Anne-Marie, 28

Social Sciences and Humanities Research Council (SSHRC), 153–54

socio-cultural engagement: in ASEAN-Australia relationship, 137; in ASEAN-Canada relationship, 137; in ASEAN-China relationship, 137–38; in ASEAN-Japan relationship, 137; in ASEAN-South Korea relationship, 137

South China Sea: ASEAN and, 38, 85, 151; Asian narratives on, 85–86; Asian vs. Western concerns and, 151; and AUKUS, 84; Australia and, 64–65, 85; Canada and, 97–98, 124; China and, 38, 51, 71, 72, 73, 83–84, 85, 137; Indonesian narratives on, 65, 85; Japan and, 85; Malaysian narratives on, 85; maritime security in, 51; militarization of, 78; security in, 83–84, 85–86; strategic integration and, 15–16; Thai narratives on, 51, 85–86; US and, 83, 84, 85–86; Vietnamese narratives on, 59, 73, 86; Western narratives on, 83–86

South Korea: Asia-Pacific focus, 42; China and, 42, 58, 113; and CPTPP, 42; and Dokdo/Takeshima Islands, 87; economics in, 47; on European states/EU, 61–62; foreign policy, 49; in GTI, 142; and India, 42; and Indo-Pacific concept, 41, 42; on institutions, 46; and Japan, 42; middle-power

Index 261

diplomacy approach, 45; national development plans, 48; "New Deal," 48; New Southern Policy, 14, 40, 46, 116, 136, 149; North Korea peace with, 58; and RCEP, 42; and Russia, 42; strategic partnerships, 152; and THAAD, 82–83, 114–15; US and, 42, 57–58, 82; Western troops in, 79–80. *See also* ASEAN-South Korea relationship

South Korean narratives: on Australia, 64; on China, 72, 96; on cross-strait relations, 91; on East China Sea, 87; on free and open concept, 49; on India, 68; on Indo-Pacific concept, 7; on Japan, 67; on New Zealand, 64; on North Korea, 80–81; on rules-based order, 7, 45; on Taiwan, 90–91; on US as benevolent leader, 57–58; on US-China relationship, 57; on values diplomacy, 49; on Western engagement, 7; on Western leadership, 96

Southeast Asia Treaty Organization (SEATO), 77

Spavor, Michael, 4

Special Fund for Asian Regional Cooperation, 136, 138

Sri Lanka: in BIMSTEC, 140; Hambantota International Port, 114

stability/instability: ASEAN-China relationship and, 71; Asian narratives and, 156; BRI and, 72; and Canadian national interests, 124, 125; China and, 9–10, 71, 73, 74; containment of China and, 72; cross-strait, 90; freedom and, 47; in Hong Kong, 106; of India, 130; Indonesia-China cooperation and, 51; Indo-Pacific concept and, 57, 93; like-minded state and, 55; South China Sea and, 71; US and, 7, 57, 58, 74, 130; Western hegemony and, 130; Western involvement and, 7, 51; Western leadership and, 26, 93; Western narratives and, 27; Western policies and, 72

strategic integration: about, 122, 149; ASEAN and, 149, 150; in ASEAN-Canada relationship, 124, 134–37; Asian institutions and, 11, 14–15, 146, 151–53; Asian narratives in, 150–51; and Asian regionalism, 150; Asian vs. Western narratives and, 53; Canada in non-ASEAN institutions and, 143; and Canada's national interests, 122; Canadian foreign policy and, 122, 150–54, 156; and Canadian influence, 16; counter-narratives and, 24; and democracy, 122; educational exchange and, 153–54; in European Union, 149; and human rights, 122; Indo-Pacific concept and, 151; interconnectivity and, 14; and international law, 122; in international relations theory, 149; like-minded state vs., 8; literacy programs and, 154; network analysis/networking and, 15, 132, 149–50; non-ideological engagement and, 11; and omnidirectional diplomacy, 16; and strategic approach, 18; and strategic flexibility, 15–16

Suga, Yoshihide, government: Japan-China relations and, 67; Japan-US relations and, 56; and like-minded state cooperation, 33; and rules-based order, 29; and Taiwan, 91–92; US alignment and, 57

Suharto, 77

Sukarno, 77

Summit of Democracies, like-minded state concept and, 55

Susmoro, Harjo, 85

Taiwan: Australia and, 88, 89, 118; autonomy and, 118; Canadian foreign policy on, 98; Chinese scholarship on, 92–93; defence of, 88; democracy, 88; Democratic Progressive Party (DPP), 87; diplomatic recognition, vs. China, 88; European Union and, 88, 89; France and, 88, 89, 118; Germany and, 118; Indonesian writing on, 90; Japan and, 118; New Southbound Policy, 116, 149; Northeast Asian writing on, 90–92; and one-China policy, 87–88, 92; people's identification as Taiwanese vs. Chinese, 88; security, 78; South Korean analysts on, 90–91; Southeast Asian writing on, 90; Thai analysis on, 90; UK and, 88, 89, 118; US and, 37, 83, 87, 88, 89, 91–93, 118; Western narrative on, 87–89. See also cross-strait relations

Taiwan Relations Act (1979), 88

Taiwan Strait, 88; Canada and, 124; Malaysian analysts on, 90; Vietnamese media on, 90. See also cross-strait relations

Taiwanese narratives: on cross-strait relations, 92; on Diaoyu/Senkaku Islands, 86–87

Terminal High Altitude Area Defense (THAAD), 82–83, 114–15

Thai narratives: on Australia, 65; on China, 73; on free and open concept, 50; on India, 69; on Indo-Pacific concept, 43, 95; on Japan, 67; on rules-based order, 45, 46; on South China Sea, 51, 85–86; on Taiwan, 90; on US, 43, 58–59; on US-EU security relations, 62; on Western leadership, 95

Thailand: alignment with China vs. US, 59; in BIMSTEC, 69, 140; and China, 10; and "Cold War 2.0," 59; COVID-19 in, 73; free market opposition in, 48; and Indo-Pacific concept, 41; and liberalism, 45; in LMC forum, 140; national development plans, 48; omnidirectional diplomacy, 147

Tiananmen Square: incident (1989), 106; suicide bombing (2013), 112

Trudeau, Justin/Trudeau government: and Canadian leadership in Western-aligned institutions, 155; and Indo-Pacific, 3

Truman, Harry, 77

Trump, Donald/Trump administration: "America First" policy, 12, 99; and ASEAN cooperation, 32; and Asia-Pacific, 6; and CPC, 93, 102; China-US stability compared, 70; defence-dependency, 6; and ETIM, 112; and free and open Indo-Pacific, 35, 38; illiberal approach to foreign policy, 9; Indonesia and, 58; Indo-Pacific vision, 14; like-minded state under, 32; and National Security Council, 32; North Korean policy, 80; and rules-based order, 29; and Taiwan, 87, 89, 91, 93; and US-China relations, 58; and Xinjiang, 109–10

Tsinghua University, poll on CPC, 105

United Kingdom: and ASEAN, 60–61; Asian narratives on, 55, 60, 62–63; and AUKUS, 54, 63, 113; and China, 78, 113; COVID-19 in, 49; on CPC, 103; and Hong Kong, 107–8; and Indo-Pacific concept, 60, 78, 145; as like-minded state, 33; and Taiwan, 88, 89, 118; and Taiwan Strait, 90; troops in South Korea, 79–80; and Xinjiang, 110

United Nations: Canada and, 147–48; Canada in Security Council, 155; Command (UNC), 80; Convention on the Law of the Sea (UNCLOS), 84, 86; Malaysian scholarship on, 58

United States: in ADMM+, 134; "America First" approach, 43; and ASEAN, 32; Asian narratives on,

55, 70–71, 130–31; and AUKUS, 6, 54, 65, 113; Australia and, 63, 64, 65, 147; as benevolent leader, 56–60; Canada and, 5–7, 9, 12–13; and China-Japan relationship, 56; Congressional-Executive Commission on China, 102; and COVID-19, 49, 60, 71, 144; and cross-strait relations, 91, 92; in EAS, 134; forces in Japan, 83; and free and open concept, 35, 38, 144; and free and open Indo-Pacific, 44; and free trade, 71; hegemony, 17, 76–78, 95, 96; Indonesian scholarship on, 58; and Indo-Pacific concept, 3, 4, 35, 40, 43, 45, 57, 77, 94, 145; and instability, 7, 58, 74, 130; international law violations, 97; Japan and, 43, 57, 63, 66, 67, 82, 96, 129; and Korean Peninsula, 22–23, 81–82; and like-minded state, 9, 12, 32–33, 34; Malaysian scholarship on, 58; and Middle East, 96; and Muslim states, 95; narratives, 21; National Security Strategy, 32; and North Korea, 37, 79, 80, 81, 82–83; and one-China policy, 89; policing in, 108; and Quad, 6, 113; revisionism by, 96; and rules-based order, 28, 29, 30, 31, 33, 44, 45, 144; and SEATO, 77; and security, 37; as shaping Asian order, 6; and South China Sea, 83, 84, 85–86; and South Korea, 42, 57–58, 79–80, 81, 82; Southeast Asian opinion on, 59; and Taiwan, 37, 83, 87, 88, 89, 91–93, 118; terrorist list, 112; Thai narratives on, 43, 58–59; threat narratives, 76–78, 96, 100; and unipolarity, 96; values, 9; Vietnam/Vietnamese scholarship and, 51, 59, 95, 128. *See also* Biden, Joe/Biden administration; China-US relationship; Japan-US relationship; Obama, Barack/Obama administration; Trump, Donald/Trump administration

Urumqui riots (2009), 112

US Department of Defense, 6; Pacific Deterrence Initiative, 29

US State Department, 110; *A Free and Open Indo-Pacific,* 35

US-South Korea Foal Eagle Exercise, 80

Uyghurs. *See* Xinjiang Uyghur Autonomous Region (XUAR)

values: Asian states and, 9–10; in Canadian foreign policy, 8; China and, 8, 9–10; diplomacy, 49; hegemonic discourse and, 38; and like-minded state, 12; and narratives, 20; rules-based order and, 45; South Korean scholarship on, 49; US and, 144; and Western alignment, 7, 11, 12. *See also* ideology

Vietnam: and China, 10, 51, 59, 128; and economic liberalism, 46; economics in, 47; and Indo-Pacific concept, 41; in LMC forum, 140; national development plans, 48; omnidirectional diplomacy, 146; and US, 51, 95, 128

Vietnam War, 77

Vietnamese narratives: on ASEAN, 44; on Australia, 65; on China, 73; on European states in South China Sea, 62; on free and open concept, 50–51; on India, 69–70; on Indo-Pacific concept, 43–44, 50–51, 95; on Japan, 67–68; on maritime security, 51; on rules-based order, 46; on South China Sea, 59, 73, 86; on Taiwan Strait, 90; on US in Asia, 59; on US military presence, 51; on Western leadership, 95

Voss, Chris, *Never Split the Difference,* 102

Walt, Stephen, *The Hell of Good Intentions,* 76

Western alignment: Asian states on, vs. with China, 72; and Canadian foreign policy, 120–22; Canadian public views on Asia-Pacific region, and, 11–12; cooperation with Asian states/institutions vs., 157; Japan and, 55, 63, 66, 68; rules-based order and, 7, 11, 74; and security, 7; values and, 7, 11, 12

Western hegemony: ASEAN Outlook on the Indo-Pacific and, 128; Asian narratives on, 130; China and, 116; and European engagement in Asia, 61; and free and open concept, 35–36, 37; and Indo-Pacific concept, 13; and security, 130; and stability, 130

Western leadership: and ASEAN, 95; Asian narratives on, 7, 74, 94–97, 128; Asian vs. Western narratives on, 17; Australia and, 65; Chinese narratives on, 96–97; competition with China, 95; and democracy, 93, 94; in East China Sea, 86; and free and open concept, 26; Indonesian scholarship on, 95; and Indo-Pacific concept, 21, 74; Japanese writing on, 95–96; Malaysian scholarship on, 95; non-ASEAN institutions and, 139; Northeast Asian writing on, 95–97; and rules-based order, 7, 54, 93, 97; and security, 93–97; in South China Sea, 85–86; South Korean scholarship on, 96; and stability/instability, 26, 93; Thai analysis on, 95; and US hegemony, 95; Vietnamese analysis on, 95; Western narratives and, 10, 23, 93–94, 145

Western narratives: appeal for Canadian policy-making, 120; on ASEAN, 25–26; on Australia, 55, 74, 129; on BRI, 114, 115–16; Canadian foreign policy and, 36, 97, 120–21; Canadian national interests vs., 10, 155; on China, 21, 26, 55, 71, 99–100; on Chinese foreign policy, 113–14; Chinese perspectives regarding, 127–28; and colonialism, 25; on CPC, 25, 103; critical analysis vs., 4–5; critical theory and, 23–24, 25–26; on cross-strait relations, 87–88; and democracy, 120; on East China Sea, 84–85; on free and open concept, 26, 34–38; on Hong Kong, 106–9; on India, 55, 74, 129–30; on Indo-Pacific, 21, 23, 41, 54, 128; and instability, 27; and international law, 120; and international relations, 25–27; on Japan, 55, 74, 129; and liberalism, 25; on like-minded state, 32, 54–55; and national strategy toward Asia, 121; and neocolonialism, 10; non-ASEAN institutions and, 139; on North Korea, 79–83; on one-China policy, 87–88; overreliance on, 20–21, 24; on rules-based order, 28, 44; on security, 21, 23, 26–27; on South China Sea, 83–86; on Taiwan, 87–89; US hegemony and, 17; and Western Chinese policy-making, 100; and Western identity vs. regional perceptions, 21; and Western leadership, 10, 21, 23, 93–94, 145; and Western perceptions vs. regional realities, 17; Western self-referential identity and, 21; and Western state benevolence, 54; on Xinjiang, 109–10, 112

Winter Olympics (2022), 120

Women-only Business Missions to Asia, 153

World Economic Forum, Davos Agenda, 99–100

World Trade Organization (WTO), 45, 58

Index

Xi Jinping: at APEC Virtual Leaders' Retreat, 144–45; and CICA, 141; Davos speech, 99–100

Xinjiang Uyghur Autonomous Region (XUAR), 18; about, 109–13; Asian attitudes and, 127; Canadian foreign policy on, 118; China and, 145; Chinese narratives on, 110–13, 128; concentration camps in, 110, 112; CPC and, 118; development of, 111–12; ethnic minorities, 111, 112; genocide in, 100, 110, 113, 118; Islamic faith in, 112, 113; religious persecution in, 110; terrorist organizations in, 112; Western narratives on, 109–10, 112